IN IT

Jonathan Robinson

ISBN
978-1502808165

www.jonathanrobinson.org

Reaction to **IN IT**

Compelling writing about the system. **Frances Crook, the Howard League**

A truthful account of the chaos and mayhem that is our penal system. The narrative put me immediately on the wings and landings of the jail. The account is both perceptive and highly amusing. IN IT shines a light. **Eric Allison, the Guardian**

IN IT is full of atmosphere – a significant writing gift. **Joanna Trollope**

One of the best ever accounts of a prison journey. The story is told with wit, verve, style and authenticity. I particularly enjoyed the combination of humour and humility. **Jonathan Aitken**

Most Interesting. **Ann Widdecombe**

A notable success. **Stephen Fry**

IN IT is a very valuable commentary on much of what is happening in prison. **His Honour John Samuels QC [Chairman, Prisoners' Education Trust]**

This is one of those books where you don't know whether to laugh or cry. Jonathan's writing is witty, concise, intuitive, insightful and at times delightfully amusing. IN IT is a MUST READ. **Tracy Edwards MBE**

Prisoners for years to come will benefit from Robinson's commitment and energy. **Inside Time**

I fully agree with your sentiment that poor and disinterested officers are the major stumbling block to enabling rehabilitation in prisons. There needs to be a sea change in this area otherwise, no amount of good intention and effort by government and others will be stymied by the "black knights" of the system. **The Chief Officer of one of the many organisations involved in the running of our prisons.** This individual has asked to remain anonymous so as "not to rock too many boats". He (or she) has wished the author all the best in instigating change.

Someone had to do something... Strange that it's an ex-prisoner...

For you know who

Foreword

By

Jonathan Aitken

IN IT is one of the best books on prison life I have read. Jonathan Robinson writes with passion and authenticity of the time he served in HMPs Bedford and Hollesley Bay. Yet although his diary-based narrative of inmate life, his ear for dialogue and his humour combine to make a rattling good yarn, the importance of IN IT lies not in its chronicles of detail but in its crusading for reform.

A former helicopter pilot who stole from his employer, Jonathan Robinson wastes no words on self-pity or self-justification. Indeed he thinks his 15 month sentence was "too lenient". Yet he soon becomes a con with a cause, which is to wake the world up to the lamentable failure of in-prison rehabilitation.

With the perspective of a talented fresh eye on a creaking old system, the author sees plenty of potential among his fellow inmates for lives that could be well and honestly lived. But he writes harshly – perhaps a little too harshly – of the Dickensian cast of characters he met who were notionally in charge of running every aspect of his prison journey. Inevitably there are good and bad members of staff. I seem to have met more of the former than this Jonathan encountered. But where we would both agree is that anything that goes on in our prisons under the heading "rehabilitation" is at best a well-meaning muddle and at worst a morass of uselessness and pointlessness.

Robinson the Crusader whose voyage of exploration on prison island bears a 21st century resemblance to Robinson Crusoe's survival story, gets to the heart of the rehabilitation crisis in two brutal sentences.

"The problem is that the conveyor belt that is prison is wasting any opportunity to remould offenders whilst they are staying. The huge /copious amounts of different agencies who work within our prisons (and who all seem to loathe each other) make the charge of the Light Brigade look like a well-planned military operation."

Well said, even after allowing for a little military or literary licence. For as Jonathan Robinson points out the reoffending rate of released prisoners is stubbornly stuck at around 70 per cent according to the official statistics and is probably several points higher in reality . This failure could almost certainly be reduced if there was a root and branch reform of the probation and rehabilitation services. They cost well over £2 billion a year and achieve little, partly because the roots of rehabilitation are not planted in prison as Jonathan Robinson urges.

Perhaps there may be hope for correcting the deficiencies so colourfully described in his book. For the present Justice Secretary Chris Grayling has now launched a policy initiative with the title Transforming Rehabilitation. Cynics may note that this label is uncannily close to his predecessor's Rehabilitation Revolution in which nothing revolved or moved! But Grayling has the zeal of a true reformer, who wants to start on the wings and in the cells using private sector providers of rehabilitation. We should cheer him on, urging him and his team to get down to sometimes gory sometimes funny but often hopeful details of prison life so well described in the pages of IN IT.

Jonathan Aitken

Author's Note

All of what you are about to read (and thank you for doing so) was typed up from a manuscript that originated from notes – on Her Majesty's Prison Paper – written somewhere around my knees or on a makeshift desk invariably two feet or so from a lavatory. Please therefore forgive any wobbly scenery by way of grotty English or grammar. The environment that my behaviour placed me within opened my eyes like you wouldn't believe and I thought it vital to transfer everything as originally written. If ever a collection of words needed sprucing up – it's what is before you. If I can ask you though – just take a seat on the ride and go with the flow… The plan always was to do something fly-on-the-wall.

Warts 'n all…

I am not at all proud of my past behaviour – but if the following can cajole the inauguration of even some debate about change, then I have anecdotally attained my goal and succeeded in doing something positive.

There is only one "add-on" to the piece. And it's heading your way right now:

I learnt with horror in September of 2012, that HMP Bedford had the highest suicide rate of any prison in England and Wales during 2011/2012. Tragically, 4 inmates committed suicide at the jail during this period, out of a population of 465 inmates.

In prison, where I fully deserved to end up, I met a great many people who appeared to be present under sufferance.

Then there were the inmates…

Please draw your own conclusions about what is going on in our prisons – or isn't – from the following….

JR

January, 2013.

"Nobody's really on the case."

Nick Hardwick, Chief Inspector of our prisons.

"Dick Clement and Ian La Frenais, the writers (of "Porridge") quite rightly, saw it as an opportunity to get some reality into the piece. You know – not all jokes. Some feelings of the sterner realities of these dreadful places."

Ronnie Barker.

"Prison would work if it was organised more sensibly – it plainly doesn't work now. Better run prisons would work…"

Ken Clarke.

"Always cast against the part and it won't be boring."

David Lean.

Monday, July 25th, 2011.

The moment I saw her I knew it meant trouble. She carried a puzzle magazine. It had seen better days. She sat down next to me and looking bored hissed for my date of birth. I answered her resisting the temptation to offer the solution to 9 across. After noting the anniversary of my arrival on earth on a dog-eared corner of her publication, she went back to her conundrum and looked even more disinterested in me. Her entrance had not been in the pages of my script.

The end of her biro was chewed.

Her presence triggered all sorts of internal warning lights. She is a security guard. She's appeared from nowhere and has taken the place of my Guardian Angel – who has had the masterly presence of mind to hotfoot it. We're in Court seven of St Albans Crown Court. And I'm in the Dock.

Her arrival means I'm not going home.

The Judge (Trevor Howard) had already indicated as such. Already I was beginning to feel like either this was some sort of out of body experience, or a film. Our brief conversation occurred whilst "His Honour" was doing something on his laptop. He was surrounded by other Court personnel on assorted tiers. It looked like *Celebrity Squares* on the telly. My new friend occupied herself with her very tired looking magazine. It was like one of those that you pick up in a dentist's waiting room.

The alarm bells should have started to ring as I entered the Court. Sitting in the waiting room listening to some trio talking about how atrocious the traffic had been on the A3, "all parties in the Robinson case" was broadcast. I got up, tried to stop my legs from shaking and following an Usher, entered the Court. My host played an eye game with one of the *Celebrity Squares* panel as to where to place me. Frantic pupil semaphore took place. I couldn't work out which member of the grid he was signalling to but clearly one of them wanted me in the Dock – from where there was only one exit – rather than a much more attractive chair arrangement that I'd targeted. The upholstery meant a suspended sentence and home.

The Dock meant *other* things.

Action had commenced with Trevor Howard asking me if I was certain I was happy to represent myself. I had no legal representation. This had caused some sort of sensation, as if I'd entered the Court stark naked. The same topic had caused consternation at the Magistrates' Court hearing a few weeks prior. I had been down the same road with the Police during all the interviews. No, I don't need legal help; I've made the mistake(s). I'm guilty as sin. Let's not waste tax payers' money on a legal team. Let's get on with this. On my last meeting with the Gendarmes, the supervising officer (Cassandra, from *Only Fools and Horses*) told me that I wouldn't be allowed to represent myself in Crown Court. I had bet her a fiver it was my right. She declined the wager.

The Magistrates had referred the case and me to Crown Court. I am here today to be sentenced.

To the day I die I'll be asking myself if Trevor was looking at me with either a bit of admiration or thinking "I've got a right one here," for cutting out the theatre of middle men that are barristers. It was difficult to tell. I had left my glasses at home and there was a very dirty piece of Perspex between myself and an awful lot of people in wigs. Regardless, the clapper board cracked and the first scene had started. The Perspex made things very difficult to hear. There was a vertical gap an inch or so wide and like speaking through a key hole, each time I was addressed, I had to turn my head to listen. Perhaps they thought I was deaf.

Because I'd pleaded guilty there was no legal theatre to play out. The Prosecution Council, a tall blonde lady (Grace Kelly) thrashed out the facts, citing a number of witness statements and summarised events to date.

One of those statements had been made by my wife.

The Probation report – a copy of which had been thrust in my hand on arrival – was studied by Trevor. He'd communicated to me already that he had to imprison me. That had got my attention. Being told that you are going to prison is like being hit by a freight train. In slow-motion. The debate now seemed to be for how long.

I'd read what Probation had to say whilst overhearing the traffic report between Surrey and London. It relayed that I was aware of my crime (I am), sorry for my crime (I am) and that the best thing for me is to continue working to make amends (I have been trying to). The worrying small print alerted the Court that if I was to be imprisoned, I was most concerned about being off-radar come June, as my helicopter flying instructor rating expires then and I need to be available to the outside world to renew it.

A voice inside me told me that at least if I am going to jail, which it seems I am – I will be out by June.

I forget if I was asked to speak or whether I just started to when the blonde sat down. I confirmed that all that had been said was true. I have behaved like an idiot. I'm sorry. I have been trying to make amends. I vocalised that whatever the Court was going to throw at me, nothing could equal the punishment that my wife has passed on me.

She left me on Christmas Eve.

Trevor responded by quizzing me about exactly what it was I needed to do by June. I replied as precisely as possible. He told me to sit down. It was at this point that Puzzle Magazine Lady materialised – with that damn magazine. Trevor studied his laptop even more. I assume checking up on the Archbold's, which in layman's terms is the Haynes guide for matters legal.

I was told to stand up. When you're in Court and they say that, you make the *Grenadier Guards* look slouch like.

The combination of the dividing Perspex and my heart thumping so loud in my ears meant I almost had to lip read what Trevor was saying. It came straight at me. Like a rocket. "Fifteen months," then adding, because I'm sure I looked confused as that would mean a release date well past June, that I would "Serve half that."

I defy anyone to begin to describe, even *half* successfully, what it feels like to be told you are going to *prison*. In no particular order I felt embarrassed, sorry, stupid, ashamed and very foolish. The emotion that hit me most was fear. By midnight tonight, I am going to be raped, sliced and murdered. As I contemplated my immediate gloomy future, I was almost disappointed that I didn't get a "Take him down." Instead, Trevor said "Mr Robinson, thank you very much indeed." I didn't know whether it was the protocol to thank him or not. I think I just nodded.

Puzzle Magazine Lady opened a secret door downstage of us and beckoned me to follow. Through it was a metal staircase. My hand was requested and she attached herself to me with handcuffs. I descended those stairs in tow of her like Neil Armstrong did that ladder, I promise you. Oddly, at the bottom of them, she released me from the cuffs. I felt for her. If I'd lost my footing, or for that matter my nerve – and tumbled she would have come with me. Once we were separated I took in my new surroundings. Metal barred doors everywhere.

Two uniformed staff.

In my mind I'm just telling myself to stay calm. Accept that you are in deep, *deep* trouble. There is nothing that you can do. Go with the flow. This is just scene two. The first scene went OK. It could be a lot worse. Alright, no it couldn't but above all else: do *not* panic. "Fifteen months," Puzzle Lady declares to her colleagues. I am walked to a room and ordered to empty my pockets. I am asked if I have anything about my person that I shouldn't have. I don't and I try to be as polite and helpful as I can be. I'm searched. All my possessions are logged by one, as the other starts a barrage of questions. I answer them as I'm instructed to remove my belt, tie and shoes. Am I white? Am I on drugs? Am I homosexual?

Christ almighty: Starsky and Hutch. No, not these two but the two rabbits in my garden. I ask my new hosts if I can use the phone. That's not allowed but because this is animal welfare they will make an exception and call for me. Even in my perilous situation, the irony of the subject matter of my first communication from Clink being about two not terribly friendly rabbits gets noted by me. I give them the number of my friend Buzz (Lightyear). He knows where I am today. He even offered to come with me. I turned him down. I needed to face the music by myself. He is an ally though. I think he is the only friend I have left.

I was teaching him to fly helicopters yesterday.

I sign some paperwork. I arrived with my wallet, my bank card, a new packet of cigarettes, a lighter, £72 in cash and Buzz's number written on a scrap of paper. I had brought it for emergencies. I left my mobile phone at home. For dire emergencies. I am not allowed to keep anything.

Panic really starting to set in now.

Get a hold of yourself, Robinson. Dignity and guts required now. Just keep breathing and try to keep calm. Take this like a man. You fucking tit.

I am shown to a cell. Spotlessly clean. I ask what the plan is. "Transport will be along at some point." Where am I going? "Probably Bedford." I get locked in. That door shutting on me a very vivid reminder of the dismal, desperate situation that I am in. Fortunately, one of them is back minutes later. They've got hold of Buzz and the rabbits will be "sorted." The message from him is to "keep my chin up." He's asked how long I have been given. One of the male guards says "seven and a half months." Puzzle Lady chimes in as they are closing the door with "*he* won't serve that long." After the door was shut I had to question in my mind if she'd said *serve* or worryingly: *last*.

I sit in my cell and look at the wall. Don't you *dare* start feeling sorry for yourself. Look at the bloody carnage you've created and bloody well live with it. If you want to stand any chance of getting through this, then it's serious stiff upper lip time. No alternative. God I wish I could speak to my wife.

She doesn't want to know though.

Some lunch is brought for me. I have no idea of the time. My head is spinning. I make myself eat. Not surprisingly I feel a bit better now that I've got some food in me. Back to pondering. All sorts of problems present themselves in my head. The door suddenly opens. A battalion of uniforms. "Transport is here." I'm searched again. Then put into handcuffs by one of the original guards. These are different to Puzzle Lady's and he sets them to a given size around my wrists, so they "won't be too tight." We walk to an exit that leads outside to a car park. One of those big prison vans is there, with darkened out windows.

The inside of my lift is like entering a massive Tonka toy. Still handcuffed to my new friend, I am taken to a cubicle inside. The door is unlocked and I inspect my space. It's about the size of a telephone box with a grey plastic seat. White walls, plastic coated. Easy to wipe. Graffiti scratched everywhere. Clean though. I'm ordered to enter. Tricky, as I'm still attached to my guard. He tells me to go in but then stick my arms back out again so he can release me. I suppose this is a security thing in case I get violent. Unlikely, as I'm positively vibrating with fear. Once in, I can't turn my body, so I rotate my top half, like Dick Van Dyke's marionette in *Chitty, Chitty, Bang, Bang*. Arms are offered and I am relieved of my handcuffs. My door is shut. Then locked. Christ, I'm one of those vans that you see on the news, carting people off to prison. The engine starts.

I then learn I am not the only passenger on board.

The noise – no, the eruption, that comes from my fellow prisoners, makes me think that we must be many in number. The Galleon crew from *Ben Hur* at the very least. A *terrifying* amount of banging, thumping, loud shouting of obscenities, yelling and kicking.

Then we set off.

Anything spotted through a window that is remotely female causes a cacophony of jarring abuse. A deafening, earthquake like cascade of noise and violence. In my mind I plead with them to stop. I don't say a word though. I just put my head in my hands.

You complete and utter *arse*, Robinson.

I don't know whether it was the shock. Or the dreadful surroundings or even the moronic noises exploding from the other cubicles but what happened next surprised me. I went to sleep. Like some piece of electronic machinery, I literally went into standby mode. I suppose I must have been exhausted. Perhaps too, it was an immediate remedy to switch off from my predicament. I didn't fight sleep. It was instinct.

I woke in a start and *immediately* knew where I was. The banging and shouting had settled down once we'd hit a dual carriageway. Maybe the other prisoners had dropped off too, like children in car seats on a long journey. I studied, or tried to, our position, by attempting to read passing road signs. Difficult, as I only had a line of fire 90 degrees to the right of me, like a porthole in an aeroplane. It was easier to read the signs on the other side of the road for traffic going the other way. The odd glimpse of signpost indicated we were approaching Bedford. I think we have been on the road for just under an hour.

A higher frequency of clattering gear changes and more acute turns tells me we are getting close. Out of my window are lots of kebab shops and discount carpet vendors. They all look the same. The dull drab weather and darkened window mirrors my mood. The combination of what I am both seeing and thinking is not helping me at all. Reminder: stay calm. Or try to. My fellow prisoners are really quiet now. Something tells me they have done this before. I have not. I'm the new boy.

I think we are here. Some turns at very slow speed. We stop and I see parked cars through my window. We're waiting for a gate to be opened I think. My only clues are noises, movement and what is on the immediate starboard side of this horrible vehicle. We inch forward about a cricket pitch length and stop again. Now my view is just a wall. It has no paint on it.

I am going to die tonight. Apart from the shame of being taken from A to B via this method of transport, I know I'm going to be picked out and targeted. I've had it. Try to go down with style Robinson. Don't give anyone the pleasure of screaming or crying during the violent and sexual attack that you are destined to receive before this day is out. I'll fight like a cornered cat. I won't last long but they are going to have to kill me before they get anything. I know to go for the eyes, Adam's apple or men's bits. The last will be difficult if there are many of them.

Eyes it is then.

We move again at walking pace. A parking manoeuvre is completed and the engine is stopped. Our carriage vibrates as the revolutions of the diesel motor cease. The cab's door opens and shuts. I wait. The main fuselage door is opened and a staff member moves about in the aisle. Voices are heard. I think of animals arriving at the slaughter house. The noise of internal doors being unlocked is audible. I'm wearing my watch but I have no idea what the time is. It does not occur to me to check. Every *second* is being utilised by observation of sights and sounds in an attempt to boost my survival expectancy. My door is unlocked and opened. I stand up. I'm very stiff. I try to stretch but am limited by space. I stoop through the door and walk towards the exit. It's still daylight outside. The darkened window in my cabin has made me think it's later than it is. I climb down to the ground. Like descending from a train at a station.

With no platform.

A Colditz courtyard. Closed circuit TV cameras everywhere. I upload as much visual information as I can. My brain is in meltdown. The place is deserted. From nowhere a female voice calls my name. I spin around and there is a woman in uniform at the top of a small flight of stone steps watching me. "This way please." I stretch properly and take in the sky. I'm not going to be seeing it again. I climb the steps and enter a prison for the first time.

Some sort of holding pen. There are about six of us. How can so few, make so much frightening noise? I just stand and observe.

The pen — if that is the right terminology — is tatty and dirty. There are perches bolted to the wall. More graffiti, scratched everywhere and anywhere. I look at the others. Very discretely. No eye contact. None by me anyway. They're all younger than me. Most are ethnic minority based. I'm the only one in a suit. All the other feet on the floor are clad in trainers. They all seem either experienced with what's going on, or resigned to our fate. Or both. Some seem to know each other. Our chamber has some windows and I look though them to take in what is going on. Some sort of giant operations room. White marker boards everywhere. Loads of information on them. Headings announce arrivals from different Courts, numbers of prisoners on remand and those convicted. Desks, surfaces of which are filled with piles of clutter, Kit Kat wrappers and division two football teams' supporters' mugs. Staff; a lot of them swearing. Filing cabinets; assorted styles. The place looks filthy.

We are called one by one. I feel like I'm on a conveyor belt. I'm no longer me, just a product. I am led somewhere to be photographed. I don't hold a number up. My property, taken from me in Court, is reassessed and bagged up. It's an efficient system. I'm told to sit down.

A female officer (Demi Moore) sits the other side of a desk. Brunette. Late thirties. I notice other male officers milling around, chatting. Lots of tattoos. Some wear T shirts under their uniforms. One has an earring. They look like a right rabble. On their belts are chains. With keys.

I am welcomed to HMP Bedford. She is pleasant to me. Loads of questions. Mr Robinson this, Mr Robinson that. *Please*, call me *Jonathan*. This — and my voice — throws her. She puts her pen down, looks up and — thank God — switches off her processing persona and speaks to me like a normal person. "I can't," she explains, almost apologising. "It's the rules." She looks at me for a few seconds and then, still in human being mode, says "look, prison's not that bad." She assures me that I can "get through" this. "Shit happens," she adds. She's read what I've done and tells me "people have done far worse" and gives me a hint that the future is now down to me. And me alone. Understood. But I still think I'm going to be dead by the end of play tonight. I don't tell her this.

She reverts to process mode. I am not allowed to keep my suit because I'll look "too much like the Governor." I will be given some clothes. She notices from my possessions that I am a smoker. I can have my cigarettes and lighter back. She asks if I would like a "smoker's-pack." Extra tobacco. Yes please, I reply. I am told that within a "day or two" I will be issued with a PIN number, so I can "use the prisoners' telephones," paid for with the money I have arrived with. The numbers I can call have to be vetted first. I give her Buzz's number. It's the only one I have. Do I want anyone called, to say I've "landed safely?" Yes please, ring Buzz, tell him I'm OK. He's going to have to be my satellite with the outside world.

Then comes the sixty four thousand dollar question. Do I want to keep my watch, or hand it in? I look at my wrist. My watch sort of identifies me. This is a tricky decision. Do I keep this part of *me*, or do I surrender it and become nothing? I'm internally begging her to guide me what to do. I look for some hint from her, as to the best way to play this. Will I be making myself even more of a target by retaining it? She reveals no clue, so I have to decide by myself. To hell with it. I'll keep it. They're going to kill me anyway. I'd rather die with a bit of *me* left. I tell her I'll hang on to it. Her face tells me I've probably made a duff decision. Again.

Thoughts that her fellow officers look like a bunch of ill-disciplined nightclub bouncers are confirmed when one of them balances an eraser on her shoulder. They all seem bored with nothing to do. There are four of them hanging around. The rubber falls off her epaulette and the gag is unnoticed. Or ignored. She does something with a computer and an ID card is produced and given to me. It has the picture of me on it taken a few moments ago. I hardly recognise the face looking back at me. I have been issued with a prison number. A1796CF. Easy to remember: "Complete Fool." She tells me to carry the card at all times. I am told that once a week, we can have "Canteen" delivered. I am given a sheet of the available options. I order more tobacco, coffee, stamps and writing paper. Like impulse buying in a supermarket. She hands over a pile of paperwork for me to keep. I take a quick glance. "Induction" information, all I will "need to know" about HMP Bedford. The interview is complete and I am taken by one of the rubber balancers to another room. I'm told to take my clothes off, down to my underwear. I'm given a gown. More of that later. Right now: it's farewell suit. I'm glad I kept my watch.

Standing in your underpants in a filthy room opposite a chap is a strange experience. I spot a sort of x-ray chair in another room. Very *Quatermass*. He asks me to hold my arms out and he examines me all over, without touching me. He orders me to pick my socks up and shake them. He checks the soles of my feet. He tells me to put on the gown. I pick it up and am *knocked sideways*.

By a speeding truck's worth of aroma.

You have never smelt anything like this, at least I hope you haven't. It stinks of stale urine. I mean *reeks*. I feel sick picking it up, let alone wearing it. On though, it goes and he tells me to drop my shorts to below my knees to see if I am hiding anything. At least, I presume (and hope) so. The gown allows me to keep my modesty. Visually, anyway. The stench could empty Kings Cross Station. Satisfied that nothing is within my pants of interest, he tells me to pull them up again and wait for some clothes. He takes my shirt, trousers and jacket. As soon as he leaves, I ditch the gown in a large plastic, waist high bin. Fortunately it has a top. If it didn't, I might as well be in a gas chamber. This could cause trouble for me but I don't care. I'm staying in my pants, thank you. I'm not wearing that again. Ever. You can stick me in your x-ray chair if you like. I don't care whether it's an electric chair. Unleash the volts. Just don't make me put that thing on again.

A trustee prisoner arrives. Ralph. (Young Dustin Hoffman). Is this the start of *Papillion* I wonder? Standing in my underpants I look more like Basil Fawlty than Steve McQueen. He tells me he will feed me and give me some clothes. I follow him down some dimly lit corridor that is all part of the labyrinth like backstage area of a television studio. The other prisoners that I arrived with loiter. We're all waiting but I am apparently, the only person who needs supplies. The "professionals" have had the presence of mind to bring their own kit. Ralph takes me to a stores room. His first priority is to find me some sheets, a blanket, some rudimentary toiletries and a towel. I'm soon clutching two green sheets and a bright orange bed warmer. I could make the national flag of India out of this. He struggles to find any clothes. Those that he does do not exactly help. But they will have to do. I'm given a T shirt, sweat shirt, three pairs of socks, four pairs of prison blue boxer shorts, a prison shirt right out of *Porridge*, a set of plastic cutlery, a blue plastic mug that when filled, I could probably take a bath in, a plastic plate that resembles a Frisbee and matching blue plastic bowl. The towel retrieved for me is the same size as a Charles and Diana tea towel. A pair of jeans – well used but clean – is handed over. Size 38 waist.

My waist size is 34.

No shoes can be found for me. Pretty soon I look like a demented Charlie Chaplain character. My own shoes and watch make me look like I got dressed in the dark in a charity shop. I carry my new worldly possessions in one hand and with the other, try to stop my trousers from falling down.

Ralph produces a meal. Microwaved fish and chips with peas – which could be placed into any gearbox you care to mention and used as ball bearings. A cup of refrigerated cold water is presented with so much flourish that it could be a fine glass of wine. The food is hard work. I feel sorry for the fish. I've never seen liquid chips before. I need nourishment though. If I've got to defend myself tonight, I don't want to be doing it on an empty stomach. I will need energy. I've got to attempt to survive.

Besides, I put myself here.

After I ate – and I'm sorry, but the peas were not happening – I heard my name being yelled. The source of this was not an officer or a prisoner but a Doctor (Robin Williams). I get told to go into a room with him and he questions me on my health. He does not examine me but I am weighed. I report that I'm fine apart from a tendon problem in my left hand which I already know about. I'm not in "long enough" for him "to do anything about it." I am pronounced fit. End of medical. I made a mental note: Don't get ill.

Doesn't matter - it's game over tonight, anyway.

An officer fetched me. It's time for the next stage of the conveyor belt. He announced that I have "been in Reception." We walked through corridor after corridor. I'm glad he knew where we were going. The more we paced the less modern the interior became. A walking time machine. Metal barred gate after metal barred gate we went through. Each one unlocked and then locked by him after we had passed through until eventually a door that when opened, revealed a view which took my breath away.

Towards the end of 1976, just shy of Christmas, I was taken to what was then, the world's largest sound stage at Pinewood studios, on the west side of London. The 007 stage had been built on Cubby Broccoli's instruction after no other structure could be located anywhere in the world large enough to house three nuclear submarines and enough water to fill the Dorchester. The production was *The Spy Who Loved Me* and walking on that set was like entering another world. I have never felt such atmosphere from the inside of a building like that again. Until now.

Entering the main wing of a prison is unreal. Just like on screen. It's Victorian, both in look and construction. High, very high ceilings. Landing after landing. Metal staircases. Cell door after cell door. The nets. I actually stopped walking as we approached the heart of it. The officer was watching me take it all in. He didn't chastise me for stopping. I think he sensed my awe. I don't think he'd ever seen anyone, so absorbed, by what I was looking at. This is like a film.

And I've been bloody well put in it.

What really got me were the efficacious nets. You're in Prison sunshine. It may look and feel like a film set but this is very, *very* real. Ken Adam, the production designer on *Spy*, got Stanley Kubrick in through a back door – to avoid publicity – to gain advice as to how to light the damn thing. This place needs no such assistance. It's right on the money.

My visit to the world of 007 was on a day when they were shooting on another stage. Films are made in a non-chronological order. The submarines were there. So too were lots of tailors' dummies dressed in baddies' clothes lying around playing corpses. What struck me was how quiet the place was. No one was about. It made the atmosphere even more electric. My arrival on "B" wing had the same effect. The place was in utter silence. Everyone had been put in their cells.

In hindsight, I thank my lucky stars that we did arrive at whatever hour it was and I didn't have to go under the microscope of the other prisoners. At least the introduction to my new home was gentle. Like an American tourist taking in the ceiling of the Sistine Chapel, I stood and stared.

I started off again and followed the officer, still holding up my trousers and cradling my collection of clutter. We walked, my jailer and I, staying on the same floor, ground level, to the end of the wing – to about the last cell on the left. The officer went for his keys. The number of the cell: B 2 5. At the same time of unlocking the door he placed a card with my name on it into a specially designed receptacle.

The door was opened.

Having only met "crew" on this "production" I now met my first "cast" member. Not by the dramatic nets that I associated with submarines but in a very Victorian cell. He was stripped to the waist assembling furniture and looked like he'd been on a shopping expedition to IKEA. "This is Robinson," said the officer holding the door open. I entered and said in as friendly a way as possible: I'm Jon. The door then slammed behind me.

The same slam as on the opening credits of *Porridge*.

Stevie (Johnny Depp) stuck his hand out and said "hello mate" and grinned. I shook it and put my Oxfam rejects down. He's late twenties, nearly six foot tall, in good physical condition and very cheerful. He has a piercing in his left nipple. He explains that he's just been moved here from another cell and that he's cleaning up and putting things back together because "it was a pig sty." A bunk bed is nearly in the middle of the room. Various bits of locker and one chair litter the floor. In one corner there is a television and a grey plastic kettle. There's a lavatory with a waist high steel door around it and a basin, just on the right. A large barred window completes the far wall. If another bunk bed was placed in here, there would be no room to stand up...

I like Stevie immediately. Maybe I'm not going to die tonight. I get stuck in and help him clean up. We make curtains out of two filthy blankets. He hangs them as I hold them. A piece of wood is his hammer and small screws are the nails. Curtain tie-backs are produced from the elastic of two old pairs of boxer shorts. Information is swapped like machine gun fire. He's in for something to do with drugs. He's been in before. In fact, he's been in and out of prison "all his life." The bed is pushed back against the wall and he surprises me by saying the top one is mine. In *Porridge* I thought the more senior man got the upper berth. He works in the kitchens and I'll "want for nothing." Our home is vaguely sorted. I notice him summing me up. He recognises from my demeanour that I've not been "in" before. He then says, in a totally non-confrontational way "what *the* fuck are *you* doing here?"

I've been a tit.

Before he lets me continue, he makes me sit down. The "first thing we are going to do is eat." Then I can tell him "all about it." It dawns on me that I have struck lucky. I have landed on my feet. It is obvious to me that Stevie is going to be my Fletcher and I his Godber. Some polystyrene containers are produced. Stevie generously passes me one and I open it up and look inside. Coronation chicken and salad. I gratefully eat. It tastes good. He watches me demolish it. When I've finished, he passes me another one. I try to be polite, I don't want to eat all his food – but he orders me to eat it. I "look like" I could "do with it." I don't argue and polish that off too. I feel human again. I am aware he is watching me. I finish.

Silence.

He's sizing me up again but can't work me out. "Jon," he says again, puzzled. "What the fuck are you *doing* here?"

It's time to fill him, and you Dear Reader, in. As to why I have been sent *to prison*.

I am a helicopter flying instructor. (Stevie: "Fuckin' hell") I've been working for an individual for the last couple of years and during that time I have been siphoning off money that should have gone into the business. The individual is more hurt and disappointed than angry I think. He's been very good to me and I've really let everyone down. "How much?" asks Stevie. A little more than £80,000. "Fuckin' Hell," he retorts. Don't I know it. I'm very ashamed. "Did you get done for fraud?" No, theft. "They don't like that. Breach of trust and all that. Why did you do it?" To make myself look better. I knew, deep down, one day I would be found out. I just buried my head in the sand. He listens in a non-judgemental way. "Twenty grand a year, top up perks" is his summary. "Everyone's fuckin' doin' it."

That's as good as maybe. I should have known better.

I don't tell him my wife has left me because of this. That I am in turmoil thinking of her and that I am absolutely terrified. I do tell him that I have already decided I'm never coming back to prison – he gave a nasty laugh at that – and that whilst I'm here I'm going to write a book.

"Fuckin' hell," he chortled, "I'm banged-up with Jeffery fuckin' Archer."

My trial with Stevie over he turned the telly on, selected one of the music stations from the many *Freeview* channels available (!) and we sat and smoked lots of cigarettes and drank tea. Prison tea bags were not bad at all. Stevie has enough small milk cartons to brick up the doorway. We talked about mundane stuff and he made me laugh a lot. I have no idea of the hour when he declared it was time to retire. I started to make up my bed. Although I did seven years at boarding school, I still let him show me how to tie up a bottom sheet the prison way. A lone pillow was already on it which I can only compare to a lump of concrete. Realising I had not been issued with a pillow case I moved to the door, where I had spotted an alarm button. Stevie stopped me in my tracks, as if I'd stood on a mine and asked me what I was doing. I explained I was going to ask for a pillow case. His response brought me straight back to planet earth. The only time I am to touch that button, is if I find Stevie "fuckin' hanging."

I slept without a pillow case.

Tuesday, July 26th, 2011.

"I gave myself up for dead before we started," said Bogie in *The African Queen* of 1951. I know the feeling. I am however, awake. And alive. The folly of hope that this is all a dream was realised when I woke up at I don't know what time. I can't even tell you when I went to sleep. I've just spent the night in a locked cell in prison. I feel completely stupid. I am so bloody angry at myself I...

Whoa, Robinson, hold it. Keep calm, *keep calm*. You're going to need to reel your neck in if you're going to get through this. Just bloody well shut up and get on with it. Right. Bollocking over. Let's take in the room. Sorry – cell. To the right; a yellow wall. Filthy. Big Victorian bricks... Do you think anyone cares where you are? Does anyone want to speak to you? Will your wife be...? Shut up. SHUT UP. The room, the room. Check out the room... Ah, right, sorry. The ceiling is rounded. Someone has drawn the features of a girl's face on it. At the foot end of the bed is our metal door. Cast iron. Dull blue. To my left and below, a loo. A steel like gate around it. There's a basin. A couple of lockers. A tiny table and a lone chair. There are toothpaste blobs on the walls everywhere. Lord, this is a God forsaken place.

You put yourself here though.

To be honest I slept soundly. I suppose yesterday took it out of me. Our door was opened and I was told to prepare myself for "Induction." The door was left open. Stevie was up and getting ready to go to work in the kitchens. I made myself get up and climbed down from the bunk. On went my jeans and went to the basin. My trousers do not want to stay up. Got hot water going and had a bloody good wash. Cleaned my teeth and put the kettle on. Studied myself in the tiny mirror. Saw a convicted criminal looking back at me. Shaved. Made a conscious decision to shave every day until this nightmare is over. Try and keep some style JR. Made some tea, which tastes horrid from a plastic cup. Keep going, keep going Robinson. You can do this.

After Stevie had left for work, I found a black biro and decided to start a calendar somewhere on a wall. That's what they do in the films and this bloody feels like one. Selected a bit of mortar, just right and above the door frame. Least likely to be spotted. Result? One black dot. One night done. Christ, what's half of fifteen months? Where are we now? July. Nearly end of. Scrub that, call it August. August, September, Octo... Someone's here...

That someone is, well, he's wearing a God Squad Collar. The Padre? The Chaplain? I don't know his correct title. But he's a friendly face and comes in. "Hello, I thought I'd come and see how you are coping." Bizarrely, he looks like Fulton Mackay. He asks if he can be of "any help?" I would feel completely hypocritical asking for help from his boss now, as I rather fear that would be attempting to shut the stable door long after the horse has departed. As he's listening he has naturally come into the cell and hovered. He suddenly galvanises into remembering something and goes to the cell door – which opens inwards. "Sorry," he says, "I just need to do that." On "that" he released the door latch. I realised straight away that this is a security measure. The door can now not be shut by either of us. Yet another reminder of where I am. He seems satisfied that I am spiritually happy. I tell him the most important thing is to get through this it's fully deserved. "That's the ticket, young man." Before he goes, he hands me a couple of small, pocket sized prisoner religious diaries.

I'm now writing this book in them.

I was called shortly after that for "Induction." I followed an officer from the cell, exiting and turning right, to the end of the wing. During this walk, I was told my "phone call was successful." Good, someone has spoken to Buzz. He knows where I am and that I still exist. Two way communication has been established.

Fort Knox styled white painted iron bars with a locked gate within it reveals the end of B wing. Walking, holding my jeans up – whilst pretending not to – along the corridor, made me realise that the whole of the building is one like one very large public convenience at a railway station of old. When I reached the bars I was told to wait. Ahead of me is a small NASA like control room. Visible within it are officers and a few computers. The staff all stand around, chatting. Looking up, two, no three floors, are some sort of offices. Bars on everything that even vaguely resembles a window or door. To my left and right, other wings branch off from "NASA." I realise that the whole thing is a T shape situation. I live at the bottom of the T. On the right.

The gate is opened and I'm directed to the wing on the left. Visibly, it could be used to "double" mine. Even the people in it look the same. On entry, another officer, by a door on the left, signals me to enter. I do and descend some stairs. A queue consisting of other miserable wretches is joined. Everyone seems to be complaining. The most popular topic of conversation is "why" do they have to "do Induction" when they've "done it here before." Curiously, they are not moaning to the authorities – but to each other. I just keep quiet and listen. Most, if not all of prisoner's comments, end with "innit."

Every now and again I notice people checking me out like suspicious used car salesmen.

The front of the queue is reached and I am patted down by an officer and told to wait in what could easily pass as a doctor's waiting room in a leafy suburb of the Home Counties. Brightly coloured fabric covered benches to sit on and notice boards on the walls. People complaining. And swearing like troopers. There are a lot more people here than were in my arrival party. Clearly St Albans is not the only tour operator. I very carefully study my fellow prisoners. They are made up of a wide variety of age and race. Most wear earrings, necklaces, sports apparel and trainers. All look thoroughly cheesed off. Most sit and stare. Some chat. A few have stood and gathered in little groups. They look like they could be on some street corner.

I am called to a booth at the back of the waiting room that resembles a set for a 1970's sitcom based in a labour exchange. I sit down opposite a chirpy, positive officer (Ian Lavender) who opens a file. He very briefly explains that this is the start of the process of working out what they are going to do with me, whilst I am "staying."

My occupation somewhat throws him for six. It is agreed I don't need any drug counselling courses or "any basic education." Indeed at this point, I said that whilst I am here I would be very happy to get involved in anything that would help others. This was notated. He tells me that at "the next stage of Induction" I will be assessed, "to see where I am." He asks if I "have any issues." My immediate concern was to talk to someone from social services to discuss my home situation. One of the posters on the wall had indicated such a thing was available. I need to sort my rent out. This was duly noted and I was told "St Mungo's who deal with that, would be in touch."

Interview over. Back to my bench. My name is called again and I am shown back through the gate and told to wait on the right, to "see a nurse." She is dealing with another prisoner, who is just being rude to her. I listen as she expertly takes the abuse like water off a duck's back, ticks her boxes in his file and shoos him away. I am called and sit down next to her. Not for the first time in prison as soon as I start talking I see surprise in the face of whoever it is I am talking to. This nurse (Joan Simms) does the same. Already the penny has dropped that I really shouldn't be here.

Please, that's *please* do not think I am saying some sort of miscarriage of justice has taken place. No, no and *no*. What I am trying to convey, is that I should have known better. End of. I hope that is *very* clear.

Even before we establish whether or not I still have my tonsils on board, she cuts in with "what the hell are you doing here?" I confess all. She looks sympathetic. "Why the hell did you do that?" To make myself look better, I explained, shaking my head. There are more pennies dropping here than on Brighton Pier. Have I "got good support from my wife or partner?" No, she left me when this was discovered I said very slowly and then burst into tears. She very cleverly steered the conversation back to things healthcare. Am I up to date with all my jabs. Yes, no problem there. Do I want a "Hep B jab?" No, I don't think so. I think I'll be alright. What about if I "get into a fight and someone slashes me with broken glass?" she asks no differently to a check out girl in a supermarket asking if I have my loyalty card.

I'll take the jab.

A colleague of hers gave me the injection a few minutes later in yet another side office, which was like a cupboard under some stairs. As I climbed the stairs afterwards to return to B wing, I realised it was a cupboard under the stairs. The injection was insignificant. The only thing muttered to me before being inoculated was "it's only a little prick."

Yep, that's me.

Frog marched back to my cell I was locked up within it. Made myself a cup of tea. Stevie reappeared at some point from work. He asked how things were going. I tried to make positive noises and enquired what the rest of the day had in store for us. He explained that I am going to "spend most of my time being banged-up." My face probably told my emotion to this answer so Stevie – being Stevie – said "I'll make you a timetable." I sat on my bunk and skimmed the paperwork I had been given yesterday, as he sat on his bed below me fag in hand, drawing up a rota on some A4 lined paper. Looking over the side of my bunk, it appears that Stevie is putting a lot more effort into his creation than whoever it was that prepared the contents of HMP Bedford's information pack. It is littered with spelling mistakes. The crux of the contents centres on the prison service statement of purpose, the race relations policy statement, the anti-bullying policy statement and the suicide prevention statement of purpose. This and some instructions and guidance on how I can visit someone in prison (that's bloody helpful) sums it up. It is printed on very thin, blotting type paper. It is safe to say that all the health and safety boxes have been ticked by my receipt of this plethora of paperwork which oddly, does not contain a timetable. Stevie passed me his home made one. I thanked him profoundly and studied it to absorb what this place has in store for me.

	MON	TUE	WED	THUR	FRI	SAT	SUN	9:00AM
9M	SHOWERS Association exercise	Work/Education	SHOWERS Association Exercise	Work/Education	SHOWERS Association	Association SHOWERS	Association SHOWERS	AM
	LOCK UP FOR LUNCH RETURN FROM ACTIVITIES							11.30
	LOCK UP LUNCH for PRISONERS AND OFFICERS							2.00
	Work/Education	SHOWERS Association/Exercis	Work/Education	Association/Exercise SHOWERS	BANG UP (CANTEEN) Exercise	Association/exercise	Association/exercise	PM
								4.00pm
								4.30PM
	EVENING MEAL + LOCK UP	DINING OUT Association	EVENING MEAL + LOCK UP	DINING OUT Association	Evening meal Lockup	Evening Meal + Lockup	Evening Meal + BANG up	
		7.00pm LOCKUP		7.00pm lockup				

Each day kicks-off at 0800. Being locked up in a morning and let out for "association" in the afternoon, dovetails with the following morning of "association" followed by "bang-up" (Sic) in the second part of the day. We're locked up every day for lunch at 1130. The afternoon starts at 1400. Evening meals are served at 1630 and then we are locked up until the following morning. This sounds grim even writing it. Tuesdays and Thursdays seem to be the highlight of each week, when "association" lasts till 1900. Non association time has been filled in by Stevie with "Work/Education" but he told me not to hold my breath. Showers can be had during "association."

God, are the rumours about prison showers true?

At around this time – strange, I'm still taking absolutely no notice of my watch – the cell door opened for lunch. I grabbed my plastic plate and bowel then joined a queue that Harrods would be proud of in the New Year sales.

This is the first time I have been out of my cell with so many of the masses present. What strikes me first and foremost is that everyone is in "street" clothes. Where are the uniforms from *Porridge*?

The servery is very close to our cell. Stevie queues one or two places ahead of me, deep in conversation. To my right, is a metal spiral staircase leading to the next landing. Half the bright yellow paint on it has been worn off. Ahead of me, high up above the servery, are massive windows at the end of the wing. They are covered in pigeon shit, like splurge gun shots from *Bugsy Malone*. I am too busy being self-conscious to take in what is on the plates of already served prisoners walking with their meals in the opposite direction. I am able though, to cotton on to someone in the queue saying something not entirely complimentary about me. "He's with ME," said Stevie, ahead of me. Not to anyone. Just said matter of fact. Nothing else was said. I could have kissed him.

I can't report what I had for lunch. I was still shaking.

The next couple of hours were spent in the cell with Stevie locked up. He helped me make a belt for my trousers. We tore off a strip of sheet.

At I don't know what time, the cell door was opened. No one came in. A voice just said "exercise." Stevie explained that I can go outside now to the exercise area if I wished. In for a penny, in for a pound, I jumped down off my bunk and went to the big gates at the head of B wing. My name was ticked and I was shown to an exterior door together with many other prisoners. Outside, I got the inevitable pat-down and went with the herd to a high fenced, green painted sort of courtyard with a yellow line painted around the outside of the ground area. The population seemed content following the "yellow brick road." Round and round we walked. No one spoke to me.

An hour or so – and many laps – later, the two officers present shouted that it was "in time." We all retraced our steps. Another pat-down, before being readmitted to the wing. All the cell doors were now open and loads of prisoners were milling around. Most saying "innit" at any given opportunity. So, this is association. On entry, the cell was empty. I sat on the chair and lit a cigarette. The noise outside displays the throbbing heart of B wing. This is a living building. Two voices get louder. One I recognise as Stevie's. The other is new to me. The owner of it enters with Stevie mid story: "so I said I'm from Hertfordshire and I'm *representing*." Much laughter. The new voice stopped talking as soon as I was spotted and Stevie said "this is Jon." Our guest is Samuel (L. Jackson). Dreadlocked, about a football pitch wide across the shoulders and armed with a fabulous set of teeth. I shook his hand and said hello. "Fuck, you're a bit posh aren't ya?" said the teeth. I shrugged my shoulders and Stevie told him something about minding his p's and q's around me. The atmosphere was friendly and everyone plonked themselves down. Samuel sat on Stevie's bed like he owned the place. I realised he had clocked that I was smoking a "proper" cigarette. He asked for one and I threw them over with my lighter. That earned me a funny look from Stevie.

After he left, Stevie gave me a pep talk. "Jon, don't give nobody nothing." I tried to butt in but Stevie cut me off mid flow, in serious Fletch mode. "Don't give nobody *nothing*, is that clear?" I climbed up and sat on my bed, legs dangling like a child that's been told off. Understood. Sorry. Before he could give me more guidance in walked the villain from the *Back to the Future* trilogy. I was so shocked by the similarity that I looked behind him to see if Michael J Fox was coming in as well. "You," he said, pointing at me, "can leave NOW. Stevie and I have some business to discuss." I looked at Stevie for guidance. Should I go and fire-up the De Lorean?

My instinct told me it was best to make myself scarce.

I may have to do my entire sentence in these clothes but I can't spend the whole of my time in prison hanging around my cell. Come on Robinson – get your arse into gear and get upstairs. What's the worst that can happen? OK, well there's that, fair enough, but you may as well have a look around. I climbed the spiral staircase with missing yellow paint and arrived on the first floor. Which here, are called the Three's. I live on the ground floor, which are called the Two's. No one batted an eyelid that the tall posh **** had ventured to another level. I hesitantly half tip-toed to the other end – away from the pigeon shit – where a bunch of prisoners were hanging about around two pool tables. No one was in the least bit interested in me. Everyone was just minding their own business. They all look different. They all sound different.

But they *all* finish *every* line with "innit."

Having given Stevie enough time for his non-scheduled board meeting, I returned to an empty cell. From nowhere there was *the* most *almighty* thunderclap bang. Half the things in B 2 5 fell over. I thought a grenade had gone off. Having regained what little composure I have left, I peered out of the door. Much rushing about ensued, from staff and prisoners alike. Stevie turned up – grinning like a Cheshire cat. What the hell was that? "That, Jon, was you first kick-off." The guy next door had "smashed up his window" and "has been carted off to the block," said Stevie rubbing his hands with glee. What's the block? "Punishment cells." Ah, the Cooler.

I've seen *The Great Escape* too many times.

At some point later, sitting on my bed half talking to Stevie and half reading something, someone else came into the cell. Young, with ginger hair. Stevie knew who he was but didn't introduce us. I just carried on reading and half listened to the conversation. I gathered our guest was leaving Bedford tomorrow "for an open prison." He was here to collect something. As they chatted, Stevie walked towards the loo, opened the stainless steel door and sat down. I concentrated even more on whatever it was I was perusing, desperately trying to make sure it was the right way up. I have already decided I'm not using the loo at all – throughout my whole sentence – I don't care how ill I get. There is just no way I can perform whilst potentially being watched. How he can do what he is doing with both me – with my birds' eye view – and a guest present, I don't know. As their conversation continued, the horrible realisation materialised of what was happening before me. Stevie was not doing what you or I do when sitting on the lavatory. He was instead trying to retrieve something. *From within his body.* I wanted the ground to open up. Judging by the noises and faces he was making, he wanted something else to open up. Yet still, he and our guest, or I suppose, his customer, just chatted on, like a butcher conversing to his clientele about the weather whilst wrapping sausages. The bunk bed was shaking by this point. At last the goods were produced. I think I was happier than Stevie. The other guy started to enquire where it was best to hide in him the goods. *Please God no,* was said very firmly to him upstairs in my head. "Under your foreskin," said Stevie.

There is a God. I thanked him that Stevie's customer wasn't Jewish.

Wednesday, July 27th, 2011.

The agenda for today is association this morning and Induction exams this afternoon. I met our neighbour from across the way after being unlocked. He enquired what the time was and spent a worryingly long period studying my watch. I should have handed the damn thing in. I felt a little more at ease when he then quizzed me as to where my shoes were from. His name is Jack (The Artful Dodger) and after we'd introduced ourselves – and checked I was still wearing my watch – I warmed to him. He's a real Jack the lad, an archetype Eastender. In short: a scallywag. And short he is: five foot two – when standing on a box. He invited me to his "gaffe, for a coffee." A volley of questions: First time in? How long? How am I finding it? Avoid so and so. Stevie is "good as gold." Don't talk to this lot, do talk to that lot. Seeing a used ashtray I asked if I could smoke. "I don't smoke but of course you can, mate." Jack explained "my Padmate smokes but I don't." Your *what*? "Bleedin' ell, me friggin' Padmate. Bloke I share the cell wiv, innit?"

So "Padmates" are cellmates. My memory of *Porridge* tells me they were "cellies." Back to Jack. Why are you sharing with a smoker, if you don't smoke? "Coz the last one who didn't did me bleedin' 'ead in." Jack told me some stories of ex-Padmates who "had done his head in." The worst it transpired was another first timer. Like me. "Nah, not like you Jon. You is a gentleman. All this bloke could bleedin' talk about woz his bleedin' bird." Jack continues: "The geezer woz struggling an' all wiv being banged-up so I tried to 'elp 'im, like." Jack would ask him if he would like to watch *Eastenders*. Response: "Me and Leisha would watch *Eastenders*." Jack would offer a cup of tea. "Me and Leisha would drink tea." How about a game of cards? "Me and Leisha would play cards." Jack – fast approaching the end of his repertoire – tried his level best to start another diversionary conversation, something about prison towels not being too bad... "Leisha had big fluffy towels." What took the biscuit though, was later that evening. The guy was getting undressed for bed and as he took his top off, well, I'll let Jack pick up the story: "The fucker 'ad her name tattooed right across 'is bleedin' back. I fought I woz hallucinating."

"B wing Library" was yelled mid-morning. Seven of us were escorted by an officer. Lots of radio work and a clearance required from some control centre before "figures seven" could go on the march to things literary. We were greeted by a very Scottish lady who looked like Glenda Jackson but sounded like a character from *Dr Finlay's Casebook*. The rules were explained, which only just fell short of "Do not eat the books." We are allowed to take out three items at a time. Let's hope no one gets too hungry. The library is clean and well stocked. Apart from the bars on the window and the prison officer present, it could be any public library. I even read the *Daily Telegraph*.

The *biggest* section available from which to borrow was of no great surprise: "Crime."

I spent the rest of the day locked up. I have no idea what happened to the exams that I was supposed to be doing. No phone PIN arrived but I did get a delivery of clothes. Not, from the system but from Stevie. Let's just say the kitchen area is down in the white T shirt department...

Later an envelope addressed to me – contents unsigned – was slid under the door. I opened it and read of the confirmation of my sentence. Fifteen months, yes, out in seven and a bit and... Hang on, what's this? "Home Detention Curfew Eligibility Date November 17th 2011." What's this Stevie? He examined the paperwork. "You're going home, on November 17th mate." I am confused. He explains: "They don't want you here" adding that because I don't "hit old ladies over the head, or am a danger to society," that I "will serve the rest of my sentence on Tag," one of those electronic, detector things. I reached for a bookmark that came with the library books. It's got a calendar on it, I'm sure. Found it and yes, it has. November 17th, that's only 18 weeks away. This might be achievable.

RESTRICTED

RELEASE DATES NOTIFICATION SLIP

BEDFORD (HMP)

Name: JONATHAN ROBINSON

NOMS No: A1796CF   Prison No: A00232   Cell: BFI-B-2-005

Sentence calculated on: 26/07/2011

Sentence(s)

1 / 1   25/07/2011   0 years 15 months 0 days

Number of days in sentence	: 458
Sentence Expiry Date	: 24/10/2012
Conditional Release Date	: 09/03/2012
HDC Eligibility Date	: 17/11/2011
Licence Expiry Date	: 24/10/2012

26/07/2011 15:07

Calculated by : ....

Checked by .... Date ....

Thursday, July 28th, 2011.

Today is Stevie's 29th birthday. His gift? He has been carted away by the Police for the day, to "help them with their enquiries." I did my dot on the wall and have also started to put an "X" on each day done, on the freebie bookmark calendar that I got from the library.

I completed the Induction exams this morning in English and maths. They both got more complicated the further into them I progressed, but no major problems. I was the only prisoner who didn't use a calculator for the latter. One poor wretch clearly couldn't read or write. I was told that I will be "called back this afternoon" for my results and then, I can be "given a job."

I then got banged-up.

In the afternoon, I hung about waiting to be called back downstairs for my results. By mid-afternoon concern firmly gripped the base of my stomach as to why nothing had happened yet. A brute of an officer (Oddjob) was approached and very politely asked why I hadn't been called. "Because your name is not on the list." He held a yellow piece of A4 paper in his hand. The list. I asked him if I could look at it. Snookered, he had no option but to hand it over. Less than *ten* names and cell numbers were on it. Mine was about halfway down. Clear, as the nose on my face. Oh look, there's my name, I said. Oddjob grunted, took his piece of paper back and waddled off. The recurring hippopotamus scene from the *Fall and Rise of Reginald Perrin* flashed before me.

Lesson learnt: if you want something done round here, don't trust an "officer" to do it for you. I went to my cell to cool off. Once calmed, I found another officer and asked, nice as pie – with cherries on top – if there was any sign of my PIN number to use the phone. This officer said he "would look into it." I thanked him and then asked when exercise was. "You've missed that, you were supposed to be at your Induction results."

At 1505 I finally got my PIN number and jumped straight on the phone. I rang Buzz, the only number I am allowed to call. Before I went to Court, one day when Buzz and I had spent the day flying, he had joked that if I "did get put away," he would come and "hover over the prison in a helicopter with a rope ladder." That conversation whirred before me as I dialled whilst reading a warning that calls are recorded. Knowing his sense of humour (delicious), as soon as he answered the phone (thank God) I told him to shut up and not say anything daft, as we were being listened to.

He sounded very relieved to hear from me and filled me in on news. Everyone knows. No one gives a toss about me (he points out he does) and the locks on my home have been changed by my landlord. Buzz has spoken to him and the message back from the owner of my home is that I have two weeks to come up with the rent or it's curtains. I asked Buzz to ring him and tell him I'm attempting to get "St Mungo's" to arrange payment of my rent. Buzz said he would relay the message. He – being the friend that he is – signed off with "ring anytime."

Got off the phone worried sick.

Hang on just a minute you ****ing idiot. If *you* hadn't been such a jerk and not let everyone down and ripped-off your boss – who was also a damn good friend and supporter of you – this mess would not exist. SHUT UP.

Stevie reappeared from his "day out with Plod" in good spirits. They had treated him to a meal at a well-known fast food chain. He also returned armed with lots of smokes supplied by the local Constabulary. He made me made me laugh by saying he had dined in the back of a police van, "ringing all his friends from the filth's phone." Dixon of Dock Green was I imagine, turning in his grave.

On Stevie's return to our ranks, he had rather more luck getting his hands on items of clothing than I did and he presented me with a brand new orange and grey jacket, "for when it starts getting nippy." He also obtained a boiler suit, which he explained, "past escapees are made to wear in prison." He tells me he "can expect a tidy sum off the internet for it."

Tomorrow, Stevie and Jack are in Court. Both are currently here on remand. They are not convicted like me (bloody amateurs). Both are hoping for bail and not to return here. I hope they get it but I will miss them.

They are my friends.

Friday, July 29th, 2011.

Stevie was up at 0630 after a knock on the door that he is "in court today." He was already packed. Various new items of clothing were buried deep among his other apparel, in huge plastic bags. He took great delight in showing me his "Sweatbox smokers' kit." A Sweatbox is the local lingo for the transport that prisoners are ferried about in – my Tonka toy. His invention: some tobacco put between the upper cheeks of his backside and a couple of matches and some strike pad in each trainer. Frederick Forsyth's *Jackal* would I think, be impressed. Less so I imagine, with what else I know Stevie has about his person. Or should I say, in his person.

What time will I know that you're definitely not coming back? "Jon, I ain't coming back," he said before he presented me with a china mug "borrowed" from the kitchen. "Drinks will taste better out of that" were his final words to me. I had my Fletcher. Now he's been taken away. My conciliation prize? A mug.

Jack came over to say goodbye. Through the locked door as we conversed, he slid yesterday's *Sun* under it. He told me I will be "banged-up for the day."

Later through my locked door, I got an officer's attention. The events of yesterday – not being called for my exam results – despite my name being on the list – were recounted. This officer I have seen before and he asked which of his colleagues it was who had not fetched me. I told him and he rationalised that the officer whom I referred to "doesn't normally work on this wing," adding "c'est la vie." How difficult is it to read a list and fetch prisoners, whose cell numbers are clearly marked on it? His advice was to "apply for jobs anyway." I dug out the job "application" paperwork from

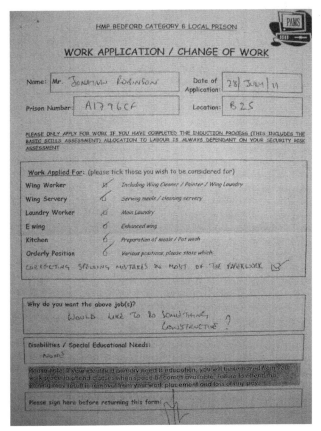

HMP BEDFORD CATEGORY B LOCAL PRISON

WORK APPLICATION / CHANGE OF WORK

Name: Mr. Jonathan Robinson   Date of Application: 28 July 11

Prison Number: A1796CF   Location: B25

PLEASE ONLY APPLY FOR WORK IF YOU HAVE COMPLETED THE INDUCTION PROCESS (THIS INCLUDES THE BASIC SKILLS ASSESSMENT) ALLOCATION TO LABOUR IS ALWAYS DEPENDANT ON YOUR SECURITY RISK ASSESSMENT

Work Applied For: (please tick those you wish to be considered for)

Wing Worker   Including Wing Cleaner / Painter / Wing Laundry
Wing Servery   Serving meals / cleaning servery
Laundry Worker   Main Laundry
E wing   Enhanced wing
Kitchen   Preparation of meals / Pot wash
Orderly Position   Various positions, please state which
CORRECTING SPELLING MISTAKES IN MOST OF THE PAPERWORK

Why do you want the above job(s)?
WOULD LIKE TO DO SOMETHING CONSTRUCTIVE ?

Disabilities / Special Educational Needs:
None

Please sign here before returning this form:

my welcome pack and ticked every box I could find. From chef to loo cleaner. I even added a box, ticked that too and put next to it: *Correcting the spelling mistakes in most of the paperwork.*

1510: Respite. An hour's exercise outside, thank God. Walked and walked and greedily gulped fresh air. On return to the wing, I was summoned to a small queue. Two civilian workers dressed in blue on the other side of a desk. Large plastic crates behind them. The penny drops. Canteen! I'm soon back in the cell opening transparent, sealed bags trying to remember what it was I ordered. It was like opening a Christmas stocking. Tobacco, cigarette papers, phone credit, A4 legal (!) pad, envelopes, stamps and COFFEE! The kettle was put on sharpish. I've been on prison tea since Monday night and I don't even drink tea on the "outside." My first cup of coffee was like drinking champagne.

If only I had been satisfied with the little things in life before...

A knock on the door and a face at the Judas hole. A piece of paper is slipped under the door. This is the menu system. I look at what option I would like to choose for tomorrow and pick the number of what I would like. What I have noticed in the meal queue is that they never say; this guy has ordered the pasta, it's always just the numeral picked. Everything and everyone here, is a number.

My "new" Fletcher arrived this evening. His name is Teevee. (Sanjeev Bhasker, circa *The Kumars at Number 42*). Indian by origin but "lives locally." Very early thirties and about five foot six. Pleasant. And funny: "Don't worry, I don't do any of that praying crap." He's in for something to do with drugs. As most of my colleagues are. He's here till mid-2012. He's clean and very respectful but does say "innit" a lot. Teevee's been shipped-in from another prison up north – I think to be closer to his family. He's not daft. Yet again I've met someone in jail who seems surprised that I am here. Any judgment though, is masked well. I tell him why I am here, how long I am here and he is philosophical. His response to my occupation is like I've told him I'm a spaceman.

I immediately start trying to climb the cliff that is to get him to change his ways. He tells me he intends to. He is lucky. His family – who are "horrified" with his crime, have a cleaning business and there is work waiting for him when he gets out. His main deterrent to not veer off the rails again though is "his missus," who will "wait for him" but has read the riot act and won't tolerate a "second time away."

I don't tell him about my wife.

Teevee is very experienced at settling into prison cells. His possessions are soon unpacked and he is at home. He has one huge transparent bag stuffed with enough tins of food to keep a third world country going for a week, which he stores under the bed. He starts to make up his berth and unbelievably, I find myself teaching him Stevie's trick of knotting the sheets at each end. A prison fitted sheet. I've been here less than a week and I'm already an old hand. He likes the soaps. He likes television full stop. I sit on the chair at our small table and write. He asks me what I am doing and I confess that I'm having a go at writing a book about my prison experience. He is very encouraging.

Then goes back to his telly.

Saturday, 30th July, 2011.

Last night I did a "*Shawshank.*" I wrote the Governor a letter enclosing every page of the Induction material that had a spelling mistake – each error clearly ringed – and requested to do "something positive whilst I am here" even offering to retype their Induction paperwork. The *bulging* envelope was placed in the wing post box. The remaining pages of my welcome-pack – without errors, are not many in number.

Lunch was a fry up. My notes say "disgusting."

I spoke to Buzz on the phone. Nothing to report other than the massive amount of support he transmitted. A very clear line made him say that it sounded like I was "next door." "Exercise" followed my contact with planet earth. I bit the bullet and started conversations with some of the gangster like walkers. Oddly, I didn't get stabbed. Some of them even laughed at my jokes.

Prison at the weekend seems to almost go into shutdown mode. There were two hours of association this afternoon. I went out to the landings after I had watched qualifying for tomorrow's Grand Prix. Nothing changes: Seb is on pole. I played pool upstairs and made an effort to talk to anyone who would listen. No one said anything good, bad or indifferent about me, or to me. They just seem to accept me... If everyone here though, is a "Bad Mother******," how come I keep beating them all at pool?

My notes say "bloody awful supper."

The evening presented me with a task that forced me to consider how James Garner's character in *The Great Escape* would have solved the problem. The challenge? To open a tin of tuna. Without a tin opener. My little grey cells went into overdrive. I looked at the window frame, the legs of the bed, the side of the bed and even the sides of the cell door. Nothing doing. Teevee watched me prowl about the room like a deranged Basil Fawlty and had the sense not to say anything. Come on, Robinson. THINK. What are tin openers made of? Steel. The only steel we have in here is the door and waist high modesty wall around the loo. I got on my hands and knees and studied the design and structure of our cell bog. Bingo! There's a sharp corner, not anywhere near potential "splash back" that should do the trick... Perfect! Two open tins of tuna.

I have just invented the world's first tin opener which you can pee in.

Sunday, July 31st, 2011.

This morning, we had association. For that; read pool. Chatted with lots of prisoners and am now on nodding terms with pretty much everyone on the wing. Does this mean I am now a "Bad Mother******?" Pool was followed by an hour in the sun. During "exercise" I walked around like Clint Eastwood, or tried to.

After exercise we were banged-up. Lunch came and went and I settled down to watch the Grand Prix. Teevee is not the slightest bit interested in Formula One but happy to let me have my fix. I think this is the first time he has not been glued to the box. He likes the soaps and the music channel, which is a massive loop of massive girls dancing to terrible music. Jenson won.

It's strange that in here, I meet and talk to people that I wouldn't normally go anywhere near. Some of them, one would almost cross the road to avoid but chat to them, I do. More vitally, they seem perfectly at ease talking with me. Why-oh-why was I so hell-bent on trying to be something better than me?

After the motor racing, by the pool table I spotted a guy who I had initially made a very large mental note to stay well away from. Today, I saw him outside his cell using sandpaper on something and curiosity got the better of me. I walked over and asked him what he was up to. Instead of him telling me to **** off, he was really friendly. To my surprise, he makes things out of matches and invited me in and showed me his entire collection. Interesting lessons learnt: Don't judge a book by its cover. More importantly: I don't need to be splashing cash – that isn't mine – or being the flash helicopter pilot, in order for people to talk to me and possibly, even to like me.

I won pool again. Many times. This worries me.

1600: Spoke Buzz. Nothing to report.

One of the more sensible officers who is aware of my Induction results, or rather, lack of them, told me he would "leave a note in ops," alerting someone, somewhere, to do something. I repeated to him that I am desperate to talk to "St Mungo's," as I have an irate landlord fast running out of patience. He said he would "make note of this." The evening meal was served shortly afterwards and we were all banged-up. Teevee and I ate together to *Carry on Jack*.

His table manners are... different.

Monday, August 1st, 2011.

Our cell is above the Cooler. Sometimes, residents of said establishment like to converse with the rest of the prison population. By shouting. Day or night. They holler at friends for banter or news. Or company. They don't always get it. I've heard other cells communicating back with material deliberately designed to provoke the poor wretch. More often than not, it has the desired effect. As I write, Dear Diary, in the evening, one of the guests below us is banging something on their door. This has caused Teevee to nonchalantly observe from his bed from where he is watching telly that "we don't half get some nutters in here, innit?"

I was up and dressed this morning by 0815. Induction results and rent situation the priorities of the day. The latter of which, keeps me awake at night. I spoke to yet another officer first thing and relayed the story that apparently some note had been left asking for my concerns to be sorted out. He didn't know what I was talking about but said "Miss Carp" would be along to see me "in the afternoon." Today is our landing's washing day and my pitiful amount of dirty washing was taken in by the "Washing guy."

On exercise, conversation was struck up with an Irish gentleman (Brian May from Queen). The combination of a *very* strong accent and speaking incredibly quickly, made it very difficult for me to understand anything and nearly everything, he was saying. I *think* he's here for eighteen months and I sort of understood that he's just been "shipped-in from a jail in Liverpool." I asked what he's in for and vaguely managed to decipher "tax evasion" followed by "ten." I responded in typical JR style, by remarking that eighteen months seemed a bit steep for ten thousand pounds.

No, no, he said, not thousand. "Ten million."

We were then, as is the norm, banged-up. The never far away voices of panic started to taunt me with pokers – red hot ones. I had to tell myself to calm down. James Herriot was utilised to distract me. Whilst turning pages on calving cows and grumpy Yorkshire-men, I would look up and stare at the door – almost *willing* it to open – to bring me some news.

A stared at cell door does not open.

Teevee is spending all his time here either sleeping, or watching the box. Don't they have telly in India?

The banging from the Cooler is now really going for it. Another cell's occupant has just attempted to get it to stop with a full blast "FUCK OFF." It didn't work.

Back to earlier and the bang-up that now fills my days. At 1455, I asked an officer (again) for assistance to sort my Induction and rent situation. I should have saved my breath. Why are prison staff so uninterested in their cargo? But I got my washing back.

At 1515, I stuck a note under the cell door, asking for an officer to come and see me.

Banging is now *really* upbeat.

1530: I stuck *another* note under the door, this time in capital letters, saying, will an officer PLEASE come and see me. I decided if a white-shirt ever turned up, to insist on talking to a "senior officer," known in these-here-parts as an "S.O."

Asking to see someone round here for help is like trying to send someone a text from a train. In a tunnel.

At 1545, the door was opened by a female (?) officer (Rosa Klebb). As she came into shot all that was missing was some stock Hammer horror film music and associated thunderstorm lightning effects. Her head was down reading my note, upon which she had one booted foot. I didn't have time to check if there was a stiletto sticking out of it. The door now open more than ajar, she shifted her attention to the part of her body that was standing on my SOS. With which, what I can only describe as complete and *utter* disinterest, my note was kicked into the cell with total disdain. It actually got some lift to it and took-off for a moment such was the gusto that she booted it with. After getting over the shock of her ill-mannered bunt, I found myself explaining for the umpteenth time my plight and asked to see an "S.O." She (?) said that she that would "see if one was available" and slammed the door.

After she (?) had departed – and the lights had stopped flickering – I remember telling myself not to become someone to whom the future is of no account.

We had eaten by 1715. As I digested my slops, I spoke with two officers. Neither brought me much optimism. One of them had told me this morning to watch for the imminent arrival of the elusive "Miss Carp" who never materialised. The other introduced a curve ball by instructing me to make two "Applications," which seem to be internal memos, for both my results and required help for my on-going rent issues at home.

I filled in this prison paperwork, thus reacting to this latest, and before now not suggested method of pleading for help and wondered what Tuesday's excuse would be.

After form-filling, we were banged-up.

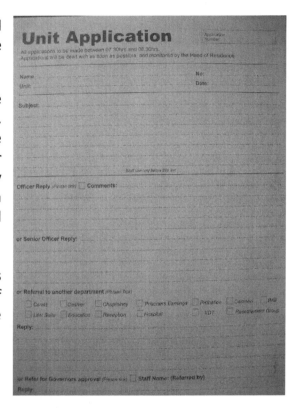

Tuesday, August 2nd, 2011.

Not a bad night. Up and dressed by 0810. I asked to see anyone of a medical disposition this morning as I have a splinter (!) in my thumb which is driving me mad. Oh for a pair of tweezers.

Banged-up.

When Teevee woke up he started watching telly!

Attempted to teach him chess. Without a chess board. Or pieces. Tomorrow we do hang gliding. At 1030, I saw a nurse. The dialogue was right out of an Ealing comedy as it was held through a waist height letter box type hole where they hand out various drugs in the hub of the prison next to mini NASA. Are drug users very short? She couldn't help – no tweezers are kept there, so I am down on the sick parade list and will get "seen this afternoon." Where have I heard that before?

Miracles do occur. When I returned to the cell my Induction results had arrived. Apparently I can read and write. And add up. Does this mean I can now get a job? Or help people? I asked an officer. Answer: "Put in an App" ("App" = "Application"). So I did. Again. And another for "St Mungo's." I am beginning to wonder if they utilise these delaying tactics on purpose, to trigger a response.

I have established the name of our resident *Back to the Future* villain: Barclay. He tells anyone who will listen what his occupation is: "Cage fighter" – I would love to see his passport – but what is really bugging me is the villain's character's name in the series of films. Biffer? Biffo? Barclay lives on the top landing and proclaims that he is "the Godfather of B wing." He's OK, and always shouts "alwite Jon" when he sees me.

1155: Lunch. Terrible. Some sort of rice thing with chicken in it. Then we got banged-up. I have nearly finished off James Herriot.

At 1415 we were unlocked and offered exercise. I shot outside like a man who had been locked in a cell all morning.

1515: Back to the cell. Canteen sheets had been put under the door. Separate sheets are pre-prepared with prisoner's name and available "spend" clearly marked at the top. My sheet simply requested tobacco, phone credit, stamps and more paper.

Played pool in the afternoon and again, kept winning. This is now *really* beginning to bother me. On the "outside" I am *crap* at the game.

I was later told that I would be taken over to the sick bay for my major surgery after lock up. It's now 2015 and no sign of an escort.

Teevee doesn't half move quickly to change channels when one soap has finished. Complete panic stations occur should he miss the opening seconds of the next one's opening titles. It's like an alarm on a warship. I am now an expert on *Emmerdale* which I thought was called *Emmerdale Farm*. He tells me they have sexed it up with its new moniker.

By 2100, something told me that my thumb is not on the top of anyone here's list, so gave up. We are settling down to watch Clint Eastwood in *Escape from Alcatraz*. Will try and get some tips.

Wednesday, August 3rd, 2011.

Prison Dictionary

"Innit"	Didn't it
"Shotting"	Selling Drugs
"Dockers"	Dog Ends (Used Cigarettes)
"Burn"	Tobacco
"Innit"	Isn't he?
"Innit"	Absolutely, old boy
"Brov"	Mate
"Smack head"	Confused Chap
"Gentle, not mental"	Go easy, old boy
"Innit"	If you know what I mean
"Innit"	Don't they?
"Innit"	Won't they?
"Innit"	Didn't they?

As anticipated, the thumb detail never turned up, so enjoyed *Escape from Alcatraz*. Now plotting – at least in my head – *Break from Bedford*. A good shouting match occurred between the locals after Clint had departed from our screen and his island. The screaming argument's subject? Lord knows.

On return from exercise played pool, had just won my third in a row (!!!!!!!!) and was waiting for the fourth victim to set them up when I heard my name being shouted from below. Believe it or not, it's finally off to see the doctor time.

The medical-man was not terribly impressed with my plight, telling me that he "didn't have the time to operate." I asked him if he was joking. Surely he's got a pair of tweezers lying about? "No." He actually *was* talking about a minor operation. To remove a *splinter*. His prognosis: "It will work its way out, once it's nice and infected" and that in the "three or four years" that he has "been here" (he must have done something really bad) he has "never had a prisoner with a splinter before."

Being walked back to B wing with my foreign fragment still on board, we transitioned the Colditz courtyard. On my return to B wing I was pounced on by yet another officer (Chuck Norris). "Robinson? You're name has been put up, would you like to move to E wing where things are more relaxed?" I remember looking over his shoulder at the pool area. I feel relatively safe here, I know some people, I have not yet been used for target practice and I have no *idea* what "E wing" is. I *do* know there is some wing here with some really unpleasant characters in it that I have heard about. Is this what he is talking about? I'm OK here, I heard myself say. His eye brows shot up to the top of his head. "Shame," he said. And walked off.

Someone vaguely familiar was grabbed and enquiries about E wing were made. "Why?" I explained the offer of relocation had come my way. "What did you tell him?" I said no. "Are you fucking mad? E wing is the enhanced wing you ****." Word soon spread that the "pilot had turned down E wing." Everyone went ballistic, telling me "it's like a hotel" and what had I "been thinking?" I've never heard of the bloody wing and I was worried I would be placed with a bunch of nutters. It was then explained to me, very slowly, so I could understand, "that the nutters are on F wing." Frog marched to the white gates by my newfound friends I signalled to an officer that I would like a word. Now I have received intelligence, I would like to move to E wing. He said he would "pass the message on." Knowing my luck I'll end up on F wing...

I have been told it's "unheard of to only be here a week and a half and be offered E wing."

B 2 5. Teevee has found a chess set. Sat down with him and went through the basics. Good to get him away from the bloody television. He has told me that since he has been in (six months), he has only read one book...

1145: Banged-up. Lunch was revolting. I have come to the conclusion that we are all made to eat in our cells, rather than a dining room or refectory, so that the most dangerous thing in the prison is split up and not stockpiled. I refer to the food.

1330: Banged-up. Library was cancelled today due to some "incident." I am thwarted to emergency rations of James Herriot.

1400: Door opened up so Teevee can go to Induction. He's already done it at HMP Bedford and at his other prison, yet they won't let me finish mine. Am I missing something here?

1515: Teevee back from Induction and the TV is on. I have only managed to use the loo once since I've been here. Teevee manages to perform with no problems, with me, or anyone else in the cell. The loo is metal, thus deposits are very audible. By the volume of the noise his business makes, I am surprised I don't have to follow him around with a bucket. It's like living with a circus elephant.

Anyone need some **** for their roses?

Thursday, August 4th, 2011.

After a game of chess yesterday evening we got chatting about prison. We discussed whether it was "worth it." Me first (author's prerogative): No. Whilst I can't turn the clock back, I just wish I had handled things not like I did. I have let so many people down. It's as simple as that. His views: "Yes." "100% yes." "Prison is easy." He made "loads of money." He "had respect." He was able to wear his "white tracksuit" and his "gold chain" and his "new trainers." Most *vitally*, Teevee was in a position to take his "missus for a kebab, whenever he wanted to."

It was difficult writing the above whilst keeping a straight face.

0855: Lots of noise – which is entirely usual, from about 0800, as prisoners got ready for "Education" or "Work." I am banged-up as I don't have a job. Despite asking for one a million times.

1055: Still banged-up. Teevee is perhaps closer to Fletcher than Stevie was, in that he just sees prison as an occupational hazard. I see it as punishment. And shame. And a possible chance to improve myself. Teevee was selling drugs the day before he went to Court. I was flying helicopters. I am NOT saying I am a better person than him. I just know I should have known better.

1200: Lunch. In cell. Banged-up. A chap decked out in very colourful gear and a turban visited Teevee and gave him some more pudding. Some sort of religious meal, I understood. It looked like Angel Delight to me. Lots of "banter" this afternoon between Cooler (below me) and some random cell (above me). The conversation was beneath me.

1500: Finally let out. Played pool. Don't ask.

I rang Buzz. My landlord will give me breathing space until the 10th. I have put in ANOTHER request to see St Mungo's. Another "app." I can only guess that the set pace of issues being dealt with – or not – here, is all part of the punishment.

1830: Banged-up. Have eaten. Teevee engrossed in the soaps. I am writing. Samuel has been moved to the Cooler for refusing a drugs test. I know NOTHING about drugs but in the short time I have been in Bedford prison I have seen more pills than in my entire life. In a commercial break I quizzed Teevee about the drug issue here. He reacts to the subject matter like you or I would discuss whether or not the cat had been put out. He reckons that some of our colleagues take their punishment and utilise the time to reflect on their past, present and future behaviour. The majority though, treat it as a holiday camp with free board and lodging, hot food and an easy place to get a "fix." Terrifyingly, some have even got themselves imprisoned on *purpose* to make money selling drugs. I hope and think I fall into the first category.

I got my splinter out today.

Friday, August 5th, 2011.

A terrible night. I turned in early, so did Teevee, with no TV (hoorah) but was woken up at Lord-knows what time, by some idiot above us playing music. I assume someone had been at the funny looking cigarettes or some other of the many substances and concoctions that are both available and on offer in HMP Bedford.

At about 0815, the cell door opened and I was told I had "Gym Induction." Off about thirty of us – under escort – went. On arrival at the huge gymnasium, we were collectively lectured by a typical PE instructor right out of *Carry on Sergeant*. He barked at us "not to break the rules" and then gave us a tour of tonnes of weight machines. On the wall was a massive coat of arms in bright gloss paint. Under the rampant whatever it was, it said "Fit to Serve." Otherwise the gym looked like any other.

0930: Four games of pool won on the trot. I'll be saying "innit" soon...

1030: Banged-up. We are to spend the rest of the day in the cell. Teevee is watching you-know-what and I have my pen in hand. I have never done so much writing in all my life and my right hand is beginning to tell me so. I suppose I am not the only prisoner here who's right hand does a lot of work... I have not masturbated since I have been here. Sex is on the back burner.

I would just give anything to *talk* to my wife.

1200: Got a letter from my landlord. Notice to quit. I am homeless. Bugger. Couldn't eat lunch.

1225: Worrying about my flat.

1226: The crossed wires of multi cell conversations shouted from cell windows are like a 1950's telephone exchange.

What am I going to do if I'm homeless? Right Robinson, GET A GRIP. There is no point in worrying about it, as there is ABSOLUTELY NOTHING YOU CAN DO ABOUT IT NOW.

The noise outside is *unbelievable*. Teevee is asleep.

1335: A note from St Mungo's slid under the door. They are aware of my problem and "will be in touch as soon as possible." It was dated the 2nd of the month...

1355: Canteen. Some respite from the pressure. I asked one of the more sensible officers if I could use the phone – urgently – and he said yes. That was the good news. The bad news was that the phones were switched off... He said I could try later.

1445: Cell to cell communication has commenced. There are (supposedly) no mobile telephones here. Just yells from windows. Although ours is open, we receive only. We do not transmit.

Teevee is watching telly.

1505: I have just asked again if I can use the phone, due to the emergency home situation. "The phones were switched off at 1500," said the officer.

1630: Played chess with Teevee. Life is crap at the moment. I am worried about my home situation. I am worried about my future. Bloody prison. I have to *keep* reminding myself that it is JR that put JR here.

No one else.

1700: Have eaten. Some sort of Chinese style, chicken leg. Not bad. Made sure I got – and ate – loads of vegetables. God, I felt so ashamed of myself looking at my fare on a plastic plate. Society has, quite rightly, put me in a place where I am not to be trusted with china.

Through the window is coming the theatre of prisoners communicating with shouts and screams at each other. They exchange insults, banter and even swap outside home addresses for the transaction of… well, I'm sure you can figure that out, Dear Reader.

1900: Finished chess with Teevee. In the nick of time, as the soaps are starting. The outside banter (which I find more interesting than the soaps), ceased and became a shouting match when a third party intervened with a "FUCK OFF" which is prison-speak for "shut up." This caused all *hell* to break loose, with many other windows demanding – with all sorts of threats – that the culprit identified himself.

It calmed down when someone shouted "dead it," which translated for me by Teevee means the "beef is dead," which I will translate for you: the rumpus is over. All went very quiet at that point. This can only mean that all the "gangsters" like the soaps too…

2000: Getting into bed. The window banter is starting again. They are obviously *Corrie* fans but not keen on *Eastenders*.

Saturday, August 6th, 2011.

The banging, shouting and "music" went on till about 0100 this morning. I got up at 0845 and felt incredibly groggy. I am writing today's thoughts and observations at 1730. I have eaten. *Dr No* is on telly. Teevee is glued to it in bed. The sequence with the spider on Connery's arm reminded me of my father. He liked the squashing bit in time to the music. Dad died in 1999. Boy, would he be in a state about where I am now. And quite rightly.

The evening banter has just started.

This morning we were opened up at 0900 by none other than the female Demi Moore officer ("DMO") who interviewed me on my arrival at HMP Bedford. She remembered my name and asked how things were going. DMO remarked again that "shit happens" and that I was a "good example of how to get through this nightmare and come out the other side." She told me I am now "low risk" and something called Cat D, which means I "can go to an open prison." The problem is that "they are all full." DMO led me to believe that my entire contribution to this production will be shot here. She knew about the E wing episode and thought it both "funny and typical," that no one had explained to me "what E wing is all about." She assured me that I am "top of the list" and gave me a certificate saying I don't sell drugs and I am not likely to escape. I have thus doubled the time I am scheduled to spend in Tom, Dick and Harry. I was handed another "work app." This one attached to the one I have already filled out (on more than one occasion), as the "forms have been changed" (!!!!!!)

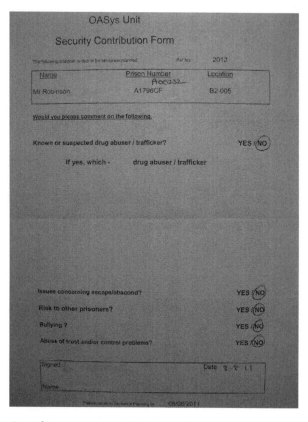

Am I being filmed? I filled in the "new" work "app" answering the same questions, again.

Teevee was told by our glamorous yet sensible officer that he is not being shipped-out. He wants to return to his old jail but can't. "There is no transport for him," said DMO. He is keen to return back to the other place as most of his kit is there and he misses his "curry club." He has told me they brew up a nice "Ruby every Friday." Their cooker is the *kettle*. I glare at him whenever he goes near ours. As much as I love a good curry, I also need my coffee in the morning...

Back to DMO. We talked of prison and I told her I thought it was doing me good. I just wished that Probation had given me a heads-up to bring some kit if it all went pear-shaped. Her response made me laugh: "Probation are a bunch of ****ing idiots with their heads up their own ****'s. They need to come and spend some time at the coal face." By this time, other prisoners were gathering round her like children do an ice cream van. She obviously carries some weight around here and actually seems to demonstrate some interest in the system's charges. Her final comment to me, before being bombarded with questions by the masses, was that "some prisoners do a mill or two and only do a year inside." DMO thinks "hmmm, it's probably worth it."

Later on the landings I continued the topic of conversation of things prison with another of the more sensible officers. It's obviously sensible officer day. I didn't spot Rosa Klebb on duty. His view – and I completely agree – is that prison is too easy. The pool tables on the landings, the telly, countless *Freeview* channels and kettles in cells that seem to just be both expected and accepted as par for the course by prisoners, almost a "right," and so on. We both agreed that once prisoners have earned privileges, then fine. He thinks National Service would reduce the quota of his guests. Looking at the rabble that consists within the prison – and I include both prisoners *and* staff – I told him he had my vote. He said the revolving door of familiar faces that "keep coming back," was very frustrating from his side of the fence. I think he meant wall. I told him that I have already clocked that not enough is done to stop people either turning up here in the first place, due to a complete lack of basic discipline and certainly not enough – or perhaps, not the right type of – after sales service to stop reoffending. Clearly prisons need to exist. Yours truly was a prime candidate that a kick up the arse was required. The problem is – it's not working.

Mid-morning and an hour of exercise. I am now on chatting terms with pretty much everybody. Pretty, they are not. Barclay – Cage Fighter and *Back to the Future* villain (I still can't remember the name) – NEARLY came to blows with an Asian gentleman, the same size as him. They were squaring up nicely. Fists and feet were flying around each other's faces – without contact – and the fuse was most *certainly* burning when the two officers present stepped in. To their credit, it was all defused with words.

Teevee has warned me that prisoners can snap with another inmate due to pressure on the home front or just sheer frustration, with no warning. I need to remind myself of this continually, especially on the landings where I will now talk, or be spoken to, by almost anyone and everyone. Like flying light helicopters, over familiarity, overconfidence and complacency *will* get one into trouble. It is inevitable that at some point with my big mouth, I will say something stupid – and face *serious* problems. I must keep my wits about me and not forget where I am.

I won pool. No comment.

1215: Banged-up. Lunch was a chilli and VERY hot. It was also I have to say, VERY good. Without doubt the best meal I have had since I have been here and as good as you would have in any restaurant. After lunch I had three "speed" games of chess with Teevee.

Then we took our clothes off.

No, things hadn't got that bad. The removal of kit was because Teevee had got his hands on some hair clippers that looked like they hadn't been used to brush the floor. Relatively new and more vitally, *clean*. I have abandoned looking like a microphone and decided I would let him loose on me. This was after I had made it *very* clear to him that I did *not* want the HMP Bedford "look." Teevee in fact, did a very good job and I told him that he could cut it (sorry) as a prison barber and earn enough to keep him in curry for some time. I then did him. His head, beard, the lot. I am now sharing my cell with a bald, slightly bearded TV addict from India.

We scheduled the coiffures to conclude at opening time, so when we were unlocked, I vacated the cell like a scalded cat at 1400 – the hour, not my speed – for the showers. Various remarks – all of a complimentary tone – were made and a rash of enquiries as to "who did it?" I think I might become Teevee's agent. Dashing for dousing, the "E wing offer officer" had some lines. I started to explain the misunderstanding but he stopped me mid-sentence (!) He had been "told of the confusion" and instructed me "not to worry." I am "top of the list." He apologised that I had got the wrong end of the stick. After my shower I played pool. Won three.

On my return to the cell I had post. In the shape of a post card. A second class stamp on it. Dated "Thursday." It was handwritten...

"Dear Johnathan (Sic) I have been asked to visit you and have made a booking to see you at 1.45 p.m. on Tuesday 9th August. I look forward to meeting you then Regards Timothy P.V."

"P.V." is prison visitor. One of the early forms I filled in after my arrival was for prisoners who have no one to come and see them, so "Timothy" and I will sound each other out on Tuesday afternoon. Nothing ventured, nothing gained.

Telephoned Buzz who was out walking his dog. I asked him to ring my landlord with reference to the letter I have received and repeat that St Mungo's have promised me that they will be in touch. Buzz said of course he would and added that he "knew my hands are tied."

1630: Banged-up. The door was opened at 1700 for dinner. In the queue my eyes wandered around the seven or so kitted in white prisoners who serve the slops. As I came to the head of the queue, with still more than half the wing in line behind me, I asked who had made the chilli at lunchtime. This caused an immediate cessation of service. You could have heard a proverbial pin drop. Even the officer present looked up. The culprit was presented. I told him that it was the best chilli I have ever had (no exaggeration) and he got a round of applause! Even from the lags in the queue behind me – and I was holding up the line! On transmitting that Gordon Ramsay had better watch out, his face was a picture. It made my day. A footnote to this: One of his colleagues said to me "not bad for £3.50, eh?" which I assume is the budget they have to work from to feed us all each day.

So I didn't need to steal money to be popular. WHAT a tit. Prison is doing me good methinks. I do however fear that I am unique within that category. For the rest of the population, it's just part of their "job." That sounds harsh I know but I feel things MUST be changed.

1925: I am concerned by the prison jacket that Stevie left me before his departure. It has an awful lot of orange to it. Not that the national colour of Holland doesn't suit me, but the other day conversing with Teevee I exclaimed that two prisoners dressed head to toe in green had been spotted, and had asked him what this signified. He thought "green was something to do with high risk, but wasn't sure." He did know "for sure though" what colour Escapees have to wear:

"Orange."

Sunday, August 7th, 2011.

0800: Awake. Sitting in prison boxers. Last night? I think I dropped off at 0130. Bloody NOISE.

0845: Just managed to use the loo for the third time since my incarceration. There is a God.

Association started at about 0930. Played pool. Lost. (Hoorah!) Spoke to Don Corleone (don't ask) upstairs, who is in Court tomorrow facing a "ten year stretch." He's representing himself...

Exercise followed. 45 minutes of walking around the pen. Talked with the heavily accented Irish tax- evasion guy again. His name is Pat. He is *full* of all the charm of the Emerald Isle but IMPOSSIBLE to understand. I hope I nodded and shook my head in the right places.

1130: Banged-up. Teevee and I are both raddled with jet-lag from the dreadful lack of sleep over the last couple of nights because of the ****ing noise. We played pre luncheon chess with alas, no sherry. I won. Lunch was "roast beef, roast potatoes and veg." Disgusting. Apple crumble for pudding. Ditto. *Carry on Behind* is on telly. Took a quick cat-nap. Got up 1250. Teevee out for the count. He's asked me to nudge him at 1330. I'm worrying about my home. I'm ringing Buzz this afternoon, during association. Sorry if this is no page-turner. I AM SO TIRED.

Through the window is the vision of prison. Don't whine whilst serving your time. Just be like Fletch and serve your stretch.

1330: Just tried to wake Teevee but he doesn't want to know. Perhaps I should turn the box on, to tempt him into consciousness.

Let out just after 1400 and got in the queue for pool. Played. Lost. Thank God. I met John (Noakes). Here for drunk-driving, "for the second time." Not only was he "pissed when behind the wheel" but also "tried to do a runner." And the bar that he had been in was only "five minutes staggering time from home." As full of regret now, as he was as full of beer then. He got four months. Despite his folly, he is a "normal" person and I like him.

1515: Spoke to Buzz and it is indeed game over at my home. Now I don't know WHAT to do. He told me that my brother has been in touch with my landlord and I've asked Buzz to speak to him, to sort out the moving of my possessions. The concern of which must take second place to the fact that I need to provide an address to this lot, before they let me go. By the sound of things, I haven't got one to give, let alone live in. First thing: Do not panic. Maybe St Mungo's can arrange accommodation when I get out. Maybe stay with someone? No – that makes no sense as I think I'll have an electronic Tag. Right, I'm in a right fix. Think, think, think.

Agenda: Speak to St Mungo's and find out what the options are. Buzz says that my landlord is in no hurry for my things to be picked up. Will just have to gather more information and above all: don't panic.

1630: Banged-up. Then let out to pick up food. Cheese salad, in a French stick. My life sucks. *Carry on follow that Camel* on telly.

1800: I need to get into my thick head, that the s**t has hit the fan – on all fronts – and to expect nothing. Then if anything good does happen, it will be a bonus. Right now, just concentrate on getting through this.

The banter has started. Guess they've been sniffing the washing up liquid again. I think it'll be a long night.

Monday, August 8th, 2011.

"Banter," I believe, is good natured chit-chat between individuals. I have come to the firm conclusion that I have misnamed the yelling that goes on at night between cell windows at Bedford prison. Is there a word that describes all- night-shouting? We have a "gentleman" in the Cooler (I think, RIGHT under us), who took great delight in keeping me up all night. The conversation (?) went from the dishing out of free legal advice aimed at one cell, to the best methods of family planning to another, with the question "yeah?" at the end of EVERY sentence. To which, I am definitely serving more than one at this present time.

Was up at 0700. On the news this morning we are being told of some seriously hefty rioting in various parts of the country last night. At least I have an alibi. It's washing day today. More importantly; I need to chase St Mungo's.

0850: An officer at the door. I have my "Tribal interview in twenty minutes" (??????????)

Wondering what on earth Tribal was I was downstairs twenty minutes later. We were met by two or three civilian females, one of whom did a very unsure-of-herself roll-call. The prisoners present numbered about eight. It seemed that at least six off her list were missing. Their possible escape did not cross my mind. I know what this place is like for rounding up prisoners and taking them where they are supposed to be...

I got seen by a young Indian lady, who was right out of any Bollywood production you care to mention but who wore too much make up. Her opener: "Where the hell have you been since you did your exams?" (!!!!!) After I had regained my composure, the "your-name's-not-on-the-list" story was recounted. She just somewhere beneath the acres of mascara rolled her eyes and asked me if I had "noticed that the turn-out had been somewhat short of the roll-call." I acknowledged noticing a deficiency in desired prisoners. "It's a common problem," she explained. I told her I have been practically begging all last week to come and finish my Induction and have filled out enough work apps to re-paper the inside of the Houses of Parliament. She told me her "department hadn't received any of them," adding that they were redundant (my word, not hers), as my "name had not been ticked off the list" (her words not mine).

She was kind enough to acknowledge that none of this was my fault and asked me for the name of the "your-name-is-not-on-the-list" officer. I told her. With *bells* on. It is only that I don't want any legal troubles that it's not recorded here. It's a bit bloody much that my "grassing" in prison, is about the bloody staff.

We moved on. The type of training and help that the system can offer me to get work on the outside was discussed. Until she learnt my occupation. When she had climbed back on to her chair she just shut her files up and said "we'd better get you on the list for a job." She then proceeded to fill out a "Work app" (!!!!) for me. She also put me down – after I told her that I will do *anything* – for a "course." In floor cleaning.

Anyone need their hangar cleaned?

She marked me down for an "urgent" appointment with St Mungo's. Whilst I had

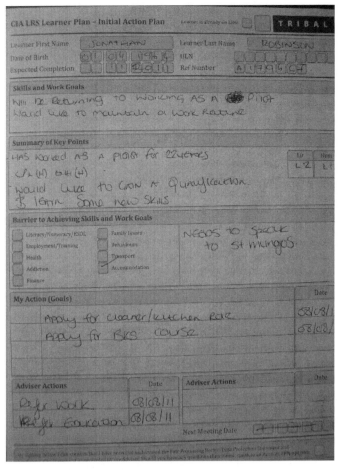

waited to be seen by her I had read one of their signs and noted that they will NOT (their capitals, not mine), supply an address for "Tag," the electronic device that awaits me. I tried not to panic as I read it.

In the library later whilst fumbling for fodder to read, I came across some book written in jail. Realised it was Jeffrey Archer's *Prison Diary* (or part, there off) and put it down like a hot potato. I do NOT want to be influenced by others who have succeeded in what I am attempting to do. Namely, giving inside experience of prison some mileage in the words department.

I got some *not* written in jail books.

Another pen has just died (number four?) I now have to write in a different colour. If this gets published, you won't have noticed that. I need to get some more biros. A breeze on the "outside." Not so easy here.

Back on the wing I rang Buzz. My brother is on the case to get my stuff moved. How and to where, I have no idea.

I am now writing again in black ink. I have just been given a pen by an officer (!) More of that later. On returning to B 2 5, I was told that my (Stevie's) mug (china) has been confiscated. "It could be used as a weapon," the explanation.

Played pool before bang-up at 1130. Won two. Shit, I'm a gangster. Lunch was served at around 1140.

I let Teevee dine first, as I simply can NOT eat at the same time as him (see the food on the beard). I was told by an officer that I have a "meeting with St Mungo's, tomorrow morning." Now that's progress.

Post luncheon played chess with Teevee. We could both be Grand Masters but only if we were both serving double life sentences. Got onto bed for a quick snooze with *Carry on Nurse*. Slept for twenty minutes. Teevee had asked me to wake him at 1415, which I did. Then the pen died, so had to go "blue." Then there was a knock on the door…

The "E wing offer officer." I am "moving tomorrow." He told me on top of this, that he will "get me a job." My mind raced. I told him I have an urgent appointment with St Mungo's in the morning and a visit in the afternoon, as I am meeting "Timothy." He laughed and asked me when could I "fit the move in?" I told him to speak to my secretary.

I then got a black pen off him. An eye for an eye. Or a pen for a mug.

The following is going to sound ridiculous but I will miss B 2 5. I can't believe I've just written that but it is true. It's been my home and bearing in mind I didn't know WHAT to expect on my arrival, I think I have been very lucky with both Stevie and Teevee, (see the food all over the scenery). I wonder what the third one will be like.

I will NOT however, miss the "Window Warriors."

1625: Played chess with Teevee. Twice. I won them both but to be fair to him – he has started beating me. Probably the past games where I have not reported the outcome, knowing me.

I can't remember what I ordered for supper from our-pick-a-number-that-is-an-option menu. I wonder what the food will be like on E (for "enhanced") wing.

1740: It was chicken (leg of) and rice. What was *once*, a probably fairly nice bit of meat had been destroyed by whoever it was that had cooked it. Certainly can't have been chilli chef from the other day. In the dinner queue, a female officer (Jean Harlow) shouted across the hungry gathering if I knew I was "moving tomorrow." If I didn't know – I know now. So does the rest of B wing. I grinned in response and said yes, then thanked her. This caused a response from the chaps that an engagement is going to be announced soon.

Dined in cell with Teevee. Simultaneously. Tried to blank his eating habits. Not easy. See/hear the chicken bones being sucked.

1745: We are going to watch the news on the Beeb at 1800. So too, is the rest of the prison. The majority of wing talk today has centred on the riots that seem to have spread like an out of control forest fire. Prisoners have told me that they "want to see their friends on the telly." It saves on visits.

1815: As soon as the piece on the riots ended which "are now taking place in Lewisham and Brixton," urgent banter started from the Window Warriors in an excited hive of activity.

1935: Teevee totally hypnotised by his soaps. It's quiet outside. Probably not for much longer. So, the last night in B 2 5. The midnight conversations will not be missed. Nor will the bunk bed heaving and wobbling like a lifeboat in a gale as Teevee, er, thinks of his girlfriend.

Tuesday, August 9th, 2011.

A quiet night by the Window Warriors' standards. Maybe they have all been moved to E wing in preparation for my arrival later. I got up at 0700 and stuck the news on. The rioting has gone through the roof, what's left of them anyway, all over London. The Prime Minister "has had to cut short his holiday in Italy" and is on his way back to the UK.

Today: St Mungo's, the prison "visitor" and a move to another wing. All that tunnelling from B 2 5 wasted. PRISON CENSOR THAT WAS A JOKE. Did the "last" dot on the wall. Here, anyway. It's 0720, and Teevee is still off with the fairies.

0815: Just BANGED on the closed door as an officer walked by. Got his attention and asked him what time my appointment is with St Mungo's. "What appointment?" his response. The appointment that I was told of yesterday by one of his colleagues that is booked for this morning. This was met with "there are no appointments this morning."

1000: Teevee up. Having breakfast. Hear the cornflakes being sucked. I've been reading. And thinking. I wish I could talk to the people I have hurt or let down. Or both. They don't want to know though.

Played chess with Teevee. Don't think he would admit it but I think he's going to miss me. I'll certainly miss him. Apart from at meal times. We all have our faults though and I bet if he was keeping a journal, his list of my peculiar habits would fill chapters in great volume. The fact of the matter is, forced together, coming from different backgrounds, cultures, class and life experiences, we have found common ground. Another good lesson in life. Anyways, Teevee is a good egg. He even looks like one with his shaved head. Lunch was served at 1200 which was horrendous.

1320: A knock on the door. "Robinson, visit." About seven of us are led through C wing, the other off-shoot from mission control. Outside, we're taken again past Reception and then up loads of stairs. Various heart attacks (by my younger colleagues) later follows the obligatory pat-down. We are then given a form of bib each to don. I'm processed, my watch is taken from me and put into a locker, for which I am given a key. All of us then enter a huge hall like space.

An officer acting as the maître de tells me "table twenty four." I nearly ask him to send over the wine waiter. My table is centre front. A yellow, plastic chair for me, which is bolted to both the floor and the table itself. On the other side of which are three green plastic chairs. All prisoners sit facing front in their bibs. We look like a table-football team. I appear to be centre forward.

Visitors start to trickle in. Indian families, the travelling community, young girls (not wearing very much) – I tend to notice these things, "mates" and some expectant mums, who look the least thrilled at seeing their loved ones. To our right, is a penned off play area with a plethora of assorted toys for different ages. I sit like a wallflower for some time. Just as I am beginning to think I've been had, I hear my name being spoken. My Christian name.

Timothy (Kenneth Connor, circa 1964) sits down opposite me. Nervous and short. His finger nails look like he's recently dismantled an old lawn mower. He has a small hard back blue note book in his hand. Across the top of it is written in black marker pen: "Prison visitor Timothy." I wonder if this is if he forgets who he is. He is friendly but both shy and unsure of me. My voice makes him even more so. The more we talk, the more embarrassed he appears to become. I sense he'd rather be talking to me at his golf club. I try to put him at ease. He opens with inquiring as to where I am from. I don't bore him with my housing problems but give him a geographical pointer. He is familiar with the area. He shifts subject to things family and asks if they are expected. I briefly explain that my wife has understandably upped-sticks due to my crime and tell him that I do not have anybody else hence the request for a prison visitor. Fully filled in on the situation, he tells me he has been "doing this for years" and he begins to become more comfortable with me now that he has some insight as to who I am and why I am here. He reveals that some prisoners who he has been asked to visit, are "so full of goodness knows what," that they are unaware of his presence. I tell him I've seen a few of them like that in here. Also "unaware…"

Of their names.

We find common ground on the complete disorganisation and chaos that is within HMP Bedford and the "useless staff" (*his* words, not mine). I gather from him that my experiences are by *no* means unique. After this moan, I think he is warming to me but still doesn't look me in the eye. Throughout the conversation, I make it abundantly clear to him that I deserve to be here. I'm not sure he's convinced. I tell him that whilst I am, I intend to make the most of it. I tell him about this book, which makes him retreat again – but only a little. At the end of the sixty minute period, he asks me if I'd like to see him again. I reply that would be very kind of him and this makes his face light up. He stands up, says in a flash; "Thursday" and is gone.

Being in prison is a surreal experience. Being visited in prison even more so. I am not sure, that even if a loved one wanted to come and see me – and you know who I am talking about – that I'd let them. I wouldn't want to put them (her) through it.

Back on B wing an officer told me that E wing staff had been "looking" for me and that they "are coming back." He then gave me some big black bin bags to collect my stuff together. On the walk back to B 2 5, many hands were shaken in farewell. Lots of smiles and many good wishes of the prisoner's best friend: Luck.

I packed my stuff. Bedding, plastic plate, books, paperwork, coffee – the lot. Teevee hovered. I felt like I was jilting him. Once packed, and to be honest I don't have very much, we agreed to a final game of chess. Two or three moves into which, a small female Indian officer (Pocahontas' mum) stuck her head around the door and said my name. Like the condemned man being led from his cell to the gallows, I was whisked out. I shook Teevee's hand. He looked crestfallen.

Via an internal route, passing through as yet uncharted territory – by me anyway – I arrived on E wing. A modern economy hotel type arrangement made up of two floors. There is noticeably much more light here. Airy. Doors open everywhere. A sort of sixth form club house. And no nets, the image of which keep trawling my mind. On our entrance, I followed the officer past a pool table, by which were some residents. Introduced myself (as "Jon"). Smiles from all. Except one. Got taken upstairs to my new home: E 3 8. It's about twice the size of B 2 5 and Dear Lord thank you, no bunk bed. Instead are two hospital beds circa any black and white *Carry On* film that you can think of. In a corner, a kettle, the same as before, sits by a flat screen television on a shelf, together with a remote control and a DVD player (!!!!!!!!!!!!!!!!!!!) Those exclamation marks are not because I am excited. They are ironic. I am surrounded by modern, symmetrical, brightly painted walls with corners, rather than B wing's Victorian arches. There is a loo and basin in the room but not with the agricultural steel around it. Instead, there is a wall. For sure – this is a step in the right direction.

The previous user of my bed had clearly departed in haste, without much regard or consideration for the next incumbent. In short: a bombsight. I was ordered to strip the bed and "chuck everything on the landing," by an officer. The mattress was too long for the bed and curled up by about a foot at, funnily enough, the foot end. Standing, staring at it, wondering how on earth I would manage to sleep this way, I saw a prisoner go past the door and called for his advice, introducing myself first.

Ben (Robert Vaughan, circa very early days of *The Man from U.N.C.L.E.*) took one look at the bed and said "follow me." At the far end of the corridor, he showed me an unused bed with a normal sized mattress on it and he told me to swap them. Mattresses were exchanged quicker than they moved that stove around in *The Great Escape* with Ben's assistance. Once we'd sprung my new lump of foam, this cheery chap then disappeared so I unpacked, trying to be respectful of another human being's "space" that I am somewhat artificially moving into. I have been told I am sharing with "Pops," which is prison vernacular for someone of a more mature age. I think I may have spotted him working in the servery. There was a pair of Granddad reading glasses next to the other bed.

I cleaned the inside of the empty cabinet before any of my clothes went anywhere near it.

Unpacked, I went – rather gingerly – downstairs and was called to the office, which looks like central control from a mini-cab company in south London. There, I was given this week's Canteen sheet. The female Indian officer then asked me if I "had a job." I admitted I was unemployed, not though from lack of trying, I pointed out. She reached for the phone. I stood and listened to her saying things like "he'd be good at that." When the phone was put down, I was told that I will be working in the prison library.

The Shawshank Redemption projected within me.

I then spoke to another officer (Rio Ferdinand) who swore – not *at* me – like a *trooper*. The F word his favourite. Told him of my St Mungo's appointment which never materialised this morning. "Talk to me about it in the fucking morning."

The unfriendly face who'd glared at me on arrival, did the same on our second encounter. With menace. A foreign gentleman I gathered. I played pool and won a couple of games. Then a few more. After a period of substantial Schumacher type dominance I totted-up how many kills I had achieved. I don't know whether to be proud or ashamed of the tally.

I had won *seven.*

Reinforcements turned up from the continuity department by means of familiar faces. Irish Pat and a youngster I have been on nodding terms with on B wing had also been upgraded to here and arrived as I surveyed my score. Pat fired off a million pieces of verbal information to me but hand-on-heart, I understood very little of it. I managed to sort out his pal's name: Freddie (Right Said Fred). Six foot tall, nearly as wide, shaved head, early twenties and a prime candidate for the England rugby squad. I chatted to them whilst having to raise my voice above the volume of the Leicester Square Odeon sized (flat screen) TV next to the pool room.

The frenzied increase in interest in the telly, by a visibly growing amount of prisoners collating around it, was the news. Rioting has gone berserk, apparently throughout all of southern England. The Beeb showed buildings alight, carnage and lots of youngsters in hoodies running amok. The talk from all sides is that we have had at least forty new arrivals to HMP Bedford today alone in connection with recent events. All of them I hear are very young. The news told us that the prisons anticipate being stuffed to the gunnels with both the existing tally and a sudden tidal-wave surge of new customers.

I lost my eighth game. To the young officer who swears a lot. He was very excited about the riots too.

Shortly after my demise at the pool table to a staff-member – which I suppose was a good public-relations exercise – I spied "Pops." It was the same person I had seen previously working behind the servery. I said hello and warned him that he had a new room-mate. He did not seem overjoyed.

Albert (Steptoe) is in I think, his late sixties. Tiny and slight. Everyone in this book has been matched to a familiar household name to help you identify them with their appearance. Albert is so close to the Rag and Bone man's dad, that all he is missing is a horse and cart and an address near Shepherds Bush.

After we had all been fed from a small exclusive to the wing servery, Albert and I talked in our room. He is here on remand. A previous trial collapsed because "the Jury were naughty." He didn't want to divulge more information on that, or what it was he did that brought him here in the first place. I respected his right to silence and told him why I am here. I didn't tell him my profession or about my wife. We went back to his issues and the most I could get out of him was that on retrial a worst case scenario "would be sixteen years." He seemed very frightened. He has no wife and his "home has been trashed." A co- defendant also resides somewhere in this prison, who "is not allowed to communicate" with Albert. Although "there have been threats." He then clammed up. I didn't want to force the issue further.

There is a new row of dots by my locker in E 3 8. Tomorrow is Wednesday. Another day in prison. At least today was a (vague) step in the right direction.

Wednesday, August 10th, 2011.

0720: A good night's sleep. It's so quiet here! Got my washing ready – today is our wash day. Albert was up at about 0700 and prepared to go to work in the kitchen. The news tells us of yet more rioting last night. I added a dot on the wall and an X in my bookmark. Albert gave me a brand new still wrapped nail brush. I looked at my nails to see if he was trying to drop me a hint but they are spotless.

The following was slipped under our door last night:

HM Prison Bedford

9 August 2011

NOTICE TO PRISONERS

Possible increase in population

We have been notified by the courts that we may be required to accommodate a high volume of additional prisoners over the next few days. As a result, the regime may have to be amended at short notice.

We will keep you informed of any changes as soon as we are made aware of these.

DEPUTY GOVERNOR

It was signed by the "Deputy Governor." In joined up writing.

0730: Unlocked. Albert took both our laundry bags. Lots of "morning Pops" to him from other prisoners. A good sign. He departed for work at 0800 but first asked me to write him a letter on his behalf about his state pension. I tootled down the corridor to see Pat and Freddie. They were both beaming about the lack of overnight noise on E wing. At least I am not the only one that was driven to distraction by the Window Warriors.

0830: Mini-cab office. Explained to a white-shirt the St Mungo's situation. He told me he'd ring them. I then had some toast! There is a toaster – and a fridge – in the pool room! I haven't had any toast since I've been here. An exploration of my new home followed. There is not a lot to E wing. Very compact. I saw my name in lights on the wing's population sheet, pinned to a notice board and read for the first time, Cat D next to my name. Believe me, in prison, things like this – and a piece of toast, are very significant.

0950: Played pool with Pat. Lost. Wrote Albert's pension letter.

1200: Banged-up. Have had lunch. Chilli again. Hot. And I don't just mean spice-wise. It was actually served hot. Again a huge difference to the lukewarm fodder we were given on B wing.

I've now been told that my "St Mungo's appointment is on the 18th of this month." On top of that I've learnt that I start work tomorrow in the library. After confirmation of gainful employment, I played pool again with Pat and beat him. Twice. And he's good. Read into that what you will.

1330: Albert came back a short while ago from work, lunch in hand. I was on my bed reading. He read and thanked me for the letter I had written for him.

1335: Door opened. The early afternoon spent not doing very much at all. We are at liberty to play pool and watch telly. I asked if we could go outside for exercise. "Not today." I hear our wing's exercise yard is very small. I just want some fresh air. The young swearing officer ("YSO") has taken to calling me Pontius. As in Pilate. Spoke at some length with Ben – he of expertise in mattress locating – about "Tag." He too is eligible for it, at around the same time as me and has told me the paperwork process involves a "twelve week turnaround." On his advice I put in an "app" to get the ball rolling for November 17th and wrote to ask if flying is permitted in the remit. Had a good chat with Freddie as well. Nice lad. Not eligible for Tag as he is here for something of a violent nature. I had a shower at 1540. Freddie told me that the showers here "are like caravan showers." Remind me to go nowhere near a caravan.

I ate at 1700 and was starving. A French stick, with ham (I think) followed by a chocolate biscuit. I was offered a pear – which I don't eat – and asked for an orange – which I do. No dice. Post supper downstairs there was a minor "kick-off" from a prisoner upset at someone winding him up. This may be the "enhanced" wing but I would not like to get on the wrong side of anyone here. I spied an orange by the pool table and asked who it belonged to. Before I got the chance to speak to its owner to ask if he didn't want it, someone else – and I saw who – pinched it. This person will be referred to henceforth as "Orange Nicker."

Got my washing back from Willy (Dick Emery's "Yobbo"). Someone else had been his locum today as he "has been in Court." He apologised for the delay in the return of my laundered clothes. I told him it was no problem at all, revealed my name then asked how Court had gone. He replied "f***ing good, a 3.1." Demonstrating again my amateur prisoner status, I had to ask him what a 3.1 was. "Three years one month." And that's f***ing good?

I saw my name on the "work-sheets." The grand title of "Library Assistant." The hours are 0830-1130 and 1330-1630. I shall practice the stamping of books later.

Thursday, August 11th, 2011.

0650: Albert and I are both up and dressed. I don't think he's very well and I am a bit concerned about him. He refuses any interest from me. Although he's in his sixties, he looks eighty. The news is on. More riots. We are apparently, very close to being "full" here with the existing ship's company plus the people we have all seen on the telly, looting and lobbing bricks.

Another piece of – unrelated – news that I heard yesterday, is that there was a "fire on C wing." Arson. In a cell. The "inside of which was trashed." "Nobody was hurt but it took three fire engines" to deal with it. The "Police are investigating."

0730: Wrote a note to Teevee, telling him where I will be working and to come and visit. Stuck his name, cell, prison number on the envelope, wrote "by hand" on it and together with the latest batch of this crap in a stamped envelope to Buzz, put the whole shebang in the wing's mail box.

The last time I spoke to Buzz, he hadn't received the latest export of this lot...

1210: Banged-up by myself having had lunch. Albert is still at work. On my return from the library, Pat told me he is being "shipped-out tomorrow" to another prison.

This morning and the library: "Movements" was shouted at 0815. This is not an instruction for us to use the lavatory but prison-speak that the commute is commencing. Downstairs, I got patted down and walked to the library which is next door to E wing. Sixty seconds later I was in it. Met Mike (Barman from the Nag's Head in *Only Fools and Horses*) the other "Library assistant" who I recognised from my last visit as a punter. Now, I'm "staff." He introduced me to Glenda (Jackson) and Gail (Porter). The civilian head and deputy head Librarians. Glenda I had seen before. Gail I had not. Glenda is even more Scottish than I remembered and Gail is her trusty Lieutenant. I got the immediate impression that Gail could sometimes, quite happily, strangle Glenda.

I was welcomed – to a degree – by a very suspicious Glenda and shown how to scan returned books. I sat at the front desk with a lap-top computer which is connected to a main computer in Glenda and Gail's office behind me.

Glenda's supervision only just fell short of telling me how to sit on the chair.

We then got our first load of customers. Overseen by two members of staff, who were in plain clothes. I learnt they are not officers but teachers, as the first intake of prisoner punters were on "Education." Those who wanted to take books out had them scanned by yours truly. Foreign books – of which there are lots – are on a different system. Newspapers and magazines can be perused but not taken out. An ID card was the required deposit to read a periodical or paper. Of the daily's, the *Sun* came backwards and forwards the most. The *Daily Telegraph*, The *Express* and a local paper were also available.

No one took the *Telegraph*.

The TV guides had been removed from the papers by Glenda. A glance at that night's television schedule also required an ID card as deposit. This, one of Glenda's ploys, to "stop prisoners nicking them," said in a very heavy Scooooootish accent.

I must now report the highlight of my stay to date in prison. Glenda instructed me that each time the *Sun* is returned; I must open it and ascertain that "page 3 is still there and not been nicked." Due to reasons that are beyond obvious I had to do this about twenty times. Whatever I was doing, when the *Sun* was surrendered, scanning or stamping, I had to stop, take the paper, open it and check that two-gorgeous- you-know-what's were still there. In good working order.

I am in prison. I am being paid to look at girls' tits.

After the Education lot had departed a quick tidy up was done and Gail told me to "stand-by to repel borders," with a big grin. About twelve members of A wing turned up escorted by an officer. Books returned, books taken and lots of coming and going of the *Sun* – with much careful examination by the author. Well, I must do my job properly mustn't I? A slight kick-off from one prisoner about a book he insisted he had previously returned but not, according to Glenda and Gail's system. To which, he was no match for. Nor Glenda's sharp tongue either. He left with his tail firmly between his legs, mumbling that it must be in his cell somewhere...

I say put Glenda in charge of the whole prison. Scratch that. Put Glenda in charge of the whole prison system. She is the only person I have encountered in this damn place that actually does her job. Very efficiently too.

Some prisoners asked for legal books which are available to look at, but not to borrow. I sat and studied them concoct their next legal move – like planning a strategy in a game of chess. Observing this lot was of more interest than the others, who sat and read comics.

If Albert, he also of E 3 8, would beat the late Wilfred Bramble – hands down – to second place in an Albert Steptoe lookalike competition, then one who made up the numbers of our second group from A wing could more than make a tidy living on the outside impersonating someone.

I thought Robbie Williams had walked in.

Not just in appearance but with the same accent too. Tattoos brought up the rear of the doppelganger for the full effect. I nearly asked him for his autograph. Our Robbie though, was OUT OF HIS HEAD. Whatever he had been at, it seemed to make him unaware of everything, including his name. I don't even think he knew he was in prison. Glenda, Gail, Mike and I all sat or stood – open mouthed – gawping at him. He did a Billy Connolly pissed walk to one of the chairs, collapsed into his seat next to their escort officer and proceeded to broadcast to the room the latest on his "grandchildren." I don't know how old the Robbie Williams that you and I sing along to is, but our Robbie can only have been in his VERY early thirties...

More books in and more books out. One of these, going in or out, was another Jeffrey Archer prison book. I scanned it without looking, nearly with my eyes shut. Some jigsaw puzzles that the library has available to borrow also went out, designed to use up that commodity that we all have to waste here: time.

After their departure Glenda announced we could all "have a coffee." I had a very nice cup of caffeine. From a china mug.

Glenda told me that my services would not be required in the afternoon. Nor were Mike's. I think she was satisfied with my scanning skills – and my natural ability to inspect page 3 – and I was rewarded with a plastic crate. I must in the morning, hit "the book-return box," next to mini NASA and "collect what's been dropped off." She didn't say she was happy with me but I will be given my "rota in the morning."

1300: Albert is back for lunch. I am writing this with a film on the telly in the background. He has just changed channels, without asking. E wing is slap-bang next door to the library but I still had to wait for "movements" to be green-flagged. That's prison. Whilst waiting for our clearance, a youngster (a teenaged John Gordon Sinclair) from B wing that I used to play pool with appeared. I am unaware of his name but he used to make me chuckle by saying "gentle, not mental" after my break-off shots. He asked what E wing is like. I didn't want to rub any proverbial salt in the wounds, so I just said it was OK. I asked him to say hi to Teevee and was then *very* ashamed when he said "alright Jon – take care mate." He knew my name.

On arrival back at E wing, when I saw Pat and learnt that he is being moved tomorrow, the rudiments of my page 3 job were disclosed. His friendly response to this cannot be reported, as my aim is to have this book sold in shops where children can wander.

1310: The menu for Friday's food has just been put under the door by E wing's "Menu guy," Alan (Alda, circa *M*A*S*H*). After he had noted my choices he said through the crack in the door that I "should help with the trolley later," as I am "probably used to all the trolley-dollies." I fly helicopters. Everyone here thinks I'm an aeroplane pilot. How undignified.

Carry on Cabbie is on telly.

1330: Unlock. Downstairs a short, well-spoken lady (Miss Marple) was walking about asking for Jonathan Robinson. She identified herself and told me that she "runs Toe by Toe in Bedford prison." I got her a chair and we sat down. Are you here as a result of the hundreds of "apps" that I have filled in? "Didn't get them," her response. A classic example of how the "system" here works. Or rather – doesn't. She has only learnt about me today, following a conversation with Glenda and Gail in the library, who have said they think I'd be good at helping people. She asked about my background, both on professional and personal fronts and showed concern about the wife situation. She asked if she could "get in touch with anyone?" I nearly said yes to this but have decided to keep her offer as an ace up my sleeve.

I just hope my wife reads this book one day.

Miss Marple asked with genuine interest how I was coping. I told her the main thing which is keeping me vaguely the right way up is writing this book, pointing out that I have neither written one nor been in prison before. We moved on to the business in hand and I said that I have heard it will take considerable time to train me. Referring to my instructional experience and calling me an "oddball prisoner," she scoffed this and said "I'll train you now."

A folder was handed over. On the front of it: "Mentor Training Pack." Run, by the Shannon Trust. On the back their aims:

To engage EVERY non-reading prisoner early in their sentence; to support prison staff to run the Toe by Toe reading plan in EVERY prison and Young Offenders' institution in the UK and to promote the benefits of peer-mentoring in prisons.

The capital letters are theirs.

We went through the contents therein. The methods used to teach possibly embarrassed adult prisoners to read were genius. I quickly adapted to their process so that continuity would be in place should anyone else from the scheme take over from me with a student. Ben came in and listened. Despite this being Toe by Toe, he was dressed head to toe in green. Like the "high risk" guys that Teevee had identified. Ben is not "high risk," and neither is his Robin Hood costume. He is a Skip Rat, a trusted prisoner who walks around the grounds picking up litter. He is kept most busy "outside D wing."

What is the best way of identifying prisoners who could do with a spot of help? Her answer was a stroke of brilliance. Firstly: "Don't bother asking the staff" (!) but instead, speak to the "menu guy" who will have "noticed anyone struggling." This I did later and Alan told me no one on E wing has any problems. There are "plenty of potential candidates on the other wings though."

Miss Marple said she would "email the Head of Security" and request a clearance for me to visit other wings. This person is "sensible but keeps cancelling meetings." We agreed to use Glenda and Gail as a post-box via which we can communicate. At 1530 I was declared an official Toe by Toe mentor. With no students. And no access to any. But she gave me a new black T shirt with the scheme's logo on it.

After this had concluded and Miss Marple had gone on elsewhere – to solve a murder – I played a couple of games of pool and chatted with Pat. He gave me a library book to return on his behalf in the morning as he leaves us tomorrow. We ate at 1700.

After dinner, I asked an officer what the score is with Tag paperwork. Do they need twelve weeks' notice? "No." Are they behind the power-curve on the timing front? "Yes." Is there anything I can do? "No."

The female Indian officer ("FIO") told me most Politburo like that "no way in hell," will my letter to Teevee arrive. Why not? I asked. "Because this is prison," she Gulag garbled.

Dialogue with Buzz on the phone. Some of my mail containing this stuff has landed safely but some is "missing." I wonder if the prison censor has taken a dim view of what I've written. It's a pain. I keep copious notes throughout each day and have "back-up" in the shape of my religious prison diaries but if some AWOL dates require rewriting so long after the event, I am worried the seams will show.

1850: Just before bang-up, I said good-bye to Pat in case I miss him in the morning. We have promised to see each other on the "out." At least I think we have.

Friday, August 12th, 2011.

I could hear it kicking-off from either A, B, C or D wings last night. The noise did not affect my sleep. But Albert's snoring, most *certainly* did.

0730: Steptoe up and seething. About "Ramadan, which if didn't exist, the prisons would be empty." I pointed out I'd still be here but this fell on deaf ears. He is visibly aging in front of me like a sped-up nature film on the telly.

We were unlocked at 0735 by none other than "your-name's-not-on-the-list" Oddjob. He went white as a sheet when he saw me. "Medication" was yelled from below, for those amongst us who pick up drugs – that the prison does know about – and I went downstairs to see if I could go over to the main wings with my crate to pick up books. YSO, who greeted me with a salute and "morning Captain," said I had to "wait until main movements." No form of initiative is permitted, allowed, expected or anticipated in prison.

0820: To the main wings to empty the book box. Mike was already there and had beaten me to it. He has a collapsible crate too. Ben's role as litter-picker-upper is identifiable by him dressed as Peter Pan. We librarians can be spotted by the plastic we carry. On arrival at the library Glenda tasked me with working through a list of overdue books. God help any poor sod who has kept something beyond the allowable time limit. The wrath of Glenda is a fate worse than death. She then told me that I will work every morning and on Wednesday afternoons. Gail told me it was her who had nominated me to Miss Marple for Toe by Toe.

Had coffee from a china cup, did much – entirely necessary – page 3 checking. The officer watching over us was the same throughout each visit of punters. I learnt from Glenda that one "can only work in the library for three months." This is not just the library job but all occupations in the prison. I understand posts can only be held for such a period, so as to give everyone a fair crack of the whip. It is not designed to stop any tunnelling efforts by moving prisoners around, nor is it because of the Geneva Convention, who I assume have decreed that this period of working for Glenda is punishment enough.

I was given a list of prisoners on E wing who have overdue books by Glenda who told me with thinned eyes, to give it to an officer. This I surrendered to YSO on my return to E wing at 1100. For the second time today, a prison officer changed colour in front of me.

Pat is still here! And to complicate matters, drink driver John has been awarded a place among us. He looked a relieved man, walking about and taking in E wing. One of the guys who I have played pool with, Harold (Steptoe), who works in Stores, presented me with a new pair of prison jeans that are my size and actually have buttons. I've been in my size 38's since day one, held up by my sheet belt and have been in danger of scaring the horses anywhere that I have been, being unable to tether my flies.

1220: Reflecting (it's all I seem to do at the moment) on this morning and the "Alpha list." This being a master call-sheet of all the "cast." Details include prisoners' names, cell numbers, sentence lengths and dates of birth. From this, I could locate the "address" of anyone who had kept a library book longer than Glenda's sense of humour would allow. What in hindsight has struck me is how young so many of my colleagues are. What shocked me more was some of them simply said, very matter-of-fact-like: "Life."

1345: Canteen was distributed in the servery by YSO, with quantities of swearing that would make well- seasoned sailors blush to their Jolly Jack Tar *socks*.

All the cell doors are open and from the many different sounds that come from them are revealed, assorted types of prisoner. E wing is a multi-racial, national, class and sentence island within an island – an artificial desert island. Although here, all the inhabitants shipwrecked themselves. Like Lemmings throwing themselves off a cliff, we have all leapt into a life that could really only end in one place. Consciously or unconsciously: our goal was gaol.

Pat is trying to discover what is going on with his pending move. John has unpacked. Things could get interesting come bed time as Pat, Freddie and John now have all their kit in one cell, with only two berths in it. Most of the rest of E wing are playing a football tournament on a Playstation (!) attached to the massive telly next door to the pool room. I played a couple of games of pool, won some – lost more and finally, Pat got moved and thus, shipped-out. John looked relieved not to have to share a bed with anyone…

I asked for "exercise" and got it ten minutes later. The yard is not much bigger than a double garage. Prisoners tended to sit and chat. Or snooze and sunbathe. Freddie came too. We sat down together and he told me his story.

He has a sister, who has had a run of violent boyfriends. The one before last was finally given his marching orders. She then hooked up with another gentleman who liked to knock her about as well. This caused Freddie's displeasure. And I hasten to add as previously reported, he is no slouch. Freddie went to have words with his sister's assailant, to read the riot act. That's my description. Freddie's was more akin to "kicking the shit out of him" but certainly; no more. Freddie found his subject in a pub, told him to step outside and basically, let him have it.

I think Frank Bruno would think twice before stepping into a ring with Freddie. Suffice to say, Freddie departed the pub with his quarry, flat on his back, on the deck, out cold.

Or so, Freddie thought.

He thought it prudent to lie low for a bit and went to stay with friends in London. About a week later, whilst crossing one of the Thames' bridges in his car – which was registered to him – he noticed he was being tailed by a police car. He had a friend on board. The shadowing police car was joined by another. Then another. Soon Freddie's mirrors were full of a flotilla of the local Constabulary's car-pool. "Funny," thought Freddie. At a red light, or some other reason to pull up, the police pounced. Without any mucking about. One of Freddie's windows was smashed. The friend on board had kittens. Bizarrely at this point, Freddie had no idea why this was happening. Flying glass, orchestrated by the Flying squad, caused the previous week's event to temporarily be erased from the forefront of his mind. It was only once he had been removed from the car and a crime was mentioned by the arresting officer, that the penny dropped.

The crime was murder.

His sister's boyfriend had died. Not from the punches, but from how he had hit the deck. At this point of the story, Freddie looked me *straight* in the eye and told me with robust orotundity that he had no idea that on departing the scene that the "beating had been so severe." Charges were later reduced to manslaughter. He's been in prison some time but is out "just before Christmas." The friend on board, who genuinely knew nothing about any of this, must have thought he was on *Candid Camera*.

1530: Showered. Got chatting to another prisoner as I dressed. Like so many of my compatriots, this is not his first time in prison. He is probably in his mid-thirties. This is his *ninth* time.

Back again to 007. Most, if not all, of the film franchise has had a henchman. Of odd stature and build. Our Nick Nack fits the bill nicely. Vietnamese. About four feet tall, with no spoken English but a hidden, deathly skill. This in his case is pool. The playing off. I was soundly thrashed.

Nick Nack is part of three or four representatives from his country staying with us. None of them speak a word of the host nation's tongue. They are all of Cato statuesque, spend most of their time in their cell and smoke like chimneys. They all smile and bow Passepartout like when they are spotted on the landing. No doubt temporarily leaving their abode to empty the ash-tray. No one seems to know why they are here. I have a horrible fear that they took a wrong turning off some motorway somewhere and that they think they are on holiday. They can't be too impressed with British hotels.

1730: Albert returned with his supper and we were banged-up. The earlier than usual lock-in because it is Friday and the "staff can go home."

Saturday, August 13th, 2011.

Albert woke me at 0500 with a bombardment of ZZZZ's. The method utilised in reaching a cessation was yelling his name – like shouting at a bad dog. I worry that the wing will think that "A L B E R T" was roared in the heat of passion.

His task today is to make the apple crumble. For the entire prison. He is very proud of this. I have tasted said crumble in the past and – very gently – asked if he has access to some cinnamon and cloves in the kitchen to nudge the taste. Yes, herbs and spices are in the kitchen but he is "not allowed to use them."

0845: Downstairs the dulcet tones of YSO were audible: "It's not what you know, it's who you blow," he concluded as he walked in with a new young black guy. I said hello, introduced myself (the obligatory "Jon") and stuck my hand out. It was shaken by a hand covered in tattoos. I wondered if its owner was a rioter.

On the landing, an old boy (Blanco, from *Porridge*) is ironing his T shirt. "Is the library open over the weekend?" On negative, he tells me he "can't go during the week" because his "work won't let him." He desires some poetry to send to his wife. I tell him I'll take his prison number, get him membership and take a poetry book out in his name on Monday. He has given me his details. I think I've just made someone's week.

0945: YSO came into the cell, doing an inspection. Not to make sure our beds had been made properly with hospital corners but to ensure no attempt has been made by us to depart the premises. I told him, pointing to the telly's corner, that the tunnel was over there. He replied with "I won't look there then" and wiggled our iron bars. They didn't wiggle back.

1000: The Gym mob has returned, rotating E wing's volume control considerably clockwise. The diversity of music blaring out from assorted cells matches the number of languages one would encounter at a United Nations' convention.

A phone call with Buzz. He received a batch of post yesterday from me but I am absolutely certain from garbled previous calls that he is missing some days in early August. We agreed I'd call him back this afternoon so we can get to the bottom of this and then if necessary, I will re-trace my steps with my biro. Got Willy – washing man – to agree to do a wash for me, despite it not being our laundry day, so I can get my new jeans done and finally stop walking around in my airship sized existing pair. Little victories...

We do have our first rioter in our midst. The guy I said hello to this morning. Age 19 and sent straight to E wing. The rest of the prison is full. When he was grilled in the pool room by the wing's population, he was asked what he'd managed to get hold of during the anarchy. His response: "A pair of trainers." I then drew his attention to his present address. He didn't say much for a while after that.

1115: Played pool with Nick Nack. Lost. He does speak some English. He can say "bye-bye." He said it quite a lot as he sank all his balls.

1200: Fry-up lunch. Stripped the fat off my piece of bacon and had a tasteless sausage. Banged-up. Washed up.

1220: Albert returns with something that *reeks* of cold egg. FIO let him in and she gave me a post card, from Timothy Prison Visitor. A change of date for his second meeting with me. He'll now be coming on Tuesday, 16th. Albert is mumbling something about being a "rotorvator (Sic), not a motivator." Over and over. And over.

1320: Albert looks very sad and unhappy. He had a nap. *Murder on the Orient Express* is on the box. Best line: "What are you reading, is it about sex?" (to John Gielgud). JG: "No, it's about ten-thirty."

1445: There is an un-covered, cooked sausage *and* egg in Albert's *locker*. Readers take note. Crime does *not* pay.

1500: Rang Buzz. The "missing" days are the 5th and 6th of August, so I have to really rack the old memory –and my back up notes.

1700: Banged-up. Have dined. I ordered "pizza" but got "chicken-wrap with chips." In fact, it was really good so for once, I am not complaining. *From Russia with Love* is on telly which is strange seeing that Rosa Klebb works on B wing. Am going to attempt to re-write August 5th and 6th.

The noise of all the cell doors being Howitzer slammed shut on bang-up was like a twenty one gun salute. But louder.

Now? I have to go back in time…

Sunday, August 14th, 2011.

0700: Albert is still asleep. There wasn't too much snoring last night but what there was plenty of – which drove me mad – was lots of kicking. He has some strange habit of being unable to keep his legs still whilst in bed. I had foot-on-sheet rustling, *all* though the night.

0810: The Jeans fit! A slight "domestic" with Albert over the definition of a boiled kettle. Despite steam pouring out of the bubbling furnace according to him, it hasn't boiled until "the light goes out." Keep your trap shut JR.

Mr Steptoe is finishing his ablutions at the basin, right next to my bed. See the wet pillow. See the teeth on his bed…

0940: Played pool downstairs. Beat an officer (at *pool*, not *up*) then lost to Keith (Flint) pronounced "Keef," who sports the most enormous tattoo above his collar-line. Willy watched the games in a most regal and officious manner. Very into the precise and exact rules he was too, to a level I can only describe as hysterical.

1120: Nattered with Ben. He comes from the area that my wife has moved to and we talked about places familiar to us both. I did not tell him about her. He is also Cat D and is hoping to move to an open prison. There is no room at the inn but he seems confident he will be re-housed. Ben is here for some naughty business deals and not a "professional" prisoner. His wife is "standing by him." Lucky sod.

Whilst Ben and I chatted Willy played pool with someone or other and lost. He is *so* angry at the world. YSO, who hasn't bothered to shave today and a fellow officer played next. At one point another staff member visited the wing in the middle of their game. I've never seen pool cues discarded so quickly in my life.

1205: Banged-up solo. Albert still at work. Had lunch. "Roast beef (?) and veg." Albert's apple crumble was... bearable.

1245: Mr Crumble returned and crashed about, despite it being obvious I was trying to rest. Told him his creation was very nice but didn't get much of a response. I realise now how lucky I was to be paired with Stevie and Teevee.

1440: Got beaten by Orange Nicker at pool. Whilst waiting for a game, I talked with John. His Tag date is Thursday. It will be interesting to see if it actually happens then. YSO played pool with a female officer that I have not seen before. The atmosphere was electric, as a whole bunch of prisoners watched a female form playing her shots. It was a pity she had a posterior the width of a deck-chair. She actually beat YSO and he was mortified. He threatened us with "placements on A wing and dodgy haircuts if anyone tells."

1645: Dinner served. A French stick. Freddie came to my cell and we dined together. I don't know whether he had detected I was down but the idle chit-chat certainly helped me.

1730: Albert back from work. No sooner did he get let in, he was let out again to go and have a shower. The door has been left open which with the quiet – everyone else is banged-up – is bliss!

1750: Albert back from his shower. Before he even sat down asked me where I was "before being moved here." I told him B wing. He asked me "which prison?" I explained B wing, here. Either he has lost the plot or he suspects me of something.

Monday, August 15th, 2011.

Albert ate a packet of crisps in bed last night. Then a Twix. Hear the crinkly paper. See the fingers being sucked.

He woke me by pouring sugar into a jar. At 0640. At that hour, it sounded like he was dropping marbles onto a snare-drum. Work today, thank God. Once there, my mission – which I have decided to accept – is to get "Old-Boy" signed up to the library.

0720: Albert's teeth are in. I suggested to him that he move a yogurt that has been on his locker for a week or so, to our "fridge," which is the same make and model as the one I had at B 2 5; The window sill. With reluctance he agreed. I didn't dare mention that the sausage that I know lurks in his locker be thrown away.

0820: Off to work with trusty crate – already loaded with a few books – and an un-opened carton of milk. "G and G" asked me to bring my own for coffee. On arrival at mini NASA, an officer was asked to open the book box which looks like a university lecturer's lectern. Once the contents of it had been noted by me, I thought of that line in *Jaws*. I'm gonna need a bigger crate.

As I sized up about a hundred-weight of books, plus one polystyrene cup, a large feather and a Mars Bar wrapper, Glenda turned up. And started interfering. As I loaded up I tried to ignore "leave that, can you carry this, can you manage that, don't do this but *do*, do that" and so on. All this right in the hub of the heart of the prison, with the hullabaloo that comes with it in full session.

I carefully carried my crated cargo to the gate and was patted down – all the books were inspected too – then continued on to the library, staying in the "slow-lane" as faster traffic zoomed past me on the superhighway. After getting the whole lot up the stairs and into the library I asked Gail if it was possible to open an account on behalf of another prisoner. "Ask Glenda and she'll say no." On her return, I asked Glenda and she said no.

Gruppenfuhrer Glenda was very gently told that the "workers" don't seem to be given the chance to get to the library. She explained that "they are supposed to be asked by the officers present if they would like to go." I revealed that's not what I'm hearing as I went-a-hunting for a poetry book, found one suitable and processed it on my ticket. Glenda, watching me with extra thinned eyes and lips, said that if "he gets caught with my book in his cell" then we will "both, get a nicking." This, I understand, would be some sort of blemish on my record. Mulling that it's hardly mustering the masses for mutiny, I told Glenda I would risk it.

Our first group of punters were from Education. The first in line for a newspaper asked for the *Sun*. Just as I was about to reach for it, Glenda told me it "had not come in today" and instead, we got the *Daily Mail*. The guy's face FELL! So did mine probably. A grinning from ear-to-ear Freddie walked in. He has got himself a job in Stores and accompanied by an escort, delivered to us two boxes of tissues. I wanted to tell him that we didn't need them, as we didn't receive today's *Sun* but I managed to keep my gob shut.

I didn't keep my mouth shut later in the day.

My next task was to go through the Alpha list. One prisoner has left the establishment. This warm feeling was extinguished when on the next wave of punters, Glenda recognised one of them as a previous customer, who only "left here last week" and is "already back."

0945: A visit from B wing. Some familiar faces and among them; Teevee! In tow; his new cell mate. A very well spoken "Doctor," (Basil Rathbone) who I immediately was suspicious of. My instinct was backed up when Glenda was all over him before he had finished walking through the door. He has, according to her, "about twelve books and one jigsaw puzzle outstanding." She restricted him to only taking one book out today. Her eyes were really thinned as she said that.

Once he-of-bad-library-credit had wandered off, I asked Teevee how he was and enquired if he had received my letter expecting him to say no after FIO had asked me what had I "been thinking," when I had the effrontery to audaciously write a note to a friend.

FIO can, as far as I am concerned, go boil her head, because Teevee *did* get my letter. So, all the drama of sending a cell-to-cell note was a storm in a tea-cup. Teevee told me it was "hand delivered by a senior officer."

Robinson: 1. Female Indian Officer: 0.

Teevee told me that he is well and asked about E wing. I advised him to put his name down pronto. He has but thought a move unlikely as he is "on the transfer-list" and is still desperate to return to his old jail and his curry club. I enquired very loudly how the tunnel was going. This forced Glenda into silent apoplexy. She positively vibrated. The officer ever-present, just continued to read his newspaper, looking bored.

After Teevee and his fellows had left us, Glenda gave me a talking to – still convulsing. She knew I "was joking" but I "must be careful" what I say or I'll start "some panic situation." I didn't hear all of this as I was too busy dispersing the earth from Teevee's trousers in the flower pots.

Prison censor: that was a joke.

It was good to see Teevee and many other familiar faces. He gave me a cheery wave as he left and quite a few of the others said "see you, Jon."

They are my friends.

They all know my name.

The last wing to visit us was 180 degrees from the friendly bonhomie of Teevee's mob. A clear signal to what to expect from this gaggle was the fact that the first of them to walk in had his hands down the front of his trousers. Whilst not actually polishing the family jewels, he was doing more than just hanging on for the ride. Others beached themselves on the benches.

Then the incident that I referred to earlier took place.

I was sat behind the desk scanning books. Glenda was stood to my right, her eyes scanning the customers. Like a hawk. Gail was on her right surveying prisoners too. The officer who'd brought them, sat to the right of her. He read a newspaper. As I processed the in-bound books of one particularly sourly customer Glenda asked him where the CD was that he had taken out. This lit the touch-paper. "I don't ****ing have that ****ing disc, I don't like that ****ing band, I've ****ing told you I don't ****ing have it." It was all **** this and **** that. (He'd make a good prison officer). On about, or near enough the tenth "****," my head shot up and internal basic decency over-took any trepidation.

Hey! Easy on the language, I heard myself say. His eyes turned on me like guns on a battleship. "Who the **** are YOU?" followed quickly by "you're not a ****ing police-man!!!" I was hoping at this point that the officer might put his newspaper down and get involved. I turned my head to him. Then Glenda did. Gail got her timing spot-on and completed the John Cleese, Ronnie's Barker and Corbett *I look up to him* sketch.

He just turned the page of his paper. I wondered what it had to take for him to get involved. Gunfire? Glenda had to respond. She explained that I might be asking him "to tone it down a wee bit." My closest involvement to a potential kick-off – due to gallantry to Glenda and Gail. I can't remember how it was resolved. I was too shocked. Not from having this brigand yelling at me but by the *complete* lack of interest shown by the redtop reading "officer" present. Those inverted commas are deliberate.

1130: E wing. Gave "Old boy" the poetry book. I explained to him that my brilliant plan had been scuppered having fallen at the first and so it was out on my ticket, asking him not to use it for lighting the barbeque.

1145: French sticks again. Albert decanted the contents of his and placed them between two bits of bread. A teeth issue I suppose. He didn't work this morning because he had a blood test. Then something funny happened. He'd been in an odd mood all morning and over lunch I had perceived that something was on his mind. At 1215 he summoned the courage together and spat it out. (Not his lunch or teeth I hasten to add). Instead, looking *very* worried, he enquired as to why I had "called out his name, last night." I very quickly explained that his body is safe from me and that it's the only way that stops him snoring.

He looked *mightily* relieved.

1330: Unlocked. Played pool. Beat Willy, who every time I encounter him, I see him not as Willy, but "Angry Man." I then played one of the Vietnamese and got whipped.

"Exercise" was called. Outside was draped in fantastic sunshine. I just sat in the yard and lapped it up. Little things like this that one can do at home (I don't have one anymore) makes you realise how good life is on the outside. And that one doesn't need to steal money to enjoy it.

Five prisoners on exercise sitting in the sun. One officer present, reading the *Sun*. Nick Nack made life interesting by lobbing an apple from his cell at one of the sun-bathing prisoners. A playful food fight ensued with the ammunition being apples and oranges. Fruit flew furiously fast (the kitchen cake-fight sequence in *The Great Race*) until finally YSO ordered a cease-fire "because of the fucking cameras."

1545: Our young rioter is back from Court. He has "made bail and is going home."

1605: At the pool table again, with the unpleasant Russian who glared at me on my arrival at E wing. I have learnt his name is Ivan (Colin Farrell). I am pleased to report I thrashed him. He lost with no grace at all and threw his cue down on my victory.

1645: Dinner served. A whole leg of chicken but just so *plain*.

1700: Banged-up by YSO. ("Later's Robbo.")

1730: Albert back. With his supper. He decimates his chicken on his bed then mixes it up with all the veg. It looks like baby food. He is sucking it now...

1750: Unlocked by an officer; "You have one hour," his easy to remember line. I guess it is association then. Downstairs I learnt that our young rioter is not going home till the morning as his parents are coming to get him then. I asked him why the delay?

"Because I'm scared of what my mum is going to say."

Tuesday, August 16th, 2011.

Not too bad a night. I still had to shout to get the leg kicking to stop which goes on all night long. Groggy, I am. When I yelled out he replied "oh yes, that's my kick-starter. I am trying to start my bike." He woke me with crashing about at 0630. His cigarette lighter had died so I lent him mine, which is non-prison issue. He studied it closely and remarked "refillable, so you're just passing through."

I am convinced that he is convinced, that I am a Stool Pigeon.

Trotted off to work at 0810 and got pounced on during my commute, by Glenda. She instructed me that Mike is doing the main hub collection with his crate and despatched me to as yet, unchartered waters. Namely: D wing.

OH LORD. It made B wing look like the Hilton. And E wing the Ritz. D wing is "jail" personified. *Huge* high, *high* ceilings. Those nets again, everywhere. Filth. Horrible. I later remarked to Glenda how shocked I was. She said I "should see it when it's busy." I'll take a rain check, thanks. I found assorted unmentionables in their drop-off box and got the hell out.

On arrival at the library, Gail and I agreed to keep chipping away at Glenda until the penny drops that there do seem a lot of prisoners who would like to go to the library but can't. She commented that this was like something out of *The Shawshank Redemption*.

0930: With most of the principals on set, Gail told us when she was on the wings yesterday she visited two Polish guys in a cell. "When I was there, one of them asked a guard for some prison shoes, as all he had were his Charles Saatchi pair. He was worried that whilst in prison, they might get spoilt." Glenda piped in: "Charles Saatchi? Don't you mean Versace?" Gail thought about this for a few seconds, like a toddler considering which gobstopper to purchase in a sweetshop and then said "oh yes, that's them," then added with her steamroller logic that the Polish guy "got his shoes."

The Polish guy has had more success in the shoe department than I have. I'm still wearing the same shoes I wore to Court. And got married in.

1030: After a period of prolonged silence we were well and truly invaded by D wing. I can't say I blame them for wanting to get off their Unit now that I've seen it.

Mike rolled-up, having spent the morning "locked in his cell." He only had to ask officers "three or four thousand times" if he "could go to work."

1103: Some other prisoners from the wing that is D. One of whom, is a "regular" and has only just come back to Bedford prison. Glenda was all over him about books misplaced during his "last visit." NOTHING gets passed her. During all this Gail told me that "Lord Brockett was here for two months" during his incarceration and that "he was a fish out of water too." I assumed from the last bit of that comment that she finds it odd that I am here. Perhaps she just finds me odd.

I deserve every second that I am serving here. What is becoming apparent to me though is the gross ineptitude in the way this place is run. This, and the very high turnover of repeat business has planted a seed in my head that change in the way I conduct my behaviour in the future, is not the only strategy that needs re-appraisal.

As the last bunch of visitors from D wing were departing one of them woke up and realisation set-in that he was indeed in the library. He addressed Glenda so: "Miss? Do you have a book? It begins with a D. It's about a thousand words. It has a red side." Glenda looked puzzled. An officer (a non-speaking part) began to drag the prisoner off-stage, as if he were a crap comedian. As I reached for my pen to scribble these events down – as is my wont – Gail said to me "is that going in the book too?" Then the prisoner – now well and truly out of shot – yelled "are they new books?" Glenda replied to him off-camera, "yes" and added "I buy them." Gail nicely wrapped this up by saying "people wouldn't believe this place."

1130: Back in the cell which I had to ask an officer to unlock for me. Albert and I have agreed to keep it locked when we are at work – we've an instinct that there might be burglars about. I quizzed my locksmith as to why his colleagues where so reluctant to offer prisoners visits to the library whilst at their work stations. He effortlessly told me to "back-off" and to "remember where I am." He finished with "be careful." The inverted commas are his.

Brick walls are all around us. Not only literally but mentally too.

Lunch was at 1200. Albert returned from work at 1230 to have his which he pulled apart on his bed.

1400: Downstairs another young rioter turned up – wearing very new looking trainers... My name was called from the mini-cab office and I got escorted over to mini NASA. About ten of us were frog marched to the visiting area. Last time we were given orange coloured bibs and resembled a Protestant fraternal organisation. Today we were all decked out in red. Liverpool fans among us were thrilled. The Chelsea followers were furious. I was given table 24 again, my regular table (by the dance-floor).

Timothy was on good form. He still won't look me in the eye but he was more relaxed. For some peculiar reason our subject matter was capital punishment. Don't get into a conversation with

Timothy if you're depressed. He took great delight in telling me "that one of the last hangings was at HMP Bedford." I made a very large mental note not to walk over any trap-doors whilst I am here. The topic then switched to things prison and I told him of my frustration of trying to get prisoners at work to the library. He commented that dealing with things here is like "swimming in treacle." He offered me a cup of coffee and as he was away from the table I took in all the other visitors. I happened to notice one girlfriend who was hardly wearing anything at all. Poor girl will get a chill.

E 3 8. My Canteen sheet met me. I filled in the gaps at stamps, envelopes, lined paper and tobacco. *All* of which are necessary requirements for the writing of this book.

1645: Picked up the poetry book from the Old boy. Got given supper. Yes, a French stick.

1745: Albert back. Asked him if he's happy with *Sweeney 2* – the second spin-off film they made – on the telly later. Alright by him, the response.

I am doing two shifts tomorrow in the library. Morning and afternoon. Alright by me. I'd do a night shift too if needed. I'd much rather be doing something, than nothing. This seems to be a common gripe by prisoners. What a shame that we can't all do something that would help pay for our keep...

Wednesday, August 17th, 2011.

Albert still has no date for his retrial and got quite hot-under-the-collar last night. I offered my letter writing services – got a flat "no" on that. He had left his cup downstairs in the pool room, so I lent him mine. He was up all night using the loo so I probably shouldn't have. He woke me – at 0500 – by making a racket and I therefore rose at 0600.

That was a mistake.

I got *bombarded* with a broadside's of pure spite worthy of the battle of Trafalgar. Out came things like "we don't get on" and "you need to move out" were snarled at me like a cornered venomous pit bull. More of Albert's battery came at me. I "look down my nose at everyone" preceded "get some ear plugs" followed by "everyone here is the same."

I didn't bite.

Instead I used my cup and made a hot drink. He then emptied my other mug of my toothbrush and made himself a drink. It was some nightmarish deleted scene from *The Odd Couple*. I kept quiet and wrote in my prisoner's diary. He challenged me again, over and over, with "what do you say?"

I eventually told him that I wasn't saying anything.

Silence, thank God, followed. The logical side of me told me that he is in a right state about the uncertainty of his future and I'm being used as a verbal punch bag for him. At no time did I feel physically in danger. He's a little old man, for Christ's sakes. My emotional side? Well, let's just put it like this. I don't think I have felt this low and dispirited since I have been in prison. Or since my wife left me.

All this after a terrible night's sleep too. I got myself washed, dressed and shaved – In the silence – by 0725. Today is our wash day and on opening I took both our laundry bags down then sought solace with the toaster. After my breakfast I returned to the cell, together with Albert's cup. He was slightly more civil at this point. I made a HUGE mental note not to snap at anyone today.

0815: Left for work. Glenda already on the move and told me to hit the main hub with my crate. There were only two books for pick up. On arrival, Mike was already there and as he is well blooded in prison-ways, I sourced his advice on Albert's behaviour. Gail's ears flapped. Mike said ask the staff to move. Gail contradicted this with "better the devil you know."

The first bunch of punters were as ever, from Education. One of whom went to sleep on one of the benches. I started to hear talk of an upcoming security audit from the officer present. For sure, recent pat- downs have been more thorough of late. Gail came up with a very valid observation: "What on earth is the point of letting everyone know an inspection is imminent?"

When Glenda is running the prison service, someone with some brains make Gail her number two.

0930: C wing customers. One of whom asked Glenda if a certain book was in stock. The officer present piped up with "that's a good one." This is the first officer at the library I have seen showing any interest – in *anything*. Glenda was taken aback too and exclaimed "an officer who reads!" just as I was about to say, an officer who *can* read.

1030: And no punters. Der Fuhrer has ordered me to clean-out the foreign section this afternoon. I refer to the gathering of books not in the English language rather than holders of non-British passports who reside in the prison. Gail and I discussed the inmates here with drug problems. There are *so* many of them. Whilst they are here, "users" are given some sort of drug substitute.

Everyone was apparently feeling less than cheery because Mike then told us of the shock that shook HMP Bedford just before my arrival of three inmate suicide attempts – two of them successful. I asked him what, if any, extra care had been put in place to assist prisoners through this time. His response soured the mood further: "Extra food..."

1055: Customers from B wing. A whole bunch of new faces too. Rioters? I only recognised two among the crowd. Teevee's "Doctor" cellmate and a pleasant Polish guy. The former told me I have had mail at B 2 5. Bloody system. Not post from the outside but internal mail. One apparently said "work will be found for me soon" and the other was alerting me that "I can start Education."

1130: Cell. I picked up the laundry and had a "visiting order" returned to me that I have no idea when I filled in. It bounced because I had not put Buzz's date of birth on it. Lunch was served at 1200. I re-submitted the documentation for a visit and a very sheepish Albert presented himself in the cell at 1220. Boy, did he stay *quiet*.

1400: Library. The first afternoon shift that I have done. Gail and I manned the fort. She revealed that Glenda has carpeted the officer who sat and did nothing when our foul mouthed customer sounded off the day before yesterday. I learnt that in her remonstration to him, the fact that the *Orderly* had to step in – whilst he just turned the pages of a newspaper – had been flagged to him in no uncertain terms.

There is something *emphatically* not right round here when a civilian female *librarian* has to narrow her eyes at a prison *officer* and tell him how to do his job...

There was no sign of any punters so I put the kettle on. Somewhat of a strange atmosphere existed as I knew from where our expected customers were due to come from in the p.m. shift. The wing that makes all here, prisoners and staff alike, sit up and take notice.

F wing.

"Nonces" are what inhabitants of F wing are dubbed by prisoners. And by the officers. This is a touchy subject. I am not going to beat about the bush; they are the sex-offenders. They are kept in complete isolation from the rest of us and I didn't know what to expect. I do know that it also houses "vulnerable" prisoners. Reading very carefully between the lines of that; if a prisoner is an ex-policeman or prison worker, F wing will be his address. To stop him, or rather, them, being got at. Feeling strange writing on this subject comes nowhere near sitting in the library actually waiting for them to turn up but that's what I did.

Two of them arrived with an officer. They came up the back stairs to avoid any possible contact with other inmates. One a youngster and the other I would estimate to be in his sixties. The officer sat down and read a newspaper. I observed our guests. Both were understandably I suppose, incredibly shy. But what struck me was that apart from the younger one needing to lose a few pounds and the older needing a visit to the wing barber, they just looked like you and me; normal.

1515: The Foreign nationals invaded the library. Loads of Vietnamese, some of them I think, from E wing but they all look remarkably alike. Ivan the unpleasant came too and asked for the *Sun* ("Sun." his solitary line of dialogue). I suppose you don't have to speak English to read that. Or those. At 1535 they left us and I was about to start work on cleaning the shelves that are foreign when we were alerted that E wing was on the way over. Freddie, Ben and John walked in, almost telling me to put the kettle on.

1615: Gail let me go. I returned with the *Telegraph*, which looked *unbelievably* out of place on my bed. FIO was manning the mini-cab office. This was the first time I'd seen her since the great letter to a cell incident. I stuck my head around the corner and with great delight, told her that my cell-to-cell mail did arrive safely and thanked her *so much* for her help. She did a fairly good impression at this point of Glenda. With thinned eyes.

Robinson: 2. Female Indian Officer: 0.

1645: French stick. In the queue I talked with Lenny (Henry, circa 1989) about the standard of food. We both agreed that the chillies are superb and that with the limited budgets, the fodder is not bad. As we chatted, I detected yet another individual trying to work out why the hell I am here. Lenny told me about an officer – currently on holiday – who I have not yet encountered but have heard much about. "A stickler for discipline and quite a character." Intrigued, I asked Lenny if it's true that this is as close as I'm going to get to *Porridge*'s Mr Mackay. He laughed loudly at this and said that I was "bang-on."

1745: Cell. Just got *thrashed* at pool by Willy, now re-named "Angry Eyes."

On the way back upstairs an officer confirmed my appointment tomorrow with St Mungo's...

1900: The soaps are on so Albert is happy. He has just offered me some Tandoori chicken. I took the offer in the spirit it was given but not the chicken. I said a *big* thank-you though. I think and hope it's now peace in our time, or to use Teevee's vernacular: "The beef is dead."

Thursday, August 18th, 2011.

Can you suck a Twix throughout a whole episode of *Lewis*? Albert can.

I am wearing my (severely short) stereotype styled sentence serving standard striped solitary shirt. Prison issue. Albert has told me it will "fetch £500 on the outside." Anyone want to buy a shirt?

0810: To work via the busy highways of fenced off walkways. Mike walked towards me with a very empty crate. He'd already done the main drop-off box so I did a U-turn and walked with him. He only had one book aboard his carrier: Jeffrey Archer's *Prison Diary*.

An omen?

Among the first batch of visitors, one of them asked me if we "had maps of prisons." I took it that he meant the inside of which (a tunnelling guide?) but in fact he was after a chart of other institutions' locations. Perhaps he wanted to tick off the ones that he's been in. Education followed. The grand sum of one prisoner turned up with an unhappy looking teacher who told me through *very* gritted teeth that his student was "getting a one-to-one service." I quickly understood why the tutor looked so miserable when his protégé grilled me. Like an onion. This chap had attitude. "How long you been in prison?" "How long you worked in the library?" "You on E wing?" and "how long you been there?" It was like the Spanish Inquisition. When his ID card was requested for the stuff he wanted to take out, he tossed it on the desk like it was a Gold American Express card.

0900: I remarked to Mike, very quietly, that Glenda really does like to interfere with whatever it is that she has tasked us to do. His line: "She would tell you how to make a cup of tea if you were making one."

0930: Punters on set but all very quiet. Their officer reads a newspaper. Mike reads a newspaper. I read a newspaper. Mike and I are prison officers, in training.

1015: Yet more punters. All – very young. Rioters?

Yes they are. And they wanted a TV guide. They huddled over it as if it were a treasure map and got most worked-up and excited about what is on television this evening. It turns out the schedule is made-to-measure for them. Their bespoke viewing includes *Crimewatch* followed by a *Riot-Special*. They acted like they'd won the lottery. The best quote: "The BBC will be well handy tonight."

BAFTA, take note.

The impression that I got from this lot is that they are *very* proud that they and their mates are all going to be TV stars.

Politicians, take note.

1030: Very, very busy with tonnes of customers. Not for the first time, I was asked by one of them where the crime section is. We could tell that it was raining outside as all the returned books and jigsaw puzzles were soaking wet. Glenda, probably looking over my shoulder as I wrung out a delivered damp digest, told me that more than half the prison population are now members of the library. She was very proud of this – and quite rightly. She does an excellent job. I think it's because of my superb page 3 work. I didn't tell her this.

1115: Two Gestapo looking officers turned up. Unbelievably they didn't ask for any newspapers but told Mike he was "coming with them" for a "random drugs-test." For Mike, "ze library is over." Out, he was frog marched.

1130: E 3 8. Harold (jeans man) has been asked to keep an eye out for a belt and a pair of shoes for me. "Not a problem." I put in an "app" (!) yesterday, asking for same. Five gets you ten that Harold comes up with the goods before the system.

1200: Lunch. Pie and chips.

1230: Albert back, muttering "same-old, same-old," over and over.

1330: Unlocked. It's St Mungo's time. To the main Units and am reminded of the noise, filth and those dreaded nets. Embark C wing and go downstairs to where Induction was. That feels like ages ago. I don't recognise anybody apart from a few officers and the Bollywood star who interviewed me before. Incidentally, when I studied the paperwork that she gave me after our meeting, I noticed that she couldn't spell pilot. My name is yelled and I at last, find myself in the presence of a St Mungo's lady (Angelica Houston).

She agrees to communicate with my landlord in the wrapping-up of my tenancy. I relay that this leaves me homeless. She "cannot assist." My brain whirring. Right. I'm going to need to get some friends (?) to locate me an address for November 17th. Like a newsreader at the end of a lunchtime bulletin forecasting thunderstorms she concludes our conversation. I go and sit on the benches and worry about what the hell I am going to do.

I have to wait for about fifteen minutes before there are enough of us to make it worth it to escort us back. When we are enough of number, we plod back to our respective wings. As I enter my cell, I feel really, really down.

What in the name of Jesus, am I going to do? I am going to have to get someone (who?) to get me an address (how?)

D O   N O T   P A N I C .

1605: Conclusion: You deserve everything that is being thrown at you.

Later I sojourn to the sodding pool room again. Steve (Davis) addressed. Tall, thin and VERY able at the table. He's heard that I am after a belt. News travels fast but he does share a cell with Harold and his employment in the prison is for the same service as his room-mate; Stores. I reveal that I've read somewhere – I think some official property list pinned to some notice board behind some race equality statement – that I am, allegedly, entitled to a belt. This causes him to roar with laughter. He tells me that he's worked in Stores since the year dot and he's "never seen any." Just lots of "size 38 jeans and size 6 shoes."

Come to prison if you're really round with small feet.

Back upstairs and find a footloose Freddie who is "hungry." I have a brainwave and remember yesterday's peace offering from Albert – the Tandoori chicken – and donate it to the cause. I hope Freddie has a cast iron stomach, it's been sitting around nowhere near a fridge for far too long.

1745: Dinner. French stick with cheese.

When released I never want to see a baguette again.

Friday, August 19th, 2011.

I have a stinker of a cold. Albert was up at 0600 and I sort-of-got-up at 0630. I am not feeling brilliant.

There was a football match on telly last night. Doors were kicked – *battered* – in the excitement of goals being scored. Right across the prison. I hope it was the football match and not a reaction to the *Riot Special* that caused the onslaught. Regardless, the brutal, violent noise was deafening. Albert has astutely remarked that "there will be some sore feet today."

On the news: "The prisons are nearly full." There are "100 new receptions a day" and the UK prison population "is now eighty six and a half thousand." The BBC went on with "there are only 1200 places left."

I sat up at that and took note. My immediate reaction was to make it 1201. "The short-term solution," the Beeb told us, is to put "three to a cell." Albert sat up at that and took note.

0730: Leapt on by FIO: "You are moving to cell number 2." Why? "Because there is a new guy coming in who can't climb onto a bunk." I was at the door of cell 2 knocking on it moments later. Inside I found Harold (Steptoe) and Steve (Davis). And one bunk bed. This three to a cell thing has started pretty quickly. I explained to them what I had been told and that I assumed one of them would be moving out. "Fuck that" their response. Harold shot out of the cell and projected himself downstairs with the speed of someone who had sat on the wrong end of a shooting stick.

Minutes later I spoke to FIO again and she told me to "disregard."

I reported to Albert that I might be moving. He looked surprised but *something* told me that he has had words with someone, possibly FIO, after our "row" the other day. I don't know why I've called it a row. It was just him being a ****. His Steptoe replica response was "who's coming in with me?" He looked worried. YSO walked by and said to me: "Carry on, Captain Birds-Eye."

0755: Work queue. Decided to just see what happens... In our small hall-way, by the wall with warship-like interior pipes everywhere, I observed FIO being jovially chastised by YSO that "she had thrown something away." This had caused her sufficient alarm to rummage through a waste paper basket. She eventually found what she was looking for. It was the Roll-call.

How, and what exactly does it *take* to become a prison officer?

0805: Main hub. Mike had already emptied the box and was waiting in line at the medical dispersal. I took his half full crate back to the library to see Gail looking very pleased with herself as she is our director today. Glenda was otherwise occupied. I got started on scanning. And I wondered how I caught my cold. The books were covered in God-knows-what.

0850: An officer turned up, looked lost, then embarrassed and then left. As he was departing, Gail said to him that she was "glad he knew what he was doing." She then turned to me and said "I could write a whole chapter in your book."

Whilst scanning, a very Irish voice say to me "are you on E wing?" I looked up and saw a sort of squashed garden-gnome apparition with an enormous scar on his face. I replied in the affirmative with a probable large amount of trepidation in my voice. "They offered me E wing" he said, "but I didn't want to go." Thank Christ for that, I thought, being very careful not to say it out loud.

0900: Miss Marple, she of Toe by Toe, visited the set. Not looking for the *Body in the library* but just popping by. She had "no news" for me.

0930: Punters from C wing. Very few of them. I asked the accompanying officer why they were so little in number. He answered that "they could have Exercise or Library." The same officer then had to listen up for a radio check to "all stations." The female controller, calling endless numbers for "test call" sounded like she should be announcing that the dog-food was discounted in a supermarket.

1020: Mike and I finish cleaning shelves. His drugs test yesterday was a "success."

1110: French ***** stick. Nearly trod on Nick Nack in the queue. YSO told me to "always look down!" I always feel down, if that's any help.

1130: A social in E 3 8 from Harold Steptoe and Steve Davis. Both of them looking very relieved that Basil Fawlty is not moving in with either of them.

1140: Went to see "Old boy" to enquire how the poetry project was going. Whilst chatting, YSO slammed the door shut so I was banged-up in the wrong cell! Had to raise hell by banging on the door to be let out and deposited in my rightful home. I was going to bang my French stick on the door but didn't want to get done for criminal damage.

1200: Albert back and moaning about the youngsters working in the kitchen, who "think a broom is for leaning on."

1250: Unlocked. Albert mopped the cell. I moved the furniture about around him. He said it now "smelt fresher." I think it smells of loo cleaner.

1330: Harold came to see me with a new jacket. "Prison-new" as it's had a previous owner. Round here you ask for a belt and a pair of shoes but you get a jacket. I introduced Harold to Albert as my tailor. The new garment is denim. So, now I have two coats. One possibly marks me as an escapee and the other makes me look like an extra from *Grease*.

1350: Spotted some milk not seen before in the "fridge" and asked Albert who it belonged to. "Us," the response. Followed by "we should call ourselves cell-mates." He went on; "even if I have the odd tantrum."

1420: Canteen served. By FIO. Nothing said.

1545: Prisoners everywhere on the wing as no one works on a Friday afternoon except kitchen staff. I still felt really under the weather. Saw FIO again and again, she said nothing so I decided to put the "move" out to pasture.

I went back to bed. With Frederick Forsyth.

Saturday, August 20th, 2011.

A fair, to middling night. 0655, as I write. Albert is stirring.

I am surprised he has the energy to do so with all the kicking last night.

From my current line of sight, my bed is on the left. Unmade. On the floor near it; loo roll. Streaming-nose for the use of, not wanking. My shoes sit there too. Still clean and shiny. The library crate and yesterday's socks make up the full compliment. On the far wall is our door, to the left the TV and kettle. On the right is Albert's bed, together with his chair. He is now getting up. At Albert's head end of his bed sit our two lockers. His, we know, doubles as a larder. In front of mine, on the right, I have put my "desk." Right in front of the loo.

On Albert's locker sits various wrapped sandwiches, a dirty plastic knife, tea bags and a plastic container. It has congealed meat on it. On my locker are books, newspapers (prison officers' treasure), cereal, and two slices of bread in a plastic bag. Bread is *very* carefully dished out in small quantities as a large supply could lead to in-cell brewing activity.

I have heard stories of the concoction of "Hooch." The basic starter kit for cocktail craving convicts contains bread or Marmite for the yeast, orange juice, sugar and some empty squash bottles. As well as this, also required is a lot of hard work and what we all have plenty of – time. Fermentation requires warmth. Some distillers drape their bodies around make-shift demijohns at night, some risk being caught by attaching them to the back of the heat pipes in their cells. The problem is, so I have heard, is the closer that their vintage comes to fruition, the more the plastic container expands. We are talking rugby balls here. One bright spark tried to be cleverer than the system and utilised the back of his wing's washing machines thinking that the bases of warmth and covert security were fully covered. He thus had substantial stock secretly simmering in his improvised brewery. What he had not anticipated, as pants, soap-suds and socks spun round, was what I presume is every illicit-booze maker's nightmare; the spin cycle. The squash bottles objected to both the bladder like expansion and the revolutions of the Hotpoint in which they were contained. And exploded.

The laundry room, smelt like a Kettering night-club for weeks.

I digress. As well as my toast-to-be, my plastic plate and bowl, plastic cutlery and my still wrapped unused nailbrush – Albert's house warming gift to me – are my "props." Aft of me is the window. To the left and behind me, is the afore mentioned lavatory with its little wall. The other side of that is our basin, placed just near the head end of my bed. A 360 degree "tour" of E 3 8.

I do NOT wish that to sound like I am feeling sorry for myself. I fully deserve to be here. I have been an ARSE. I have earned EVERYTHING that I am getting. Except maybe Albert.

Talking of whom, he has a recall to the doctor following his blood test on Tuesday. He is worried that the results have flagged something. I am trying to be supportive.

0755: Mr Steptoe is examining his teeth whilst sitting on his bed. He doesn't need a mirror. They're in his hand.

0810: Finished cleaning a small radio-cassette player which is Albert's, which has been gathering dust under my bed. As a thank-you he passed me the chess board and all the pieces in a bag. On the outside of which, is crusty steak and mushroom sauce. This made me nearly retch when spotted. I dread to think how old the remnants of some previous meal are. I asked him when he last played, a month ago, maybe two? "Longer than that." Christ alive. As *soon* as he goes to work that bag's going in the bin and I'll switch it with the one that's got my bread in it.

0845: Swapped bags. There's a new guy opposite who I met briefly last night. Vinnie (Jones). His left arm is covered in enough tattoos to make up Tokyo's subway system. He's "in" following a "punch-up that got out of hand after a skin-full." It seemed like a good idea at the time – apparently – to take his clothes off in a car park. As one does. A drinking pal, also frighteningly drunk, objected to the timing and location of this disrobing and a fight started. Vinnie got his "head cracked open and the other guy lost an eye."

I have just remembered something from Miss Marple's visit to the library yesterday which in turn, has triggered flash-backs from our first encounter which had also been temporarily erased from my memory. She told me (again) to "read the prison book that Jonathan Aitken wrote, during the serving of his sentence." She added that "he struggled too." What hit me, on both occasions, was the "too," implying that I appear to be displaying outward signs that I am struggling. I thought I was doing alright.

Porridge, film of, is on telly later. Ha!

1200: Lunch. Albert came back at 1230 with some "home-made" shortbread the size of a paving slab, which was still warm from the oven. It was delicious. We talked of his upcoming doctor's appointment, which is clearly worrying him. As I learnt the other day – the hard way – he has no one else to talk to, let alone to open-up with. I know the feeling. Too well.

Albert didn't say anything about the clean bag that the chess pieces were in.

1445: Watching *Porridge* on the "inside" is absolutely *unreal*.

1530: Am still in the company of Norman Stanley Fletcher. At the same time, I have done what only I could do. I have accidentally locked myself *in* my cell. I hope someone notices my absence before supper, or I will have to hit the "emergency" button. (Room Service).

1540: Heard Ben outside my window and peered out. Spied him the other side of the fence post Skip Rat duties, locked out. He shouted at me to get some staff to let him back in. I then admitted I had been about to ask him to fetch them, to let me out.

Have you ever seen Ben, the other side of a locked fence – dressed head to foot in green – saying rude words? I have.

I had no option but to tell him to hang on whilst I rung for room service.

1600: Ben in the cell for a social and to thank me for getting him back in. He's thanking me for that?

1645: "Chicken Kiev." Straight to the bin my "Grease Kiev" went.

1730: Albert back from work and looks like he's been in a steam-room. He hasn't, he's just been "cooking the chips for the entire prison." I didn't admit that mine had gone where the chicken went. He was let out straight away for a shower and the door was left open.

1820: Door closed. For sure the extra time of the door being left open is the main perk of being lumbered with him. He has just made himself a corned beef sandwich. I then wiped up all the bits of spilt meat off the floor.

1845: Albert now eating a cold sausage. Please NOT THE ONE FROM THE CUPBOARD.

Sunday, August 21st, 2011.

I spoke at some length to our sole (E wing) young rioter, who arrived on Tuesday. He is (a very young) Rodney (Trotter). I don't know if it was my "posh" voice but he exhibited huge signs of regret over his behaviour. I got the impression that he like his predecessor, had been on the end of a substantial "third degree" from his parents so I did not give him a hard time. Besides, I'm in prison and a tit too. Rodney, small and slight, has not been to jail before. He told me that he felt daft about getting involved in what we have all seen on the television. He hadn't gone looking for trouble but just found himself swept up in the frenzy. I don't think he took anything of value or did any damage but because the Courts have hit back in such a Draconian way, he is among us. His only consolation being that because the rest of the prison is full, he has been billeted in E wing from the get-go. He told me that come Court, he was going to hold his hands up and plead guilty and hope that it would be recognised that he has done a few days in jug, learnt his lesson and move on. I asked him if indeed that was the case. He paused, panned his eyes around our surroundings and gave me a "look at where we are" grimace. All he "wants to do now," he added, "is get a job and not get into any more trouble."

Prison allows jungle drums to beat very efficiently. Rodney had heard that I am allegedly handy with a pen and asked me to write something for him for his Court appearance. Trying to be as avuncular as possible, I said that I would, if he really meant what he had told me. I had no doubt from the look on his face that he was sincere.

I lost pool to a Pole, Colin (Firth) who does a Rolf Harris running commentary as he plays. I thought I was at the Crucible. Angry Eyes stomped about, looking deranged.

1150: Lunch was served. "Roast beef, roast potatoes and vegetables." I ate the veg. The meat and spuds joined the Chicken Kiev.

1230: Albert, looking like death, returned. He has the afternoon off. He told me I think four times, that it was he who "made the spuds." On about the second announcement of this amazing feat I surreptitiously checked the contents of the lavatory bowl to confirm that my quota of his creation had definitely departed, having cut out the middle-man of the prison food service; me.

1330: Unlocked. No one, apart from Rioter Rodney on E wing, says "innit." Is this how they decide who comes here? They do say ****, a lot. And **** is popular. So too is **** ****. Downstairs Orange Nicker was playing pool and in the busy room, someone called him a ****. He looked up. And looked at me. He obviously knows that I think he is a **** but he was trying to work out whether I had said he was a ****. He doesn't know that I don't use that word. Women don't like it. The penny eventually dropped that someone else had called him a ****. Which he is. A right one.

"Exercise" was yelled out. I was sitting outside in the sunshine about ten minutes later with Michael Winner. He has not been imprisoned – yet – but had borrowed Vinnie's *Sunday Times*. I read that he is selling up his house and that the "prisons will be full in two weeks." Why don't they use his residence? One good turn deserves another: Mr Winner mentions me in one of his books so now I am doing the same by writing about him in mine. I hope he sends me a cheque.

Returned to the wing and rang Buzz. The good news is that the "missing days" have turned up. The prison censor had not stuck their oar in. Rather the author had stuffed too many "days" into one envelope and the Postal service had objected to carting half a week of jail mail around the country on the fare of one first class stamp.

I asked him how the originals compared to the "re-writes." He told me the match wasn't too bad. Good; my back-up system works. The bad news from Buzz is that he has no news on anything positive about my "old" home or my possessions. This caused a boiling over of lava like panic inside me. I tried not to let him know in my voice as I spoke to him. He's not daft though and I'm sure detected this.

1645: French stick. Borrowed more of the *Sunday Times* from Vinnie and tried to pretend I was somewhere else. At around 1650 we were banged-up.

1820: Albert is sitting on his bed with his teeth in his hands, cleaning them. With a J cloth.

This experience is hell. Like I imagine, a long film shoot in some God forsaken country at some God awful location with a God knows what cast and crew. My "shoot" still has more than two months to go, nearly three.

Prison? Take it or leave it. I plan to do both. Take it *and* leave it.

Monday, August 22nd, 2011.

Another night of kicking and snoring. Albert was up at 0600. He packed, and then re-packed his sugar. Then he did it again.

He's just told me that "Old Boy" collapsed in the gym yesterday and is "in hospital."

In the work queue John asked FIO, who was in the mini-cab office but on this occasion not riffling through dustbins, if there was any update on his Tag which was due last Thursday. "When your sentence is complete," her very helpful response.

Glenda swooped down on me like the Caped Crusader and told me she and I were "going to D wing." I was glad to have her with me as my bodyguard. On arrival at this loathsome dreary place, I started to take the books out of the box. Glenda told me as I was doing this, to "take the books out of the box." Same old Glenda!

Gail relayed to us that she had a barbeque over the weekend. I told her the highlight of mine had been reading the *Sunday Times* in the sunshine and she very cleverly pointed out the "little things one doesn't realise one has, until one is inside." All this excitement was whilst Education were still with us and as they were leaving, Glenda got a bee in her bonnet about "one of the Chinese," who she was convinced had "walked out with one of our books." A Chinese takeaway.

My morning task was to count the members of the library within the prison, whose population is something like 450. Of that, I worked out that 232 have signed up. This computed despite Gail mucking about, trying to put me off! I threatened her with murder in the library if she carried on.

1100: Glenda got a phone call from "Admin" who told her "that starting tomorrow," I am on a "three day BICS course" (British Institute in Cleaning Services, or similar). Glenda was livid, as she'll be a man down. I asked the officer present what this was all about. He looked at me over the top of his tabloid newspaper and said that I "will get a certificate." Gail and Mike immediately started to go for the kill. Comments like "can you smell bleach?" and lots of sniggering ensued. Both of them are highly amused that the pilot will soon be polishing floors. After washing up the coffee cups (Mike: "You'll be good at that") it was back to the wing.

1150: French stick.

1230: Albert back. I told him about the cleaning course. In true Steptoe mercenary mood he started to talk of money. He said that he thinks I'll be nominated to do "post incident" cell clear-outs after God knows what has occurred. At "£20 a hit," which lit his fire.

At 1335 a helicopter came over the property that was so low that Albert looked like he was going to hide under his bed. The noise of the whirring rotors made me realise that when I get out I want to go back to WORK.

Meanwhile back on planet earth, I washed my white T shirts in the basin. And thought about flying. That aircraft coming over had the same effect on me as that spider did with Robert the Bruce.

1700: Dinner served. Some sort of curry. I learnt that Freddie is on the cleaning course too. No word on John's Tag or Harold's release, due this Friday. They don't like talking to you in this place.

Albert back at 1730. He told me twice that he "dropped the custard" and then topped that up with "there was a suicide attempt this afternoon on A wing."

Unlocked at 1820. Went downstairs. "Old Boy" is back from hospital. One good piece of news.

1855: I am so very, very tired.

Tuesday, August 23rd, 2011.

0715: If I've got my diary right, today I meet Mr Mackay. ("Fletchaaaaar!")

0727: Albert's teeth in.

I have a visit this afternoon. Timothy?

In this world of hype, so many times does something get so incessantly raved about that on witnessing the goods oneself, things are never quite as hoped. In the work queue I saw for the first time the officer that I have heard so much of. The Mr Mackay type – which had led me to imagery of a swagger stick and some medals on the left lapel at the very least. However, I did not get an iconic Mackay from *Porridge*.

I got Butler from *On the Buses*.

The BICS course. Four of us were ready to clean up. We climbed some stairs. Spotless they were too. On arrival at the theatre of polishing, I realised I was entering the cleanest place in the prison.

There were different types of floors, for different types of cleaning, everywhere. It was like a TV studio. We sat down and were straight away told that "tomorrow wasn't happening," and we should go to our normal jobs. The course will "now carry over to Friday." Great, I thought, well one of your lot can tell Glenda then. I pitched in with the fact that I have a visit this afternoon at 1515. The officer said that we should be complete by then. "Keef," the tattoo above the collar ("TATC") fellow turned up with another prisoner. They are already BICS qualified and were picking up some kit to go and clean something. They collected and gathered more than a mop or two and I learnt that they were off to clean up the cell that was set alight on C block a few weeks back. They left us looking like they were off to wage a chemical war.

Our Instructor took great delight in announcing that if we were doing this course "outside," it was cost us individually "£800." With the use of a white-board with the TINIEST writing I have ever seen, we were told the basics of BICS. Freddie had not brought his glasses and he can't read a motorway sign standing in front of one *with* them, so he struggled. We all had to squint like mad to read anything. It was like the bottom line at an eye test. Soon, we were all experts on the ratios of chemical to water and the masses of health and safety signs, one of which looked just like Jarvis Cocker. After an exhausting thirty minutes the officer said we could have a coffee break. Caffeine uploaded, our instructor told us that we would be "knocking off early," as he has "been summoned by the Governor" but "wants to take a shit first."

What does it take to *fail* an interview to become a prison officer?

At 1000, we learnt how to use a mop. When the officer told us that "if we look after our mops, then the mops will look after us," I didn't dare look at Freddie, who was struggling not to break out in hysterical giggles. At 1015, we learnt how to sweep a staircase. As I had a go, Freddie very helpfully said: "Shoddy workmanship."

The officer hadn't been joking when he had said he was cutting things short. I was back in the cell by 1030. Glad I haven't paid "£800." Saw Albert and asked how the doctor's had gone. He woefully said "everything is still working" and walked out.

I shall give you an example of how this place is run by revealing what is on the film production type call-sheets downstairs that effectively lets everyone know the order of play for each day. According to the script, I am this afternoon doing BICS training whilst simultaneously working in the library. Oh, and at the same time, I'm receiving a visit. My stand-in has a busy afternoon then. After reading this I went to the pool room for a game. I won the first and as the second was being set up in walked, with no form of ex-military swagger at all, he just sort of rolled-in, our Mr Mackay. This was to be the first time I had heard him speak. Except he didn't. He just shouted.

"I SAID 1115 FOR BALLS. IT'S NOW 1130."

Not only is the appearance nothing like the late Fulton Mackay's brilliant characterisation, neither is the voice. He sounded like a wounded bison. A deaf one at that. Some small place in England is I noted, missing its village idiot. This bloated walrus then squelched out of the room. With my ears still ringing, I collected up the pool balls to take to the mini-cab office, full of huge regret. An interesting character he is not. Just an overweight, always shouting, nothing like-I'd-hoped-for officer, who like so many of his colleagues, just seems pissed off that he's here. As Timothy PV calls them: The clock-watchers.

1200: Lunch. A "Thai curry." Ha ha ha ha. Banged-up 1220.

1400: Back on the course and learning how to pilot a Buffer. A Fly-mow type contraption that I held on to for dear life. A spinning-polishing head at floor level with me and handle bars for operation of, at the other end. To move it to the left, lift the handle bars up a notch. To the right, lower them a tad. Or was it the other way round? I was just a passenger. I thanked God that I had four walls around us, or I'd be halfway to Northampton with a very clean strip of the M1 behind me. I was assessed as I pretended to know what I was doing and then signed off for solo. Unbelievably, I now have a licence to clean. Felt a complete fraud.

After I was relieved of my command of this machine with seemingly, a mind and will of its own, the "course" finished for the day. I asked the officer to ring the library, to tell Glenda that I would be with her tomorrow. He made the call and went an odd colour as he spoke on the phone.

1450: Albert asleep. He probably needs to catch up after all the kicking last night and the worrying and fretting over his medical appointment. The latter, he has my complete sympathy for, the former, makes me want to kill him. The Canteen sheets arrived. I filled in my order and went downstairs to wait for an escort for my visit.

I forget what colour tabards we wore today but again, we looked like some football team or other. Someone else played centre forward. Our manager put me on the right wing. And I did play Timothy PV.

I had so hoped it might be you-know-who.

Timothy has regressed in the shyness stakes and didn't look me in the eye at all. We talked about his wife, who is under the knife a week today for her hip-job. He asked about my wife and I immediately switched subjects to this book. He wants to know the title so the optimist in him can keep an eye out for it in his local book shop. I'd like to know the title too.

On Timothy's departure I thanked him for his kindness and wished his wife all the luck in the world and was returned to my cell. Albert was still in bed. I fear one day, he'll go the whole hog to match the Steptoe character in full and I'll find him naked having a bath wearing a hat in our basin.

As I write to draw today to a close, I've just been handed my French stick. There were two officers downstairs. One was supervising Angry Eyes and Ben as they dished out our supper, the other was the Walrus. He was in the mini-cab office.

And was fast asleep.

Wednesday, August 24th, 2011.

Two letters arrived under the door overnight. Both internal mail. One was from St Mungo's confirming our appointment on August 18th…

The other was of much more use. And interest. A written communication from the Tag people. Brief and to the point: My Tag paperwork will be "executed on November 8th." I hope I won't be. They didn't bother to answer any of my questions vis-à-vis the possibility of flying whilst kitted out in their apparatus but at least it's a start. I shall put in another "app" with the same questions as the previous one, again.

Up at 0630. The BBC is telling the world that Libya is in jubilation after a massive uprising. Most of the people brandishing arms wouldn't look out of place on B wing.

0810: Library. Conversation between a prisoner from Education and Glenda (who is certain that she knows who the prisoner is talking about): Glenda: "Was he tall?" Prisoner: "No, short." Glenda: "Moustached?" Prisoner: "No, clean shaven." Glenda (still not giving up): "He was a local chap *wasn't* he?" Prisoner: "No, he was from Sunderland."

Good old Glenda!

When not stifling sniggers at Glenda's sultry stubbornness, I worked through the Alpha list. As I flicked through the pages, checking this and ticking that, a familiar name leapt off the page at me. I am very sorry to report, that Stevie is back in HMP Bedford.

Oh Stevie, why, why, why? What has happened? You *promised* me. Shit, shit, shit.

Nattered with Gail about Glenda. I told her that all the officers are absolutely terrified of her. I still think Glenda should be put in charge of the whole prison.

1010: Three days of no work because of the upcoming bank holiday will be painfully slow so gathered plenty to read. As the gathering of punters plodded out it was Gail's turn to get agitated about someone who she thought had pinched a book and "put it down his trousers." She repeated this so many times that I thought she wanted to go and look down the trousers herself.

1110: B wing and not one familiar face. Glenda on the war path for Teevee, "who owes a CD." Poor Sod.

1135: Returned to the wing.

Then my day was rocked.

It wasn't a Staff member. It wasn't anything in writing. It was *Ben* who told me.

"You're being shipped-out mate." *What*? "Suffolk, Cat D." When? "Friday." How do you know? "Seen the list mate." What bloody list? "Go and speak to FIO."

I found her but as usual, she wasn't the least bit interested and ignored me.

Lunch was taken to the cell. I couldn't eat. Down the loo it went and I just sat there completely dejected.

Downstairs, Lenny was positioned near the servery for possible seconds. Why is it that no white-shirt ever tells you what's going on? "Ha!" his response. Freddie walked up. "I hear you're moving." Every bugger knew. Except me. I hung about the mini-cab office pleading with God to give me an officer who would talk to me.

Found one. I have heard that I am moving and can you help me? "What's your name?" He consulted his script. "Yes, on Friday, to a Cat D, Hollesley Bay on the Suffolk coast. There will be no walls, no wire and you'll have your own key. You'll get a job. Don't be late any evening or you'll be back here." When on Friday? I have a cleaning course to complete and what about the library? "The cleaning course has been cancelled (!) Go to the library on Thursday, but not Friday."

Cries, no, *screams* of "ROBINSON" came from upstairs. Up I went and found FIO looking for me. Yes? She reacted with no more than the normal distaste and said "behind your door." I wondered if she had left me a present and went to the cell and actually looked behind my door.

There was no gift. "Behind your door" is prison-speak for "go to your room."

Albert came back at 1230 and looked nonplussed on hearing my news. I told him that I hoped he would get someone nice to replace me. He replied "a female please." He then asked why am I "getting preferential treatment?"

So, we're back to him thinking I'm a spy again.

1400: Library. Gail thought I would be sweeping stairs and was most surprised to see me. I filled her in on both the course being cancelled and my move to somewhere called "Hollesley Bay." She took this in her stride and passed me a book – thick as the *Yellow Pages* – so I "could read up," on where I'm going. It was some sort of prison guide. I looked up Hollesley Bay and was completely *stunned*.

It is in Woodbridge. I pretty much grew up down the road from there, in Aldeburgh. Both my Grandparents and favourite Uncle are buried there.

It's where I took my wife for the second part of our Honeymoon.

I don't know whether it was neurosis, guilt or shame but I immediately assumed that this was part of the punishment and the system really wanted to rub my nose in it. Almost as if they'd put me on a chain gang re-surfacing roads outside my wife's parents house, which is where she is.

As a child, when my Grandfather was still a practicing surgeon ("still cutting," as my Grandmother used to say) I would meet him at Liverpool Street station and off to East Anglia we would go. He'd drink an umbrella stand's worth of whiskey and soda and got me totally tanked on small tins of cider ("don't tell your Grandmother.")

I haven't been able to even *look* at cider since.

My late, favourite Uncle, who got me into helicopters – who would be so ASHAMED of me – retired, died and rests in Aldeburgh.

OH GOD PLEASE HELP ME.

Right, just hang on just a second you arse-wipe. Many, if not all of those visits were paid for with money that wasn't yours so JUST SHUT THE FUCK UP.

I have now got a hold of myself. I just know it's going to feel very, very odd going there. Bloody hell. I cannot put into words, either spoken or written, my thoughts. The last time I was in that part of the world, I was with my wife. Someone has a cruel sense of humour. This, like so many other prison experiences, is like a film.

"Come to the library tomorrow anyway," said Gail. She was glad I had turned up because Mike hadn't. Probably locked in his cell again. I made some remark about something, I honestly have no idea what and Gail stopped what she was doing and said that she'd "never met anyone" like me, "in prison before." The shame of knowing that I should have known better is uncommunicative.

Whether Gail knew what I was thinking – *never* underestimate a woman's intuition – or not, she changed the subject. Mike then rolled-up. Sure enough, he'd been "locked in his cell all afternoon."

1415: A visit from "that" wing again. One of them looked exactly how I originally thought they would all appear.

1445: Education hits the library and within their ranks; Teevee. He was "very chuffed" for me about the move and said "it's Cat D, innit?" I did tell him that I am beginning to feel positive about moving to an open prison. I didn't tell him that I just wish it wasn't where it is.

About ten non English speaking prisoners mulled around, not one of them anywhere near the foreign national books. I got talking to their teacher, an attractive smiley lady (Lulu, circa 1990) who was grinning but – only just – bearing it. We talked of the uphill battle of teaching them English whilst in jail and she revealed that "the keen ones soak it up. Those less interested, however…" As her voice trailed away she looked around the room and shrugged her shoulders. How does teaching in prison compare with on the outside? She is "safer in prison," her worrying reply.

1650: E 3 8. With a French stick. I've had half of E wing telling me I "will love Cat D prison." I "will have my own room" and all sorts of weird and wonderful new privileges at Hollesley Bay not accessible at Bedford (other prisons are available). At the time of writing (1800), my head is still spinning as to my new home's location. Albert returned at 1730. I suppose I should look on the bright side – only two more nights of kicking to endure. When the Judge told me that I was going to prison and I feared a right-kicking, I never imagined it would be Albert style.

Earlier this afternoon, after reading up on my new home, I flicked through the pages to discover what had to be said about my current abode. In summary, it related that Bedford is a form of transient prison. It told of Victorian architecture and "small cells." It said it was "reasonably safe." I have no axe to grind at all with what this publication publicised about this penitentiary. What it does *not* mention is a *complete* lack of interest by *most* of the staff. Where do I start? Sleeping on duty, Kicking notes back through doors, not following simple lists of prisoners to collect and deliver somewhere, playing pool. I could go on. I can only assimilate that the majority of prison officer training is taken up with sitting in a circle, and reading out THAT line. Come on now, all together: "Make an app." And again: "Make an app." You there, you're looking too interested, do it again: "Make an app"…

Tomorrow? Another day at Bedford. But the last day. Then a new chapter begins. At a new prison.

Near Aldeburgh.

Thursday, August 25th, 2011.

Albert kicked nonstop with no respite, all through the night. I'm sick of it. Thank heavens I'm moving tomorrow. I think I was awake from 0215 until I don't know when. I have tried picturing in my mind that I am asleep on the deck of some marvellous boat and that the noise is the wind on sails. It doesn't work.

0800: Glenda and I passed each other on the stairs. I told her about the cleaning course being scrubbed (sorry). She already knew about my move. Nothing, I mean nothing, gets past her.

0820: Alpha list and *straight* to the page that Stevie appeared on yesterday. He has left us again. I hope he is OK.

0825: Teevee turned up, asking "for a final game of chess." Explained – with Glenda clucking behind me – that I can't because I'm at *work*. He reluctantly accepted this. We said our goodbyes and promised to write to each other. His final words to me: "All the best, mate."

There is a Grand Prix on this weekend. Spa, in Belgium. I've never been there. My wife promised she would take me sometime.

1015: A foreign prisoner with no English at all – and I mean *none* – visited to view the volumes. A lot of universal sign language went on between him and the hapless officer. If you're foreign and do not speak English, do not come to jail.

In fact even if you do speak English – do not come to jail.

1120: The last scan. *Thunderball*. 007 appears again amongst these pages.

1130: I am now an ex-librarian, back on the wing. No more page 3 inspecting for me.

1200: Lunch served. Pasta. Banged-up.

1230: Albert back. See the pasta being sucked.

1330: Unlock. Played pool. Beat John, lost to Angry Eyes, who is irate that I'm going to an open prison ("why can't I go to an open prison?" said, over and over to an officer). Wrote a letter to Timothy PV informing him of the move and thanked him for all his time and support. Addressed it to Timothy PV, via the prison Chaplain and wrote "By hand" on the envelope, sticking it in the wing mail box.

That'll piss FIO off.

Played pool again. Beat "Steve Davis." Bloody hell!

1535: Penned the statement for Rioter Rodney, reading him the riot act first to keep his nose clean. I wrote of him being sorry and having done a lot of reflection in prison, he would now like to start again. It was not hard to write, the sentiments echoing mine to a tee. I warned him that it was likely he would get some community service and was encouraged that he said he'd be happy to make amends by "getting his hands dirty." He's been here two weeks.

And he's nineteen years old.

I finished by telling him that if he is EVER back in Court, the Judge will only just fall short of putting on the Black Cap and throw a *very* large book at him. I told him to get a job, find a nice girlfriend and to pull his finger out. "That's what I want to do," his reply.

It's a very strange feeling that today is my last day at HMP Bedford. I wonder what the future will bring. Albert told me earlier that I am the "fourth person to be shacked-up" with him since he's been in E 3 8. On asking him what the others had been like, he went very quiet. Somewhere out there are three other people who go puce when they see sails on a boat.

1630: French stick. Please God, let there be no baguettes at the "Bay."

1700: Fetched two enormous transparent "HMP" bags for my "ship-out" in the morning.

1745: Rang Buzz, who now too has experienced how things are done the "Bedford way." He rang the prison to arrange to come and see me. They put him on hold. For "forty-five minutes." On top of that, they didn't tell him I am moving…

1845: Banged-up, for the last time, here. So many thoughts. If B wing was "death-row," E wing the budget European hotel, what will Hollesley Bay be like?

Albert is on his bed having just finished his sarnie. He's just taken his teeth out.

Friday, August 26th, 2011.

The night? Don't ask. But – that's it! No more kicking. The relief... I am full of elation. I write this at 0630. I woke like an excited child on Christmas morning.

0700: Albert up. I have written a note to Glenda and Gail and placed it in one of the books that Glenda is coming to pick up this morning.

Having hardly slept a wink last night I will probably snooze on the way to Suffolk. I'm good at sleeping in Sweatboxes. How long will it take to get there on that bloody bus?

0745: Ha ha ha ha ha ha. And Ha. Just been told that my "transport is cancelled." Ha ha ha ha.

The bed was stripped I was packed and ready for take-off. Lesson learnt: In prison, do NOT count your chickens. The Walrus was asked why. "Could be for any number of reasons," he managed to gurgle without shouting, then added that he "has been doing this job for thirty years and the left arm never knows what the right arm is doing." It was the most sense that I've ever had out of him. He then said that I "should go to work." I told Harold, who is leaving today and he understandably started to panic that they were going to muck him about as well. Soon, the whole of E wing knew.

I had put my sheets in the laundry bin amongst Lord-only-knows-what and asked Angry Eyes if he could help me with an emergency wash, explaining the situation. "No chance," his answer.

Great.

I feel sick. Not because of the sheets but I'd had my mind set for the move and more importantly, no more "kicking." You IDIOT. This is PRISON. Take *nothing* for granted.

The Walrus then told me that I'm "goin' Tuesday." Yeah, right. I'll believe that when it happens.

In the queue for work I was told the library doesn't need me – they have a replacement already! Bloody hell Glenda, couldn't you have waited for the body to go cold first? Can I go anyway, to get some books for the weekend? "OK," said the Walrus, but I only have "ten minutes." Raced to the library. Took the thank you note out of one of the books to be returned – I'll reinsert it in the next batch.

Library. Gail: "WHAT are YOU doing here?" Explained. Noticed a "new" library guy, sitting in *my* seat, inspecting page 3. Bloody cheek. Turns out he used to do the job before me and Glenda has informed the management that she wants him back. No one round here argues with her. Did a

Supermarket Sweep in one minute flat grabbing a couple of blockbusters to while away the time that includes a bastard-bank-bastard-holiday. I would, if had the time, have gone to the "crime section" and looked for *How to Murder your Cellmate.*

Returned to the cell which Albert was cleaning. "Doing a spring-clean," he murmured. It's the end of August and it's raining I told him. His stuff was everywhere.

I give up. I lay on my unmade, stripped bed next to my two plastic bags and watched the practice session from Spa on the "Red button." In prison.

1030: Utilised the sodding crap caravan showers. Played pool with Albert and lost. Cue "Steve Davis": "What are you doing here?" (A potential title for this book). Relayed the story. Again.

1045: Christ; I could do with a cry. And a cuddle. And some love. I am all at sea. Or not, as I'm not going to Hollesley Bay. Not today anyway.

I put myself here though. Arsehole.

1100: Ben was informed that Tuesday is apparently when I'm off, noting it was unusual for me to be telling him what is in store for me, rather than the other way round. Orange Nicker and an officer (the late *great*, Lionel Jeffries) who I've not seen before, shot the breeze. An old boy with a moustache covered in a sea of nicotine stains. Towards the end of their conversation he with the 'tache got up, walked towards me whilst pointing out of the window and said "see that?" directing my eyes to a white door on a building near a far wall. "That's where the executions were. The topping shed."

And I thought I had problems.

1145: French stick.

1300: Just woke up. I apparently needed some sleep. Funny that.

1430: Canteen delivered. Smokes, coffee and stamps. Then I just hung idly around – deliberately nowhere near the topping shed. The whole wing is preparing for the nothingness that is the weekend in prison. And this one, a three day event.

1700: Dinner and bang-up. Cottage pie. I have tried to be as open and transparent as I can be so far within these covers whilst within these walls and so must therefore admit that dinner wasn't bad at all.

Some dialogue followed with my Steptoe lookalike. He opened up a bit. I wonder if somewhere, deep inside him, he might even be sorry to see me go. I told him I'd drop him a line from Suffolk. "Naaaah, you won't," (RIGHT out of *Steptoe and Son*). I suggested, very, very gently, that Albert accepts a visit from Timothy the prison visitor. He reacted like I'd asked him to give the Walrus a left hook. Lots of calming down followed. Albert has had no visitors ("I don't want them") and I think he could do with talking to someone. Admittedly during the night I wish it was St Peter. I continued to carefully coax him into agreeing. Talk about hard work... I tried the telly angle, saying that Timothy would happily discuss the soaps if that's what Albert wanted to talk about. I repeated that he did not want to talk about the case or to pry. Just to have a chat. He is convinced that the entire world is out to get him. I tried the age angle and told him that Timothy is of Albert's generation and pointed out that he's always going on about the "youngsters here being idiots." Still no mustard was cut.

Biscuits brokered the deal.

I kicked myself that I didn't think of this earlier. When Albert learnt that he would get a cup of tea and a biscuit, (sorry Timothy), he relented.

When I get out of prison, I shall always be looking over my shoulder for a *seething* Timothy.

Saturday, August 27th, 2011.

Mr Steptoe told me last night that he has been asked who he would like from E wing's current crop to move in with him to replace me. His response was not unexpected; "None of them." Colin the Pole had been suggested but the notion had been shot down by my patient, understanding, easy-to-get-on-with, hygienic and very still at night cell-mate. I came up with "Old Boy" but got a filthy look by way of response. Maybe he was concerned there would be a mix-up over false teeth in the mornings. I cut to the chase then and asked him who he would like. The reply was just a very slow quiet shake of the head.

0630: I have to admit I slept well. Or, as well as one can do in the company of the thrashing around of legs, which did yet again woke me. At what hour, I have no idea. I calmly said – twice: Will you please keep your legs still. A voice came back at me in the pitch black and said "next year I'll get a go-cart." Then the kicking stopped.

WHY didn't I try that before?

The weekend. "Normal" people will be cock-a-hoop with the prospect of three consecutive days off consisting of well-earned downtime. The contrast in here is vivid. I say again that everyone here and most especially me, all deserve to be incarcerated but when there is nothing to do, the walls around us become insignificant and the mind and all the subjects it raises, takes over the toil of the jailer.

I keep reminding myself that I wouldn't be here if I hadn't been such an arse. All this to "buy love" which has spectacularly backfired on me with "bye love." I have completely blown it with people and in particular, one who I love (present tense) who loved (past tense) me, for trying to be something other than what I am. Here though, people have accepted me – during the lowest, most desperate period of my life – for who I am. Now there's a lesson in life.

1045: Following letter writing to Timothy to match-make him and Mr Steptoe I played pool. Lost to John who is no nearer or wiser about his Tag. He only has "three weeks left" of his sentence and thinks he might "just sit it out."

Angry Eyes stomping about challenging anyone for a game of pool for the wager of a "chocolate bar," which he says over and over.

1130: Downstairs to ask for more washing up liquid. You Dear Reader, pop out to the shops for such errands. I go to a mini-cab office. After I had picked up a bottle, I saw Nick Nack walking about.

In tears.

To FIO's credit, through sign language she was trying to understand what the problem was. Nick Nack had streams scrolling down his cheeks and was actually shaking. My immediate thought was for someone to get on the phone for an interpreter but I didn't get involved.

1200: Cell. Have had lunch. The rumour in the queue is that Nick Nack is being bullied by the unpleasant Russian, Ivan the Horrible. The conversations flying around made it pretty obvious that Ivan is not popular on the wing. On a happier note, Ralph, he of Reception and giver out of oversized jeans and peas that are like bullets was in the lunch queue and is now a resident of E wing.

1230: F1 qualifying. Albert back with his lunch. See the egg on the wall.

1340: Unlocked. Albert to work. Went next door to "Vietnamese Central." It looked like forty of them are living in there. Hundreds, no thousands, of unwrapped packets of noodles filled the place in the great fog of cigarette smoke. Through sign-language and some very basic English I gathered that Nick Nack is "OK" but I could be wrong and they may have been trying to update me on the plot of *Hollyoaks* which they were all watching.

1400: Seb on pole.

1500: Angry Eyes hurling apples from the pool room window at the Skip Rats. After he tired of this playtime he then ate one of his missiles.

Unpleasant Russian has been kicked-off the wing. Taking his place is none other than my page 3 inspector replacement.

1545: Played pool and lost to one of the Vietnamese who was taking a break from *Hollyoaks*. In the queue for the game, *the* story of the day unravelled. TATC has apparently been slowly tap-drip feeding Rioter Rodney that "the wing has swimming lessons" (!) and Rodney "bit." His first mistake was to believe TATC. His second, was to ask the packed pool room "where the swimming pool is." I think the laughter could be heard all over the prison. Rodney has not heard the end of this. When I played him, I asked if he wanted to play from the shallow or deep end of the table. Other comments came thick and fast, the best, as he retreated – still glowing crimson, was someone asking him if "he was floating off?"

More unanimous delighted conversation on the demise of Ivan the Horrible.

1700: Pizza (cardboard) and chips. Banged-up. Thinking about whether or not I really will go on Tuesday.

1740: Albert back.

1800: Door opened for Albert's shower. He has his uses. I understand he's found someone in the kitchen who he'd "like to have move in" with him.

1910: Door still open! This probably sounds extremely petty to you, Dear Reader. Here though, it's luxury. That is, until one of the youngsters from downstairs started mucking about on our landing. Micky, (any 19 year old football player you can think of) got shooed off by the author.

1915: Door shut.

Sunday, August 28th, 2011.

0705: Albert only woke me once during the night and another polite verbal request to please keep his legs still did the trick. He rose at 0630, in a foul mood. Out came the same sort of comments – but not as bad – as during the "tantrum" last (?) week. I ignored them.

ONLY ONE MORE DAY TO GO!

I am a complete and utter fool for thinking that I might actually go. So I will shut up.

0835: The Walrus was in evidence and in the mini-cab office I asked him if I was still moving on Tuesday. From behind a tabloid newspaper I heard "yes."

1045: Micky, he of mucking about outside my door yesterday evening has just been to see me cap in hand. Not yet twenty years of age and right on the cusp of approaching a fairly vital fork in the road of his life between sorting himself out or becoming a "regular." Looking like a young footballer as he does, he kicked-off with asking "for a favour." I listened to what he had to say.

He has heard that I am "OK at writing" (!) and can I "write him a letter to give to the Judge showing remorse?" What are you in for? "GBH." My response threw him: No. Instead, I suggested, would it not be a better idea if I wrote something for him to read out, so the Judge can hear it straight from the horse's mouth? I saw a light bulb come on and he agreed. He exclaimed that he does "mean business" and that he "doesn't want to come back."

1100: Wrote Micky's Court speech and handed it over. Told him to read it very carefully and come back to me. Tomorrow is his twentieth birthday.

1115: Micky: "It's perfect." Frog marched him to Rioter Rodney and told them to both practice on each other and to make it sound good. They looked like naughty schoolboys.

This ironically is exactly what they are.

In the TV room one of the Gym mob was checking out the girlie channels, which unfathomably to me, are available to us – in prison. I told him I can't look as it's too much torture for me. He accepted this but pointed out that he is going "to be here a long while, so needs it." As much as I have enjoyed page 3 inspections and that I've admittedly always been-first-to-the-lifeboats for bedroom hostilities, what I would give absolutely ANYTHING IN THE WORLD FOR, is to *talk* to my wife.

I suppose I am doing that through this book.

1200: Banged-up with lunch. Lamb pie. The Grand Prix on the box.

1230: Albert returns, clutching two enormous bottles of purple fizzy drink that look like something that would make Superman nervous. He has "swapped the radio-cassette player," that I cleaned for him and these "drinks are the down-payment."

1430: Seb won. Downstairs Angry Eyes playing pool and just being… *him*… Please, please, please, please, please, please may I be moved on Tuesday?

1620: E wing and no doubt the whole prison, is going mad as events unfold at football matches. Some listen to radios, the rest are glued to tellies. Noises of delirious euphoria are coming from all directions, followed by tribal teasing to enemy team supporters. Bets are flying around like Albert's legs. Stakes vary from "£1" to the wretched "chocolate bar." Words I can only now associate with Angry Eyes, who just goes on and on about the bloody things. When I'm out, I never want to see so much as a Penguin. And I do not refer to small flightless birds found near David Attenborough.

1630: Dinner served. French stick and…a chocolate bar. ARRRRRRRRRRRRRRRRRRRRRRRGH.

The Queen, the Helen Mirren film is on later. Have seen it before but feel duty-bound to watch it again whilst "working for Her Majesty."

1642: WEIRD to be watching HRH on telly with cries coming from everywhere else of "Rooooooooooooooooney."

1650: Someone's team has scored and a cell door – on this level – is having the stuffing kicked out of it by way of some moron displaying his side done-good. The Walrus is on duty and has gone berserk. "ANYONE KICKING THEIR DOOR WILL BE TAKEN OFF E WING," shouted the blubber.

1700: Ad break and menu just slid under door. Picked my option for Monday. Ironically, the fish choice was selected. The same meal (well, I hope not exactly the same) that I had on arrival at Reception. My stay at Bedford is to be bookended by fish and chips.

When I leave, do I ask for the bill?

Monday, August 29th, 2011. (Bank Holiday)

A terrible night. Vietnamese central next door had what sounded like an all-night party. Then it got even worse. On the second (polite) request for a cessation of kicking – that would make Bruce Lee envious – I got a Dam-Busters worth of verbal abuse. I "don't work," I "should get a single cell" and so on and so forth. I didn't respond.

I feel like the condemned man the day before the execution. Five neat lines of vertical dots of seven on the wall. Tomorrow, five plus one and then HOPFULLY, a new wall to carry it over on.

More and more people have been saying to me "last day" and other similar lamp-rubbing jinxes.

1100: Back in cell. Played pool. Before a match with Angry Eyes who was "£6 up," he asked me if I wanted to bet on the outcome. At least the offered odds where "£1" rather than the ghastly type of confectionary nourishment that I can't even say out loud anymore let alone write. I declined. "Chicken," he clucked after failing to keep his competition with Ladbrokes going via me.

I thrashed him.

1200: French-sodding-stick.

1215: Was that the last lunch here? Albert back soon afterwards and does his normal take everything out of French stick and stick it between two bits of bread whilst humming routine.

1300: Had, or tried to have, a cat-nap. Difficult with Albert eating crisps. I don't know whether he gets more satisfaction from eating them or the noise he can make with the packet.

Was that my last nap at Bedford?

1335: *Midsomer Murders* on the box. Albert's humming along to the theme tune. Out of time. This he does to most things on the telly. His favourite being the ads.

1340: Unlock.

1430: Micky mulled. I asked how the speech practice was going and wished him many happy returns. I then studied what the "sheets" say we are all doing tomorrow.

They announced that I'm working in the library.

This didn't start panic stations because I'm long enough in the tooth with the prison system to know that disorganisation is rife here. I thought I'd go and enquire if the staff could shed any light on this official documentation, to see if someone knew something that I didn't. The Walrus was on duty in the mini-cab office but I couldn't speak to him.

Because *again* he was *fast asleep*.

1545: Ben has visited E 3 8 for a social. I revealed to him that Hollesley Bay is only minutes from family familiarity. I couldn't go any deeper and disclose my problems with my wife. Instead, I managed to open up on one emotional front and confessed that I am – and this sounds dreadful – pleased that my father is no longer living as he would just be so disappointed in me.

Ben agreed. His father is still alive and struggling to come to terms with the fact that his successful son, with the "big house and the flash car," was not all he seemed to be.

It must be terribly tough for a father to see his son locked up. We both went quiet when we in unison voiced that we wished we'd settled on baked beans – which would have been basic but honest. Ben said that prison had taught him "to respect people, money and honesty."

1620: Down the other end of the corridor, John and I stared out of the window and looked at the massive wall between us and the human race. The memory of the look on his face as he focused into oblivion will I hope, stay with me for a very long time. It was that of a small boy summarising a destroyed model aeroplane. His main topic was of regret. The icing on the cake of his comments was:

"That it is time to hit the re-set button."

Tuesday, August 30th, 2011.

Just as I was drifting off, the kicking started. I made some remark. The owner of the legs said that I was a "sarcastic c***." It worked though because the next thing I knew, it was the morning.

0730: Unlocked. The note to G 'n G was passed to the New library chap ("NLC") hidden within my returnee books. Downstairs Glenda appeared from nowhere and asked me where my "taxi was."

Started asking any white-shirt, newspaper reading or not, if I'm going. No one as usual, had any idea. At 0855 got a "you are going." Went upstairs, stripped the bed – again – and packed – again. The bed took longer than the packing. I have hardly anything.

0935: Told YSO, downstairs, that I was ready for a porter. Everyone and I mean everyone, keeps asking "if I'm going."

Except Albert, who earlier simply walked away without a backwards glance. I'm sorry, Albert. I tried.

1020: Downstairs still trying to establish what is going on. One prisoner playing a computer game on the telly, Angry Eyes at the pool table going on and on about a "50p bet."

YSO observing Angry Eyes. Author observing YSO. I asked him again, if there was any news and he yelled back: "I don't know, they've switched contracts."

Only a jerk of an asshole helicopter instructor could be hoping to be moved from one prison to another on the day that a new company has taken over the tender of shuttling prisoners around the country. If I am going, it won't be with the same "carrier" that brought me here.

1030: Considered un-packing. Stood and looked at my "kit" on "my" bed. Look what your life has come to Robinson.

1120: Pool. YSO trying to help Nick Nack "phone-home." Yes, just like the film. Except E.T. was taller than Nick Nack.

I watched from the other end of the corridor as YSO dialled about a million digits into one of the prisoner telephones, the ear-piece next to his head as he listened to the phone system trying to make contact with somewhere the other side of the world. He heard a voice and planted the receiver against Nick Nack's head without sleight-of-hand.

Nick Nack's conversation lasted a conservative twelve seconds before the phone went dead and cut him off.

I never want to hear wailing again like what followed, in my life.

Screaming, with tears pouring down his cheeks, Nick Nack flew up the stairs as though he had been shot out of a cannon. All *hell* broke loose. Prisoners and staff appeared from doorways like a French Farce. YSO turned to me and said – with urgency – "go to him. Now!" and then disturbingly added "make sure he doesn't top himself."

I think I did the stairs, four at a time.

Nick Nack doesn't live in Vietnamese central and it took me a few seconds to establish which cell was his. Not helped that when I did find it and him, he had huddled into his bunk and due to his size you never would have believed that there was actually a person in it. I wondered what to do. Another concerned prisoner turned up who "used to share a cell with him." How does Nick Nack take his tea? "White with loads of sugar." Raced to my cell to put the kettle on and reclaim about half the sugar that had previously been given to the awkward one. Returned to Nick Nack's cell with a bucket sized mug of steaming, very sweet, prison tea. The other prisoner left so I gently prodded the tiny bundle under the covers and he gingerly sat up. He looked terrible but accepted the tea. I backed off and sat-down on a chair and smiled. He got down from the top bunk, which looked ridiculous as he is so tiny (why the hell is he in the top one?) then sat next to me. Like Robinson Crusoe addressing Man-Friday for the first time, I pointed to myself and said "Jon," trying to discover what Nick Nack's real name is.

Got nowhere establishing his actual moniker but he picked up a pen and paper. A stick-men illustration was shakily drawn and I gathered – I think – that he had just spoken to one of his three children. He was still very upset so I kept encouraging him to drink the tea. Other prisoners turned up and we debated whether this is all because of the Ivan incident or if something is wrong at home. NLC turned up and so did Colin the Pole. It turned out they are Nick Nack's cell mates. At least these two are sensible. I left Nick Nack with them and went to find some staff.

YSO assumed I was on site to badger him about my move. I made it crystal clear to him that my re-housing was secondary to Nick Nack's welfare and insisted that he got on the phone to find an interpreter.

1200: Lunch. Banged-up. All of lunch, the whole nine yards, went straight down the loo.

1230: Albert back. "Where's them milks gone?" (Sic). I told him that I'd taken half of them. Inside I was seething. Most of what I'd left for him was mine.

1400: Unlocked. Checked on Nick Nack. Still miserable. Went downstairs to try to discover *any* news on *anything*.

1425: Whilst standing by the mini-cab office, an officer appeared on the wing. Looking for me. I am going!

BLOODY HELL.

In a flash belongings were gathered. I walked out of an empty E 3 8 and returned downstairs. The officer nodded at me and opened the gate. I stepped out of E wing. For the last time.

I am taken to the main wings with my prison suitcase, a solitary, large plastic bag. I walk slowly. I look at the nets. The high landings. The Victorian cells. I feel like the "film" again. The officer tells me to wait by mini NASA whilst he rounds up other prisoners. How many are being shipped-out? "Four." I stand in slow motion. I take in the wings. B wing ahead of me, A and B wings to my left and right. I feel like a lone chess piece on an enormous un-worldly board.

The Jean Harlow officer is standing watching me take all this in. "Hello," she says. "Are you leaving us?" I tell her where I'm going. She continues to study me as I absorb all the sights, sounds and atmosphere of the main wings. I can't begin to describe to her the experience of my stay at HMP Bedford. She listens and I think, understands.

Four of us are soon following the round-them-up officer outside. Two of my fellow transients say to me "Library Guy!" and grin. One of them, Gordon (Patrick Stewart), tells me he "didn't realise" I was a prisoner on his library visits and thought I "was staff." This, I decided, is good. I still seem to appear normal. I assure him that I'm one of us.

We are led through a door, up some stairs to a room next door to Reception.

I am taken by myself to a side room, then frisked and told to "get down to my underwear." I nervously look around for that ghastly gown. There is, thank God, no sign of it. Once down to my pants the officer says "that'll do for me," so I get dressed again. I'm taken to another side room and see my suit in a dry-cleaner's type bag and other possessions of mine that remind me of me. My wallet, my tie and my belt. My fellows have loads of kit. One has nine bags.

I have one.

One of the many receptacles is full of food-stuffs and is leaking. As we are all processed we're told to not "slip on the apple juice." As this conveyor belt grinds away with us all side-stepping an enormous river of sticky liquid, we introduce ourselves to each other. Gordon, I learn is in for roughly the same time as me. His fellow library visitor, Andrew (Jon Voight, circa 1970), the same. Nine Bagger (Genghis Khan), considerably more and "has been to Hollesley Bay before." How does THAT work?

We meet our "Crew." A male (Les Dawson) and a female (Les Dawson) duo. Some sort of human legal hand-over takes place and they frisk me as well. To tick their boxes, one of them asks me if I'm "happy to travel" and do I "know where I am going?" I tell them Yes and Brazil.

The four of us are led outside to our Sweatbox. I am shown my phone-box compartment, on the right. I seem to only be placed on the starboard side of such vehicles. I am locked in and hear the other doors of my fellow passengers being shut and locked too. About a minute passes and the engine starts. My eyes are glued to the view from my porthole. I want to enjoy the sights of Bedford Prison being removed from me. We pull out of our parking space and a three point turn, to a degree, is conducted by our pilot.

Genghis looked like he might have been a prime candidate for some form of physical or verbal demonstration but no one kicks or shouts. It is then really silent as the engine is doused for what I presume is some formality at the gate. From memory, we have to stop outside, then get let in somewhere with a wall, then, no doubt a gate is shut behind us and then one is opened in front of us – and then we're out, we're free, we've left.

Except we're going to another prison.

Our driver goes to start the engine to be let in to the place with the wall. It doesn't start. He tries again. It still doesn't start. He tries a third time with the same result. "Fuckin' hell," shouts Female Les. "Fuckin' hell," shouts Male Les. Goodness gracious, think I.

I may not be the world's greatest pilot but I know a little about engines. Through my locked door I call for the attention of Female Les. I instruct her to tell Male Les to start the engine without doing ANYTHING to the gas pedal. This message she relays, adding profanities to which a rugby team's tour bus would have to consult a dictionary for their meaning. And blush.

The engine starts. The relief is tantamount. We edge into the walled area and an officer who looks like he's been working on the motorways comes aboard and has a nose around. Satisfied that nothing is untoward, he exits, the door is shut and we wait for the gate ahead to be opened, revealing non-prison territory to the nose of our vehicle. The van pulls forward.

And we leave Bedford prison.

Goodbye B wing, goodbye E wing. Thanks for… making me… *consider*…

I try to sleep but can't. I just sit there looking out of my window as the world rushes by. I sit and think. I get quite anxious. I must try and stay calm.

Stay positive. It can't be any worse.

A conversation takes place between the Les duo about our fuel status. I gather we are not going to make it. The roads that we are on are littered with petrol stations but neither Les knows which ones will accept the card that we carry in order to pay for it. Eventually, Driver Les turns into a well-known brand of petrol providers as we are, I gather from the urgency of his voice, running on fumes.

It's bizarre sitting in a prison van on a garage forecourt, surrounded by normal people going about their everyday business. I watch some mum filling up a silver Toyota, whilst telling her son that if he doesn't shut up there is going to be "hell to pay."

Payment is the subject of much heated and urgent dialogue between our Crew. Driver Les is not at all certain that the "card will work here." Bossy Les is telling him to just "get on with it," and if they don't accept it, she "will call for back up." Diesel is soon flowing. I call for our cabin-crew attendant's attention and she comes to my door. If we can't pay, how long it will it be before back-up can get here? "About an hour." Think Robinson, *think*. My possessions are on board… My wallet… My bank card… There is about £200 available on it… I make the decision that if their card is refused, they can let me out and I'll pay. I don't care. I do NOT want to sit here any longer than I have to. They will probably need convincing but I will insist. Someone can pay me back later.

This plan becomes redundant when Driver Les climbs back into his cab, payment successful. I can't see him but I can sense his relief. We are soon off again. With the fuel needle at a happier place for him on his gauges.

Before I know it, we are crossing the Orwell Bridge and my thoughts go haywire. The last time I was here, I was with my wife.

SHIT SHIT SHIT.

I see familiar buildings. That ugly B.T. monstrosity. Roundabouts that as we used to pass in my excitement of nearing Aldeburgh, would cause me to demonstrate my crap Suffolk accent by way of yelling *I can't read, I can't write but I can drive a tractor*.

SHIT SHIT SHIT.

It is horrible being so close to such fantastic memories. Mrs Robinson, if ever you read this, I am sorry. I believe that I have NOW been punished. This afternoon's route has been the icing on the cake for anyone who wanted their pound of flesh. Of that you can be *very* sure.

We continue for probably about another thirty minutes. Driving through what looks like the middle of nowhere. At about 1815, the view from the window and our slower pace indicates that we have arrived. We slowly drive around a series of buildings that could double as a 1950's military camp. There is a problem however.

Driver Les doesn't know where to go.

In his uncertainty we drive all over the campus, which begins to resemble more and more the set of *Hi De Hi*. Just before Paul Shane materialises, Nine Bagger, who is familiar with the lay of the land – having been a guest previously – shouts directions from his telephone box booth, like a navigator to his pilot in a Lancaster bomber during the last war. Driver Les though, is no Richard Todd.

On my arrival at Bedford I didn't but here I do check the time as I climb out of the bus. It's about 1825. We've stopped by a one storey brick structure that looks like a field hospital. A white barred gate on the outside of it brandishes our welcome. Driver Les goes walkabout, Cabin Les organises unloading of bags from a locked compartment. Soon, the tarmac is covered in huge plastic bags.

And apple juice.

We are led inside. A well-lit corridor with a line of cell doors on the right. Halfway down of which, is a fish tank the size of a bath. On the left, a kitchen area, a few doors then a 1970's hotel reception desk. More cell type doors lie beyond that. We are told to wait in one of the rooms near the desk, the walls of which are covered in information posters and employment course flyers. There is carpet on the floor and comfortable chairs to sit in. We all plonk ourselves down. Genghis looks at me distastefully, no doubt internally cursing the manufacturers of fruit-juice cartons.

We are called to the Reception desk individually. Two officers man it. My possessions are logged and my picture is taken again. This time I do hold a number up. I am still A1796CF. As my photograph is taken, the snapping officer remarks "that's the first time anyone has smiled." I am told to go back to the others whilst they are called in turn. I ask if I can smoke and to my astonishment the officer says "yes, of course" and that he'll "open the gate" for me. Within a minute I am standing at the rear of the building smoking probably the best cigarette I've ever had. I'm in a sort of agricultural looking area. I can imagine farm machinery and the like once lived her. Trees line the horizon.

And no wire.

Gordon is called to see "the nurse." Then it's Andrew's turn. When he comes out, they are both told they are "being transported now to the wing" and I watch them board a tatty blue Ford Transit as my name is announced. I enter another room and sit opposite an attractive young nurse (Sylvia Simms, circa *Ice Cold in Alex*). She "already knows" about my hand problem. She asks if I have any other issues and when I tell her that I'm fine, she says "that's good" because she "doesn't normally work here." My medical complete, a frozen microwave oven fish and chip meal is thrust in my hand. It is exactly the same as the one Ralph fed me with on my first night at Bedford...

Following his medical Nine Bagger and I are loaded onto the Blue Transit. The driver is a prisoner (!) and as we pass assorted gatherings of buildings – all from various eras – he warns us that "the staff here are very grumpy." He explains that we are going to the "Induction wing which is called Hoxon." We drive up a hill for about sixty seconds and after passing an enormous green metal fenced eye-sore covered in razor wire, we turn left. A sign says "Hoxon Unit." The Induction wing it may be but it looks like the villain's lair from *On Her Majesty's Secret Service*.

We unload and climb a couple of steps. Bond it is from the outside but the inside makes me feel like

I've entered a 1970's Spanish hotel. On entry is a full size snooker table covered in what looks like a football pitch's amount of green. It's so vast you could land a small aeroplane on it. A couple of pool tables are to the left of it and then acres of space with an open dining room to the right. Another fish tank sits between the spaces. The far wall is occupied with huge car-showroom sized glass sliding doors in wooden frames. The view through them is of gardens and a line of trees. Benches and tables are positioned in dribs and drabs.

We enter a modern looking office. A long white desk separates two officers and me. Everything is spotless. No one reads a newspaper. I am given a key to my room (!), number 48, which I take down from a wooden key board on my left. Again – very 70's. An ID card is presented to me.

We pass the games area and come to a staircase. Upstairs leads to more accommodation, downstairs and to the right, is where 48 can be found. I put the key into the lock of the non-metal door and open it.

In shot: a close-up of a small but perfectly adequate clean and tidy room. A wardrobe on my right, a bed with wooden storage shelves beneath it. The window – with curtains – occupies the far wall. The left far corner has a locker, on top of which is a telly. To the left of that a desk and chair, above which are shelves for books. The room throws out preliminary atmospherics of "use this place to study and better yourself." I move to the window.

I have a sea view.

I am called for shortly afterwards back upstairs to a classroom type arrangement. Gordon and Andrew are already there and Nine Bagger arrives. Student type chairs make a crescent around the room, each with a small writing surface attached to the right arm. On these, are A5 sized Hollesley Bay Induction brochures, photocopied on that awful prison blotting type paper. At the "teacher's" desk, sits a bemused looking trustee prisoner who is going to be our guide. He tells us he is "Elk." (Fagin, as played by Alec Guinness, in *Oliver Twist*).

Elk tells us that we are just waiting for a few stragglers "who have also arrived today." A handful of tired looking prisoners shuffle in. One sits behind me and to my right. I sense him suspiciously checking me out. Elk starts off with a "welcome and sorry for all the fuck-ups" and that he "knows it's late" (1915). He'll share now "the bare bones of what is Hollesley Bay" and over the next few days, we "will get the works." The basics that we "must take on board *now*," are right out of the pages of Colonel Saito's opening address to the POW's in David Lean's *The Bridge on the River Kwai*. There are "no walls around us." If we cross *any* the "out of bounds" signs, we "will be on the first bus out of here, no matter which prison it's going to, even if it's *Durham*."

We are given menus and Elk asks us to select for the "next two weeks." Canteen sheets are produced for the immediate processing of goods. T.V. aerial leads and bedding rolls, which are the same uniform orange and green as at Bedford, are dispersed. Mine is neatly tied up by a piece of plastic string.

We don't need to leave our mail unsealed, we can send out what we like. My initial reaction to this is I can make this book juicier but in fact, everything penned from Bedford got past and passed by the prison censor. Our phone PIN numbers will be carried over.

I ask Elk what the score is for getting kit and he tells me "we will visit Stores tomorrow." Whilst it's not quite titters that go around the room, I get the same feedback to my "posh" voice that I got at Bedford. Elk's eyebrows certainly go roof-wards. He goes on as the Canteen orders are efficiently brought in by an officer, that we are to be "in our rooms by 2300," that this is a prison "where people work," so we are "to keep the fucking noise down." He tells us to be on time for the "Roll-check in the morning at 0730" and adds that we are all to "muster at 0830 for the tour." This is to be accomplished after we have "reported to Julian in the morning and completed any odd jobs that need to be done." With that, he closes and everyone drifts back to their rooms to make their beds. It feels like the first day of school.

2345: I'm sitting at the desk in my room finishing this. I am tired. I couldn't cope with the fish and chip meal so instead had eight (!) pieces of toast and some coffee in the spotlessly clean dining room. There is an enormous electric urn with hot water for tea and coffee, an endless supply of bread and a toaster the size of a cattle-grid. Next to which are bucket sized reciprocals filled with tea, coffee, jam sachets and butter packs.

The best thing? There is no lavatory in my room. Communal loos are just down the corridor. And I have my own door handle.

I made it. This, with a bit of luck, is the beginning of the end. I'm in bloody *Suffolk*.

And I'm STILL in PRISON.

Wednesday, August 31st, 2011.

I have not slept like *that* in AGES. The last day of August! A gift from Hollesley Bay which has already been redubbed: "Holiday Bay."

I hope Albert's new cell mate is not too shell-shocked.

0800: Breakfast and "task" complete. I reported to Julian (Christopher Lee, circa *The Battle of the River Plate*) who almost apologetically asked me to empty four bins. Separate toils were given to Andrew, Gordon and Nine Bagger, who commented to me "fuck job, innit?" (Sic). It seems that word has followed me from Bedford...

0815: Hanging about in the massive hallway to meet Elk. Other newbies converge. I've hung my key on the board so staff can see whether we are here or not. As soon as we're all together, one prisoner walks off and Elk does not look amused. Attempting to both pacify him and break the ice some remark is made by me along the lines of being happy that I am finally here – my transport was cancelled on Friday. His response brings back flashes of the shambles of HMP Bedford: "There never was any transport booked on Friday."

Jovial Julian cranes-in to view and is asked if I'm to do the bins each morning. He nods and we formally introduce ourselves. He's certainly more posh than I am and has been in "six years for fraud."

We eventually start off on the tour. About seven of us. HMP Hollesley Bay is a campus with a public road bisecting it. Elk is very careful to point out to my colleagues, most of who have been in "closed conditions" for some years, to be very aware of the cars. He is not trying to be funny. The readjustment required for some of my fellow fledglings is already apparent.

He meticulously points out the Out Of Bounds signs and repeats that whilst there are no walls here, these signs are the wall of death. We traverse the big green monstrosity, covered in wire and Elk tells us that it's a "Young Offender" Institution.

The silence coming from it is deafening.

We pass a chapel, "Stow" Unit and walk down a pathway that parallels the road. Elk shows us where Plastering takes place and the Painting shop. There's a Bricklaying school too and even a Forklift driving course. It is becoming blindingly obvious that this place is designed to provide a trade.

For the storeroom, see *Carry on Sergeant*. Pile after pile, not of combat fatigues but prison jeans, prison T shirts, prison boxer shorts, prison… You get the idea. A Quartermaster runs the show, who looks as bedraggled as the prisoners present working there. He tells me to "fill my boots" and take whatever I need. The T shirt pile is attacked first and I try to pick the non-burgundy colours that prison provided possessions prominently are; purple. A bright orange one catches my eye and a Cambridge blue one throws itself at me. I pick it up and read the slogan across it… *ALDEBURGH 2011.*

Someone up there, or probably *down* there, has a sense of humour.

Teetering over to a table to wrap my new possessions in a net washing bag, the plunge is taken and feeling like I'm ordering a bottle of Claret, ask the Quartermaster if there is any chance that I can have a pair of shoes. "What size?" Seconds later, I am holding a bag with brand new prison pumps in it. At least they are not purple.

We leave Stores and cross the road. Elk points out the library on our right and "Wilford" Unit, ahead and to the left of us. A 60's building which could double as either an East German lookout post or a Police station post a riot. A very tatty Union Jack hangs limply from a flag pole. We continue on. On our right, various administration offices are housed in what resembles an old music school. We get to the end of a path and Elk points to some Portakabins at about our ten o'clock and a hundred yards away. "That's Bosmere Unit," he says "and beyond it is Cosford Unit." The former looks like the sort of thing that people who work on the M25 make their tea in. Between us and the building-site looking accommodation that is "Bosmere," is a massive field for "Exercise." We turn right. "Healthcare" is pointed out; a huge redbrick building that could portray a schoolhouse – or at a push the Bates' residence from *Physco*. Further up the hill, on our left is "the Gym."

Elk turns to us all and announces "that's all folks." I can see in his eyes he is saying "don't fuck this up."

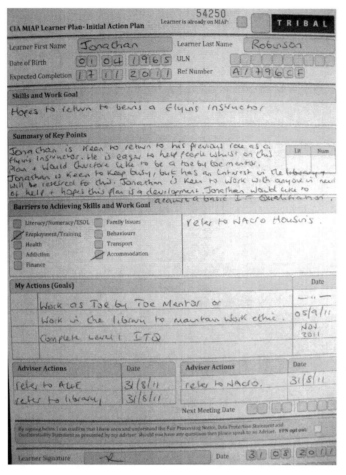

0920: Hoxon and a Tribal interview. The same lot who couldn't spell pilot in Bedford. This chap seems more switched on. Frank (Bruce Willis, circa *Moonlighting*), discusses my housing issues and what I'm going to do whilst I'm here. The former is addressed by starting a process with something called "Nacro Housing" and the latter gets covered by me alerting Frank that I will do *anything* and I am quite happy to shovel shit. He makes me laugh by saying that I'm "not really a shit shoveller." He notes that my previous job at Bedford was in the library. I tell him that I am signed off for Toe by Toe and that I got absolutely nowhere with that in Bedford and am keen to work in that direction whilst I am here.

Frank "will be in touch."

1045: Dialogue outside with Robert (Shaw, circa 1964). An "old hand" who knows Aldeburgh and laughs when I tell him the T shirt story of this morning and how I think it's all a spurious ploy to punish me further. Robert has been here – and in other prisons – for some time...

1100: Interview with a nurse (Sue Pollard). The inside of Healthcare portrays a leafy village Doctor's surgery. Nurse Sue would not be out of place in such a setting either. As she is making an appointment for me to see the Doctor about my hand, a colleague of hers enters the room. This individual would perhaps not slide so easily into an NHS practice in the Shires.

The door of the room burst open like a scene from a cowboy film. The colleague (Ruby Wax), dressed in the same uniform as Sue, stomped in carrying a rucksack. She looked like she had been mucking out horses. A cupboard was opened, the rucksack *thrown* in it – with enough force to blow a safe – and a proclamation of "I'm packed" was made. Sweetness and light, it was not. I asked our new arrival if she was leaving us. A mumbled expletive prefaced an affirmative and she left us to it. As the door *slammed*, Sue said almost like Basil to a guest that Manuel "is from Barcelona," that I have arrived "during a difficult period of transition." Switching situations concerning Spanish waiters in Torquay hotels back to things *Hi De Hi*, I asked Sue if we were happy campers. The reply: a *very* firm "no."

The library was routed to on my way back to the Unit to sniff out the possibility of getting a job therein. The prisoner running the show, Brett (Anderson, circa Suede) was friendly enough. On learning that I had worked in Bedford's library, Brett told me he had done the same "a long time ago." I asked him who the Commandant had been during his scanning career there and he said "some Scottish Lady." When I proclaimed the name Glenda he said "that's it!" then went a funny colour. Brett told me "there are no vacancies in the library."

1200: Another exterior two-shot. This time with Walter (George Cole). He did "18 months" thirty years ago. Back now with a "two year sentence." Why on earth the gap? "Stupid greed." I tell him why I am here and he listens sympathetically. A nice chap, who is "looking forward to his first Home-leave this weekend." Prisoners here are tap-dripped back into society with gentle visits back to the earth's atmosphere with exeats. An enormous man, Oliver (Hardy) turns up and goes on about the complications of keeping his "car here." He reels off a long list of the obvious such as road tax, insurance, the vehicle's log-book and the registration documents but "cannot understand" why he "must have road-side assistance cover." Walter: "So if you break down, they can tow you back to prison."

1200: Lunch. The best meal I have had since I've been in prison. Loads and loads of salad. I must try and put some weight back on.

1300: Library. Monday's paper was read and two books borrowed. Barry Norman's favourite films and Paul O'Grady's autobiography. Like a magnet, I was drawn to Jeffrey Archer's *Prison Diaries* in the (like Bedford) *huge* "Crime" section. Thirteen copies of them! A mental note was made to send Hollesley Bay fourteen copies of this.

If it ever gets published...

1400: An interview with a friendly female officer (any prison officer from *Within these Walls*). Am I OK? What will my address be on Tag? No, I can't fly on Tag – but "fill out an app to the Tag Lady who is switched on." My "Home-leaves" will be at the end of October and November and do I want Christmas leave or New Year's leave? I thought I'd be out on November 17th? "Apply for them anyway."

The influx of questions ended at 1530. Reams of forms to go on various "Home-leaves" (where the *hell* to?) have been filled out and an "app" to get the ball rolling with "Tag lady" to see whether or not it is possible to commit aviation whilst manacled.

Played pool with Gordon and Andrew. They are cheery souls and it is easy to see why they were made Cat D and re-homed here. I was then summoned on the Tannoy, yet again. This time to see the prison Chaplain. A Lady (Irene Handl, circa 1969 – decked-out in *full* collecting-jumble-for-the-church-bazaar regalia).

I assumed it would be a spiritual chat but God works in mysterious ways and instead was asked again where my Tag address was and told that I "won't be able to fly on Tag." I thought that anything that got me geographically closer to her "boss" would please her... Perhaps when I meet "Tag Lady" we will discuss Mathew, Mark, Luke and John...

1715: Dinner. Dined with Gordon and Andrew and confessed to them about the book. If they didn't think I was mad before, they do now.

1930: In my room following a very long conversation with a chap who was amongst the ensemble gathering of sleepy stragglers who arrived at Elk's briefing for newcomers on our first night. Rod (Jason Statham) had initially inspected the goods in a most veracious James Cagney manner but after he had completed his analysis he relaxed his guard with me and I breathlessly settled in his immense charisma. Early thirties with the shoulders of Hercules and bears an uncanny resemblance to *any* character you care to mention from pretty much any Guy Ritchie film you can think of. He certainly knows half the dialogue from *Snatch*. I hit it off with him immediately. We sat outside on the terrace and talked and talked and talked...

Rod is on this "production" for his interest in things horticultural. He had a very large amount of a certain species of plant that grew in lofts in great number. The numerical quota referring to both the amount of greenery and the number of lofts utilised. He is a season ticket holder in the services that prisons provide – I got the impression that he's got prison in his *veins* – and has been around the block more times than you care to mention. He is not a fan of the staff within the jail system but indicated on a number of occasions that he needs to turn a new leaf.

I both anticipate and expect some scenery-chewing turns from him, as these events un-fold.

He told me that he had "clocked" me when I'd asked Elk a question during the night briefing and had noted that I had apparently responded to Elk's answer with "righty ho," which Rod Explained, was a "first" for him in prison. I told him why I am here and that I have been a tit. He was not judgmental but did say "yes you have." He's seen me scribbling notes and guessed that I am writing a book. Not for the first time in prison, Rod radiated that I'm "clearly, a fish out of water."

2000: Getting into bed with *Lewis*. The first episode in ages watched without the sound of a Twix bar being mutilated.

Thursday, September 1st, 2011.

0725: The holiday hallucinations have hung over from yesterday's evening chat with Rod, which was just like striking up a conversation with a fellow-Brit on a beach. But with no wives in-situ.

I miss being loved very much. It is worse than prison. Noted however, is that the love I "bought" with stolen money, got me here. She texted me after she abandoned ship at Christmas saying "everything was make-believe." I have written back repeatedly over the last, now eight months, saying that the love wasn't. But nothing.

Picked up milk in the Roll-Check queue, during which you sing out your room number and a white-shirt ticks off your name – a massive human Bingo game. I did the bins again which took me five minutes.

0800: Outside with Barry Norman. I had contemplated taking Paul O'Grady with me but worried about starting a rumpus by reading a "gay" book. I personally don't care one iota, POG makes me laugh but I live in a sensitive and volatile climate.

The first thing I was asked on sitting down was "what book are you reading?" I was glad it was Barry on my arm and not Paul.

0930: In front of the same *Within these Walls* female officer ("WTWFO") as yesterday and answering the same questions again. She "assures" me, that this is "the last bit of Induction." I repeat again that I am most interested in doing something constructive whilst I am here. She hints to me that instead of waiting for "work to come to me" why don't I "go and look for it?" adding that "Alan, in Education, would be a good port of call."

I read that as "get on with it."

Rod asked me where I was going and could he join me. Walking down the hill I trod purposely. So much so that he requested if we could "keep it down to a slow jog."

Education was found in the music school buildings. Rod went upstairs "to talk to Nacro." I took in my surroundings. What greeted me was more like any "talent" I have yet come across, right up there with Robbie Williams and Albert Steptoe from Bedford days. "Alan" looks so much like Alan Rickman that I wondered if we were switching from *Prison story* to the sequel to *Robin Hood, Prince of Thieves*.

I introduced myself. I told him why I am in prison, what I do on the outside, that I'm Toe by Toe trained and that I would really like to do something helpful whilst I am here. Tribal had acknowledged I was not a "shit shoveller" and that I was trying to use some initiative further to my most recent Induction interview. In true Rickman style, he faffed for a few seconds, I think even nervously knocking something over before he came up with the notion of "going downstairs" and for me to talk to the "computer room," to ask if they can use me. I thanked him and left.

Said room was in the bowels of the music school. An IT training platform if ever there was one. More computers sat idle at desks than at Canary Wharf on Christmas day. The conversation that took place was nearly out of *Fawlty Towers*, for if I resemble Basil, I was addressing Polly. She told me "that she would love to use me" but has been told "from on high not to employ people as they are bloody useless and let everyone down." I thanked her and left.

Standing opposite Alan again, I recounted the conversation with Polly. Much thinking took place. Something else was probably knocked over. His next idea: "Go and talk with Miss Mary upstairs." Up the stairs, I went. And found Miss Mary (Joanna Lumley, circa 1966). Her first line once I had identified myself: "You're the Toe by Toe guy."

Hoorah. Something had got through the Chinese whispers process that is the prison communications system.

I explained my plight. She revealed that the "Head of literacy" had "just resigned" so I "should seek out John." I thanked her and left.

Back in Alan's office I brought him up to date and asked him where John could be found. As I spoke, the Rank gong should have sounded. My prey entered and looked *so* much like John Mills (circa *Morning Departure*) that I nearly called him Johnnie. He has the height, face and voice. He even has the beard.

Mr Rickman explained the score to Mr Mills and (Sir) John invited me back upstairs to "sort this out." He asked me to "tell all." Sensing a straight-and-to-the-point trait, I gave him the abridged version; flying instructor, tit, five weeks in Bedford, here till the end of November, Toe by Toe trained, would like a job that uses my brain and most importantly; whilst I am here, I would like to do something that might actually help some people. I would like to put something back-in. I closed with: End of pitch.

He straight away provided me with the names of two prisoners who have "asked to learn to read" and as doing so, made some comment that I was "exactly what he needed." He told me that I can "use these rooms" and to "get on with it." At last, I thought, I can do something positive. One of the names, currently on a "bricklaying course," he wanted me "to go and see now." Telling John I would report back to him, I thanked him and left.

I walked to the school that is Bricks. On entry to a small aircraft hangar sized structure filled with half built brick walls, I asked someone if they knew where my man was. A huge hulk (Lou Ferringo) was pointed at and I went over and said hello. After telling him why I was here he looked grateful that I had appeared. I told him I would just go and get the OK from his Governor to talk to him. Into a small office in the back I trotted and found an instructor. He thanked me for the explanation and told me to "carry on."

Back to the Hulk. He was very shy so I used as much tact as possible, remembering Miss Marple's advice that a lot of illiterate prisoners are "very embarrassed." I didn't want to bombard him with spiel, especially with my "posh voice." I told him that I was on his side and would like to help. He was most receptive. We talked about the frequency of meetings and he explained that he was anxious "not to miss any bricklaying." We settled on convening once a week. Mondays, 0900 at Education.

Alan's office for an update. He was taken aback by my let's-get-on-with-this attitude. He made positive noises though as he picked something else up that he had knocked over. He relayed that the other prisoner who John has asked me to track down "will be in the building this afternoon" so I should return later to "enrol him." He introduced me to Jennifer (Mrs Pike from *Dad's Army*) who "will sort out pay." I objected to that. Toe by Toe is voluntary and I don't expect to get paid. "You'll be working in Education so you must be." Jennifer told me that she was "coming over to Hoxon this afternoon" and that we could thrash things out then. I thanked them and left.

Back to John's rooms to update him. He seemed pleased that I had grabbed the nettle and told me that he'll "be away for a week" but to "crack on." Not for the first time today, I thanked him and left.

I felt elated! At last, something positive and constructive to get my teeth into. As I walked back, I made a very large mental note not to "fuck this up."

Diverted to the library, remembering that Miss Marple used Bedford's as Mission control for Toe by Toe. I met Hollesley Bay's Glenda, who is Sally (Glenn Close, circa *Jagged Edge*) and she was only too happy to help. I am to "use the library whenever I want to." She seemed pleased that something was actually being done and asked me "how long" I am "here for." On being told the approximate ten weeks that I have left she said: "Not enough."

1130: Unit. Relayed to WTWFO that I have made some positive headway and she gave me one of those "I told-you-so" faces.

1200: Lunch. Filled Rod in on events and he observed that it is something out of *The Shawshank Redemption* but said it like Bricktop, from *Snatch*.

1300: My Home-leave request forms have been returned to me as they "want an address."

1330: Outside with Rod and a new guy, who arrived yesterday. I thought I'd had it on lookalikes with the Rickman/Mills combo but things come in threes. The new guy Don *is* Chris Moyles. *So* much so, that I nearly asked him how the Breakfast show had gone this morning.

Rod's voice and stories are very "Guy Ritchie film." The banter between Don and Rod made me start looking around for Madonna's ex-husband plus crew. A very funny story ensued about an armed robbery that went wrong, a car crash and machine guns in a hospital. I don't want to go too far with relaying this, as I don't want to wake up with a horse's head in my bed on the (please God) publication of this. What I am happy to divulge though, was Don's comment about the heist that ended with him being with us. And you have to picture Chris Moyles visually, with an over-dub from a Ritchie film:

Don: "So we did this security van."
Author: Had you done a lot of reconnaissance?
Rod: "You ALWAYS do a lot of reconnaissance."
Don: "Nah, we didn't do any reconnaissance."

As all this went on my pen was in overdrive. Don saw me scribbling, did a Robert Redford double take, then carried on with hilarious antics without a word of my jet-speed jotting. I would occasionally interrupt with a question – this difficult with the hasty pen work going on whilst nearly wetting my pants with laughter.

My writing-down-of-everything caused Rod to caution me after Don had toddled off. In the friendliest of ways he warned me to be careful with my questions – he knows that my over-zealous curiosity and endless filling in of paper is for this – but others do not. They "may even think" I am "Old Bill" and "could become suspicious."

1345: Jennifer arrives. It is elected that we will speak "back at her office," after she has finished here. Apparently my name has been cast as Healthcare Orderly but she can "pull that," as she knows I "want to work in Education." She adds that when I come over, she will "introduce me to the other prisoner who wants assistance." I relayed that I was all set with the first victim for Monday.

Shortly afterwards I am sitting in the dining room with her and fourteen other newbies. Jennifer reveals all the courses available to us – kitchen chips to computer chip qualifications. I am impressed.

There is a "six week lie-down" required after arrival, before prisoners can be considered eligible to work "in the real world."

Following the fresher's festival Alan's office was routed to. I found him and Jennifer in conference. Both looked preoccupied. On the conclusion of their confab, Jennifer asked me "to come and meet the Head of Education." I followed her into a small back office where the holder of this title lived. As I walked in a very young man (Brains, from *Thunderbirds*) stood up and shook my hand.

His phone rang and he motioned me to sit. Jennifer left us to it and I studied a very blank wall-planner above his desk. His office was full of files. The phone call completed, which seemed to be a very long- winded way of confirming some meeting or other, he asked me to bring him up to date with the morning's events. I gave him the whole shooting match in detail and included the fact that I had kept both Alan and John up-to-date with regular bulletins. I can't remember how his office was draped in floor furnishing but when I had finished, he pulled the carpet from under me.

I can't "start this until the 12th." This said whilst a wall-planner was pointed at. "Because at the moment we are green" and "we don't go blue until then." I asked what on earth he was talking about. This caused a biro to be tapped on the wall-planner with obvious frustration that I wasn't up to speed with his colour coding. There was more coming my way as the Bic was again hammered on the plastic coated calendar: "This will only happen," if the Tutors "want" me there. I am to "scrub the Monday appointment." The question of "who" had told me to talk to John was discharged, then "John has no power" was gunned. The coup de grâce came with "the Governor won't like it."

I wanted to thump him.

Instead, I tried to make him see reason. I went through the facts. My understanding was that Toe by Toe is available in all prisons, that I was trying to help people (with *learning to read*) and that I had attempted to use some initiative. I repeated again that I had regularly reported back to staff with what was going on. He then rather queered my pitch by saying – vehemently – that "there will be no Toe by Toe in this prison."

I hope this gets published. I hope it gets read by the powers that be. I would *love* to be a fly on the wall (planner) during any subsequent conversation in the future between the "Head of Education" at HMP Hollesley Bay and the people that are the Shannon Trust.

With an awful lot of tongue biting, I asked him if he was aware of *how* what he was saying *sounded* and that it appeared to me, that he was perhaps a little too preoccupied with colours on charts. No dice.

I was *seething*. The way forward was requested through clamped jaws. "Go back to Tribal." I didn't storm out but I wasn't exactly Nureyev as I stepped out of the office with the wall-planners.

By fluke, Frank from Tribal was in Alan's office. He gathered that he was not in the presence of a happy pilot and with a sideways movement of his head, signalled me to follow him to his office. On hearing the lowdown, he was sympathetic and indicated that "red tape is all over the place." He told me "to leave it with him" and that tomorrow I will see on the notices that I "start work in Healthcare on Monday."

Hoxon was *stomped* back to. En-route, Elk was commuting and got the receiving end of my vented frustration. What is the point in prison, of stopping people who are trying to help others, I asked him. He said "don't try and beat the system."

I wasn't trying to BEAT it. I was trying to HELP it.

1600: Hoxon. Fuming. Relayed events whilst still fit-to-be-tied to the entire company. Andrew's reaction: The prison system is not used to someone "using their brains." It just wants to "incarcerate us, feed us and release us."

1700: Dinner. My notes say "so so."

I feel pretty down in the dumps. I thought I'd cracked it. I haven't forgotten why I am here. It just seems barmy to me that the system doesn't want to help. It would make sense if I'd opened up shop with tunnel digging lessons or how to print twenty pound notes.

I wonder why the "Head of literacy" resigned...

Friday, September 2nd, 2011.

0910: Muster for Gym Induction. Five prisoners short and Elk is thoroughly cheesed off.

On arrival, an Orderly (Anthony Hopkins, circa *Magic*) showed us the ropes. Lots of "innits" flew around from all parties. The gym was huge. Walter was on a treadmill ("alright Jon") and Elk peddled like mad on an exercise bike. As the tour continued, our guide explained that there are "no free weights here," as prisoners were "taking steroids" and "looking like Arnold Schwarzenegger."

1015: Unit. My two neighbours either side of number 48 are both still in bed. I can hear different TV stations being watched from each room. It's absolutely stunning outside. Rod has told me that "lifers are just so used to being stuck in a cell that they struggle to adjust to the freedom here." He reckons that anyone who has done more than "five years behind the door," is "fucked."

1030: Mediterranean conditions. All characters clutch their massive plastic mugs. We resemble some ridiculous over-grown Kindergarten. Sad though, that there are almost as many prisoners inside their rooms, as there are outside enjoying the weather. I suppose once a lifer has metamorphosed into Abel Magwitch, the sun is of no interest.

1100: Locked Paul O'Grady in my cell. Now there's a title for this book. I am today wearing my Aldeburgh T shirt which I have discovered, has the name of the Institution next door to us – the green place with all the wire – printed on its back. One of my fellow prisoners on seeing it, asked where the "*hell*" had I got "*that*." When I simply said Stores, he was most surprised. My clothing collection capabilities are obviously not very good as when I wore the orange top, picked up on the same expedition, I also got grilled as to its origin. Turns out that orange is the colour that "Young offenders" are made to don.

1200: Lunch. Very good, had loads of salad and queried if it is grown at the prison. "No." What a stupid question. I mean it's OBVIOUS isn't it, that with HMP Hollesley Bay being SURROUNDED by green fields, and with half its inmates happy to spend all day in bed, that getting some people to grow some lettuces is an INSANE notion.

1245: Library. Rod came with me to research funding to complete various qualifications on his release. Don arrived looking just like Chris Moyles – I even call him Chris now – and took out one of Jeffrey Archer's *Prison Diaries*. Traitor. As Library Brett scanned it, he said that "Archer was here for a bit."

1420: Got grilled about helicopters and where and when they can be flown. I answered the questions but made it very clear that I wasn't *remotely* interested in any potential shenanigans involving things rotary. The case of a now convicted prisoner who was squirreled (that's a helicopter joke) away over the channel by a certain pilot was discussed.

Oh – it wasn't me, if that's what you're thinking.

The conversation switched to which Units are more favourable than others if we are moved. Chris Moyles wants one in particular because his Co D (Co-defendant) is already there. So is "one of his mates." So is his "wife's cousin." I asked him if he gets a family discount... He won't get any visits. Most of the people he knows are already here.

1610: Elk waiting for a new influx to arrive. Apparently one has turned up under his own steam (!) from HMP Ford, also an open prison, where the "riots were, last Christmas." Has Elk ever been a guest there? "Yes." Which is better, here or there? "Here," by "miles." There's a "fence around Ford."

Back to sunbathing. One of the...er...larger of my colleagues, taking in the rays whilst dressed only in his shorts, was not amused when someone told him that passing local shipping had reported the sighting of a whale.

After Supper Rod came by. He's asked me to pen him a letter to apply for funding. He was a bit embarrassed but I told him not to be silly.

2100: Returned to 48 from snooker. Played Rod and won but was then beaten by Chris Moyles, but only by the black. I've never played snooker before with an armed bank robber.

Not that I know about anyway.

Saturday, September 3rd, 2011.

Awoken at 0600 by a ghostly clicking sound of light-switches as the night-staff glide along the corridor checking their charges.

On emptying the bins the back-stage area of the servery requires trespass. Returning, I got chatting to the chap who runs the servery. Like clockwork. Heston (Blumenthal) was in Belmarsh before coming here. He told me a few horror stories, including one about an officer who gave him a "back-hander." I do not refer to a transfer of funds.

To date, this is the first inkling of violence committed by a member of staff. Hitherto I have only witnessed ineptitude. And this is hearsay but the way in which Heston runs the servery, does make one think though.

0930: Back on the Unit after watching football with Rod. On arrival about thirty very enthusiastic prisoners were warming up. Some in blue, the balance in yellow. No officers were present. I know nothing about football but everyone else seemed to be an expert. Various skirmishes with debate took place about who was playing in what position and on whose side as a number of balls were kicked about. The yellow team had no goal keeper.

Kick-off time, scheduled for 0900, came and went but no Ref in I gathered the shape of an officer, materialised. By about ten past the hour, the unanimous decision was made to start without him. Much to my surprise, a game of football broke out. Ten or so minutes later, the man with the whistle arrived. And went berserk. "How dare you start without me," he ranted. "If you ever start again without me there will be no football."

Rod and I looked at each other and without saying anything, decided to leave.

Back in my room I wondered if I really was beginning to lose the plot as I was certain I could hear Spanish being spoken. Either the Tannoy was trying to add to the holiday hotel feel or the Basil in me was being haunted by Manuel. I stopped to listen. Great relief came over me when I figured out that one of my neighbours has got hold of some sort of language course on tape. One of the poor souls who finds it so difficult to exit his room is having a crack at another tongue.

1115: A letter from the Tag people. Within it, loads of blank spaces to fill in. The crucial one being an address but in the small print, a glimmer of hope; if I don't "have one," one can be "arranged..."

1200: Lunch. Absolutely revolting. However, we each got a real tomato. I heard that there is a remote possibility that these might actually have been grown here. Now there's an idea...

1230: Rod suggested "tea on the lawn." I half expected him to set up croquet hoops and make Pimms. He got talking to two of the newbies from yesterday's batch. I introduced myself to the one nearest me and learnt that he is Lennox (young Frank Bruno). His pal is Irish. And I think is what we currently categorise in our politically correct world as a Traveller. Have you seen *Snatch*? You know the Brad Pitt character? You get the idea...

Personally, I couldn't understand one word of what "Brad" was saying. I just found myself nodding and shaking my head when the moment felt right, like I used to do with Pat at Bedford. I didn't get challenged to a bare-knuckle fight or ordered to supply a caravan so hopefully didn't upset anyone too much.

1330: Outside. From my line of sight I can see twenty four cell windows. Sorry; rooms. All of them are wide open. Four of them have the curtains shut. That's four individuals just whiling away their time on their beds watching television.

A beach towel hangs from one window. And this is prison?

1530: Hoxon's "Washing man" (Mickey Rooney) had some lines with me. Short and in his sixties. Tattoos everywhere. "Here, because of something to do with guns." "Lots and lots of guns." Mad about "motorcycles." And "guns." Being released "next week on Tag but cheesed off" as they won't let him "go on holiday."

1600: Chris Moyles back on the Unit following a visit. I thought everyone he knew was already here.

1700: Dinner. "Halal Vegetable Curry." Spot on.

Buzzed Buzz. The good news is that everything is up to date concerning this lot. The bad news is that he's had my brother on the phone who seems to be under the impression that I can phone any old number. Which I can't. Buzz and I agreed that it would probably be a good idea to touch base with him.

The necessary paperwork was completed in order to speak to a sibling and handed in. I asked how long the vetting process would take and was told "Tuesday, latest."

After which, I sat with Rod and we composed his letter for funding. He was so pleased with my scribing services that he let me beat him at snooker later.

After this massive victory I got talking to a newbie. Alistair (Al Pacino) is in for something to do with naughty dealings with money – I can't exactly point any fingers – and very nice. He's currently shacked up with Gordon, who had the misfortune on our arrival to be given a two-man room.

As we conversed I was thanking my lucky stars that I was given a single room on my arrival here.

Sunday, September 4th, 2011.

During my bin chores, last week's *Sunday Times* magazine was found. There is another ST reader on Hoxon. Whoever you are, thank you very much.

0830: Read about this place:

"Hollesley Bay was opened in 1887 as a colonial college for training those intending to emigrate. It became a Borstal in 1935 and a youth custody centre in 1983. In 1988 it was given status to house life prisoners nearing the end of their sentence. Now, the establishment provides different regimes for adult category D offenders."

When I am "out" and next visit a zoo, I shall look at the animals behind bars and commiserate with them.

Soon, our Induction period ends and it is highly likely that I will be moved to another Unit. In a perfect world, I would like to stay here with the gathering of friends I have made. Strange that when I heard I was going "away," I thought it was curtains for me. How wrong I was.

Knowing my luck I'll get moved to the motorway tea cabin Unit that is called Bosmere. I already refer to it as "Bosnia."

1200: Lunch with Chris Moyles, Don and someone who I've not met before – I'll call him *"Sunday Times"* as unbelievably, especially after what I wrote this morning, it is he that takes it and I have read today's Michael Winner column.

1400: Outside with Rod and Moyles. Our resident Disc-Jockey lookalike entertained us with a story of past antics in Australia. Again, I can't repeat too much of it but it involved a "New Age Traveller," with facial piercings – "All that shit in 'er face." – "Cocoa the Clown, some pills and an aeroplane." The afore- mentioned flying machine had to stop en-route for fuel somewhere which led to "sentences of ten and fifteen years." This chapter ended with "it was all sorted by Stan, back In Colchester."

Don avoided a "longer stay" in Australia by "jumping on a plane to Singapore."

This was followed by another episode of happenings in the land of Bruce and Sheila. A misunderstanding between "8" and "8000," together with a mix up of "160.00" Australian Dollars with "160.000" in the same currency and a very confused Australian gentleman who I gathered, didn't quite grasp the concept of bulk buying.

1700: Dinner. At the table, Moyles, Rod and *Sunday Times* man – who's name I still don't know (sorry) but I think he looks like Dennis Waterman (circa *The Sweeney*). He has kindly said he will throw me the rest of his newspaper.

As well as no walls or wire here, there is no Cooler. Miscreants who play up at Hollesley Bay are not sent to segregation cells, they are simply shipped-out back to "closed conditions." I'm hearing stories that our population has today decreased.

1915: Watched a program about wounded veterans trekking to one of the Poles. This threw my problems right out of the window and made me realise that I must stop moaning. There are people out there with a lot more troubles on their plate than me. And they didn't cause their mishaps.

Monday, September 5th, 2011.

Walter was first in shot, dressed to the nines for his Home-leave. He looked like a child who'd been told he was going to be let loose in Hamleys.

All of the "experts" involved themselves in offering advice. Prisoners on Home-leave, which lasts five days, are not allowed to consume alcohol under any circumstances. Steers to Walter varied from how to get around this problem to what time he should have lunch on a given day. I think one person even told him what to have for lunch.

Prisoners mean well with their suggestions. It's clear that Walter is going on Home-leave for all of us. I begin to see how important "home-runs" were from Colditz during the last war.

I start work in Healthcare today. Andrew also has a new role as of this morning. He's starting on a painting course – walls, not pictures – and thus will be redubbed "Pablo." Additionally, Rod has christened me with a new title. My fellows now get my attention by calling "Biggles."

Whilst talking to Moyles, I learnt he had spent some time in a German prison "and no Jon, there were no machine gun towers." Don, how long have you *done* in jail?

Some totting up later: "Nine years."

When he starts to go on "Town-visits" and "Home-leave" the system wants to monitor him and he will "have to stay in a hostel." I asked him where that will be. He "doesn't mind. It can be anywhere." Then as an afterthought a caveat came: "Except Newcastle."

Why?

"Coz they talk fuckin' funny up there."

0905: Departed Hoxon for Healthcare. En-route spotted *Sunday Times* man dragging a lawn-mower backwards over some rough ground. He does look like Dennis Waterman and it did look like a scene from *Minder*. I still don't know his name and very embarrassingly he gave me a cheery "morning Jon." I need to pull my finger out and find out what he is called. Especially as he lets me share his newspaper.

Healthcare was *full* of prisoners. Staff were searched for in the hubbub to announce that the new Orderly was here. In a side office, I located Rachel (Michelle Yeoh, circa *Tomorrow never Dies*), who like Glenda on my first day at work at Bedford, eyed me suspiciously. Meeting my second boss was much easier on the eye. With absolutely NO surprise to me or her, she had NO idea that I'd been posted to her charge. She fired up her computer and somewhere, found that what I was saying tallied. Once satisfied with that, I got grilled.

If someone with any sense is going to put Glenda in charge of the country's prison system, then I too have a nomination for Rachel's services. MI5. She quizzed me to the extent that John Humphries could learn a thing or two. Once I'd fended off the Paxman like probing, she relaxed a little and asked me if I have had, or do have "anything to do with drugs." On my absolute fulmination of this, she announced that was fine "because the Orderly here has to be clean as a whistle," and that "murderers make good Orderlies as they are so good at cleaning up after themselves."

Tact is a vital necessity for the role and I am to turn my eyes and ears off whilst I am here. Patient confidentiality exists for prisoners too. She took this further and instructed me that I was not to get involved with "anything – even trouble." I told that I would only wade in if I thought life was at risk. She then warned me that there have been "problems in the past with prisoners getting over familiar with the (female) staff." I responded that this was noted and before she gave me a "Tour," she instructed me that I am never to enter any room unless it is manned by staff.

I was shown around. The main ground floor was taken up by a waiting area with plastic chairs, a table and a fish tank, centre stage. On the left, after entry, is the main Treatment room, next door to a very modern looking dental area. "Room 10" was beyond that, where I was interviewed by The Sue Pollard nurse and got the rucksack throwing demonstration. An old fashioned stair case – a *very* close match to the one in *Physco* – is in the middle of the ground floor. To the right, Rachel's office and a drug dispensary unit that was right out of *One flew over the Cuckoo's Nest*. We climbed the lino-covered stairs to the first floor. To the right, the mental-healthcare unit, ahead, on the nose, the doctor's consultation room and to the left, a staff kitchen. By which, were two large brown filing cabinets full of cleaning supplies. On the rear wall, two locked lavatories.

Rachel said "keep the place clean" and that there will be "mail to be delivered to the Units most days." She will pay me the very grand sum of "three pounds a session." With that, she left me to it.

I found a vacuum cleaner and did the carpeted area upstairs. Then mopped every bit of lino I could find. I didn't dare confess that I never finished my "BICS" course at Bedford – and was thus furbishing illegally. Whilst swabbing the decks, I met Stanley (a very young Richard Pryor) who works in mental healthcare, and Philip (Philip Seymour Hoffman), one of the male nurses. Both were down to earth and very friendly. Everyone called me Jonathan which was a huge bonus. By 1040 there was nothing else to clean so Rachel told me to "go home" and that she would see me in the afternoon.

1200: Lunch. I can't report what I ate as I was, and am, too shell-shocked. *Sunday Times* man joined Rod, Chris Moyles and I and his name is none other than DENNIS!

I didn't bother telling him or the others that I had already decided that he looks like Dennis Waterman. Strangely, Rod had already given him a title: Elbows. I sat next to Dennis during luncheon and I can see his point.

Healthcare. And mopped the stairs. Then did – under the escort of Philip – the "drugs" area. A secure room containing a big open space with a dividing wall though it with a "them and us" partition. Then still under Philip's supervision, I vacuumed the Head "head-doctor's" room and remarked to Philip that this was the cleanest room that I had seen so far. That's, explained Philip, "because he's never here." There was nothing else to be done after this so I was released.

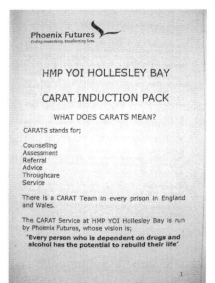

1400: On arrival at Hoxon I got jumped on by two civilian female staff and invited to a "CARAT'S" meeting. I thought they had said carrots and wondered if I was going to handle some rabbits. It turned out that this was an anti-drug program. ("Counselling, Assessment, Referral, Advice Throughcare Service"). These two very young females looked like half The Spice Girls. Sporty spoke first to the amassed five or six prisoners and then Baby told us that if we "do want to take class A drugs in prison." Can we please "do it in small amounts."

1430: Chatted at length to Heston. He's been in a couple of years and in talking to him we discovered common ground on our views of the prison system. Heston described it to a T: "Too much warehousing and not enough fixing." Neither of us could see any logic whatsoever in continuing to give the drug users their substitute – and very expensive – "fixes" and this reverted us round again to the lack of "fixing."

I told him my story adding that I felt very ashamed and stupid. He told me that I "appear to have survived so far."

News travels fast in prison. Among the headlines is my new place of employment and I got sidestepped later by a "professional" pedigree prisoner with a word of warning about Rachel. He told me, under "no circumstances," to make any "funny remarks." Not even a "you look nice today." He admitted that she is the "fittest female in the joint" but will not take kindly to anything untoward. I thanked him for the heads-up and told him of the warning she had already fired in my direction about over familiarity. He then told me that the "female in the dentist's, does have a sense of humour," which I thought strange as he spoke because my source had most of his teeth missing. I thanked him again and assured him that I would both walk on egg-shells with Rachel and keep a look out for the dental assistant. To satisfy him, I explained that Rachel is not my type anyway and he gave me a "are you mad?" look. Before he started to get nervous about visiting the showers I confessed that I am partial to blondes (one in particular) and that I had already let Rachel down gently when she had asked me what I was doing on Saturday night.

1615: Letters to Ben, Teevee and Albert have been penned. I was minded not to rub salt into any wounds. I told them that I'm OK and that it's good to have no walls and no bang-up. I think I may have dropped in that the wine list is very poor. I passed my best to them all and just refrained from asking how Tom, Dick and Harry were progressing. I assume Ben and Teevee will be pleased to hear from me. I'm not sure about Albert but I did promise.

1700: Dinner. Present: Don (Chris Moyles), Rod (Guy Ritchie film dictation machine), author and Dennis (Elbows), who I still think looks like Dennis Waterman.

As we ate, Don continued with his travel stories and I asked him if apart from the UK and Germany, had there been any forced leave in any other country's jails. "No." I think five seconds passed. "Apart from Mexico." Wishing I had Rod's Dictaphone skills, the table hushed.

"A bunch of Brits out there for the World Cup." One with "bright red spiky hair and boss-eyed," were on their way to a match. "Oh, the bloke with the hair, he had a mole too." They drove in a "big red rented Yank-tank," from across the border. "The U.S. of A." Big it needed to be. Eleven were on board. Preparation for the match was carried out by way of the consumption of "three or four gallons of beer." Per person. Including the gentleman at the helm – he "with the red hair." As they approached the match venue the alcohol caught up with "him with the mole" and a quick snooze was decided upon before kick-off. The Destroyer length vehicle was "parked-up," in some residential area "near a bus station." Whereupon it seemed like a "good idea at the time," to the rest of the passengers on board to "handcuff the now sleeping boss-eye to the steering wheel and to give him a haircut."

I think the whole dining room was listening by now.

The sheering of hair, red in colour, commenced. The noise of which "woke ex-spiky hair up." With one side of his locks shorter than the other and still locked to the steering wheel, "he started the engine" and "roared" the car towards the nearby bus station "demolishing it." Rod, transfixed at the story, asked why.

"Because he didn't want his hair cut."

Don vacated the car, now half in, half out, of what used to be a serviceable bus station. Dust, rubble, masonry and bits of cut red hair, were everywhere. The previous owner of which, vacated the vehicle, or tried to, as he was still manacled to the wheel. "Some other fella got out as well" but "eight were still in it." They started to protest that "the beer now tasted gritty." Some keys were located, and as their driver was released, "Old Bill turned up."

The three who had got out were "thrown in the back of a van." The gritty beer drinkers were "left alone" ("they're probably still there an' all.") Don, the "other fella" and the chap with now half a head of red hair, soon found themselves in a cell "with one rat" and a squadron of "flying cockroaches." Opposite their new accommodation was a cell "stuffed with drunk Mexicans, about forty of them," all making various sexual requests and or threats to the "Gringos." This "and the rat," kept Don awake "all bleedin' night."

The next morning, "all three were let go with the equivalent of a six pound fine." The "other two, made it to the next match," the "hand of God match, you know," said Don. He "couldn't go though," he had "to go home."

Why? We cried.

"Had to go to me mum's wedding."

Rod noticed a newbie on the scene who he knows from another prison, a lifer. "Who has so far served seventeen years" – my time in prison is about the same in weeks. Rod remarked that he knows this guy will be struggling with the openness of Hollesley Bay that we all take for granted after just one week. This very tall individual entered the dining room, scanned the area, turned and left. Without getting any food. I asked Rod what we should do. "I'll sort it," he said.

And so he did. As I sat on the terrace digesting Moyles' Mexican mishaps, Rod appeared with this new chap in tow. I was introduced as Biggles (thanks, Rod) and I shook the hand of Mathew (Kelly). The Kelly and Statham doppelgangers lit cigarettes. I was very low on tobacco and Rod knew this. He told Mathew, who then immediately offered me some of his. I voiced that I was OK. "That's Biggles being polite again," said Rod. Mathew insisted and thrust a cricket ball of the stuff in my hand.

Statham was very crafty in getting our new incumbent out and about. Off, to the far end of the gardens, the three of us trekked. Rod pointed out the sea and Mathew did with his face, what I would do probably if my wife appeared from around the corner.

Rod reappeared at my room later. This time flying solo. He needed a new-and-improved version of the previous letter that I scribed for him. Frank in Tribal has given it the green light but "someone else in Resettlement" has suggested more information be added. I sat him down to gain additional data.

He left school at the age of fifteen. Without any qualifications. His mother died that year, leaving his father to bring him and three brothers up. For a period they were homeless. Rod turned to crime.

During the time served at his previous prison he started to get concerned about not having any bits of paper to his name and – pulling his finger out – got his head down to gain some qualifications. He now has twenty six certificates with a further two still owed.

I hope with the paperwork that I am doing for him and from what he has told me that we can turn him around. I hope also in doing so, it helps turn me around too.

Tuesday, September 6th, 2011.

It rained all night long and we were battered by some very strong winds. So strong, that I had to get up in the night to jam my door shut. Coffee and toast was had with Moyles, Rod and Mathew, who Rod wants to replace Dennis with at "our" table. I'm not getting involved. One is my newsagent, the other my tobacconist. Neither is my baker but I know which side my bread is buttered.

0835: Wearing Stevie's "Escapee" jacket very self-consciously for the first time, Rod's latest letter was slid under his door and I left for Healthcare. Initially as a punter – I'm due to be seen about my hand – then as staff. I wondered if my jacket was going to cause me grief...

As per the norm on my anticipated fears in prison, no one batted an eyelid.

0850: Sitting in the doctor's waiting room admiring a very clean floor, a young lifer (Dexter Fletcher) – "who is out next week" – opened communication with me. He has done "seventeen years, mostly in Parkhurst." I asked him what the plan was. He rather sadly I thought, told me he was going to "sit in the garden of a rich woman in Croydon," who he "has met whilst in prison" and "get her" to "get him" a "motorbike."

0920: A lady doctor (Another Glenn Close lookalike) examined my hand. Again I heard that I'm not here "long enough" for her to "do anything." So I got cleaning. Which took me five minutes. Rod turned up to see the doctor. I enquired if my recent secretarial scribes were to his satisfaction. He sleepily dug it out of his pocket and read it like a morning newspaper on a commuter train.

1000: To "Nacro" to see if they had received my "app" with my queries about "Tag and flying" and to find out what the form is on the address, or lack of address situation. Ended up sitting opposite a young lady called Zara (Philips) who was very helpful. A birthday card sat on her desk and I enquired when the big day was. "Today." I wished her a happy birthday. The card was not the only thing that caught my eye. Zara wore a spectacular top. The view was stunning.

Whilst trying to concentrate on my issues rather than the voluminous valley, she found me in her computer. "The flying issues will have to be sorted with the Tag lady." She though, "can get things started on the accommodation front" (I was absorbed by another front). She told me to fill in some forms for approved accommodation for ex-prisoners. If something "comes up" from friends or family (Ha!), I "can always cancel it." This was beginning to sound promising. She then said that she would try and get hold of the woman who runs the Tag system, to get to the bottom of whether or not aviation would be permitted. As she shifted for her phone, the view got even better. Also by very good fortune, the Tag lady was at her desk and answered Zara's call. I understood she already "knew about me" and then came the brilliant news that "flying will not be a problem." Things were really looking up. I was just trying to stop looking down. I thanked Zara very much, making sure I looked her in the eye as I stood up – and nowhere else. I wished her happy birthday again and walked out elated. Light has been illuminated at the end of the tunnel. I just might be able to turn things around.

Dennis was met on the way back and told him my news. He works with the garden team and as they chopped back hedges he was very supportive. I scanned his fellow workers to see if there was a John Thaw lookalike but if there was, he was lurking in the topiary.

1100: Hoxon. Mail for me. More internal stuff with "November 17th" plastered all over it. Fine by me. Bring it on. Signed it and returned it to the office.

1200: Lunch. Rod, Moyles and Dennis/Elbows, depending if you were sitting next to him or not. Mathew didn't join us. Or anyone. He just picked up a pork pie, which was less than half the size of the lump of tobacco he gave me yesterday and retreated to his room.

My attention turned to our Disc Jockey lookalike. Apart from Germany, Mexico and the UK, had he been to any other nations' lesser-known hotels? A spoonful of something covered in custard was put down whilst some thinking took place. "Sweden," was said and then the spoon was picked up again and placed in the orifice which had added Scandinavian stir to the script. Rod, Dennis and I put our spoons down. Go on, I said. We leaned in.

He and a "mate had met a couple of sorts on a booze-cruise," and ended up I think, in Malmo. For reasons beyond me they decided "on the spot," to "rob a suit shop," that they had spotted. (Is this why Don has been allocated work in Stores, where they keep all the clothes?) They "got caught." How, I asked, did they catch you?

"Coz we woz in it."

Carted off again in a van – never go on holiday with Don – they soon found themselves in a police station. And charged. Then "put into a lift." On the next floor was "the Court." They were sentenced then put in the lift again. On the final floor: the prison. "All in one building," then added "sweet." "At least it saves on Sweatboxes," said Dennis with much nodding and agreement from around the table.

So Don, apart from Germany, Mexico, Sweden and The UK, is there anywhere else? A pause. "Switzerland." Another pause. "And Luxemburg." I asked Don where he was planning his next holiday to.

"Ipswich."

1330: Left for work in pelting rain. Wore my Escapee jacket which is 100% man-made something and because it was so mild I was sweating buckets on arrival. Philip asked me to do the floor in the Treatment room and to vacuum "Room 10" – the rucksack hurling practice room – which had apparently been used by the staff for their lunch as it was filled with sandwich wrappers from Tesco and crisps were all over the floor. I wondered if Albert had been a guest.

She who shall not be complimented on asked me to do a mail run. Envelopes with prisoners' names, numbers and Units on each one, containing forthcoming medical appointments were put in my hands. I broke them down to the different Unit locations and realised I would be visiting each one. Carte blanche to check out Hollesley Bay. Due to the inclement weather, I nearly asked Rachel for a life-jacket.

As the post was sorted, I noticed that Healthcare's fish were looking a little green around the gills. That's just a method of speech, I am no Vet. The water was very cloudy and the level looked low. Rachel was asked who was in charge of our aquarium and told me that I "could have the job" if I wanted. I explained that whilst reasonably handy with a plate of Dover Sole and a glass of white, my expertise in things marine stopped somewhere around there. I relayed that the fish on Hoxon look well looked-after so I would endeavour to find out who my Unit's fish foreman was and get him to come and take a look. She agreed that was a "good idea." Left Healthcare to do the mail run and was wetter than the fish before I reached the bottom of the steps.

On my travels it was concluded that I really do want to stay on Hoxon because the other Units were what can only be described as dumps. Bosnia is a pile of caravans, Cosford looked like the abandoned set of *Crossroads*, Wilford was filthy and Stow looked nothing like the school at all.

Hoxon's bunch of mail was saved till last and on climbing the steps it stopped raining. Went to the office and gave the officer the Unit's medical mail. He looked up from the computer game he was playing, unenergetically eyed the names on the envelopes and lethargically told me that "two of the addressee's are no longer on this Unit."

It turns out that Healthcare's computer system is a different one to the rest of HMP Hollesley Bay. The officer irritably minimised his game and brought up the Units where the two ex-Hoxon residents now live.

So back out I went. The law of Sod dictates in matters like this. Both prisoners had moved to the same Unit and it was Cosford, the one furthest away. Then it started raining again.

1445: Hoxon. By fluke someone was tending the fish as I walked in. We started talking about Healthcare's poorly looking aquarium. I introduced myself. Rick (Paul Simon) listened and said "no problem," he'd "take a look tomorrow." I passed instructions to tell Rachel that I'd sent him along and this thrilled him as he "knows her" and in "his head" she is "his girlfriend."

1500: Still raining-cats-and-dogs outside. Went to get coffee and grinned at Gordon, who's now "working in the kitchens," so he's now called Gordon Ramsay. Whilst filling my cup I observed Mathew and other newbies filling in their Resettlement forms. I heard him question one of the staff about what to do with the "work experience section," as he's "been in prison for seventeen years." He was ordered to "leave it."

1700: Dinner. Messer's Moyles, Robinson, Statham and Kelly. The first time I've seen Mathew sit down and eat something.

1800: Tried my brother but the phone system wouldn't let me dial his number. Visited the office and enquired what the situation was having been previously told that it would be done by today. The officer's response: shrugged shoulders. A pair of them.

I am going to attempt an early night. All in all, not a bad day. Great news about flying and Tag. I still have a feeling in my bones that a massive uphill struggle awaits me on release. I must though, on all accounts, use this as the making of me. Rod remarked earlier that he thinks I'll come out of this, on the other side, "as a better person."

I hope he's right.

Wednesday, September 7th, 2011.

0800: Rachel was informed of yesterday's treasure hunt for prisoners and that her computer is not talking to the prison's. She replied that "they don't talk to each other." Met the dental team and sounded out the "assistant"; Renee (Zellweger, circa *Bridget Jones' Diary*) who I'd been told has a sense of humour. I couldn't see the joke of her asking me to mop her floor when the drilling had been done but that's life. The time mutilation of molars was expected to end was requested. "About four."

0830: Met another new face. A civilian female staff-member but not in uniform, exiting "Room 10." I said hello and asked if she needed anything done. The list of desires was long and only just fell short of moving the building to the right a bit. Worse was that it was enumerated in a very broad Welsh accent and for a moment I feared the owner of it might start singing at me. This was Kathy (Bates) and her manner was formidable. When the long list ended I politely pointed out that half the tasks on it had already been completed and most of the others were not possible because I have been told those places are off-limits unless I am escorted. Her reply, in heavy Welsh:

"You have a bit of an attitude."

I bloody do now.

I managed to bite my tongue. Where the hell is Philip? I need to have conference with him NOW and find out who the HELL the "Welsh Dragon" is. Noticed she was wearing a wedding ring.

Her poor husband.

Mopped loos, vacuumed, emptied bins, poured boiling oil over the Welsh bint (that bit in my head). Saw Rachel, told her that "Rick the Fish" was turning up at 1330 and left sharpish.

0930: A Goon in my room ferreting a "volumetric check." Can I get "all my things into two normal sized suit cases?" he asked. He looked around my measly possessions and announced that I can and went next door.

I could get my possessions into a *shoe* box.

0945: Outside with lifer Mathew. The first time that we have properly spoken. Discovered he is from North East Yorkshire. Asked if he has family – he does – but didn't probe if he has a wife as I think that MIGHT be why he is here. Rod has told me that most of the lifers have "bumped-off their old ladies."

1030: Eavesdropping on a conversation between Mathew and a younger prisoner, who has been inside "seven years." His age; 21. He is telling of "learning more about crime whilst inside, than anything else." He has "no qualifications but would like to be a fireman." Someone in his "young offender's prison was stabbed last week – for a milk." The following words are *his*, not mine:

"These places put all the young bad eggs into one basket. They continue the gang warfare that existed on the outside and fight each other on the inside, brewing a new type of criminal."

I wrote that down verbatim. Mathew watched me. Out of the mouths of babes...

1200: Lunch. Relayed the Welsh Dragon story. I am dreading work this afternoon. Maybe she was just pissed off about the match result last night? (England 1. Wales 0.)

1400: Went to work early to avoid the wrath of the Dragon that is Welsh. Rick the Fish stood on the outside of Stow Unit like a lady of the night. He alerted me that he'd been to see the aquarium and it needs something called "filter wool." He told me that he had reported this to a member of staff. The tall chap? I asked, referring to Philip, who is my height. "No, the short one," said Rick which was odd because Rick is tiny.

On arrival Philip proclaimed that he thinks my title of "Rick the Fish" is "brilliant." Philip, you should spend some time in prison. "I Do." I suppose he has a point. Philip is very easy going, charming to everyone, patient with his patients and calls everybody "Sir." Except me.

No sign of The Dragon.

Mopped Philip's floor and met another member of staff, Benjamin (Ben Kingsley, circa *Coronation Street*) who I think is a male nurse although he doesn't wear a uniform so he may have some other function. Spoke with Renee about the length of the dentist's waiting list and asked her to make me an appointment. Renee said she would get back to me and could I "mop her floor at four."

The Dragon turned up.

1500: Met Rod. Not that one but another of the same name (Woody Harrelson), who was in the waiting area. A lifer. Fourteen years served. Out next October. I didn't tell him when I'm off – I have learnt that with the long haulers it's just not the done thing. My sentence is known in the trade as a "shit and a shower."

This Rod is "shocked" by the behaviour of some of the "youngsters" in prisons past. And what they are "allowed to get away with." At the top of his list is the "trousers below the hip" mob who "show their boxers."

We talked of the absence of any class system in prison – which I like – and I confessed to him that on sentencing, my first thought was that I was dead because of my posh accent. He smiled hauntingly at that. I went on: people have just accepted me for being, well, me. Prisoners don't judge you in here for *what* you are. It's *how* you are. The hinted ghost of a smile that Rod reciprocated with endorsed that I had hit any nails lying inactively around firmly on their heads.

Later, whilst killing time before I could get into the dental area with my bucket I grabbed Philip and hissed at him to give me some intelligence on the Dragon that is Welsh. I recounted the welcome that she had given me this morning. "I'd heard," he grinned. "Ignore her." She is "like that with everyone" and Philip has had to "duck to avoid the flak in the past too." He pointed out that she is "under stress about NHS cutbacks."

Under stress? I wish she was under a bus.

1600: No sign of a wrap for the teeth team. By quarter past the hour I was almost begging Renee to go home, so I could do her floor. She eventually came out and asked if I could do it "tomorrow" and added that I have an "appointment with the dentist on the sixteenth."

1620: Number 48. Door open and Rod walks by. The walking film encyclopaedia. I asked him for the name of that film that Kathy Bates is in with James Caan about a psycho nurse.

"Misery."

Half the landing had heard me. Another voice, further down, commented "that Welsh tart in Healthcare." It seems that I am not alone in the mantra of character analysis of the Celtic beast.

1700: Dinner. Moyles, Rod and me. No Mathew as he has been roped in to work in the servery. After dinner, Moyles is planning a visit to another Unit to see his Co D who "Probation have forbidden him to talk to."

1755: Canteen sheets arrived. Filled in my order, handed it in and moved to the telephones to attempt speaking to my brother (a *very* young John Gregson).

1815: I got through to him and we spoke for about ten minutes. He was very jolly and supportive but I hated it. I feel so stupid calling my "kid brother" from where I am. I am so ashamed of myself. During the call I decided not to ask for any more help whatsoever but just to relay information that I am alive and coping. I said I would be in touch.

I don't half feel sorry for the Welsh Dragon's husband. That's worse than prison.

Thursday, September 8th, 2011.

Slumbering down the corridor at 0620 Dennis was up and on the phone. As I write, an alarm clock is going off in someone's room and is either being ignored or its owner is a very heavy sleeper.

0715: Grabbed Dennis in the dining room and asked him who on earth he was speaking to at such an ungodly hour. "Kids, wake 'em up for school." Breakfasted with Moyles, who is not normally to be seen first thing (doing his breakfast show I suppose). He has an "early job interview for driving the vans." As Moyles munched, he asked me a strange question. "What's the name of that bloke who was in *The Sweeney*?" Which one? John Thaw or Dennis Waterman? On Waterman, he punched the air. "I knew it!" he cried. What? He pointed at Dennis on the other side of the dining room and with a mouthful of toast spluttered "that's Dennis' name: Dennis Waterman."

Not for the first time in prison, I thought I was being filmed.

I told Don that according to the telly we are in for almost hurricane like weather over the next few days. "I was in an 'urricane, in Cuba." I stopped eating. Did you go to jail in Cuba? He stopped eating. "Nah." A bite of toast. "But…" I stopped eating and put my toast down. All ears. When he was in Cuba – during said 'urricane, he was running for cover along "some street" in the pouring rain. He was just a "Brit abroad" ("we'd gone wiv bleedin' Thomas Cook") and accidentally "bumped into someone." Nothing unusual in that. Nothing out of the ordinary either that the collision made the other gentleman "drop something."

A 9mm Browning automatic.

Don's wife grounded him "for the rest of the holiday."

0800: Dennis was cornered and confirmation sought that he really is called Dennis Waterman. He is. I didn't even start to tell him the similarity had already been noticed and more to the point, noted. I think he knows about this book. He's lived all his life with a famous name, so is used to it. As a footnote to this though, he told me the name of his "mate" that he used to hang about with…

"Simon Templar."

Swapped some more of the *Sunday Times* with the friend of the *Saint*. On the way back to my room met a newbie who "landed yesterday from Belmarsh." Introduced myself. His name? Rod. (Charles Dance, circa 1981).

Another one…

0815: To the office to make a plea to stay on at Hoxon. Spoke to one of the more sensible officers

(Clint Eastwood, circa *Where Eagles Dare*) and asked what does one have to do to stay on. He told me I was "clearly mature and sensible" (??!) and he "prefers" people like me "rather than the difficult ones." However, he "does get grief for surrounding himself with the easy ones."

Talking of difficult ones, rumours are rife that yesterday someone "kicked-off on Cosford Unit." The story is that the culprit was a bit of a Kung-Fu expert and prior to dispatch to another prison – in handcuffs – "chopped" an officer "who is now in hospital."

0825: Rachel was already at her desk madly typing whilst occasionally shooing off prisoners who float by for a fix of flirting. She has a stable door to her office and she sensibly keeps the bottom one shut. Lags look like nags as they hang over the ledge of lust, tongues lolling with eyes on bean stalks as they attempt conversation about what always sounds like utter codswallop. Rachel takes it in her stride.

The Dragon was about and being far more civil. I wondered if she was better behaved because Rachel was on set. A very short male nurse (a younger Godfrey, from *Dad's Army*) paraded too.

0905: Philip and Nurse Sue rolled-up. Rachel told them both that they "have to go to the suicide meeting." Neither looked thrilled.

0910: Some photocopying completed and I am promoted to Healthcare Stapler Operator.

0912: Rick the Fish turns up to speak to Rachel.

0915: Break stapler.

0916: Switch the (obviously faulty) stapler with Philip's.

0922: Finish stapling and am told to "come back in the afternoon."

0935: Hoxon. Saw Don whizz by in a van on the walk back so it looks like he got the job.

0937: Whilst making coffee and toast I break the toaster.

What is wrong with me today?

And why do 99% of the youngsters in the two prisons I have been in, all try to sound like they were raised in Harlem?

Went outside to not be near any more machinery and overheard a conversation about "bent officers." Apparently, some officers in some prisons will, for a price, bring in items that would be perfectly legal on the outside. Mobile phones for example, which are verboten in prison. This is done by way of "emptying and opening the wrong end of a carton of orange juice" and filling it with individually sealed phones of a certain make and model that is I hear, very popular in the penal establishments of the land. The bottom of the carton is then re-sealed and hey-presto. Talking of bottoms, the particular shape and size of the most desired mobile device makes it easy I hear, for self- storage. A whole new meaning to the phrase dirty phone-call...

Gordon is no longer Gordon Ramsay. He has left the employ of the kitchen and is now working in Stores in the vacancy I assume produced by Don, who with his vast getaway driver experience has moved from there to Vans. Gordon is now to be redubbed on the call-sheets as Gordon-the-Gopher.

1200: Lunch. Salad. Tones of the stuff. Dined with just Rod as Mathew "pot washing" in the servery and Don still doing his demon Damon Hill activities up and down the hill. After lunch picked up my Canteen delivery and gave back some tobacco to Mathew.

I had a quick word with the officer with whom I'd talked to this morning about staying on board Hoxon and asked him if I could apply to become "enhanced." He told me that I "meet the criteria and to leave it with him."

1330: I still can't put my finger exactly on the description of this place. HMP Bedford was easy: Victorian. HMP Hollesley Bay is a mishmash of age, look and feel. Anything from a 1970's average school's grounds through to an ex M.O.D. site, with touch and goes of disused airfield, stabs of film studio, beats of an old music school, dents of a building site and a dig at an agricultural college make up the Bay that is Hollesley.

The place is *full* of tractors. All driven by bearded, shaven headed Asians, who drive like Cambodian taxi drivers in the rush-hour. I spend my commutes having to avoid them by jumping out of their way. All those tractors. All those fields. All the workforce here. Yet the only thing put on our plates so far that was allegedly grown here have been some tomatoes... To be fair to the never-driven-in-a-field tractor peddlers, it was not one of their battalion that tried to wipe me out today, but our female prison Chaplain. I recognised it was her car as I leapt out of the way by her personalised number plate.

I wonder what St Peter would have to say to me on arrival – before no doubt being sent basement-way – having been dispatched by the "God-squad." In prison.

Once at work presented myself to Rachel who deployed me on Rounds. On the way out, I asked Philip as he was eating his lunch how the suicide meeting had gone. He just sighed.

Around the grim Units I went. On arrival at Bosnia I got the po-faced officer to double check on his computer that the names and Unit addresses tallied. He'd just been sat looking out of the window when I walked in.

Part of my drop-off route involved Reception with the paperwork I'd stapled together this morning but I couldn't gain entry. The inner door was open but the outer gate remained firmly locked and I couldn't make myself heard over *Home and Away*. At the next Unit – Wilford – I got the officer off his computer game and asked him to telephone Reception to alert them that a prisoner had failed to break in. This he did and back I went. I had more success this time and handed the pages over to one of the goggle-box fans. I left for Stow Unit and he went back to his telly. On the uphill leg, Rick the Fish travelled down the incline. With a green plastic bucket. Off to do something technical to our fish-tank.

1500: Coffee in the dining room. Two others prisoners are at the toaster wondering why it's not working...

Whilst by myself – and pause for thought – more reflecting took place. Came to the conclusion, not for the first time in prison, that I am an utter *tit*. I must change my ways. I am so angry at myself. I'm sorry for all that I have done. I also feel ridiculous that it's taken being thrown into jail for the yellow card to be noticeable to me. I don't begrudge the punishment but the fact that it took putting me in here to wake me up and that the required catalyst was clink to buck-up my ideas is just, on paper, so crass.

Fact is though, even if they had given me ten years, my wife leaving me is the ultimate punishment. She told me, I think the last time I saw her, that her folks "never liked me." I can see their point.

I really *do* need to sort myself out...

Rick the Fish returned to the Unit mission accomplished. I thanked him on behalf of both Healthcare and the fish.

1500: Locked myself out of my room! Went office-bound to ask if someone could let me back in and lots of statements were made as to how much I will enjoy camping. After all the hysterical comments I was readmitted. Frankly, I am surprised it has taken me so long to do this and I'm sure it won't be the last time.

1700: Dinner. "Seafood Pasta." Disgusting. After dinner played pool with Gordon and lost.

Which is how I feel. On top of that; lonely, angry, frustrated and hurt. I remind myself, again and again, that this is all down to me.

I wish my wife would talk to me.

I don't want to attempt to turn this book into *Crime and Punishment*. It is simply designed to illustrate day to day life in prison and all my thoughts. And what I've seen and learnt in my short time with what is wrong with prison. I hope that the combination of the funny stuff and my regret and sorrow lead to a firm pointer that crime doesn't pay. Seeing as this is also written with the idea of getting potential criminals to think twice before proceeding with misdemeanours can I point out in no uncertain terms that as well as the stigma of a stay in prison, you also stand a very good chance of being abandoned by loved ones.

Believe me, when you ARE in prison, the imagination runs RIOT of what the consequences of that can and will bring. It is horrible. Trust me on that one. The reader may gather I hate myself right now.

You are getting everything you had coming to you Robinson. You don't even deserve Open prison.

Friday, September 9th, 2011.

Assaulted the bins and questioned Julian about the future-perfect prospects of staying on at Hoxon. He told me that he is "sure" that I will, as my name is "ticked each day" for having done my "job." He went on: "Ticks mean prizes." Staff "move people that are non-ticked." As we talked some lump walked over and asked Julian for a job. He was told "that's OK, nothing today."

Back in the room with the news on. Then, the local news stopped me in my tracks.

"A man from **** will be sentenced later after being found guilty of..." This continued as a mug shot of an individual came up on the screen. It was Matchstick man from B wing at Bedford. I've beaten him at pool.

0810: Still reeling from the news feature, went work way. On arrival Rachel (four foot ten inches?) and "Short Man" (five foot nothing) were talking about "height." "Short Man" is called Dave and his accent reveals broad Birmingham breeding.

The fish looked magnificent.

Diminutive Dave was asked to open-up upstairs so I could get cracking. My initial matching of him to a younger *Dad's Army* Godfrey was reinforced by our first proper conversation. He didn't sprout of his sister Dolly but did recount his frustration of being "unable to buy Hampshire watercress in Tesco." It comes I hear, "from Holland." I pointed out that our current location is closer to the land of Edam than it is to Hampshire.

0840: Philip heard of my shock about seeing someone I knew from Bedford on the telly but just shrugged his shoulders. I did some cleaning then reported back to our Mr Seymour Hoffman, who remarked that "the place has never been so clean" and left at 0850.

On the walk back, coming in the opposite direction, a new-to-me prisoner (Peter Sellers, circa *Dr Strangelove*) approached. As we closed on each other he smiled and realising that I have finished my morning's toils said "now go back to your cell and think about what you have done to society." He was making a joke and spoke with a North American accent.

The irony of this, is that this is EXACTLY what I do ALL THE TIME. I wonder if "NGBTYCATAWYHDTS" realises this.

1000: Unit. Rod was asked if he wanted the surplus stockpiled sachets of porridge that are not my cup of tea which for some reason beyond me, I have been squirreling. His reply was *right* out of the pages of Dick Clement and Ian La Frenais: "I don't like *Porridge* porridge."

1130: Dialogue outside with Rick the Fish and Robert. We wondered how Walter will feel following his Home-leave. I imagine coming back after nearly a week in your own bed is probably worse than initial arrival.

They were amused and slightly put out that on my arrest, when asked if I had anything to say, I had responded with "bang-to-rights." They seemed convinced that I should have "fought it" but I told them that I wouldn't have been able to live with myself if I had hurt anyone else further. Both arguing the toss and or denying it would in my opinion be the lowest of the low. Besides, I am not a "professional" criminal and now classify myself as Failed Amateur Criminal (Retired).

Both of them saw the piece on Matchstick Man. They told me that he will be working for Her Majesty "for a very long time."

1200: Lunch. "Roast beef salad" plus "French stick" (probably imported from Bedford) with "tropical coleslaw." I queried this title but Rod announced that he'd found *the* piece of pineapple.

1300: Rounds. At my first port of call, Cosford — the *Crossroads* set — a face figured that I recognised from Hoxon who has been shipped-out to this Unit. He didn't look terribly happy. Continued my *Postman Pat* duties and on the penultimate drop-off at Stow, saw another jetsam ex-Hoxon face that I hadn't noticed on the missing list. A foreign gentleman. He didn't seem terribly pleased to see me. "You on 'ere?" No, I replied sweetly, I'm just delivering letters. This was the individual who had eyed me so distastefully during Elk's briefing on my first night at Hoxon. He has made it very clear that he thinks I'm a "grass."

1430: Outside and soon joined by the mob. Moyles in high spirits and full of boundless beans. Mathew was grilling him of all the prisons that he has been in. My ears pricked-up. A list was itemised, all of which we knew about. An additional one though appeared over the horizon by way of Don saying "Scotland." Then added: "Nearly."

A bunch of "football fans" had journeyed north of the border to see a match. By train. Much lubrication had occurred (again). On arrival, a visit to a public house seemed in order. At the packed bar — and remember where we are — one of Don's companions decided that the singing of a ditty would be a favourable pastime to accompany the beer. A song commenced, the title of which perhaps questionable considering the audience: *"Who's afraid of the big bad Jock."*

Have you ever seen a pub go quiet? Don has.

On the opening of the third verse the publican, counting four of Don's group and about sixty of the opposition, shrewdly shut-up shop and the shutters came down with all the speed of a falling guillotine blade. This was the green-light invitation for glasses to start flying. "Blood was everywhere," types of which donated from both north and south of the border.

Once the weapon supply had been depleted or rather, smashed to smithereens, a new arsenal was required and armaments were provided by way of a magazine of pool cues.

It was pure folly though and Don and his side did all that they could do by courageously "legging it." Walking wounded, they were. A visit to a local hospital was out of the question as both their appearance and injuries would no doubt cause unwelcome interest from the local Constabulary. One of their number "had their hand hanging off," so it was elected to take the train "from Dundee to Edinburgh" and "go to the hospital there," to get patched up. The plan backfired though when the

Police, who had been alerted that the cast from some horror film were aboard the train, "stopped it, boarded it" and said "you cunts are coming with us."

Don, fearing another nation's jail was shortly to be added to his curriculum vitae, was more than relieved when they "were taken to the 'ospital and not the nick."

1530: Walter is back. Looking shell-shocked.

1640: Found a notice on the boards – dated 2008 (!) – announcing that "prisoners can apply for outside charity work at ANYTIME." The "mandatory lie-down period is not required for this type of work." Why has no one told us this? Went in haste to the office to ask where I could sign up. Received the standard stock line…

"Make an app."

1700: Dinner. "Balti pie and chips." I didn't even put it in the Pigswill bucket. I don't want to get done by the RSPCA.

1800: Rang my younger brother who clearly felt uncomfortable having his older brother call from where he is and I don't blame him. I made the decision then and there not to bother anyone again. I must sort this and myself, out on my own.

YOU got yourself into this mess Robinson. YOU get yourself out of it.

Saturday, September 10th, 2011.

My imagination is running riot about what my wife is doing. At least she knows where I am.

0900: Left for (watching of) football. Pitch side, Parkhurst asked me to sign a "spectator sheet" thus documenting my attendance. I suppose for boxes to be ticked in the event of trouble. He told me that he'd been "rushed to hospital on Thursday night," because they'd given him "the wrong drugs." Ipswich? "No, Methadone."

On kick-off, the first comment I heard came from one of the Yellow team. "Them got twelve, innit?" I got counting and indeed, there were eleven yellow men and twelve blue ones with one referee who had turned up this time. As Parkhurst told anyone who would listen about his hospital visit, I noted that there was so much spitting on the pitch that I may as well have been watching a water polo tournament.

Lunch was at 1200. I should have worn my *Grease* jacket.

1400: Seb on pole.

1500: The Tannoy announced that my presence was required. An inordinately large female officer told me that her "colleague at the end of the corridor," was looking for me. I turned about and indeed saw an officer (Tim Roth, circa *Reservoir Dogs*), holding a bicycle at the end of the passageway. "Are you Robinson, in 48?" said the bike stand. I nodded assent and learnt that I was "going, with him, to Stow Unit to do an Oasis (Sic) review." Noel or Liam? I asked. His answer worried me. "OASys (Sic) is for all the lifer prisoners." I *very* firmly transmitted that I was no lifer. He told me that he "knew that" and that my name had been "pulled out of a hat."

This officer has a reputation. And a nick-name. From both staff and inmates. For ease of avoiding trouble on publication of this drivel (there's optimism for you) let us agree that this officer was and is known, as the "Terminator."

En-route to Stow the Terminator asked if I was "local." I told him no, but shamefully admitted the Aldeburgh connection. He chuckled and told me that he used to work in one of the hotels there...

The world's a small place. An even smaller one in prison. Some dates and names were thrown into the ring. It transpired that this individual had waited tables for my late uncle. And spoke highly of him. Guilt spread through me like spilt ink... I felt terrible.

A row of windows ran across the far wall of the office on Stow. As he did things to a computer I sat with searchlight like sunlight aimed at me, like an interrogation scene from some war film. This interview "would be good for Tag," he announced and you name it – we discussed it. As we progressed through the data bank of questions he kept saying that the "computer was concluding it was very unlikely I would offend again." My "risk was 0.0001%." I told him that when I get out, I'm not even going to break wind in a supermarket.

The Terminator had a heart. When we discussed my wife leaving me he did the equivalent, whilst working on a computer, of putting his pen down and told me of stormy and choppy waters that he and his better-half had been forced to navigate.

They had been separated a year. He'd been working overseas since the cessation of smooching but civility still existed. One day on a building site balancing bricks in Germany, he concluded that something needed to be done and got on an aeroplane and hot-footed it home. He rang her and invited her out for a drink. After her agreeing to this she told him to hang on as there was someone at the door. She found her husband holding the phone in her porch. They have been together ever since.

We resumed the review. My thoughts now on my crime were questioned and discussed. I repeated my sorrow, regret and evoked my intentions to expiate matters. I told him – with complete transparency – that I think prison has done me good.

He put his "pen" down again and asked me what I'd "heard about the kick-off with the Karate Guy." Without singing like a canary – I don't want to sleep with the fishes – I told him what was already common knowledge around the Bay: A kick-off by a prisoner handy at martial arts, an injured officer and a "ship- out." The Terminator leaned forward and told me the story...

Cosford Unit. A prisoner who had been "with us for a considerable time" and has been "good as gold," suddenly presented himself to the Unit office announcing that he "wished to be returned to closed conditions." This "was quite out of character." "Staff were concerned" and tried to find out the reason for this odd request. They got "no response" and the gentleman "returned to his room." Mystified, "an officer followed him." On arrival at the cell, the officer "found the door open, the prisoner stripped to the waist whilst covering himself in baby oil." This is an old trick to make the achievement of a firm grip on an un-cooperating prisoner difficult, if nigh-on impossible. The well-oiled prisoner then "attacked the officer." Mayhem ensued. "Five or six officers attended and subdued the assailant. All have bites and one has nearly lost an eye."

How is his colleague now? "He is alright." I relayed my wishes for a speedy recovery.

I questioned what on earth had brought this on. Especially with the no previous problems. "No idea." Now intrigued, I enquired as to how much observation we are under, other than "Roll-checks." He admitted "very little" as officers "don't have time."

Time enough to sleep on duty, play pool, read a Fleet Street Editor's *dream* quota of newspapers, play snooker and play computer games seconded my mind.

Back to the interview. I will "definitely get Tag." However, by 1640 we were only "halfway through" and we still need to cover any "known association on the outside with anyone dodgy." I told him the only person I know is Rick the Fish. This caused an immediate stoppage of the typing department. I speedily explained it was just my moniker for the fish guy.

He saw the funny side but I have to learn to shut up. Things like this could cause problems with Tag and I want to get out of here and ring my wife asking her out for a drink as I push her doorbell.

Well, one can live in hope can't one?

We agreed to re-convene tomorrow but not, at my request, during the Grand Prix. He laughed at this and told me that he will be on duty at Hoxon on Sunday and that we would "wrap this up."

Supper had with Rod and Dennis. Moyles joined us later post driving duties. He didn't eat as he'd already "stuffed his face with cake in the kitchens." I repeated all that I had been told about the Cosford kick-off. All were incredibly sceptical. I repeated again and again that I was only relaying what I'd been told. This was their point. The Terminator wasn't there either and he was telling me what *he* had been told.

After dinner, caught up with this masterpiece. Rod and Moyles both bored and kicking their heels in the corridor, complaining about the "fucking seagulls always waking them up in the morning." Don gave me a demonstration of the noise which is just what you need when you're trying to recount a day in prison in very grotty handwriting. He wouldn't shut up, so down went the pen and I let him continue. I could sense a story coming...

"Whilst in Belmarsh," it was not the Seagulls that got up Don's nose "but the pigeons." The large gathering of which was mainly caused by prisoners throwing bits of bread out of their cell windows thinking of days past in Trafalgar Square. The pigeons learnt that they were on to a good thing and started collating in droves and shrieking at the first sign of daylight for their breakfast on a regular basis. Moyles' cell was on the ground floor and no doubt the Hovis baying cries made things very difficult to conduct a breakfast show. One morning as he grimaced at another landing crust, he decided to "grab the bull by the horns." Through his barred window in his best hard-man voice, he vocalised his bull-grabbing so: "WILL YOU CUNTS STOP THROWING BREAD DOWN HERE."

This was heard as the announcement of the open season for loaf lobbing. Half a Mother's Pride lorry's worth was soon cascading downwards to Don. The view from his window was like a Christmas nativity scene, such was the quantity of sliced-white descending majestically earthwards. I assume the pigeons thought it was Christmas too. Moyles managed to see the funny side of this but still closed this episode with "bunch of cunts."

1930: A heavy downpour and outside with the mob in it. The usual suspects, plus one. A newbie (Frank Skinner) and an unhappy one at that. The reason for his displeasure was simple. Our flat roof was flooding. An overflow pipe situated right by his window, was subjecting him to the Chinese water torture. The more it dripped, the angrier he became, which increased the delight in everybody else no end. After he stomped away in disgust, Rod scampered off to fetch a large plastic dustbin lid which he surreptitiously strategically placed right beneath the offending pipe. A lot of schoolboy sniggering could just be heard over the snare-drum like sound. The percussion section was aided by horrendous fart sounds which came from Moyles' direction and he admitted that he may have overdone it a bit with the cakes earlier.

The furious prisoner returned not seeing the funny side of things at all. As everyone fell about in hysterics, Rod smirked, Moyles broke wind and I told him that we'd thought he'd take it like water off a duck's back.

Later in the evening Moyles recounted yet another story. A "broke" Moyles and "friend" had received information of a big fat juicy safe filled to the brim with what makes safe-breakers sit up and take notice. That was the good bit. The less attractive side to the plot was the safe's location. "Three hours away," by car. On arrival and after whatever-it-is that safe breakers do had been done, it became apparent that either God, or the owner of the safe, had a bigger sense of humour than Moyles and Co. Their booty came to the stupendous amount of twenty six pounds.

Moyles shamefully admitted that it wasn't even enough "to pay for the petrol home."

Sunday, September 11th, 2011.

Ten years since 9.11. Mathew had unenthusiastic news first thing. "They want to move him to Wilford Unit shortly." We talked of how prisoners like to moan – myself included. Even if there was "free beer" at Hoxon, we would all still complain. Probably that it "wasn't cold enough," concluded Mathew.

0900: Moyles on the phone to Mrs Moyles busily sorting out logistics for a visit this afternoon and the execution of remotely getting both her and their teenage daughter in the same car at the same time. "There will be war." Mrs Moyles "has borrowed a Sat-Nav from next door." She doesn't "need to program the address into it" though, as Hollesley Bay is "already in it." The "husband" of the woman next door is "in this prison too." Moyles has shaved for the invasion and it has taken ten years off him. (That's him – not his sentence).

0950: Sorted paperwork with Rod. I need to do two letters for him.

1200: Lunch. I don't know what pudding was supposed to be but it went straight to the bin. Some sort of lemon sponge. Anyone need their loft insulated?

The Italian Grand Prix.

1430: Seb won. During the post-race interviews my name was called and the interview was continued from yesterday. A similar bank of questions came my way. This curtailed at 1600 but we are still not wrapped so agreed to meet at Stow Unit at 0830 on Tuesday to get this in the can.

After the most awful of evening meals Mr Waterman suggested "team pool." Mathew and his team mate (bloke writing the book) were soon squaring up to Dennis and Moyles. The target being the "first to five." It got to 4.3 to them and then Moyles sank the black to claim victory.

Yours truly had to make the tea as the losers' forfeit.

I have never experienced so much camaraderie before in all my life. I tend to rather… er… take my time between shots and comments like "bloody hell, Jon, I'm out in October," had me in fits of giggles.

Mathew blamed his (appalling) standard of play on the reasonable excuse that he couldn't see anything so we dispatched him to his room to fetch his glasses. On his return and for the rest of the evening, Mathew Kelly was addressed as Dennis Taylor which confused the hell out of Dennis so we resorted to Elbows whenever anyone referred to him. When the mob communicated to me, the printable prefaces were Jonny, Jono, Jon-Boy and Chopper-man. However Rod kept to his customary Biggles.

Monday, September 12th, 2011.

Got into bed last night with my book and the bloody hero's wife has just walked out on him. I can't escape from this anywhere.

Heston told me of his recent Town-visit – which is prison-speak for going home for the day. On his experience he was most reflective and summarised his time spent with his family with the observation that life is not about "flash cars, big houses and new clothes but throwing pebbles into the sea with your kids."

If that's not *the* quote of this book, I don't know what is.

0800: Work. I got busy and mopped the – staff only – loos. Which, with their cleanliness and supply of Andrex were too inviting not to utilise… Kitchen workers' perks are extra food, mine are the bogs in Healthcare. After road testing the lavatories I emptied the building's bins into the huge skip sized containers outside. During which, I found myself humming *My Old Man's a Dustman*.

Please don't think that I mind emptying bins and the like. I put myself here. I just wish I could use my brain a bit more and possibly use some of my alleged noddle to help people. I must hunt down Frank in Tribal and see if he's had any luck with the "Head of Education." The man who won't allow Toe by Toe in this prison…

Hoxon. Some commotion on the corridor was audible so went for a look-see. A drugs dog – "Rusty" – and his handler (Bill Oddie) were doing their stuff. I watched a very intelligent Spaniel as he sniffed out everything he could. The walls, fire extinguishers and even a warning sign about slippery floors were snuffled at. The handler was asked what Rusty does when he actually finds something. "He freezes," he said icily.

1015: Wrote a note to Frank in Tribal asking for an update on the Toe by Toe situation and went outside to read. A strong wind blowing made the sunbathing days seem like many summers ago. It's not cold but it's certainly not warm either. And not hot enough by any means, for the wearing of Bermuda shorts but those who converse with the preface of "bruv" and sometimes "blood," still insist on wearing them. Whilst displaying their underpants.

I sat in Hoxon's gardens and thought of the time between my wife leaving me and Court. I would hold her pillow at night and clutch her dressing gown. Texts from me to her telling her this were ignored.

Damage. Damage. Damage.

1200: Lunch. French stick (!) with cheese. Dined with Rod and Elbows. Elbows being called Elbows because I had to sit next to him. I moved my chair right around to the corner of the table and I'm still calling him Elbows. I could have sat at the next table and he would remain addressed so. Mathew joined us post servery duty and looked at me oddly, clearly wondering why my plate and I were teetering on the crevice that was the cliff-top corner of the table top.

Rod held forth over lunch delivering a soliloquy on how to "deal with Probation" after release. I am fast gathering that prisoners see this body as some form of Gestapo movement. My experience is only based on the lady who I met before Court who was absolutely fine with me. Apart from her telling me that I wouldn't be going to prison. Regardless, even if I do meet a bunch of long black leather coated individuals who – and this was made *very* clear – have the power to send me back to prison, if they say "jump," I shall ask how high…

Mathew then dropped a bombshell that he is being moved to Wilford Unit tomorrow. I keep calling it Wilfred. I will miss him. The bombshell turned into a blitz when I remarked that Moyles was late joining us. Rod broke it to me in pure Jason Statham style that he has been moved to Bosnia. Our loss is the Caravan site Unit's gain, which I'm sure will be a happier, funnier and sunnier place with his presence.

1310: Healthcare. Revealed to Philip that my main source of laughter has been exported to Bosnia, which he took too literally and I had to quickly explain that the establishment has not branched out but that I have a habit of renaming things. He looked quite relieved.

Mopped the stairs and that was it. I take longer going to and from work, than I actually do at work. On my way past what Mathew has told us is to be his new home – Wilford, an extraordinarily throaty car pulled along-side me and stopped. Clearly a Getaway Driver coming to see a pal. An awful lot of spoilers and wings had been bolted to this contraption and everything wobbled as horsepower rumbled at idle. The driver's window slid slowly southbound. The *antithesis* of prisoner voices identified himself – wrapped in Emerson Fittipaldi sunglasses – as "one of the Institute of Directors," here for "the lunch" and asked me where he "could park."   A vacant spot was pointed at.

1430: Unit. There's a pile of bed-packs by the main door. Each one rolled-up and tied together with the same plastic binding that mine was bundled together with. I kept my bit of string. Not as a keepsake but as a tool. It sits around my neck and my ID card hangs from it. If I had some straw I'd look like a scarecrow.

Sitting in Hoxon's gardens a gathering of people appeared from the north end having by-passed the green Cathedral. This lot, who looked like American tourists were in fact conducting some form of inspection. Two of them were in bright red tops and resembled holiday reps. The effect added to by the fact that they were so tanned they were almost mahogany in colour. I wondered if they were going to have a go at selling me an excursion. They passed me by and entered the main arena of the games room, looking like they were going to purchase some post-cards. Heston remarked that "you can't work for the IMB (Independent Monitoring Board) unless you have a tan."

Walter, Rick the Fish and Robert; Hoxon's *Grumpy old Men* sat on a bench. The word cunt was used a lot. Not directed at me but aimed at anyone who had incurred their displeasure. The staff, someone on the telly, the Judge who had sent them here, the bloke who had serviced the car and even one of their sons-in-law were all identified so by this hammy breed. It was like listening to lost tapes of *Derek and Clive*.

We dined at 1700. Rod, Dennis and I talked about things not being the same without Moyles and Dennis asked "why does everyone call Don, Chris Moyles?" The *uncannily* close resemblance was explained and then Rod took things further by telling Dennis what we all call him! Poor Dennis went crimson in colour and we fell about. Rod, who was sitting next to Elbows, asked him "if he wanted to see the bruises."

1805: Phoned Buzz. He has done – and passed – all his exams! (Written examinations are a requirement for gaining a pilot's licence). I was thrilled for him. He told me that he'd done "a bit of flying" but was "missing his instructor." We discussed him coming up to see me but struggled to pinpoint a date. It was his diary that was the stumbling block, not mine. We agreed to talk again on Thursday to nail a day. He asked me about things marriage... I replied by asking how he was.

2030: Returned to 48 from the tables following a doubles tournament. Dennis opted out so it was Mathew and I against Rod and a young lifer whose name remains a mystery.

Tuesday, September 13th, 2011.

0815: On key-drop, the officers told me that they will complete my paperwork for "enhanced status" today. Their final words to me before I left: "Don't count on Tag."

Stepped aboard Stow and found the Terminator who told me he would "be with me in a bit," before suggesting that I should "hang-out." Various familiar ex-Hoxon faces were about – again who I hadn't noticed on the missing list. Nine Bagger dollied in and inquired "what you doin' here, Bruv?" I answered that I was here for a meeting which was a crassly stupid thing to say, as enough people already think I am some sort of *Brubaker* spy.

Stow's notice boards were window shopped. Literature about the status that is enhanced were displayed. In a nutshell, I can have a Playstation in my room. I wouldn't know how to turn one *on*.

The Terminator called for me shortly afterwards. The clock on his office wall was stuck at 1600. Enquiries about the injured officer led to the news that "he is out of hospital and will probably take early retirement." We moved on to the matters in hand. More of the same questions trickled out and he kept telling me that his machine was concluding still that I was "low risk." My emotional well-being was a temporary focal-point during which I aired my desperation about my wife which was noted. We talked about me putting something back in, either by attempting to stop people from coming here or helping those who have just got out as the existing process doesn't seem too successful. The Terminator stopped typing...

"A very well-known footballer," had tried something along these lines, at a Young Offenders Institution. Some keen and enthusiastic inmates were corralled together and "all moved to one wing." They "lived, worked, ate and trained together." The result was a "success."

More stories tumbled out. "One of the gentlemen from the Iranian Embassy siege was here." The worldwide headline grabbing events in which the SAS swooped in by helicopter – like Milk Tray men – and blew everything up. "This prisoner was very polite and intelligent." The "odd thing was" that when he received visits it was the "team who had sieged the building that came to see him." All "dressed in sunglasses" and "the visits had to take place in the chapel." No one knew if "he had befriended the SAS or whether he was passing on information."

A final funny story from the Terminator. A certain "high security prison was due to have an inspection," to which all staff (and from my experiences to date, probably all the inmates) had been given a "heads-up on." One prisoner within those walls was "under 24 hour observation" and was being "very carefully watched." Or at least, was supposed to be. When the inspectors came by to witness the "observation in progress," they "found the officer asleep."

Shades of the Walrus at Bedford.

We finally finished the interview. As the above will testify, most of the time taken was used up by chatting. I was asked if I'd "like a copy of the report." I was handed 40 pages.

Frank of Tribal made a cameo appearance on my commute back. Incidentally, the Terminator told me that Frank "used to be a Screw" (Prison officer) but I "don't know that." I asked Frank if he had received my note requesting movement on the Toe by Toe satire. "Yes. It's on the Head of Education's desk." The fan of wall planners. When will it be sorted out? I asked. The day after my Tag? "Probably," said a rather embarrassed Frank.

After ten minutes of vacuuming at Healthcare back to Hoxon. Mathew about, who has now been told that "he is moving to Stow" but "no idea when." The young lifer who played pool with us yesterday evening is with him. Kevin (Bacon, circa *Footloose*). I tell them – from my travels – that Stow looks acceptable but not to go anywhere near Cosford or Bosnia. It transpires that Kevin is "moving too." Where are you going? I ask. "Cosford."

1220: In my room after a veggie burger. Dennis has "done his back in," quite badly and it showed.

1330: Work. Mopped the stairs and the Treatment room. Discussed with Philip the switchover from the NHS to the private sector. He proudly showed me his new badge and said "would you like fries with that?" We got a heads-up that Dennis was hobbling over to us with his bad back. I quickly briefed Philip about Mr. Waterman's eating habits. Philip, now fully seasoned, gave me a knowing look and shooed me away when Dennis limped in.

Consultation complete, Mr Waterman exited the treatment room mystified as to how and why a medical expert had told him that "he would feel better if he managed to keep his elbows in whilst eating." One look of my face and he caught on. The comments made, are both unprintable and physical impossibilities.

Escorted the walking wounded back to Hoxon. The plan to write this up. Wrong. Tannoy: "Mr Robinson report to the office." Duly turned up and got told to report to what sounded like "Emu." Is Rod Hull here? Michael Parkinson's assailant it was not, but "OMU" (Offender Management Unit).

Having positioned myself to the heart of the Bay, some exterior metal stairs were climbed which were like an executioner's scaffold and an office scenario was entered. A sliding glass enquiries window on the far wall, not dissimilar to a village post office beckoned. Got someone's attention and told them my name. A familiar faced officer arrived and the plot unravelled further. "Need you for Oasis," he puffed.

Erm...I finished that this morning. "Oh yes? Who with?" Relayed which officer and offered to go and get the copy of the report, if he liked. "Oh sorry. Go back to your Unit and ask them to send Mr._____ over."

It seems, Dear Reader, that within prison management, the left arm *really* doesn't know what the right arm is doing. A bit like Elbows at meal times.

In the book I'm reading there's just been a wedding scene. No guesses who I'm thinking about. If the roles were reversed, would I be doing the silent treatment? No way in hell. I always promised that I would be there through thick and thin. Don't give up Robinson. Never *ever* give up.

1700: Dinner wasn't good – greasy chicken. Didn't eat much. The boys noticed and asked what's up. I'm sick of the crap food. Rod immediately donned his Fletcher hat. "Are you not here to be punished?" "Are you not in prison?" This made me think. Afterwards, I thanked him. He does after all, have a point.

In the coffee queue Julian relayed to me that Guns/Tattoos/Bikes man is going home tomorrow – for keeps – and "doesn't want to leave."

Wednesday, September 14th, 2011.

Mathew has educated me that on release, I will feel like I have a "massive motorway sign" – which "everyone can read" – over me, saying "I've just got out of prison." Rod added with his sustained sardonic state that I won't need a sign if I "wear that top." I'm in my bright orange young offender apparel. I look like a giant Satsuma.

0800: The longest conversation yet to date with Rachel. She has relaxed her guard with me. So much so that when we were talking about arsonists – don't ask – she referred to them as "stupid fuckers."

Welsh Dragon was on the prowl so I got busy. Rachel told me that "some people are turning up" from outside to "do some tests" and asked me to prepare one of the rooms upstairs. A man and a lady turned up – both of whom looked like accountants. One had a laptop and needed "somewhere to put the needles." Heroin addict accountants? The female later asked me how to get an "outside line on the telephone." I told her I'm not *too* familiar with the phone system as I only use it to call Australia. Went for reinforcements. Found Philip who effortlessly said "dial 9."

Overheard Rachel talking to the Welsh Dragon about the "upcoming meeting." WD said that "she thought she would be in Spain." I know Anglo Spanish relations are not too hot post the Armada and the on-going Gibraltar debate but isn't us sending her to them a little over the top?

0845: Escape Healthcare. Tribal Frank features on my way home. He is the only person – outside work – who *always* calls me by my Christian name. In frivolous full. He raises my short hours – acknowledging that there is only so much to be done. I repeat my frustration of being unable to help people who *want* to *learn to read*. I sense his annoyance too. He hints that there will be stern words from him soon. He tells me that he "knows the system," as he "used to be a prison officer." (I of course, know this already but feign surprise). He closes with "it's a shame" that I'm not "here longer," to allow more time to "sort this out." I promise him that I'll lob a brick through a jeweller's window so they can bring me back.

0845: Hoxon. I retired to number 48 to write. Five minutes later Dennis appeared at my door. Hindsight tells me that because I had removed myself far from the madding crowd he had seized the moment to come and talk. And not about the price of beans. I cleared my armchair of the *Sunday Times* (his) and my escapee jacket so he could sit down with his bad back.

We talked until 1015.

You name it – we covered it. His crime, my crime. Other people in prison. We conversed of the future, the past and the present. He told me he couldn't get through this "without his missus." It was time for me to put my cards on the table and I told Dennis – I think the first person in prison who is not staff – about my wife. He heard the *whole* story.

He summed things up rather neatly. And very accurately: My Tag date is November 17th, my conditional release is March 2012 and my ultimate discharge is November 2012 – but the sentence of my wife and my love for her, is "with me for the rest of my life."

I already knew this. I described how she used to make me promise her that I would never leave her. I found myself having to defend her silence to him. I tried to rationalise her pulling-up of every available drawbridge by the fact that I hurt her and let her down. Period. Dennis said that he was surprised that I'm holding it together. I am too. I don't have any options though.

I repeated that I will not give up. She was my best friend, I quoted from Hollywood's golden years and the premise for a film that never failed: Boy meets girl. Boy loses girl. Boy wins girl back.

1020: To Nacro to attend something about "Prison Employment Workers." Am I going to be asked to join a union? Knocked on the door and met an Orderly behind a desk who had *all* the necessary credentials to be a Bond heavy. In towering contrast to his appearance a most stately voice declared from an office beyond "you're early." The owner of the palatial palate appeared and I met Victoria (Wood) who regally runs the show. If ever they shoot a live action *Wallace and Gromit*, I've just found Wendolene. I was invited to her chamber and she explained why I am here: What am I going to do work-wise after I am released. Do I have a trade and do I have a job?

After relaying that Zara is signing me up for a hostel I told her my occupation – which she took in serene stride – and warned me that "the hostel will be expensive." Her solution to this was that I "must sign-on as soon as possible." The Benefits Department "will then pay the rent." We then addressed the flying side. What do I need done – to be able to work. My flight crew medical has expired, so too my LPC's on the two aircraft I predominately fly (yearly flight checks that helicopter pilots have to complete). Victoria took all this in and asked for a ballpark figure for the costs of "getting all that sorted." I estimated about eight hundred pounds. Her response *floored* me: "That shouldn't be a problem."

She educated me that there are numerous bodies that are happy to help get me back to work and picked up her phone and dialled a number. Before I knew it I was talking to a complete stranger from one such organisation who very kindly said "how can we help you?" I told him my situation. "What do you need?" After I had gone through the basic ingredients, he said "no problem," I can even "have some of it now – or wait till November and have the whole lot." Due to not the best of aircraft availability at HMP Hollesley Bay, I told him November would be fine and gushed thanks down the line.

Victoria said she would fix up another appointment with me for September 27th so we could fill out the required paperwork.

After this amazing bit of news I expressed that I am interested – in the future – in getting involved with helping. She made a note of this. I exclaimed how surprised I was that there were such groups offering assistance. She said that the people who *want* to be helped *can* be helped. Her proudest story was of one of her successes "who was on Stow last year and is now working in Harrods."

1145: Dining room. Encountered Mathew looking dastardly delighted. "Don't eat the soup." Why not? "I made it."

Was his victim poisoned?

1150: Rod joined us and announced that the young lifer, Kevin, has been shipped-out to Cosford. Poor sod. Somehow the conversation then veered to the legal system and the Courts. Mathew piped up with asking us if we knew what a Kangaroo Court was. We did. He had a story…

"Back in a proper prison" with boarding school type dormitories "some items went missing." Everyone "knew who it was" and the suspect was put under observation and "caught at it, red handed." It was unanimously agreed that the "accused should be tried by a Judge and Jury, in a Court" – which was the dormitory. The "Jury" consisted of twelve men (no women were available), all "honest and true" (convicted prisoners). The "Prosecution Council" was an "Ex-solicitor, banged-up for fraud." The accused defended himself. The "Judge" wore a mop head.

The accused was "found guilty" and "never stole again. In or out of prison."

1345: Work. I misidentified the people who arrived this morning. They are not accountants but medical people here to administer staff jabs. (Why can't the staff here do them?) Attempting to find something to do, room 10 is entered. WD lurks in there. Bugger. Ask her, in my sweetest voice if there is anything she needs doing (Pull the pin on the grenade? Serve the hemlock? Pull the lever on the trap? Load the gun?). Instead, I empty her bin. After an exhausting afternoon I leave at 1400, having done a grand total of fifteen minutes work. At Hoxon, a hand written note greeted me, on a scrap of paper, saying that I am "now upgraded to enhanced," signed by an officer.

Now, where's my Playstation?

1625: Elbows at my door. Can I give him a haircut?

1640: Dennis' haircut complete. He's still talking to me. I now have a new name on the call-sheets: Sweeney Todd.

1700: Dinner Pizza (?) and chips (?) Gave the boys my chips and in return, got a pile of oranges and yogurts. I asked Mathew what the latest gadget was, when he went away seventeen years ago, that he couldn't live without? He thought for a few seconds, casting his mind way back.

"The telephone answering machine."

Thursday, September 15th, 2011.

Got into bed last night at 2035, to read.

Then the fire alarm went off. But only for about five seconds. Is it? Isn't it? Mass confusion. Do we? Don't we? Decided, I do. General muster and Roll-check in the gardens. A full moon or certainly nearly a whole one. The muster wasn't though. Ten minutes later the stragglers appeared, to much applause from the rest of us. No one seemed to know whether it was a legitimate drill or not. The Terminator did though, as he stood outside with a clip board taking names.

0700: Everyone moaning about the fire alarm. No one is sure whether it was a drill or an error, or just five second of noise.

0800: Rounds. All Units. Prison officers in the offices looking very bored and talking to each other on the phones.

0850: Unit. Scribing Rod's letters. Last night's stragglers have all been given IEP's (red marks against their records). I heard one senior officer saying to one of the newly convicted that "it could have been done better."

0950: First letter done for Rod. Had a question about the second and walked down to Bricks to see him. As he answered my question I surveyed the "Wall." Hadrian would be proud.

1030: Second letter complete.

1130: Chatted at length with Mathew. His goal: "To be a baker in ASDA." He asked me why the hell I did what I did when I've got "the looks, the intelligence and a good job." The insecurity and my upbringing as a child, I feebly justified. He said he understood. He "feels like a dick about himself too."

My outside charity work "app" has come back saying I "still need between four and six weeks lie-down." This *completely* contradicts the notice displayed on Hoxon's bulletin boards. Yet again, the left arm has no *idea* what the right arm is doing. "HMP": "Hopeless management prevalent."

1150: Replied in writing quoting the notice number which says in *very* plain English "lie-down not required."

1200: Lunch. Rod, Mathew and *another* Rod. This version: Old Rod (any David Leanesque lag).

1345: Rounds. A civilian boiler man (Arthur English, circa *Are you being Served?*) steamed about and told me the cost of Hoxon's daily oil bill: "Seven hundred pounds."

1400: My socks and my pants from Court – my only underwear – have disappeared from my laundry. I now only have prison gear. Made a mental note to study other prisoners' ankles.

1445: I am a prized tit. Went through all my clothes to see if I was being daft but they were not there.

Gave up and decided to have a snooze. Then I found my clothes.

I'm wearing them.

1530: A two-liner with Old Rod. He did "five years, thirty years ago, for handling proceeds from an armed robbery" and now back in "for supplying drugs."

1600: A two-hander with Mathew. I don't think Old Rod looks like a drugs dealer. "Well lad, what do you think drug dealers look like?" From my Bedford experience, mules and runners all seem to be Asian with white tracksuits. The Masterminds I assume all resemble characters from the *Godfather* films. He says I'm half right but do I think that *he* looks like a drugs runner?

In the early 90's Mathew would "go on the ferry with a pal, from Hull to Rotterdam and purchase items." There were "no security checks on re-boarding" and they would arrange for "ferry staff to deliver their goods safely to their home address." Some "decent money was made." He also enjoyed a "supply business too." Customers would "request a certain television," and he'd hit electrical stores with "stolen cheque books." So he was a "thief, drug peddler and a fraudster." And "that was all."

"Until the murder."

It is not every day that such talk comes up in my life. The closest I have been to murder is *Colombo* on telly. And prison food. But it's Mathew who has brought this up. And he knows about the book. Sensing my chance I cagily ask him what happened.

A person he had known for "some time" had been getting on his nerves. One day, Mathew decided "that enough was enough" and "decided to go to his house and kill him." As he talks my eyes are darting around to see if anyone is listening. We are at a table right by the row of trees. The CIA would struggle to eavesdrop. Had he warned the person that was incurring his displeasure? "Oh, yes many times." So what happened? "A spur of the moment thing." Mathew "plus friend, decided then and now, that this was going to happen." How? "We went to his house." Was it day or night?

"Day, It were a *Wednesday*, Jon."

On arrival did he suspect trouble? "He knew he was in for a beating but didn't know I was going to kill him." Did you warn him what was coming? "No." Why not? "Because he would have tried to get away." So what happened?

"I shot him in the head."

Mathew is a quiet and gentle. I can picture him helping old ladies get off the bus. What happened next?

He "left the area and went to stay with pals." His friend "took the weapon." He has "seen neither since." Two weeks later, "armed police turned up." If the death penalty was in place would you have still done it? Without any hesitation, without the blinking of an eye, he answers.

"No."

1700: Rod had been roped into servery duties so ate with Mathew, a library guy (Kabir Bedi) who's name is unknown and his pal (Albert Moses) who is uncredited too. Library guy is going on Home-leave tomorrow. At least I think he is. To be honest, I'm still reeling from Mathew's conversation and everyone else might as well be talking in a foreign language.

Later, Elbows played pool with the most enormous Bond villain type to appear so far in this log of events. All he was missing were metal teeth. Mr Waterman, being ever friendly, informed me I was to play the winner. I watched as this *huge* bulk of shaven headed mass defeated Dennis so up against this monumental monster I went – and beat him (am I mad?). As he graciously shook my hand he eyed me up – probably calculating how much concrete was going to be required to dispose of the body. Mine.

Word went out that that a card game was on the tables for the evening. They plan to play something beginning with a "K."

Witnessed Belmarsh Rod, Mathew, Greg (Gregory Peck, in his early twenties), another chap with whom lots of nodding has occurred, Heston and Dennis play in the dining room. Two packs of cards were utilised and you have to pay attention. Much ribbing and laughter collated around and many unprintable words were said. Dennis won the first two rounds, 50p being the prize for each hand. A real feeling of camaraderie cuddled the room. Imagine the brotherhood of soldiers and multiply it by ten. I am again subconsciously reminded that in prison, one is accepted for *how* one is.

This is something I am *determined* to take out with me when I leave.

Another day complete. Each day here, even if it starts like the day before, seems to bring some new thing into my head. In prison – when I'm down – I'm *down*. When I'm not down, does that qualify as a high? Is it *wrong* – am I wrong – to admit during these highs, that I am actually *enjoying* it here?

Friday, September 16^{th,} 2011.

Dennis doing his chores – mopping – as I half sleep-walk to get coffee. His luck at the tables "went downhill" after I retired. I didn't know I was his rabbit's foot. The game is called "Kaluki" – which sounds to me like the title of some 70's film with Omar Sharif.

Sherriff Rachel's orders: The room next to the dentist's "needs a good going over," plus "Room 10." I mop the loos, empty the bins then survey the dentist's room with Rachel and WD. We agree that as it's still being decorated, there is no point in doing anything technical with it so it was decreed for me just to render room 10 ready.

During this, I asked Rachel why the on-board staff couldn't do the staff jabs. "Because someone else has the contract."

Overhear dialogue between Rachel and WD about whether or not the latter is "staying or not" post switchover to non NHS management. At this point I must confess that ever since my baptism of fire on my initial meeting with Ms Kathy Bates, she has been very friendly. Perhaps she was just pissed off with the football result of the night before our first scene. I'm not sure that the cloves of garlic and the wooden cross that I carry to work each day are still necessary.

0915: In room writing. Spanish lesson taking place next door.

1130: Writing down a list of name replacements for this. Everyone must be given a new moniker – I don't want to embarrass anyone in the future. It's harder than I thought.

1145: Told the boys – or some of them – their new names. Uproar. They all want to be called "Knuckles."

1200: Lunch. Turkey salad. Ate Mathew's as he doesn't do salad. He can have my chips this evening.

1315: Left for work.

1319: Arrived at work.

1320: Left work.

Hoxon. A game of al-fresco chess with Dennis. Got thrashed. Not helped by Rod and "Card Greg" giving a running commentary on each move like surveying Generals overseeing a battlefield from afar.

Rod then borrowed my key to put "something in my room that I will like." Ventured to 48 to investigate and found a brand new duvet set on my bed.

And my television upside-down.

The rest of the afternoon was served chatting in the sunshine with Dennis, who is out – for keeps – very soon and we discussed what he's going to do. The top of his priorities list being a "haircut, a bath, a nice meal" and getting to know Mrs Waterman again…

1700: Dinner. Pie (?) peas (?) and chips (?) Revolting. Chips to Mathew who told me that I "look depressed."

1745: Played pool with the Enormous Bond Villain ("EBV"). Lost. I'm not stupid.

2020: A social from Rod. We talked about this book. He's quite excited that he has a starring role in it. We discussed the long term temptation for him "to make a fast buck in the future." Rod says that he "wants to go straight" and "get a job and a house and not to spend another five years in prison."

2045: I still only have a very small grasp on the game that is Kaluki. If one is late declaring, then there is a points penalty. Slurping one's tea earns the same reward. Mathew told me that he was "close to bubbling." All participants questioned this – with good humour – and he explained that "it is what his therapist has said when he's cheesed off." Straight out of pages penned by G. Ritchie Esq. Rod's response was "what, on a mad killing rampage?" Then, with all the timing of the same director, a

Tannoy announcement: "Sorry, Gentleman but the showers are closed. The ceiling has caved in."

I quipped that the Irish residents had dug their tunnel in the wrong direction. Heston: "Fifty points for racism!"

Saturday, September 17th, 2011.

0810: A visit from the guy who limps. Al (Murray) introduces himself and has a question. "Are you the guy writing the book?" On confirmation of this: "Gawd, love a duck," followed by "fuckin' hell – feel like a right cunt asking you that."

0820: Tannoy: "Will Mr Je… Jo… Ji… Jh…" An officer desperately trying to pronounce the name of someone not from these shores. A Beat. "Will room 28 come to the office please."

0935: Departed for the library with Dennis. Fortunately he does not walk with his arms protruded. He revealed confessional like that he goes to church every Sunday. This organisation I had *not* pictured him within. He "prays for us all." Somewhere in the back of my mind I asked him to double the output on my behalf. I wonder if he sticks his elbows out when he's in communication with him up there?

Back on the Unit Rod joined me in the sunshine. The future and all of us behaving ourselves being the primary topic. I voiced a question to Rod: Who do you think I'm most concerned about? "Me." Yes – and I'm going to be all over you like a cheap suit.

Who is going to keep an eye over me?

Heston hove to but not in his usual, calm and methodical state. A Governor was on the prowl. Our Kitchen-Captain was worried because a "ladle was missing" and this would "cause complications." Rod admitted that he had "probably left it in the custard yesterday" and it'll have "gone back to the kitchen." This caused consternation because "this Governor already has a beef" with Heston and "this could lead to trouble." A plan was hatched to get word to Chris Moyles and his van to "get another ladle shipped-in during a meal delivery."

1145: Tannoy: "Gentlemen, this place is not a kindergarten, will you please behave like adults." No one knew what had caused such a proclamation.

I have post from Ben. He of the green get-up and fellow resident of E wing, Bedford, but the address at the top of his epistle, is *Wandsworth* prison…

15th Sept 11
Hi Jonathan,
Where do I start!! I'm glad you have landed on your feet mate it sounds infinitely better than B Cat. I showed Freddie your letter and he says hello. My life took a drastic turn on the 9th when I

had a Court hearing. It was meant to be held at _____ but for some reason it was moved to _____ Crown at the last minute. Transport fucked up and didn't get me there until lunchtime and the hearing didn't go ahead but I was told I was not going back to Bedford. Instead I am now in Wandsworth! The first 5 days was nearly constant bang-up and right back to square one but I managed to secure a job which means I have been moved to a workers cell (They are on the main wing but are unlocked as Bedford E wing). I am now "Activities Orderly" and get paid seven pounds forty a week, I was on thirty two pounds a week in Bedford! I am 3 hours from my house and have lost the two kids' visits I had for yesterday and next Wednesday... To boot if you read this month's "*Inside Time*" (Author: An internal prison monthly newspaper), Wandsworth is slated for most areas. Social gets cancelled, exercise, gym and library also. The place is massive and has huge staffing issues. The Governors are so busy nobody seems to get their issues dealt with and HDC (Author: Tag, or Home Detention Curfew) is never on time. Now I am a worker I should be able to get more sorted out as I get to know the staff better but it has been awful so far! I also got told I am standard unless I have proof of my enhanced from Bedford! With a bit of luck I should get moved to Ford Open prison as I am Cat D but like I said things here do not seem to happen as expected. My only saving grace is that I took all my stuff with me even though Bedford told me I would be coming back. I imagine you are reading this slightly gobsmacked and it is really shit but fingers crossed I get sent to Ford! I hope you are still enjoying Woodbridge mate and have answers to your HDC and flying questions, write me back and let me know.

All the best Ben.

1200: In the lunch queue the presiding officer called for quiet and I wondered if he was going to say grace. He didn't and instead boomed a bollocking. En-masse. "Stop putting water under cell doors." There have been "five complaints." So that what the Tannoy was all about.

1305: Wrote back to Ben to keep his chin up. Then went on to complain about the constant water skiing and the topless beach being too crowded.

1700: Dinner. Mathew eats nothing other than chips.

1900: Buzz is kindly coming up to see me next Sunday. I filled in a "visiting order" for him, car registration, date of birth, address and inside leg measurement.

Then, because I'm such a party animal, at 2040, I turned the light off and went to bed.

Sunday, September 18th, 2011.

0720: Cornered by an officer (Ernest Borgnine): "I hear you're a helicopter pilot." Discovered he's an ex-engineer. We talked of flying whilst on Tag and he suggested that I request an interview with a Governor to thrash out the inevitable situation of being stuck in a field and being unable to get home.

Update on Heston's ladle lather of yesterday: "All is sorted." All ladles present and correct. Chris Moyles was the cavalry. I say no more.

A young man (Christian Bale) – no name yet – who had borrowed my mirror has just returned it. On handover, his line: "Sweet." This is Hollesley Bay's "innit" as everyone round here seems to say it almost as much as the burghers of Bedford used that other expression. Whilst on the page it looks like something the late John Inman might have mouthed, here, it is *nowhere* near that context.

Returned from the library at 1015 with Tony Blair's *A Journey*. Whilst perusing different books, I made a big mistake in opening up *Suffolk from the Air* and the Aldeburgh pictures cast my mind back... places we went – places we stayed.

On money that wasn't mine.

1200: Rod served a pudding that looked like wall-paper paste. I understood it was rice pudding – not for me, thank you. Andrew said he would have mine. Perhaps he plans to redecorate his room. Because Rod and Mathew toiled, it was just Dennis and me of the regulars. One of the vacant spaces the other side of the table was taken by a newbie. This was Russell (Grant) who has arrived from Ford open prison. Which is the better of the two? "Here. By miles." The "food is better." I hope my horoscope doesn't include a move to Ford.

1640: Tannoy: "Mr ___ get out of your bed and into your head and GET TO THE SERVERY."

Post dinner – Halal cheeseburger (!) – half the Unit played Kaluki. All participants were getting a little tetchy. Every now and again I was asked to do a star jump, not because they enjoy seeing me prance like Basil but our lights which are movement detector activated, kept going out. That never happens in Monte Carlo.

Monday, September 19th, 2011.

On the news: The "Dale Farm" eviction today.

Back to last night's card game and the atmosphere around it. Everyone was on edge. Comments and challenges flew around the table like a scene in a western before the shoot-out. Eyes were darting as if Sergio Leone was directing events.

Maybe with my luck with things love, I should take up cards.

0710: More and more footsteps outside. The noise of walkers is always the same. The miles of endless polished floors in the country's prisons make everyone sound alike. I defy anyone to make a different noise whilst treading them.

0730: Last week it was pebbles in the sea. Today it's "sticks in the forest," with which Heston summarises a day spent with his clan.

0835: Back from work. On arrival, Rachel, in the biggest pair of Elizabeth Taylor sunglasses that I have ever seen, was drinking water from a pint glass. I remember hangovers. Dave was complaining about his "man flu, his legs and working over the weekend." WD was suspiciously friendly. Is this because Wales are still in the Rugby world cup?

If they get knocked out of the tournament I've had it.

0900: Glorious outside. Going out with Tony Blair.

0945: Summoned by Tannoy to meet "one of the Governors." I knocked on a door and yet again met an owner of a familiar looking face: Noddy Holder stood before me. He of Slade. (The band not the prison). This Governor, wearing a suit that looked like it had been slept in, asked what he could do for me. I listed my concerns of the combination of Tag with a curfew and flying. It is inevitable that at some point I am going to get stuck somewhere. Flight safety is hugely affected by decision making and the added pressure of "get home-itus," which has led to the boosting of coffers of many undertakers' takings on too many occasions already, will only be affected by the pressure of a return leg because of the apparatus around my leg and I don't want to be read about in a newspaper. I made it abundantly clear that I did not want to be recalled back to prison. Ever. Noddy replied that if he "had a pound" for every time he had heard that, he "would be a rich man."

He proposed another meeting in mid-October and applying for longer curfew hours. "When people on Tag are late" – it's him "that gets the heat."

1145: Rod's vocal menu: "Fish-heads in a bucket." In fact got a cheese and onion salad which was very nice indeed. Two inspectors lurked, which probably explains why it was rather good.

1325: Healthcare and a request to Dave for odd-jobs. A light bulb flickers as he searches his memory for something filed away that actually needs doing. The bulb illuminates. Please can I clean the office chair in the Treatment room. "There are bits on it." I venture upstairs to fetch the vacuum cleaner.

1327: Treatment room. WD plus the Rucksack Hurler within. Damn. I wrestle the R2D2 sized cleaner and anaconda like hose through the doorway. Rucksack Hurler: "Are you supposed to come in here?" I quickly regret not bringing my wooden cross and garlic and relay that Dave has asked me to do the chair. This explanation warrants her unable to continue the abrupt hostility.

1334: The chair cleaned, I leave work.

1510: A call for me on the Tannoy. "Go to Nacro." Off to Zara's office I go – full of anticipation of what today's top has in store for me. On arrival: no top. And no Zara. Instead, I get her colleague who introduces himself as Peter (Darling from *Blackadder* adorning a Peter Gabriel beard).

His top is rubbish.

The genesis of what he says is a replica of what Zara and I have already covered and I gently tell him so. He apologises and back to Hoxon I retreat. Whilst I appreciate the help, is there *any* communication within the countless agencies that make up the prison system?

1600: The large gentleman, Oliver, who is always – and I mean *always* – first in the food queue at meal times is back from a Home-leave. (Town-visit: one day. Home-leave: five days). How did you get on? "The food tasted good."

Just realised why so many second helpings have been available over the last five days.

1610: Neil ("Crazy Frog"), an Indian gentleman who has been with us about a week and I have been chatting. He's come from HMP Pentonville and had a tale to tell of his arrival there…

"Winter time, cold and at night," started Neil. An officer was on "meet and greet duty," as they decamped from their Sweatbox, which in this instance "was an icebox." It was "too cold to stand around so everybody was told to make their way up the stairs to Reception." A request obeyed by all. "Except one." This individual, realising that they were not being observed, "hit the deck and rolled under the truck." Then "like Spiderman," held on to the exhaust and axle system for dear life before being wheeled – literally – straight out of the gates. "It was some time before CCTV was checked and the staff viewed how their missing man, had become missing."

"Chappie," Neil concluded, "handed himself in a few weeks later."

A second, more serious story came from Neil about having to cut down an individual he had "found hanging – who was still alive." For reasons beyond obvious Neil "had no knife" so had to use his "lighter to burn through the ripped sheet." The "chap survived but it took an awful long time for staff to arrive…"

1700: Dinner. Large gentleman always first in queue; first in queue. Dined with Dennis and Mathew – who has started a bricklaying course today, which was his trade seventeen years ago. I asked if anything had changed. "Frog up now – it used to be Frog down." *What*? "The hole in the brick lad," said Mathew, like I was an idiot for not knowing this. Rod joined us post dishing-up duty with enough food on his plate to feed all the occupants of Dale Farm, who got a reprieve today.

Am settling down for a night-in with the telly. Thoughts whizzing around my mind. I keep trying to remind myself: Make this the making, not the breaking of you.

Tuesday, September 20th, 2011.

Woke 0500. Clicking light switches…

0815: Healthcare. On site: Rachel and Philip. In the quiet, I asked him how best to deal with the lobber of Rucksacks. "Ignore."

Rounds. All I need is a white coat and a stethoscope. Returned Hoxon at 0900 and took Tony Blair outside. A quote threw itself at me from his pages: *"Never give up. Simple but essential. Never stop working on it and never give up on it… and remember: it is better to try and fail than not to try at all."*

We like.

1115: An irate Greg appears in front of Tony Blair and me. I attempt to discover the reason for his demeanour. Greg "was called on the Tannoy for a meeting" and on his arrival "was told to wait five minutes." Here's someone who needs to cool-it methinks. I ask Greg how long he's been in. Still fuming, he says "five years." How much longer? "A minimum of a further year," providing he can complete an "anger management course which parole is insisting on." The required course though "is not available in this prison." I try to soothe the seething with some advice. Namely, under his own steam, to attempt finding a distance-learning course of a similar type in the library which might both help him and show good willing to the parole board. Whether or not that's a good steer, I don't know but it mollified him.

1200: Lunch. First in queue guy; first in queue.

1300: Neil hovering in the hallway looking for a "tall person." He felt I would do. His window in his ground floor room was stuck open and as Neil is only five feet and a bit, he required the use of my legs. After a simple whack to the frame he invited me for a social. As I rolled a cigarette he rummaged amongst paperwork looking for something. I surveyed his room. Loads of cards of support adorned the walls and as is so typical of people from his country, joss sticks sprouted from countless makeshift holders like telegraph poles on a railway line. He found what he had been hunting for and passed me a laminated A4 letter. At the top of it the HMP logo was emblazoned in all its splendour.

For any of you, especially ex or serving prisoners reading, who may of thought that Neil's fables of yesterday contained top-spin, you can rest assured that the letter I saw from someone *very* senior at HMP Pentonville, thanking him for his assistance in the unfortunate incident when a prisoner tried to take his own life, added serious credence to Neil's story.

And it must have been a legitimate prison letter. It contained spelling mistakes.

I told him that he had done a very courageous thing. He revealed more of the events that occurred with connection to the poor wretch but I don't want to go into too much detail. Suffice to say that Neil has had a pretty horrific time of it and is not sleeping. As I was off to work, why didn't he come with me? We could then get him on the list to have a chat with someone.

Down the hill we trotted. On arrival I found Dave and gave him a brief outline. He said he'd see Neil straight away. They were in the Treatment room sometime. When eventually the door opened and Neil reappeared I asked him if all was well. Yes – and he has a full blown appointment in the morning.

Tony Blair in the sunshine.

1600: Wrote a couple of letters to begin the investigation of how to get what you are now reading into book shops.

1700: Dinner. Mathew, Dennis and my new neighbour, a gentleman from Iran (Omid Djalili) who I think is called Shiv. Some sort of lamb concoction for dinner. Rod rolled-up after his servery duties with enough food on his plate to make a whole herd.

A lot of new faces on the Unit, one of whom I misidentified as one-of-us, although the subject wore suit trousers. Andrew was convinced it was staff and only when the chain and keys were clocked did I admit defeat.

Off now – 1910 – to watch the card game.

Whilst observing suits of cards being up-turned, the half-suited newly identified staff member turned up and perused the players as well. Turns out this is "Governor Two" (Rodney Bewes, circa 1965). One below our glorious leader – who I have never met. He surveyed the progress of play and then said in a heavy Geordie accent, that he "was pleased that they weren't playing for counters." Various responses of "oh no Sir," "certainly not Sir," and "definitely no counters here Sir," were exclaimed. "Good," said the Governor. "We've got people here with serious gambling issues and prisoners in here can start playing with Monopoly money…"

Mathew: "Oh no Sir, we're just playing for points."
Belmarsh Rod: "Yeah, just points."
Heston: "No counters here."
Deputy Governor: "I'll leave you to it then" (Exeunt).
Mathew (to Greg): "You owe me seven chocolate bars you cunt."

2015: In bed with Tony Blair.

Wednesday, September 21st, 2011.

0630: Dennis on the phone.

The BBC is telling me that Penny Farthings are back in production and are now being manufactured in Leicester. "We wanted to keep this a British affair," said Mr Bali, the factory owner.

On bin-bag collection Julian told me that "L.A." – the other library guy – is back from Home-leave and has declared that he "wishes the library had burnt down," in his absence – such is his distaste of working in there. This, Julian went on, "is quite funny because Library Brett is among us for arson."

I have the dentist this afternoon at 1405. Rachel moved my appointment.

Rod came my way with a question: "What's the name of the big Scottish Fella who has replaced Stanley at Healthcare?" I told him that I had no idea but would endeavour to find out.

0810: Healthcare. Asked Rachel to open up for me upstairs and followed a very nice view as she climbed the steps ahead of me. She's in a Mrs Peel get-up today.

See the boots.

For sure, this morning Rachel looked terrific. As we got to the first floor – with my eyes on bean-stalks – she went towards the kitchen and asked me about the Neil situation. After obliging her she made some positive noises. It was hard work not to goggle at the black leggings and just concentrate on the speaking end. She re-visited "prisoners' involvement in issues." I recounted my HMP Bedford library incident when a prisoner was laying in with foul language to Glenda – and I'd stepped in. Rachel, leaning against one of the kitchen surface tops, said that she "feels much better when Philip is around" and "even more so, now that Robbie is on board." Who? "The big Scottish chap who has replaced Stanley."

Rod's question answered.

She went on. She "gets grief from prisoners sometimes" but "lets it go over her head," then added "I mean *please*? Would I be interested in a *prisoner*?" She was looking me straight in the eye at this point. I tried to change the subject. Is Robbie the big guy I've seen with arms the size of my waist? To this, Rachel lifted a leg up, right out of the "are you trying to seduce me?" scene from *The Graduate*, stroked the interesting end of her legging clad limb and said "his arms are bigger than my *thighs*."

See the thighs.

Make of the above what you will.

0840: Returning to Hoxon I couldn't seem to stop humming the *Avengers* theme.

1030: Neil back post medical appointment. He has been "referred to Robbie."

1200: Greg was prodded if he'd had any further thoughts of seeing if off his own bat, he could get the ball rolling for some sort of anger management course. Mathew was listening and I suggested again to Greg that action like this would surely help his case with the parole board – *Won't it* Mathew? "Yes, it fookin' well will."

After lunch another postcard from Timothy prison visitor with again, a second class stamp. He wrote that the "increased freedom and trust at Hollesley Bay" can only do me good and that he "will visit Albert." In hindsight, that is one event I would *love* to be a fly-on-the-wall for…

Paperwork was also received from OMU – with questions about flying – signed by someone called Nadine.

1255: Library. Very busy so sat in the corner and read the paper among the hullabaloo. In the middle of the mayhem a very excitable chap came in and with high volume quizzed Library Brett on the availability of a book on "pre-homo-sapien life." I suggested a Guide to Stevenage which although I say it myself, brought the house down.

Onwards and upwards to OMU. Climbed the scaffold, opened the door and walked straight into a most *almighty* bollocking. I am apparently, according to some *irate* senior officer, supposed to ring the bell and wait. I went back out, rang the bell, and waited. About ten seconds elapsed and a small civilian female (Hilda Ogden) opened it and asked if she could help. I apologised for barging in and told her that I thought I'd upset an officer a teeny bit. She rolled her eyes and gave me a "you don't have to work with them" look. I asked if she was Nadine. "No," but she would take my paperwork and "make sure that it was passed on."

At Healthcare there was no work to be done. What's more, there was no dentist either. Renee, the dental assistant was in a right state and had a "string of patients" to be seen but couldn't "get hold of the sodding man because his phone goes straight to sodding voicemail."

1500: Grabbing the bull by the horns – probably whilst it is still *in* the china shop – the following letter has gone out to some publishers who I looked up in the library earlier.

Dear Sirs,

Forgive the strange request but am nearing the end of a spell in prison and have written/am writing a day to day book about it. Funny, sad and ironic (I was in during the riots) and a lot of observation on the "system." I wonder if you could point me in the right direction as to "what to do with it." (Clean replies only please). Release date of "Author" November 17th. Release date of book, up to you.

Jonathan Robinson.

1545: Replied to Timothy, prison visitor, thanked him for his card and wished him luck with Albert. He's going to need it.

1700: In the dinner queue Mathew was poked about Greg's reluctance to shake some branches over his anger management course. "Greg wants to talk to the Probation people first," so as to not "rock any boats." Why is initiative so actively discouraged by the management? "All things management are stupid because they think we are stupid."

1800: Buzz has received the visit-paperwork and is coming to see me.

1940: The end of a social from Rod. He needs me to do another letter for him. We talked of Greg and his problems. Rod pointed out that it is tough for Greg to take advice from me and much harder than I realise. Greg will be shocked "that the tall posh twat is trying to help."

Thursday, September 22nd, 2011.

0645: Some alarm clock is going off – and has been for a good ten minutes now – its owner continues to sleep.

0651: Alarm switched off.

Part of prison punishment is being unable to address problems on the outside. Just serve your time and-get-on-with-it. Nothing though, beats the wife situation. Nothing. I could be writing this whilst waiting to be taken in front of a firing squad and still the heartache would outweigh the punishment of silence.

0730: Bins done. Dennis, as ever, up. And swabbing the decks. My therapy is writing. His seems to be mopping.

0745: A newbie (Mick Hucknall) walked about. I learnt that he was "here two years ago" and got "ghosted out, for being over familiar with Rachel." He's a lifer and is the *complete* opposite of Mathew.

Rachel – who like Glenda at Bedford's library is always ahead of the news – interrogated me about Mick Hucknall. I was rewarded for this by following a spectacular view up the stairs. She's in the same leggings and boots as yesterday but in a different top. I tend to notice these things. Working in Healthcare is no bum deal.

Mopped, cleaned and vacuumed.

Finished five minutes later and picked up letters for Rounds. WD was talking about "voluntary redundancy." Rachel countered this with something about "Hugh Jackman in the bath." Philip looked perplexed.

0830: On my travels I again recorded the eerie silence that sounds from the green Cathedral. Never a squeak.

0930: Outside with TB who I have nearly finished off. Russell's about and tells me his story. Not a dissimilar plot to mine, except a great deal more money was involved – and he denies doing it. He is being shipped-out to Bosnia on Friday and knowing of my visits to all the Units on my Rounds, he asks me what it is like. I didn't want to dishearten him with my thoughts that a new series of *Auf Wiedersehen Pet* could be shot there so redeem that they all seem very much alike. For sure though, if Bomber and Moxey aren't spotted soon on Bosnia, then at least the cast of *Stalag 17* will be...

Speaking of ship-outs, Elk has told me that on average, between one and ten prisoners a month are re-housed to closed conditions.

1110: Tony Blair is finished. I know the feeling.

1150: Spied the senior officer of yesterday who likes the ringing of bells so lingered nearby as he talked with another inmate. Their conference complete, I approached him. "Yes, Mr. Robinson," said Shouter. My name is known in some lowly places. I apologised and tried to explain that I was simply dropping off a letter. He accepted this and thanked me. As it was so close to lunch I nearly asked him for a nice table by the window but didn't want to bolster Elk's statistics of "between one and ten."

1205: Lunch. Mathew announced that he is "going to give up smoking."

1210: Dennis went for seconds and returned to the table with a French stick and proceeded to make himself something resembling a tuna torpedo. A snack for later. After putting it into a bag he then started chatting to the table next door and I had the not very bright idea of hiding his maritime missile. On my knees, under the table it went. Mathew gave me a "you are an idiot" look. It was meant as a harmless schoolboy prank.

Dennis didn't see it so.

His conversation next door complete, his eyes returned to the table. Assessing that his tuna had disappeared he said in a *very* pissed off manner "give it back." I grinned like a moron at him which instead of making him laugh, had the complete opposite effect. He stormed off.

Oh Shit.

Mathew, realising this had back-fired, cautioned me and said "in prison, some people are funny about their food. Now go and say sorry." I beat any sprinter's-that-you-care-to-mention-time to Dennis' room. As he furiously tried to open a sealed Canteen bag I told him it had been done as a joke and nothing else. He vaguely accepted my apology but like the bag of Canteen that stayed steadfast shut, so did his sense of humour.

Back in the dining room whilst washing up Dennis reappeared looking sheepish. He apologised to me "for overreacting." I told him again it was meant as a joke and he said he knew, but had his "prison head on."

1310: Library. Left Tony Blair on the counter and read the paper.

1330: On getting to work – it was locked. Everyone "was in a meeting somewhere else." I got talking to a prisoner (Leonard Nimmoy, circa 1970) who was here to discuss his dietary needs, telling me he "was a vegan" (not a Vulcan). He was cheesed-off because his "needs weren't being catered for" by the catering department.

1400: Benjamin arrived with the new "Head Doctor" Robbie. He with the arms bigger than Rachel's thighs… Not only does he look *exactly* like Robbie Coltrane, he *sounds* like him too. I am in the company of *Cracker*. I explained my predicament and it was decreed best for me to return to Hoxon. I asked Cracker to let Rachel know that I was on call, if required. Got an "och, aye" or similar in return.

On the way back, Dennis was about so we sat on the steps by the main gate (!) and smoked a cigarette. There is no actual "gate," just a flight of steps next to a sign that says "Deputy Governor" in the car park. As we lolled, we looked like some lost publicity shot for *Withnail And I*. Back on the Unit had a coffee in the splendid sunshine with Julian and gathered he is loaded with an arsenal of *Withnail* quotes. You'll have needed to see the film to understand that one.

1810: Following dinner, hit the office to ask if it's acceptable to pass over letters on a visit, with reference to Buzz coming to see me this weekend. "Not a problem" said the officers. Hoorah! Something that makes sense…

Limping Al came-by 48. He told me that I should "interview" his pal "for the book," who has just arrived from another prison. The reason for this nomination was that this chap "is really interesting." And also a "transvestite." I thanked Al but explained I don't do interviews – this book is solely about what happens. "Too bad," said Al. "Oh well, never mind," then added that his mate "was pissed off at the moment anyway." Being polite, or trying to be, I asked why.

"Security took his curling tongs."

Friday, September 23rd, 2011.

Woke 0630. Mrs Mop, up and mopping.

My locks are beginning to outnumber those in the prison and have asked Dennis how handy he is with his clippers.

0715: Rod announced – in a *foul* mood – that he has given up smoking. He then banned me from speaking to him until after the Roll-check at 0730. The alarm clock that "no one turns off" is his!

0800: Work. Swept some floors. Dave very preoccupied by the computer. Left work at 0825. L.A. journeyed down the hill and "couldn't believe" that I was "done already."

Back on the Unit I discovered my spoon had gone-west so asked Julian for a spare. In between many *Withnail* quotes he suggested sourcing me a "real spoon" – as in metal. I thanked him but expressed my mettle to remain a transient prisoner and my objective of not settling in too much during this daunting endurance test. I have not seen the inside of Julian's room but I have the feeling it's both wallpapered and carpeted.

0900-1000: Hoxon's gardens. Any un-required reminder of my current status and address was reconciled by someone insisting on spitting – whilst making *horrific* noises – every ten seconds or so. One of the clan who like to show their underpants to the world and walk about with their hands down the front of their trousers. Neil appeared sidestepping the spittle and asked me when I'm going to work. On hearing that I'd been and was now back, he proclaimed that he was "going to put in an app," requesting that I'm given "hard labour." Knowing my luck, that'll be the "app" that actually works. Neil tells me that I'm living "far too close to the life of Riley."

1100: Hiatus with Heston. At last night's card game – which I was not present at – players got so fed up with having to do star jumps to keep the scene lit, that at one point Mr Blumenthal "threw his slipper" at the sensor and "got a direct hit."

Incidentally, that's the light sensor I'm talking about – not the prison censor.

1130: Julian joined the jollity. I learnt that he is with us for something to do with "fraud and computers overseas." He drinks coffee like it's going out of fashion and as he got up to go in to replenish his mug for the umpteenth time, I told him that when I get out I'm going to buy (with what?) stocks and shares in Starbucks. Elk had joined the fray by now ("morning Captain") and dryly said "don't mention stocks and shares in front of him."

Neil returned from Healthcare, still looking like death warmed-up but making positive noises. He had a "forty five minute session with Robbie."

1145: Elk pointed out to a sunbathing always-first-in-the-queue gourmand that it was "getting close to time." I've never seen anyone – of that size – move so fast in my life.

1200: Lunch. Guess-who, first in the queue.

L.A. boulevards up. And not a happy bunny. He is being driven "to distraction" by Library Brett with his "constant sarcasm."

1245: Library. Don lazed in. "Allo mate, wot you doin' down 'ere?" it was good to see him. Until he wheedled that I'm "goin' grey."

1330: Work. The place empty apart from Dave and a student nurse (Little Mo from *Eastenders*) – with us to learn the ropes – who whacked a package in my hand and grinned. I peered within and found pairs of glasses – for delivery around the glasshouse. I was *very* tempted to put a pair on and do my Michael Caine impression but managed to not make a spectacle of myself.

In true prison tradition they had their new owners' names on them but no Unit information, so Dave had to nervously fire up the computer to get correct addresses. Dave and computers are like Mr Barrowclough and his wife in *Porridge*. The first name pulled out of the hat didn't exist. He eventually cracked the code and I worked out that I only had two Units to visit, Wilford and Stow.

Wilford. Explained to the officer why I was here and for whom the glasses were for. "He's not in this prison anymore."

Stow. The customers for glasses actually did still live there and optics are off-loaded.

Hoxon. On key pick-up was told to "hold fire." Thoughts of an enforced move to another Unit came to mind. The officer told me that "somebody" wants to see me but he couldn't remember who. My mind whirred. His dawdled. Nadine? Like a bingo player calling house, the white-shirt exclaimed "yes!" as his ducks fell into a row. "Go to OMU," he blurted.

Climbed the scaffold repeating to myself to ring the bell. At the summit, stopped and rang it. The door was opened by a twenty-something who kept calling me Mr Robinson despite me calling her Nadine (Ruby, from *Upstairs Downstairs*). We went through the business of Tag and aviation. I will not fly overseas, I will be home (where?) by 2100 each evening and won't attempt any long-haul stuff, which in helicopters is anything more than an hour away. I asked if all these requests were beyond the remit but she very fairly pointed out that it's my "living." She'd taken copious notes and was thoughtful for a minute. "What does your Probation officer say?" I had to almost apologetically say what Probation officer? She went white at that. "How about your personal officer?" What personal officer? I have never *met* my personal officer. The only member of staff who I have spoken to about Tag and helicopters was someone at Bedford who had told me that I won't be able to fly on Tag as "the Governor wouldn't like it" in case I "fly to Mexico."

Nadine – who had now turned a greenish sort of colour – said she would make some calls and get back to me "on Monday."

1430. Unit. Played proverbial pool with a rather brash and unpleasant newbie (Donald Pleasance, circa *The Great Escape*) who had a very squeaky high pitched voice. He beat me.

1600: Dennis "wants a chat." We retreated to number 48. Some outside events have occurred and he needed to talk some things through. I am not going to repeat them here and no, it was nothing to do with his marriage. What I will reveal is the real pain prisoners go through when we are unable to fix anything that may need attending to on the outside. I have trained myself to accept that they can only be dealt with once this is all over. I tried to be positive with Dennis – who knows all my troubles – and pointed out that eventually, everything will fall into place. This earned me the proclamation from him that I'm "the coolest guy in the prison."

1700: Dinner. Always first in queue guy, first in queue. As Heston served me, he alarmingly exclaimed "just the man." I gave him a quizzical look. Can I "help out over the weekend?" The next server on the conveyor belt was Rod who lavishly said that it was he who had "volunteered" me.

I had conference with Heston immediately after eating. He is a "man down over the weekend." I perceived myself in a chef's hat being Jamie Oliver. How can I help?

"Clean the tables after each meal."

After we agreed terms – which was me saying yes, Heston and I talked things prison and what it has taught me: 1. Be myself. 2. Be comfortable being myself. 3. Everyone's the same. 4. I'm actually quite a good guy. I relayed how I've started to consider and become aware of the changes in me now but have concerns about returning to my old ways when I get out. I told him that I know this is going to take some very hard work. Heston listened sympathetically.

Then he told me to clean the tables.

1845: Rod roamed. "Still off the fags but struggling." In his tow was a new youngster, Rupert (Grint), whom he knows from a previous production.

2030: It's all change. Loads of newbies are around and many people have been shipped-out to different Units. My immediate neighbours are gone, the Spanish learner and the Iranian guy. I now have two new house-guests either side of me. Both convicted murderers.

I bet I'll sleep well tonight.

Saturday, September 24th, 2011.

Up at 0600. One of the killers snores and I do not refer to the band that was doing rather well before my enforced holiday.

0700: Tables done. The newbies are walking about resembling some nature program when animals are released back into the wild.

0730: Bins done. A towel clad newcomer was sighted on his way to the showers at 0728 and it was gently suggested to him to wait until after the Roll-check to avoid, what is called in the trade, as a "Nicking."

I'm now a prison pro.

How do *some* people get moved here? If this is supposed to be the stepping stone for prisoners back to society, then society has my sympathies. That man who walks about with his hands down the front of his trousers is spitting again. *Everywhere.*

Rod enters the scene with his disciple Rupert, the new youngster alongside. Mr Statham immediately starts complaining about my cigarette smoke. His devoted protégé nods approvingly.

O930: Library. An aggrieved L.A. looked both miserable to the customers and daggers at Brett. I got stuck into a newspaper and then took down more addresses of publishers to write to about this dreary collection of garbage.

1030: Hoxon. It's BOILING. Various stories earwigged ranging from "smelly Keith," "Lee – who always smells of diesel" and the "aggravation of getting to Canada."

1145: Mathew and L.A. surveyed the fodder with me in the lunch queue. I remarked that I couldn't half murder an Indian. L.A. – from India – looked worried.

1305: Tables done. I am now, I have just been informed, doing them "until the end of play on Tuesday." Marvellous.

1345: Qualifying for the Grand Prix of Singapore. I think it's hotter here…

1550: Did three letters to publishers between Q2 and Q3.

1605: Seb on pole.

Went outside with Dennis and Robert. On Monday, Dennis has only one week to go. I shall miss him.

1700: Dinner. Chilli. Very, very good but not as good as *that* one at Bedford. Did the tables afterwards then got severely thrashed at pool by Neil.

1900: In bed with the telly.

I hate this and I hate me. A good experience I suppose.

"Experience is the name people give to their mistakes" (Oscar Wilde).

Sunday, September 25th, 2011.

Dennis is now very tanned. A deliberate ploy, as he plans to tell all of sundry on his release that he has been in Dubai. I alerted him of my sense of folly of this strategy. For two years? Come off it.

I'm going to blazon to anyone who will listen where I've been. And hope that it's changed me.

Robert and Rod sauntered up. For some reason, Dennis took this opportunity to tell Robert all about this book. Robert's verdict was that it will be something similar to what Jeffrey Archer penned during his incarceration. I reacted by saying it's more a story of the discovery of me – pointing out that I have not read the Archer book. Everyone listened to me in silence. I summed up with Heston's comment to me a few weeks ago. Flashy cars and snazzy houses are not the meaning of life. Throwing stones into the sea with your kids is though.

The silence that had occurred during my description of these pages became a stunned hush with that. Rod didn't speak for ten minutes. When he did, he said with sheer honesty "that hit a nerve."

I sat in the sun and read Dennis' *Sunday Times*. Michael Winner has finally tied the knot. Wonders will never cease.

1145: In the lunch queue I found myself next to Greg. Without being asked, along came his story. He "was first in prison for GBH. A fight had started with the neighbours following a row with the missus." He's with us now for a similar loss of temper when "the other two fathers" of his "missus' kids, came round for a word." Things got out of hand and "knives were involved…"

After a non-eventful lunch settled in my room to watch the Grand Prix. Caught the lights going out for the start when the Tannoy announced that visits were also underway. At the office, I signed some paperwork confirming what I was wearing. Not a fashion statement but to make matters easier to confirm it's me that returns post visit and not a bewildered Buzz.

The officer told me to come back in half an hour so raced back to number 48 to watch the cars. Seb, Seb, Seb. Lewis appeared to see the red mist again…

Thirty minutes later a bunch of excited prisoners boarded one of the Bay's Transit vans so we could all be driven down the hill to the visiting centre, which is slap bang opposite Healthcare. Dennis was on board and remarked that it was "like a beano." This was met by someone else saying that on such excursions "nothing female is safe."

On arrival I was allocated Table 2. The space here for temporary respite from our living hell is nothing like Bedford's. A large church hall type set up – the same sort of arena that *Dad's Army* paraded in. Coffee type tables and armchairs were plonked everywhere. Blue ones for prisoners. I was given a yellow wrist band. Visitors started to arrive wearing red ones. It was like Glastonbury.

Excited children, older parents, young wives and girlfriends came in with different pace. The latter of the group, not wearing very much.

One looked so much like my wife that for a fraction of a second my heart missed a beat. My emotional side *willed* it to be her but logic overpowered my genuine desperation. It couldn't be her. I hadn't sent her a Visiting order. I can't tell you the pain. Pure hypnotising agony. You have no idea.

But one can live in hope.

Soon everyone had arrived. Except Buzz. I started to get anxious. At 1350, it was announced that prisoners and visitors could go outside if they wanted to. Next to Healthcare is a collection of tables and benches in a stockade fenced-off area. I have long dubbed this the "Beer garden." An officer was asked if I could go outside.

"Nah."

So I sat and waited. Where the hell was Buzz? Had something gone wrong? Shit. More torture. As I was contemplating the prospect of being stood up – by a bloke, *in prison* – in, thank God, he walked.

I have never been so glad to see someone in all my life. The first human in nine weeks...

I shook his hand like I've never shaken a hand before. Buzz looked at me like I've been on another planet. I suppose I have. "You look well," he said. "You've lost some weight but you look good." Not as good as he looked. We talked and talked and talked. He filled me with chocolate. And I mean *filled* me. Luxury of luxury he had also come equipped with a packet of my favourite cigarettes.

He has heard that someone else is "living in my flat." I wondered what has happened to all my possessions. Shit. Shit. Shit. He promised to "make some calls," and it was agreed that I'd call him tomorrow at 1800 to gain further intelligence.

Buzz is very keen to finish his licence but is not keen on the locum instructor. I told him I'm keen for him to break his legs – so he can't fly until I'm out. He laughed but we both agreed one step at a time.

Words cannot do justice – certainly not mine – to describe the loyalty from this man. Apart from spending two hours in the car to see his imprisoned flying instructor and the drive back, he is probably down a hundred pounds in petrol too. When your luck is down, you find out who your friends are.

Buzz is my friend. Light years ahead of anyone.

I pointed out the wife lookalike. He agreed the similarity. I seized the nettle and asked him if he'd heard from anyone else...

"No."

Soon, far too soon, it was time to go. Him, not me. I thanked him and thanked him and thanked him for coming. I think I'd still be shaking his hand now if he hadn't taken it back.

He left me with a tiny glimpse of my world outside. My old world. *Some* of which I want to return to.

He'd brought copies of his student records. Trainee pilots are followed about by a plethora of paperwork. I need to reconcile them. I wonder if this has ever been done in prison before?

The return leg to Hoxon was ghastly. Outside life had been brought so close to me that I could almost smell it. The re-entry to the Unit was a firm reminder that I am here to be punished. And quite rightly.

I had it. And I threw it away.

Monday, September 26th, 2011.

Following much thinking further to Buzz's visit Tribal Frank was asked on the way to work if Probation will provide after sales service and assistance on avoiding potential rocky paths. "Speak to Robbie in Healthcare" was knowingly advised...

HMS Healthcare. A prisoner (Guy Pearce) fed the fish. After preliminary introductions it was decreed that Rick the Fish "did a blinding job," via recent servicing of the now gleaming aquarium. Then followed brief details on why I'm here – and confirmation that I do not intend to return. "Good," he said. "Anyone who comes back in is an asshole." When is he out? "September." Affirmation that my billet was Hoxon was enquired. Yes. "I liked Hoxon. This time and last time." You've been here twice?

"Yeah, I'm an asshole."

Mopped anything walkable on and gingerly asked Dave to set me up an appointment with Robbie. Gingerly, because this task would involve Dave using the computer.

0915: Hoxon. One of the gardening team, the chap who advised me to play it cool with Rachel when I first started in her employ, Morris "Minor," (Compo, from *Last of the Summer Wine*), pruned the palm tree nearest me. He caught me looking at a northbound jet high overhead. Cotton wool vapour trails were discarded behind it like railway tracks. Another one, twenty miles or so astern, tracked the same route. An airway (an aviation highway for airliners) I supposed. "Do you think that's going somewhere nice, like Spain?" he asked. I explained to him that it was heading north/north west so, because the world is round, probably North America. "How do you know that?" I fly. "Fuckin' 'ell, what you doin' in this shit 'ole?" A very good question.

What a *jerk* I've been.

1140: Tannoy: "Mr. Robinson, to the office please." Here we go, I thought. "Get over to OMU," said a sourly officer. Over to OMU, I went. Climbed the scaffold stairs again and rang the bell. A jangle of jailer's keys followed and I'm opposite the officer who yelled at me. "Have a seat in here please, Mr Robinson," he said without yelling.

Nadine tracked into shot accompanied by a female who looked like she should be related to Miss Marple of HMP Bedford. We were introduced. This was Judi (Dench), the Tag Lady, who is effectively my ticket out of here. We adjourned to the side office. During the dialogue Judi monitored both my words and demeanour most M like. The combination of both Tag and flying was aired and – thank God – Judi confirmed "that it will not be a hindrance," providing the "address issue is sorted." I asked once that is, when will I go? "Oh, you're going on 17th November." With that she gave me the name and number of my Probation officer – a female – and suggested I got in touch...

After a late lunch I asked the office if I could use their phone. Permission was granted and tried my luck. The number rang but no one answered. Returned to 48. *Butch Cassidy and the Sundance Kid* was on telly. When Sundance's girlfriend, the school teacher lady, tells him she is leaving, it reminded me of... well, you know.

1330: A second request to use the phone and got a "help yourself." Success. She knew my name and was helpful and jolly. Very Scottish – like Glenda – and everything I said corresponded with her hymn sheet. Above all else, she had a sense of humour. She ended the call with "see you in a few weeks."

Rolled to work feeling like I'd been pushed by a giant wave. The *real* work, I know, will begin when I'm out. Right now I'm still surfed-up on this desert island.

Nothing doing at Healthcare. Nothing new in that. Enquiries were made if Robbie was in residence. "Yes," but with Neil. So I waited.

Doing so, overheard a *fabulous* conversation:

Dave: "You do not have concussion."
Prisoner: "I do."
Dave: "You do NOT have concussion – I will issue you with Paracetamol."
Prisoner: "OK." (Stops scratching head).

1400: Robbie seemed taken aback that I wish to talk to him "professionally." He asked me to see him "for a proper session," tomorrow at 0930.

1415: Hoxon. Heston mopping. Is it a competition against Dennis? Does this man ever stop working? (Is he related to Dennis?) He told me he "used to be a senior nurse." When he is out, he'll "be a house husband." He wants to teach his kids all the stuff his dad, "a raving alcoholic," never taught him. "Like carving a chicken."

Carry on Abroad on telly. I think it was filmed here.

1600: Outside with some new faces. One chap "doing five years" and one youngster: "Six months and out on Tag next week." We agreed that the *beginning* is the end of the time *in* prison.

1700: "Curry." Neil almost walked out in disgust.

1745: Tables. Doesn't anyone here, have the ability to keep their food on their plate whilst eating?

1805: Andrew popped by. He's "moving Unit on Thursday," and not thrilled about it.

1810: Buzz has spoken to my landlord and all my belongings have been packed up and put in boxes "in the garage." This news filled me with anxiety but there is nothing I can do about it now. He closed with his intentions to post me a large stamped addressed envelope for the return of his student records.

I'll despatch them by return of post to show some form of efficiency.

Tuesday, September 27th, 2011.

0630: A blanket of fog outside. I didn't sleep terribly well due to one of the killers snoring all night long. A real ground-trembler.

0820: All aboard Healthcare. A mass of activity on the decks. The dentist in – a new one. Am handed a mop by Renee almost before I'm through the door and told to attack the room abeam the dentist's which has finally been painted. Do so, then get asked to "lose the curtains," which have been painted around! The curtain top is about twelve feet above the floor. I bet you I'm the first prisoner here who has been told by staff to climb the bars and "rip the curtains down." Once the windows were de-draped the room looked like a photo in a newspaper after a bomb has gone off. Most of the new paintwork also joined the curtains on the floor. I cleaned up everything. Again.

Now I was in Renee's good books for ripping her curtains down she said that she would try to "fit me in today," on the dental list. I did the loos and bins and then told a disinterested Rachel that I was going to wait outside for Robbie. This I did and various prisoners walked by remarking "how hard" I'm working.

0920: Robbie arrived in an expensive car of German manufacture with his fog lights on, as the weather was still set for a Sherlock Holmes scene. He asked me to give him "five" and then come and give him a "kick."

Five minutes later we opened proceedings. The subsumed page-headers: Insecurity. The theft of the money. I'm an idiot. My wife has left me. She is not even talking to me. Hurt. Despair. I explained how I have now learnt I can be me and accepted, even in prison – and I feel stupid. I voiced that I'm scared of doing it again. Despite me HATING it here, it would be daft not to accept that my duff decision making might not go away. He was shocked about my wife's behaviour.

I had to defend her.

He probed about my family and what support I was getting. On the brief explanation that I am very much solo on this shoot, the future was touched on. What future? He announced that we should start a process to build up a "ring of steel," to stop this happening again. Mondays at 0930 were earmarked and are "to be continued on the out."

I liked him and felt good. He was amused by the book, the writing of which would have been loopy not to disclose. I questioned if it's being written purely as a defence mechanism. I got a Cracker-look for that but he agreed that "there are some real characters in here."

1200: Lunch. Mathew, who is "definitely leaving for Stow on Friday," greets me with "hello Jon boy." When I looked at what I had been served, I was stopped in my tracks by what appeared to be brake pads on my plate. Some sort of burger in a bap.

1300: Tables and finance letter done for Victoria's funding man. Let's hope the outcome of the request for sponsorship is as good as my table tops.

1330: Rupert proudly showed me an essay for his Open University course. I gave loads of praise and encouragement.

Receive a message from the office on key-drop, that I am required for a "Business Link workshop," on Thursday 29th. I have no idea what that's about.

Nacro. Victoria's sidekick Barbara (Streisand) is at her desk and we are introduced. They both look like ladies who lunch – the office reticent of Delia Smith. My letter is "fine" but Ms Wood "needs emails" to have – in writing – the cost of everything. She lets me use the imperial phone and with my heart in my mouth I speak to the outside world. From prison. I ring a helicopter company that I know – and who know me – and speak to someone asking them to send an email with costs. No flinch from their end when I read out a prison email address. That's a start then. Also spoke to my landlord's assistant (my landlord also being a CAA approved doctor), to get her to email the cost of a flight crew medical.

Again, she reacts like I spoke to her last week...

With the phone calls complete and me feeling odd – like I did after Buzz visited – Victoria asks me to fill in some forms with her Orderly. His typing is interesting to say the least but he's being helpful. This done, it is agreed I will pop in on Thursday afternoon around the Business Link Workshop (!!!) to check that "all the emails have landed."

1430: Healthcare. Five minutes later (together with a dentist's appointment for Tuesday 18th) leave for Hoxon as there is nothing for me to do.

Back home spied Rupert and Mathew locked into a Playstation game. On a day like today... Headed outside where Rod joined me. I told him of Rupert's essay. Rod looked thoughtful and said *very* Jason Statham like that Rupert "has a vicious wire," which Rod "will have to defuse."

Morris appeared. I gathered from his attire (teeth in, black t-shirt and special occasion's ear ring) that he had been somewhere special. He had. And I got told all about it. He and "another prisoner have been entertaining the local grannies in the Faith room." The mind *boggles.* "Bingo, board games and feeding them." And by the sound of things – a great deal of flirting. He rounded this off with "it's nice to do something good."

The fog then rolled in like a wave. One second it was glorious, the next, we had zero visibility and it was cold. Very cold. A tanker sounded its horn with irritation.

1630: Dennis suggests now is a good time to attack my locks.

1645: Prison haircut complete. Slightly wonky but it'll grow back quick and besides, it won't need doing again till I'm out. Leapt in the shower. Various comments made about my new look, of which none are printable.

1700: Dinner. Looked horrible so gave it a miss.

1900: Seven letters written for Rod.

1910: Coffee pit-stop. My haircut causing much amusement. Dennis has now told me he has "never cut anyone's hair before."

Wednesday, September 28th, 2011.

0620: Examined my hair in the mirror. I think it looks fine – when my head is tilted 30° to the right. Considered in bed last night about the irony of being in *prison*, sorting out my *helicopter licence* yesterday. It sounds daft doesn't it? I have made the decision that the first thing I do when I get out is to go to Aldeburgh and leave some (not expensive) flowers at my uncle and grandparents' graves.

0820: Bins done (no tables!) and off to work. I'm wearing purple prison sweat suit trousers and my blue Aldeburgh T-shirt. Heston remarks I "look like a children's TV presenter." I suppose the wonky hair doesn't help.

Noticed one killer packed up and ready to be shipped-out to another Unit. Mick Hucknall. Wished it was the other one who snores.

0835: Rounds. Hot.

On the walk back to Hoxon, that chap who a few weeks ago said "now go back to your cell and think about what you have done to society" reappeared – and with the same line. I updated him that he had previously fed me these instructions. "Is it working?" he laughed most P. Sellers like. No, I responded with my best Inspector Dreyfus drawl.

It *did* work though...

0945: Hoxon. Hot. Julian scoops me up asking if I can watch out for "Sanjay, who is dropping off some cleaning chemicals to the Unit." No problem. Julian says Sanjay is better known as "Chemical Ali."

1005: Mick Hucknall outside moaning. Something had got him started. Mathew catches me making notes.

1220: Lunch complete. French stick (!!!!) In the queue, Neil's solitary line to me: "You're looking more and more like a Lag each day." Thanks Neil.

1320: Healthcare. Rachel asks me to "blitz the windows inside – but behind the bars – (like me) – in the dentist's two rooms. This done, ten minutes later I'm on my way back to Hoxon. A very relaxed Frank is loitering and report that I saw Robbie.

"I know."

Hoxon. It's HOT and we're back to Spanish hotel mode. Staff patrol the grounds. Gordon whispers "let's hope they don't find Tom, Dick or Harry." The youngster who I chatted to on Monday is going home tomorrow. He tells a nice story that he doesn't want his family "who have been brilliant" and supported him nonstop "to waste petrol money," so he is going home on the train. He wants to return to his "school caretaker job."

1700: Dinner. Chips to Mathew. His orange to me. In the queue, a very unhappy Lennox. Brad Pitt has been shipped-out to another Unit.

Thursday, September 29th, 2011.

The TV tells of another hot one. Dale Farm on the news. This will run and run. I can hear "Mrs Mop" up. Who will do it next week?

0800: I bade goodbye to the young School caretaker, shook his hand then set off to work in the sort of weather that makes German holiday makers put towels out at ungodly hours. A Teutonic greeting from Don and: "What happened to your hair?"

Work. Conference with Philip about my hand. He says he will get me to see the doctor again on Monday. I mop the floors and leave.

0830: Hoxon. My door has gone! Dust and bits of wood laid the scene. The SPG had not been-a-visiting, for a civilian carpenter toiled. "New fire regs," he carped as he pointed out a special seal in the middle of the replacement "which takes longer to burn." Anyone fancy a BBQ'd imprisoned flying instructor?

One of our new "Young offenders" (Jamie Bell) converses with me. So young. Very polite. Very northern. As with all arrivals, he's shell-shocked by the trees, grass (the green stuff on the ground) and the freedom we are given here. He asks me – the pro that I am – about visits. He is keen for his "mum to come here as soon as possible." Not for his sanity, but hers. He voices that his mum thinks "prison is like Strangeways" and he wants to "reassure her." He adds that when she does come, "she will go to the mystery place" (the green Cathedral), that is surrounded by typical prison fences and razor wire "because that is what people think prison looks like."

This young man – "Strangeways" – has Tag right after me. Not been in long. "And not coming back." Interesting footnote: The crowd that he used to hang out with had been identified previously by his mum with the following observation: "They're not your friends." Mums are always right.

If you're young and reading this – firstly – thank you. Secondly, listen to your mum.

1100: Outside with Rod. And the spitting man, who is driving me nuts. Hear the *noises*. "That is a really nasty habit," remarks Rod to me quietly. And he's has been around the block...

Post arrives...

JEFFREY ARCHER

Dear Mr Robinson,

Many thanks for your letter of 20th September.

Getting published is extremely difficult. I suggest you first try to find an agent. If an agent likes your manuscript (send them a synopsis and a copy of the first couple of chapters), they will not charge you a fee until they have secured you a publishing deal. You can find lists of agents in "The Writer's and Artist's Yearbook" which should be available in the library.

Best of luck with this, and in the future.

Yours sincerely,

Jeffrey Archer

So, Dear Reader, I had taken the plunge and written to my new pen-pal for advice. I am very grateful that he has taken the time to write back. Clearly all my letters to date to *publishers* have been a waste of time. I must start to bother these "agents."

1200: French stick. Andrew has his last meal at Hoxon.

1330: Depart for the "Business Link workshop." Divert to Victoria's office, to make sure the emails have arrived about my future. "One has landed," says a harassed Victoria in a Wendolene Ramsbottom state of kerfuffle. Sensing nuclear fallout, I leave Victoria's bunker and go and wait in the corridor with some very bored looking prisoners. We are herded into a classroom-set next door and everyone sits down. I find myself sitting next to Andrew (!) who just moved house. He is "in a sharing room" on his new Unit. What's your new roommate like? "It's Gordon."

Of the Bedford four, only the author remains on Hoxon.

It's an extremely hot and sticky afternoon and I do a headcount. Eight prisoners and one wasp complete the tally. A civilian female arrives and introduces herself. This is Felicity (Kendal) and she explains that she is going to go through what it takes "to start up a sole trader business." Most of the fellow students look bored. One eats an apple. Two talk to each other. Whilst she is talking.

What exactly does it *take* for prisoners to become Cat D and to be moved here?

She asks each of us to tell the room what we do. Oh no. Please no. I make all sorts of emergency promises to God to get me out of this. No escape. So after hearing Plumber, Green grocer and similar, eyes swivel to me...

Instructor, I say ashamed. "What sort of instructor?" Oh God please no. But there's no way out... I teach people to fly helicopters.

Hear the *silence*.

Felicity rescues me by moving swiftly on. We are told, amongst other things, that "people buy from people" and that we should "work smarter, not harder." Our hostess is by this point working the room and catches my eye. She tells me that as she is about to start on "how a plumber can start his own business," that this is maybe a "waste of time for me" and hints that it's OK for me to tiptoe out. I thank her and excuse myself. But not before one prisoner gets up, without saying a word to her and walks out.

On my departure, Felicity tells me that she flew gliders "and went solo at 16."

1500: Hoxon. A new door greeted me. I attacked the post-grenade carnage both in the corridor and number 48.

1700: Supper. Straight in bin. The place full of very noisy boisterous newbies.

1815: Phone call with Buzz. He has been busy. Including doing his Qualifying Cross Country. (A terrifyingly long trip in a helicopter when the student is by themselves).

1820: Writing, until nearly 2100. The time Included meeting my new neighbour (Bono), who is in Mick Hucknall's old room. Another killer. And another one opposite too. Whilst I'm talking to Bono in his room, there's a moth whizzing around and I catch it in my hand. It's now dark outside. He sees me do this and goes very quiet. When you're in a confined area with a convicted killer, with a live moth in your clasp and he goes quiet, what do you do?

I went to the window and let the moth out.

"I'm glad you did that," said the killer.

"I'm a Buddhist."

Friday, September 30th, 2011.

0815: Mopping at work complete.

0900: Hoxon and it's already hot. As I passed Wilford on the way "home," I thought about Gordon and Andrew. Wonder how they're getting on?

Two Young offenders sit near to me on the other bench. One of them "Strangeways." We talk about the contrast of here with other jails. My time-served-to-date is requested. This is the end of my 10th week. "You're lucky," they say. I know what they mean. A short sentence and shipped-out to an open prison. They ask when my Tag is. "Strangeways" comes out with: "I don't want Tag."

??????

He doesn't want the "restrictions of Tag," but would "rather have Home-leave every month," so he can go out and "enjoy" himself. He digs himself a deeper hole with the news that he has a "job offer on the outside" ("which I don't like"). This causes me botheration. Some guidance is called for: Look, you're going to have the stigma of jail for the rest of your life. How is it going to look in the future that you stayed in, so that you could go out to get pissed? Think about the future. Admit that you screwed up – but start showing people you mean business. You've got a job offer on the outside. Go to work. Earn some money. Don't think about now. His friend (shaved head, tattoo above collar line) says "that's what I've been saying." "Strangeways" looks at me, thinking. I can see cogs going round.

"I'm gonna get Tag."

1120: Mathew materialises. "I've been terminated." He is not moving. He's "been packed since dawn."

I'm glad he's not moving as I'd miss him. He's too stubborn to admit he's relieved too. But I know he is. So much so that he's gone off to see if he can move to my corridor and have a sea view.

1155: Alistair has news on Gordon and Andrew – and it's bleak: "Wilford Unit is filthy and they don't get any breakfast."

Lunch. Mathew *definitely* back to his old self by complaining to us all that we hadn't put our "stuff out early enough to bag the table" and that he had to "fight-off newbies." We all say sorry like naughty school boys.

Library. I take out a Ken Follett book – *Jackdaws* and hunt for the book that Jeffrey Archer suggested I should look at which "should be in the prison library."

It is.

"The Writer's and Artist's Yearbook" is a *Yellow Pages* of what I'm going to need. Full of agents and more interestingly, loads of tips. I look to see if I can borrow it but it is for reference only.

Then, another coincidence – the Jonathan Aitken prison book catches my eye that Miss Marple, the Toe by Toe lady suggested I read. Gail too, if memory serves me right. I pick it up gingerly. I have not and will not look inside – but I want the publisher's address. I know J.A. and the Yearbook have said to get an agent but I have now written so many letters to publishers that one more can't hurt.

Arrive at a deserted Healthcare five minutes later and find a desperate Dennis loitering outside. He's in a state about when he should pick up his "fit-for-release-certificate." Despite him and I both knowing that Philip wants to see him on Sunday morning at 1100, he asks me to check with Philip that his "appointment on Sunday is still on." "Yes it is," says Philip, not quite in despair but clearly ready to join our ranks by murdering Dennis.

That would work. He could have Dennis' room.

1410: Unit. I settle down with Mr Follett. Prisoners are sunbathing, snoozing, chatting and passing time in the sun. Some are stripped-off to their shorts, until loud shouts from an officer: "No sunbathing during the core working day!" T shirts are reached for by bronzed prisoners with much haste. Julian is now the colour of a decent cup of coffee, with a dash of milk.

1700: Dinner had with Mathew (secretly very glad to still be here), Rupert and Mr. Waterman.

1830: Wrote to Jonathan Aitken for help/advice/phone numbers of his daughters.

Saturday, October 1st, 2011.

0705: "Pinch and punched" Rod, an *exceedingly* brave thing to do bearing in mind his normal disposition in the morning but he responded with "that's good luck, welcome to October."

0920: A letter of support to Dennis half completed, I set off to work with a Geordie chap (Tim Healy). "Four years behind the door and two more to go," announced right out of *Auf Wiedersehen Pet.*

A thrilled-to-be-working-at the-weekend Philip found. There is a pile of HIV leaflets available for waiting patients to peruse and instead of reading them, poorly prisoners seem magnetically drawn to tearing them up – into tiny pieces. Philip and I talk about the leaflet shredders and he agrees with my *Telegraph*-reader views that instead of feeding them a substitute drug – which will lead to cravings on the outside – and thus the revolving door that is prison – they should simply be weaned off. I know nothing about drugs and I am probably opening up a can of worms by expressing my views in this pile of written rubbish but I do know that Philip agrees with me. And *he's* in the trade.

0955: Library. Rod and Rupert were within – and panted like dogs. Both had been for a run and sweated like glistening racehorses do at the end of the Grand National.

I got into the book J.A. advised me to consult. "How to deal with rejection" was studied as I'm sure it will be the most useful and apt information for me in the months to come. Library Brett and L.A. were asked if the "reference only" books can ever be borrowed. Brett bellowed with a look that would have made Glenda in Bedford's Library *more* than proud and L.A. winked at me…

The time now, as I write this is 11.24.

Checked some other books for any unhit publishers and stumbled across the Jonathan Aitken book again.

Realised with sense of *doom* that I misspelt his surname in my letter to him yesterday. (At least I didn't misspell his Christian name).

1045: Unit. A chat struck up with the newbie lifer opposite. He is Stuart (Richard Whitmore). "Eleven years done so far."

1124: L.A. Bel-Airs into my room. Together with the *"Writer's and Artist's Yearbook."*

1145: Lunch queue. As Mathew tells me he is "now leaving on Monday," someone walks to the servery who I have not written of before but Rod – the all-knowing oracle – has dubbed him "A.P." The reason for the lack of appearance of this gentleman in these pages is explained by his acronym.

"Arrogance personified."

1200: Lunch. Had a go at the "Halal veggie sausages." Mathew, who has worked in the kitchen, gave me a look and said "you're a braver man than me, lad."

After lunch some mail. A note from Buzz with an SAE big enough to post myself out of jail in – for his student records:

Hi Jonathan,

I hope you're well and the days are flying by. Here is the SAE you need for my flight log, etc. I know I will hear from you over the next few days so until then be good.

All the best Buzz.

And a letter from one of the publishers saying that they will have a look...

Outside later with Dennis and a heart-to-heart. I try to transmit how before prison, I wouldn't have spoken to some of the types we have here. I wouldn't have given them the time of *day* in fact. Here has taught me humility. And not to judge a book by its cover. And a revelation – that I didn't need to change *my* cover. I confess that if I had been myself – not exaggerating what is in fact OK – then everything else would have been just peachy. All due to, do you know what Dennis? "Insecurity," succinctly suggests Dennis. Dead right Dennis. The fact that my stupid bloody insecurity has involved taking money not mine, lying and being a shit still makes me bloody angry.

The vultures began to circle overhead Mr Waterman. Demands start flooding in for what is not going with him. Before he knows it his watch, shorts and various T shirts are pledged to colleagues. Someone has asked for his plate (from home) but Dennis declines this. It is part of a set and he has promised Mrs Waterman to bring it back. He asks me what I would like. I'm embarrassed and I find the taking of things whilst the body is still warm too much. "That's prison," he says. We settle on his *Sunday Times*.

1700: Dinner. Mathew in a strange mood, due I am certain, to his upcoming move. When young Rupert leaves the table he suddenly says "he needs sorting out." What? "His manner." For sure, Rupert has the "young lion" walk, talk and vocabulary that so many "Y.O.s" do. I remind Mathew that Rupert is young – and would have learnt such bravado at his previous establishment. Mathew doesn't buy that. "He needs punching in the mouth." Wouldn't it be better having a chat with him? Rod would be good at that and Rupert looks up to him. "That's one of the things that annoys me about you Jon, everything in prison can be sorted out by talking. He needs a good punch in the mouth."

Sunday, October 2nd, 2011.

0700: Dennis' last full day. My letter to him is on his desk. I was going to reproduce it here but some things are best left to the imagination. Snoring Killer is moving to Wilford tomorrow. No more snoring. But who will replace him?

Outside with Dennis, Robert and Geordie, who "can't believe Dennis is going tomorrow." Robert tells me that he "times things in three month sections." I ask Dennis if he feels like an astronaut who is blasting off to the moon in the morning. He doesn't answer – too overwhelmed.

Ironically, he's *returning* to earth tomorrow.

0950: Buzz's student records are now up to date. Rod and Geordie have collected conkers. Much excited schoolboy talk occurs of locating bootlaces and some vinegar. Their quandary: how can the holes be made?

The very high pitched voiced gentleman ("HPV") perches on my bench. Lily white, he strips-off next to me and insists on tapping his feet. I depart to the other end of the terrace. Especially after his opening staccato gambit: "Good out 'ere, innit?"

1055: Healthcare. The tables outside packed with the football match mob. Andrew amongst the terraces. Wilford sounds *terrible.* I'm so glad I'm still at Hoxon. At Healthcare, Philip was "all OK and still here." Dennis, Robert and EBV were in residence for Dennis' certificate. Did he take his equerry reinforcements in case he didn't get it?

1145: Hot. Eavesdropped a conversation between Neil and another ex-Pentonville prisoner, about the "bald headed officer" who use to smuggle stuff in (Fairy liquid). "Got 5 years." Then a general agreement that "bent officers should get much harsher sentences."

I stress again that everything in this book is as I hear and see it. I have no idea how substantial all the stories I pick up on are. I suppose you, Dear Reader, can look things up on the internet as you wade through these drab pages and check if things ring true. If they *do,* can someone please make my wife sit down and ponder my pleas to her. *Please.*

1200: Lunch. "Nut roast." Nut brick more like. Mathew still in a funny mood and sloped off. That left me stuck with young Rupert who is not the biggest conversationalist in the world. He likes to chomp away at his meal hardly saying anything at all. I bought up the subject of his essay and that hit the ignition switch for a most enthusiastic lecture from him. To date, the longest piece of dialogue divulged from him whilst dining was about a certain fast food chicken chain.

The new lifer opposite, Stuart, tells me he's… in a spot of… bother. He's been offered a job in the library – and accepted it – but had not met Library Brett – or heard the grim behind the scanner stories from L.A. before signing his life away (no pun intended). He asked me how to escape the situation. I said to speak to Frank in Tribal. It's all I could think of.

1255: Reading the J.A. book. "Enquiry" letters to agents. "Double spacing," bloody hell. What have I let myself in for? I have started to write out agent's addresses on envelopes. Lots of them.

1420: Outside and Rod comes over to my patch. The conkers from the morning have now become a sizeable collection and inevitably, a play fight starts. All waged in good humour. Until Rod misjudges quite a hard long shot. If I asked him to throw a conker again – at speed – *right* across the entire gardens and hit "Big Len" (Ross Kemp), in the mouth (whilst he was *asleep*), he wouldn't be able to. He'd only be able to do it once...

And once he did.

"WHO THE FUCK THREW THAT?!" Heard the herd on Hoxon and half of Holland.

I have *never* seen Rod move so fast. He put Geronimo to shame. Big Len – who could crush anything in his *hand* – was up on his feet. Rod was by his side saying sorry almost before the projectile had hit the ground – after it had been deflected by Len's upper right molar. All of Rod's defusing skills are utilised in seconds. He turns the Guy Ritchie character caricature charm factor up to warp factor seven. Luckily Big Len sees the funny side. Or it may have been both Dennis *and* Rod leaving us tomorrow, with Rod in a box.

After supper, during which Mathew was in a filthy mood, Dennis, EBV, Robert and I sat outside and kept the tobacco industry rolling. As the theatrical and atmospheric smoke wafted in the air, a very last day of term feeling also surrounded us. Only for Dennis though. Everyone is sad he is going. Thrilled for him – a home run – but sad. EBV said anyone who "fucks about on licence is a cunt."

1800: Buzz's flight test is soon (like a driving test – but in a helicopter). Have you ever phoned from prison and explained the required drills for landing a helicopter in a confined area?

I have.

Monday, October 3rd, 2011.

Dennis' D day.

Stuart, our library lifer, writes an awful lot – and leaves his door open whilst doing so. Last night I asked him if he's writing a prison book.

"Yes, been doing it 11 years."

Christ *almighty*. Then I realised he was smiling at me. Very funny. I like him.

He introduced me to his Bono lookalike pal, the fellow lifer who I had the moth scene with. Unbelievably, he's a Rod – another one. I now have a Rod to the left of me and a Stuart on the nose. When do the Faces check in?

Dennis has been ordered by Robert to partake in a "final breakfast." A prison tradition. He puts enough prison cereal in his plastic prison bowl to block up the channel tunnel. How did he sleep? "So so, but woke up at 0430." I leave him to eat, wake Rod – the Statham Rod, not the Bono one. You too, are confused? – and return to my room.

So its absence is not noted, the J.A. book has been returned to L.A. I've written enough envelopes to literary agents to fill a fridge. Individual letters also need to be penned – and then the problem of the amount that I need to get-out needs addressing. The system allows us one a week. I'm hoping to ship-out five a day. A mass break out then. *The Great Envelope Escape*.

How-to-land-a-helicopter-in-a-confined-area prison-phone-calls are recounted to Elk. He chuckles but points out if I was "in a higher security prison" I'd now be "in a Sweatbox, on my way to another higher security prison."

0815: Light rain. Dennis steps off Hoxon for the last time. I carry one bag, he carries the other. Various people shake his hand. As we walk down the hill, he starts coming out with all sorts of neurotic suppositions. Will his wife be here? Will they change their mind? I try to reassure him as we close on the main gate and climb the stairs. This is it. Dennis unnecessarily says he's really anxious and thanks me for "being here."

"You're at the wrong place. Go to Reception."

The field hospital set is full of other leavers. Being here brings back memories of my arrival. I stay outside – in case they confuse me with someone else and send me home. An officer's line to the others gathered: "Go away – in the nicest possible way," and they are released. As they rush past me one of them chimes "let's get the fuck outta here."

Dennis is processed. I watch him stand at the desk. The place where I last saw my suit, belt, shirt, tie, and wallet. He is given bits of paperwork to sign. I'm rolling two smokes as he's "too nervous to make them." As he is being warned that he may never go near a firearm, firework, air rifle or starter gun an officer approaches me…

"Are you his lift sir?"

I'm wearing a prison shirt – with my prison ID around my neck and a prison (Dennis) haircut.

I am tempted to say yes and ask the officer to carry the bags to the car, *very* tempted. Prison though, has taught me to keep my mouth shut so I identify myself. The officer looks rather embarrassed. Internally, I am thrilled that I still exhibit traits of a normal person.

A problem arises. Dennis' debit card is missing from his personal property. A call is made to the main gate and confirmation is made that it is there. Dennis is dispatched. We leave with his bags as a black Mercedes, as long as a cricket pitch, bowls up.

The Waterman clan. He invites me over to meet his wife and kids. They all shake my hand. They look very relieved. His wife says on our introduction "very nice to meet you." His daughter, in her early teens – but going on 25 – wears high heels and is going to be a knockout. Dennis, you're going to have your hands full there...

Just as well he's not allowed firearms.

We put the bags in the boot. I joke with them that I'm getting in too – and I'm tempted, believe me. He explains to his wife that he needs to go and pick up his card and we walk back to the main gate.

The card collected, we smoke a final cigarette. He will read my letter when he gets home. We get to his car. I open the front passenger door like a doorman outside the Savoy. We shake hands. He hugs me. He gets in. My final line to Mr Waterman: Look after your family.

And he is gone.

Healthcare. Feeling thoroughly miserable. Philip tells me Robbie is ill and there is not much that can be done (cleaning wise, nothing to do with Robbie's prognosis). The loos upstairs are mopped as I mope. Disappointed that the Robbie Rendezvous didn't happen, Hoxon is returned to at 0905.

0915: Unit. An officer is told that Dennis is gone ("oh, you mean Waterman") and that I met his wife and kids. This earned me a bollocking for "associating with the public" and that I could have "been given drugs to bring back in and to watch out." I offered myself to be searched but didn't reveal that I nearly got into the boot of Dennis' car.

Stuart's door open. He recounts that he was in an open prison before – but was "put back in closed conditions by Probation." What on earth had he done to force them to play that card? He is "in prison for murder and when working on the outside," at his last open prison – he "met and started a relationship," with his female boss (!) and "did not disclose it." On a Home-leave, he did not "go home" but went to his boss's house – at her invitation (!) "Probation were *not* amused." Straight, Stuart went, "back to closed conditions and behind the door." Another Cat B. "Once Probation, the Governor and Lord knows who else, were happy that all parties were happy," it was confirmed he could "go back to open conditions." How long did that all that take?

"Seven months."

We talk about time. I explain my units are of full weeks. He is a lifer. His unit of time?

"Seasons."

1200: The "last supper" with Mathew – who "is going." Lunch is a French stick… Young Rupert joined us and was bemused by Mathew's reaction to both my I-wanted-to-get-in-Dennis'-boot and the phone-call-from-prison-on-how-to-land-a-helicopter-in-a-confined-area stories. Mathew thinks I'll be shipped-out.

My ears pricked up on hearing Aldeburgh being talked about at another table. "Young Jimmy" (Osmond) – young being the operative word – *very* immature, is going to be "working there, in a charity shop."

1245: I'm getting quite good at moving mattresses around in prisons. Rod has just frog marched me to a vacant room where there *were* two…

1255: Nacro. The Victoria line: "Most of the emails have arrived."

1340: Healthcare. Rachel tells me that I have a dentist's appointment tomorrow at 1000 and sends me on Rounds.

1500: Writing letters for this bastard book.

Dear _____

Please forgive the hand written letter. This reaches you from prison. If you're still reading – thank you. I am a middle class, middle aged helicopter pilot nearing the end of a short stay for theft. During which I have written/am writing a book on "day to day life inside." Funny, sad, ironic and topical – I was in during the riots. Jeffrey Archer, who wrote me a very nice letter, has pointed me towards the *"Writer's and Artist's Yearbook,"* within which, I found you. I am writing to ask if I may send you some pages following my release – and much typing! – in November. I only hope that you find my words more interesting (and funnier), than we find the food here…

In advance, many thanks,

Jonathan Robinson.

1700: Dinner. "Cheeseburger."

1800: Writing this – then more letters. This, after having locked myself out. Again.

1845: On the telly, the Dale Farm saga continues. "The Prime Minister now involved." A whole bunch of letters done.

1900: *The Great Envelope Escape* discussed with Julian and Rod. Do I risk five a day or do I get other people to write the envelopes to disguise them? The Envelope Escape Committee is deliberating.

Tuesday, October 4th, 2011.

There are an awful lot of literary agents in the UK.

Healthcare. Nurse Sue held the fort, the waiting room *packed*. Benjamin lurked in Rachel's office and wouldn't let me take the mail for Rounds. Being tactful, I discreetly asked Sue to alert him that it's OK and I'm not trying to escape. He then rather reluctantly gave me the mail. I did some vacuuming and general cleaning up around the masses. During which, I noticed that most of the drawing pins that I had used to tidy up the notice boards in my early days in the role of Healthcare Orderly have been liberated – no doubt for putting up pictures of loved ones in prisoners' rooms.

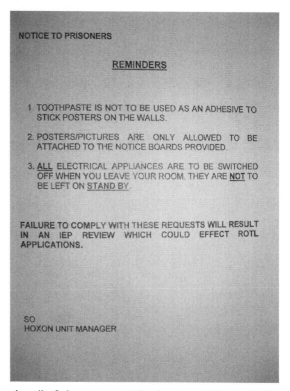

No such pictures adorn my walls. My behaviour has made everyone run for the hills.

One very pasty individual loitered. He looked terrible. His eyes sat in a very blank, expressionless face. Again a line from *Jaws* uncoiled before me and Quint's slant on sharks: "Lifeless eyes. Black eyes. Like a doll's eyes…"

The Fish man fed the fish. A feeding frenzy feast for fish followed, with the water rippling like mad. All parties watched. Apart from one, who walked about banging on the walls, doors and windows. This mob were waiting for something other than the dentist…

Things became somewhat more apparent as to why this etiolated lot hung about when Nurse Sue announced "meds." For the second time I witnessed a rushed frenzy. Not for fish-food, but for the dispersal of drug substitutes.

The scampering dependants made the earlier stampede of the fish look organised.

Renee extracted me from the mayhem to see the dentist. I didn't mention the fact that I had been swinging from on-high around his windows recently. Instead, sat down and the back of the electronic chair reclined. The closest I hope that I am ever to get to an electric chair in prison. He peered into my talking end and recounted those letters and numbers that dentists do. My release date was asked for and he reported no problems but said he would give me a quick polish.

1030: Rounds, including a touch-and-go at Victoria's station. Everything sounded pretty much in place for the funding. I am to return on Friday morning.

1300: Following lunch more agent letters then left for work at 1315. I stopped at the library at

1325, which was cutting it fine as it closes at half-past the hour and Library Brett takes great delight in chucking prisoners out like closing time in a pub. A notice had sprung-up announcing that Joanna Trollope is coming to Hollesley Bay to give a talk about writing (!) in November. I put my name down under Victoria's and Barbara's. Therefore at the moment, I'm the only prisoner on the list.

Healthcare. Did a quick inspection to see if I could spot anything that needed to be done (showing initiative, I'll get into trouble) and there wasn't. Picked up one letter for Bosnia and briefly saw Mathew, he now of Stow Unit, who said he was "OK."

1335: Hoxon. Yet more writing of both this and agents' letters.

1430: Finished first lot. Now starting the second batch.

1500: Calculated that five a day is cutting things very fine re timing. Going to risk ten a day...

1620: Bono Rod has returned from the "taking of the minutes" for the "prison catering meeting." I shot outside to gather what had happened. First of all, the "Head of catering did not turn up" (!) "Servery Heston represented Hoxon blindingly" and then it "just turned into a shouting match."

1640: One more letter to make it ten, for Wednesday night's drop-off.

1700: Dinner. A "Black history month homemade curry." Not at all bad. Neil though – from India – said "it's not Indian because it has raisins in it." It was difficult to make that out though, as he had a mouthful of curry at the time.

1845: A break from (bastard) letter writing to grab Heston to gather any more titbits from the catering meeting. "One of the Unit reps kept saying after every suggestion, point or idea, that this is shit or that was shit and this is all shit and then walked out."

1930: ****ing letters.

Wednesday, October 5th, 2011.

0820: Rounds. At Stow, Nine Bagger looked at me suspiciously and asked, in a not too terribly friendly fashion: "You still on Hoxon?" Gave Genghis the affirmative, returned to the Unit and wondered if I would get rumbled about the sack loads of post I am illicitly despatching (most people try to get things into prison, I'm trying to get them out). Nothing was said. Peeked in the post box – it had been emptied. Fingers crossed.

0845: Writing. More letters. If you're reading this, it worked.

1110: Went to the office to get more paper (!) The officer's comment: "He's writing us out of house and home!" So they must have cottoned on.

1120: Piles of sealed envelopes now fill my room.

Lunch. "Hot pot" – or similar. Not bad. Mine eaten after successfully knocking over a bowl of soup. Out came a mop and bucket and a tepee sized Health and Safety Traffic cone – which in any role other than nanny-state-mollycoddling would have warranted planning permission – was placed by an officer over the accident scene. As Heston dined I passed favourable reviews of the Hot-pot. "Do you mean the Cumberland pie?" After back-tracking on my mistaken identity I voiced apology for the soup incident and that I'd been careful when mopping not to place the suds bucket too close to the soup container in case anyone confused the two – for fear that the contents of my pale tasted better...

1330: Healthcare. Philip most excited as he has something for me to do. A highly technical job of manoeuvring some plates back to the officer's Mess. As I always seem to get bollocked for going through doors in prison, he is asked if there is a tradesmen's entrance. This throws him – but then he remembers that the Mess is "closed now" and suggests I "come in later tomorrow."

1430: More letters.

1530: A flying visit from Bono Rod – who has been told he's being moved to Stow – and lifer Stuart – who has heard he's staying. Rod Stuart is no more.

1610: A room inspection by two officers. Why is my bed is not against the wall? Rationalise that the cot's non-regulation position is so I don't whack the wall when I'm in it. This is accepted and they continue their nosing of other rooms. Stuart thinks "someone important" is coming to the Bay tomorrow.

1615: Tannoy: "Listen up: We know there's one mobile phone on A wing and one on B wing. There is an amnesty if you hand them in now." So the room inspection was a ruse to find phones with hidden electrical equipment. The normal fee for being found in possession of anything cellular is instant ship-out to closed conditions.

1700: Dinner. Young Rupert proclaims that he "can't wait to get out and eat proper food."

Such as?

"KFC, Nando's and McDonalds."

Thursday, October 6th, 2011.

Peeped into the mail box – which had been emptied. Will I get carpeted today for my envelope export?

Unto the breach. Does WD not have a hair brush? "There are letters and Unit Rep sheets to be delivered and Dave is upstairs," she fire-breathed. Is he hiding from her? Reporting to Dave with the plate detail task for Philip he is challenged with what's the Mess like? Consulting my notes as I write this, his reaction is: "goes white."

Swabbing the Treatment room, WD starts telling me how to mop. During this advice I concoct exactly in my mind, what I'd like her to do with the mop.

0855: Loaded with enough plates to last a season of Greek weddings, the aisle to the Mess is trekked. A "Prisoners not to go beyond this sign" warning-sign is passed and a lodge type building is tentatively approached. The bullet is bitten and entrance made. Another sign says "Leave radios and keys at front desk" – a bit like in westerns when cowboys are instructed to remove their weapons in the saloon bar. The dining area is surveyed...

I believe they made 12 episodes of *Fawlty Towers*. If ever they decide to do more – I now know where they can shoot the dining room scenes. All that is missing is Andrew Sachs...

The plates returned, double back to Healthcare. Robbie is about – "Sorry for getting ill." I shake his hand and welcome him back to the fold. He's done his knee in "whilst trying to find a runaway tea spoon in the dishwasher..." Play resumes with him on Monday, at 0930.

Benjamin pounces on me: "Where are the plates?"

What exactly does Benjamin do here? All I ever see him do is walk about with a clipboard. He's a very nice, polite, softly spoken Indian gentleman.

Is he the Plate Inspector?

Rounds. The standard mail plus "Unit Healthcare Rep Sheets." Hit Bosnia. A disingenuous newspaper reading officer is asked if he knows who their Healthcare Rep is. "Look at the boards," is muttered from the other side of the *Daily Mirror*. Their notice boards reveal who the Travellers'/Anti-bullying/Diversity Reps are but the identity of the wobbly caravan site's Healthcare Rep remains a mystery. I return to the *Mirror* reader and inform him that I have had no luck but am ignored. The sports-page is instructed that I'll go and attempt to find someone. A sort of positive glottal sound gives me the green light to go-a-snooping. The interior of Bosnia is a Portakabin City. The floor creaks as I pace and shifts like being on a small boat. Continuing onwards on my maize like mission, a door is found open to someone's room. The occupant is a regular extra often seen during scenes at Healthcare. Unbelievably – it is he who has the role of Rep. The paperwork is surrendered.

As I leave, noting that the *Mirror* is still being read, I think how lucky I am to still be on Hoxon.

On my way to Cosford the sheets are counted. I'm one too few. At the office, I enquire if can I use their copier. "Don't 'ave one," says a consummate *I'm not interested* voice from behind this time, the *Daily Express*. Again, there is no Healthcare Rep sign up so find a name in the office – as quietly as I can – don't want to disturb a chap from his paper.

Return to Healthcare to get a further copy made. This done, set off for Wilford. As I do so, a gaggle of civilians head towards me. The visiting VIP's? As they near I recognise their host. Our "Head of Education," accompanied by a posse of four suits. He spots me and looks *very* nervous. I quickly have to decide what I'm going to say should one of the suits ask me what I think of the Education facilities here. Back to westerns again. The two cowboys approaching each other, each one waiting for the other to "draw"…

We pass.

Mr Head of Education, I do hope you, or more importantly, your superiors, are enjoying this book.

Wilford. Two officers are in office. One on the internet, the other eating crisps (cheese and onion). Do you know who the Unit Health Rep is? Pre-empt their answer by reading a name on their board next to the title of "Healthcare Rep." As I'm about to write this individual's name on the sheet, "Cheese and onion" wipes off the board saying – with a mouth full of crisps: "He left last year."

Cheese and Onion then looks at Wilford's resident's names saying "let's pick someone sensible." I suggest Andrew. "Good idea," says the crisp eater. Andrew will love it – lots of nurses to hang around with.

Well, Philip and Dave are nurses…

Stow. The same scene is played out again with no one knowing – or interested – who the Rep is.

0940: Hoxon. Heston's Healthcare memo slid under his door. The "Door men" are back – slowly working down the corridor. The room next to mine is being trashed.

1200: Chilli.

1328: Arrive at Healthcare for work.

1329: Leave Healthcare. Work accomplished. It's not exactly sewing mail bags is it?

1400: Letters to literary agents…

1445: Letters now done up to Tuesday 11th. The last batch possible due to the paper and envelope supply. There is none left.

1620: Whilst playing pool the Governor – and I mean *the* Governor appeared on set, plus 1. I assume the plus 1 was a VIP as his host gave him a tour which was worryingly reminiscent of Rigsby showing some unsuspecting potential tenant around the premises in *Rising Damp*. The VIP didn't look convinced.

Our proprietor (Marty Feldman) is *tiny*.

1700: Dinner: Kebab. Bin. Sorry – not eating that.

1805: Mail drop-off. The mail box still attached to wall – despite a hundredweight of letters to the agents that are literary.

Friday, October 7th, 2011.

0805: Healthcare. Dave and another new student nurse (Myleene Klass) told me I was "first in the queue" for the doctor (at 0900) so zoomed out to do Rounds with letters addressed in WD's dreadful handwriting.

0905: Waiting prisoner patients have no patience.

All of my colleagues were getting vocal about the whereabouts of the doctor and the "order of the queue." I said nothing. Things must have got desperate when even WD said "where's the doctor?"

0910: A flustered female doctor breezed in, who looked like one of the female assistants from *Dr Who* in the 70's. My hand is "not worth doing anything with" but she will let me have some Selenium – the antioxidants I was on before my holiday. WD said they will be here on Monday afternoon and I will be "allowed to keep a week's worth in my room."

Unit. Rod – Guy Ritchie Rod – and Stuart have moved rooms to another corridor.

1110: Rod comes to see me with a response from one of the letters I wrote for him. It demands form-filling but sounds optimistic.

Warning staff I may be late for the 1200 Roll-call (responded by grunts) an audience with Victoria is trod to. HRH goes through my paperwork in the most regal of fashions. Everything that she needs "is now in" and she "is away next week."

1145: Luncheon. Stuffed my face with loads of salad.

1230: Multiples of prisoners are moving off Hoxon today to other Units. The roulette ball still hasn't fallen on my number. Thank God.

1255: Catch HPV talking outside my door and see him carrying bags. Ask him if he's moving (trying not to sound too hopeful) – "yes," said falsetto in my ears. Where to? "Bosnia." (*Everyone* is now referring to Bosmere Unit so...)

Hope the windows on the caravan site are plastic...

1300: Bono Rod gone.

1305: Work. All staff discussing "the upcoming redundancies." I gather that some big meeting is happening on the 13th. WD suggests to me I take the day off then, "as the language will be fruity." It must be said that WD has lightened up a *lot* since our first skirmish. Mathew walks in and enquires as to when his optician's appointment is – 1500 – as he requires replacement "Deidre fookin' Barlow glasses."

1345: Unit. I have a near heart attack when my pile of literary agents' letters is seen sat stationary on the officers' desk. Why haven't they gone to the post room? Have I been rumbled?

1430: Waiting for a call to the office. I am certain I'm in it. Up to my neck.

1500: Why the hell are those letters sitting there? Thinking between the lines – they won't open them – I don't think they're allowed to – but maybe a Governor is? I am convinced that there will be a call on the Tannoy later: "Whoever the mystery writer is, please come to the office."

1505: In attempt to distract myself – I offer Neil a game of pool. I must be desperate, he's a demon and always beats me. It is though, a good excuse to go to the office and try to get a surreptitious update on the outgoing post situation by way of collecting pool tools. In I go and ask if I can take some cues, trying to be nonchalant. "Help yourself," says the officer. Thanking him, my eyes glance to where the letters were. I scan the desk surfaces. I don't have much time to walk from where the shafts live to the door without looking suspicious. My eyes dart everywhere. Nothing. As I leave I see them. In the outgoing mail tray.

I breathe again.

1700: Dinner. "Chicken Tikka pie." Straight in bin. Spoke to Julian and with his First Assistant Director's hat on he's getting my stand-in to do the bins tomorrow and Sunday morning so I can watch the Japanese Grand Prix. I will step back into my dustman's shoes on Monday morning.

1730: The best use of "innit" yet. A chap running down the corridor towards me, clutching a woolly hat on his way to outside association – and it's cold. His question?

"I can wear this, innit?"

1940: Following a few rounds of pool I walked into the dining room. The vision before me absolutely made my evening: Two tables had been placed together, with two green prison sheets over them. Littered about were 180 cardboard (each individually cut out by Greg) chips and eight prisoners playing full scale poker.

Further to yesterday's hunt for Reps, I have told Greg that he should be "Gambling Rep." This was met with his intentions to put a roulette wheel into operation at the other end of the dining room tomorrow.

Saturday, October 8th, 2011.

I am pretty much out of paper.

It dawned on me last night after Greg's quite brilliant grand opening of Casino Hoxon that there probably will be roulette tonight. I caught him eyeing up the dart board that no one seems to use and I imagine he will turn it on its side, employ a table tennis ball and get spinning.

Seb on pole – then menu filling-in followed by a Tannoy announcement that they are the wrong ones. Post for me. A standard letter received from a publisher saying "send it in."

Whilst doing something or other near our entrance, a pair of young unfamiliar faces appeared (Beavis and Butthead). "Where's the Reception?" Right and right again, I said directing them to the officers' office. It then occurred to me that they were looking for the main Reception – so I chased after them. Are you outsiders? I asked like some Amish elder. "Yes we're here to visit ____." You're in the wrong place! Where you want is down the hill. Scarper – and don't say you've been here or you'll get shot...

1530: More literary agents' letters.

1645: Dine with Geordie. He passes some nice comments about how I handle myself here. I'm told I'm polite, can give and take a joke and am a "very well educated man" ("canny, like"). I look over my shoulder to see if he's talking to someone else. I divulge that I am sure on the outside, when I tell people of my sea view and telly, that they will say what was the problem? He agrees with me that you've got to experience this to believe it.

Please don't.

1810: Nearly at the end of the long line of letters. There won't be a literary agent left in the country who doesn't know about this. Poor sods.

1830: Letters finished!

1930: Returned from a few games of pool and a Casino visit. Shades of Wyatt Earp and Doc Holliday caused Casino continuity but less people were playing cards tonight. I think Greg's cleaned them out...

Sunday, October 9th, 2011.

0832: Jenson's race. Seb third. Seb 2011 world champion. I wonder if you-know-who is watching this. She used to enjoy watching them with me.

1010: Sitting outside in desperately drab weather. A lone seagull pads around. It's just him and me. He looks even more bored than me but less depressed.

I saw two seagulls outside my window the other evening. One was tub thumping its feet like mad – to attract worms – and the other stood there and watched. Fred Astaire tapping-away was saying "if you do this, you get food. Honest" and Ginger Rogers was thinking "oh yes? Pull the other one..."

I taught Fred Astaire's widow to fly helicopters. Now look where I am. I am *so* ashamed of myself.

A prisoner throws bread from a window for my lone seagull. Suddenly nine more appear which quickly turns to eleven and I'm in a Hitchcock film.

1130: A knock on the door. Stuart – with.....The *Sunday Times*!!!! Where did he get it? "A spare one." A close look at the top reveals a familiar name: "Waterman." Dennis – you forgot to cancel your papers...

Immerse myself in the paper and before I know it, lunch is called. The IMB are here – witnessing the felons' feeding fiesta.

Coincidence – or conspiracy? – lunch turns out to be the best meal I have had in prison. A homemade beef pie – with lots of meat and *full* of flavour. On the menu was rice pudding – I gave mine to Stuart, which seems a good deal to me – a bowl of wallpaper paste for the *Sunday Times*. My theory of conspiracy was settled when some chocolate cake appeared that was not like the normal chocolate cake. This had bits of chocolate in it. Heston was grilled if things had been adjusted for our visitors' presence. He said that the pie has been on the menu for ages. Whatever, I hope the IMB come to Hoxon more often.

Before I came to prison I believed in coincidence. Now I'm a cynic.

1515: Rod comes for *Shawshank Redemption* help with spelling, editing and a general critique of his work to date on his BTEC course. On the whole, a very good effort. After a bit of poking, some corrections are made – and a few suggestions thrown into the ring – and he goes off to write – not before I have to storm a cell/room full of various prisoners about the volume of their Playstation antics. Rod gives me a knowing smile which I take to mean: "You're learning." Not a peep since.

1700: Dinner was served and it was absolutely *fantastic*. I had seconds. Two very good meals on the trot. Relayed this to Heston and he asked me to write same in the comments book.

2030: Visited the Casino. Going in full swing. Asked Jimmy, the youngster, when he's starting in Aldeburgh: "Wednesday."

Very close to home.

Monday, October 10th, 2011.

Jimmy has been given the full lowdown on Aldeburgh. Describing the places where my wife and I frequented was horrible. I tried to convey that it is from another era and that locals won't take kindly to any brash bling bravado. I *think* the penny dropped. Who would have thought when I was there last, that soon I would be describing it to someone in prison.

It's not like I don't deserve it though is it? I have, or am due to have, a session with Robbie today to help me not to go anywhere near the behaviour that bought me here ever again. Ever. My plan? To get out of jail and try to win my wife back.

Meanwhile back on planet earth. Officer Clint Eastwood is back with us, with a heavily bandaged wrist. It looks like a gauntlet... He got another gentle reminder that I am very keen to stay on Hoxon. His response gave me hope. "You are staying" and then added that I am "an asset to the wing." How, I have *no* idea but I really do *not* want to be moved.

0750: L.A. and Stuart looking miserable. Two weeks this Thursday the former is wrapped. Soon he will be L.A.X. Stuart is down because he's starting work in the library today. I wonder if they're plotting something horrendous for Library Brett...

Neil appears looking much more cheerful. He's also starting a new job today: driving the vans. I told him I'll make sure I look both ways VERY carefully before I cross the road.

0835: Work. WD relinquishes that "D day" is on Wednesday, for the announcement of "who goes/who stays." I gather it won't be done in person but by email. Quite a lot of spluttering prisoner patients amble on set. Some giving me the once-over with the George Raft routine. Robbie arrives at 0900. Are we still on for 0930? He seems unsure and will get back to me. So I do Rounds – to Bosnia. This done, return and do the kitchen – well, empty their bin. The "drinks list" on the wall catches my eye:

Rachel: Pint of water.
WD: Coffee, black, 2 sweeteners.
Philip: Coffee, no sugar, strong.
Sue: Tea, white, 1 sugar.
Dave: Tea, white, 3 sugars.
Robbie: "Magners."

1015: Back at the ranch and a gossip with Heston. We chat about young Jimmy and how working in Aldeburgh could make or break him. Heston rather sadly points out that young prisoners "don't give a monkey's and just want an easy ride." I point out that, in essence, is what brought me here and I should have known better. I'm ashamed that it's taken a stay in prison to teach me this lesson. Heston encourages me to go further...

I was too insecure to be what is me and had to make myself more attractive and successful. Purely to be loved. I have learnt in prison I do not need to do that. I hope I retain what I have learnt. He suggests as a constant reminder "getting a swallow tattoo" on my hand, between the first finger and thumb – that seems so popular amongst our population.

Ah, the Bic biro prison tattoo parlour, I say.

He enlightens me of the way of manufacturing tattoo ink as utilised at HMP Belmarsh. Prisoners would steal the rubbery plastic bungs that can be found underneath a bog (sorry) standard lavatory seat and then melt them on glass with a cigarette lighter. "The carbon residue would then be chopped up with an ID card and ink was the end product."

1125: A message from the office: Robbie will see me at 1400.

1135: Young Rupert is being shipped-out (of the entire jail) on Wednesday. "A relative of the victim works at the prison." Rupert shocks me that he "wanted to jump across the table" and "bite the ears off the Deputy Governor" on being told of his marching orders. It's sad to hear his news, but sadder still to hear his reaction. Rod was right about the "vicious wire."

Five of today's agents' letters mail-drop put in the post box. There are seven remaining. I will do those tonight. Ten remain to escape tomorrow.

1200: I have written to the literary agents that this book contains irony. Ironic that this morning I got told that I am "staying on Hoxon." I have just been told I am moving Unit. To Wilford. I have said I do not feel comfortable and want to speak to a Governor. The officer seemed puzzled that I hadn't been told over the weekend.

My heart is in free fall.

1220: Called back to the office. If I refuse to move I will be "put on adjudication with the Governor tomorrow." I have been told to have my kit packed by 1300, or face the consequences of being "shipped- out, in handcuffs, to closed conditions."

I bloody well rubbed the harbinger lamp this morning didn't I?

Repeated that I feel safe at Hoxon and that various other Units that I have visited on my Rounds contain occupants who are not terribly fond of the tall posh one. I question the officer to confirm that he understands I want to see a Governor for my *safety* and am I to understand that if I do insist on seeing him I will be put on adjudication?

"Yes."

Return to 48 to pack. Word quickly spreads that I am being ushered off the premises and my twin mattresses and chair are taken. All my stuff goes into three large HMP bags. Two that came with me from Bedford, although I only used one – and half of it at that – and one, supplied just now from the office for my duvet.

The TV aerial lead and pillow are handed in and my bags are put in the hallway. Stuart helps me. Limping Al sees me and asks if I'm OK.

Back in 48, by myself, I say goodbye to the room. Goodbye sea view and goodbye home.

A white transit arrives. Two other guys are moving. One to Stow, one to Bosnia (I suppose things could be worse).

We leave Hoxon. Shit Shit Shit.

Stow is stopped at to unload the first deportee. Then we arrive at Wilford. I deplane and leaving my bags outside, go into the office. The officer behind the desk makes me think I've barged onto the set of another remake of *The Ladykillers* – but with the *original* cast – as the vision before me is Arthur Mullard. A real wobbling wheezer Mr Bumble. I identify myself and at least he seems to know who I am. I relay that I have not eaten and that I have a Healthcare appointment at 1400. He rings Hoxon to find out why I have not had lunch and it's explained to him it's "all been a bit of a rush."

And some. Why is everything to date in my prison experience *so* disorganised?

The Mullard officer – who also sounds like him – sends me to Reception to pick up a meal. I know it will be one of the fish and chip efforts. It's not. It's a rice and spinach thing and rock solid.

Healthcare. – I can't face entering the set that is Wilford right now. Robbie and staff are sitting outside. Robbie, sensing all is not well – walks over.

He seems astonished that I have been threatened with adjudication for questioning my safety. As we talk, I drop the spinach and rice thing in the bin. A loud, unappetising thud acknowledges receipt of it. He suggests that we defer this afternoon's session and I give things time to settle. "Can we do it in the morning?" OK, I say and if I'm murdered in the night will he please remember this conversation? "I'll shout it from the rooftops." He "doesn't understand the complete de-stabilisation so close to Tag."

Wilford – and my new room. I am entombed in number 30. Recently vacated by someone who I gather, has departed in a rush by the look of things. There are mountains of spilt sugar and rubbish *everywhere*. And no chair.

And this is an *open* prison? The airlock utilised prior to re-entry to earth?

Someone is asked where I can find cleaning stuff and with all my possessions on the bed, I get busy. Very busy.

1445: All surfaces now wiped and the floor mopped. I start to unpack and take in room 30. The view from the window is the car park and the scaffold stairs to OMU. No sign of the hangman. Yet.

1515: A friendly hello from a chap opposite. This is Harry (Enfield). His door is open and the view past him is the closest I've seen to Groutie's suite-like abode from *Porridge*. He is wearing a dressing gown. Not quite the Mr Bridger smoking jacket from *The Italian Job* but very close. "Have you come from Hoxon?" After a gulped yes he tells me Hoxon is "gold five-star and this is silver two-star." The "youngsters on Wilford are ****ing idiots and very noisy." I ask him who the escape officer is on this Unit as I scan over his shoulder for candelabra.

1520: I *have* to go out for a while so venture to Zara (Top). She's in her office – thank heavens. Checking out this visit's top, a summary of the meeting with Judi is passed plus preparatory Probation phone calls. Her verdict: "Things are all in order." She will make some calls and can I "come back tomorrow at 1130." OK, I said, standing up trying not to look anywhere other than eye-level.

Healthcare. Rod is roving and he asks if I'm "alright about the move." I think my face answers his question. He tries to say some positive things. The staff are told of my Dale Farm eviction from Hoxon. All of them are very supportive and tell me I can "hang out in Healthcare" whenever I like. My drugs are not in. Benjamin tells me "they will be in tomorrow."

So that's what he does. He's the *chemist*!

1600: Return to my new room, on my new Unit, to write. Almost prefer Bedford to here.

1645: Downstairs bump into Andrew, who has heard I'm here. Gordon is soon at his side and they are both very welcoming. We get in the food line. A certain bunch of prisoners don't queue – they jump it and go straight to the front. I ask Gordon if anyone ever says or does anything. "No." I can't remember what I ate. They have grim news. "Nothing ever happens here." There is "never any coffee or butter on the wing." There are "no kick-offs" but Gordon warns me candidly "not to talk to anyone about the book." People here, he says, "are very clicky."

As we eat my eyes wander. If the interior of Hoxon was a 1970's vintage Spanish hotel, the inside of Wilford could match the interior of a 1960's new-town working-men's club. After a three week sit-in protest by coal miners – in their work kit – such is the filth and mess everywhere. Some faces I recognise as either ex-Hoxon or as customers from Healthcare. Someone I spoke to there comes over and says hello. A start. I tell him I'm sorry – I can't remember his name.

"Rod."

The penny drops. This is the Woody Harrelson Rod who on early days at Healthcare told me of his shock of what the youngsters get away with in prison…

1800: On Andrew's advice, I reposition a lone chair from outside the showers to my room. The corridor is dominated with a mass of different, very loud music – if you can call it that. This is going to be hard work.

Everyone has been asking – why did they move me? All seem flummoxed.

1900: Reconnoitre with Gordon and Andrew. They instruct me to get as much coffee and stuff over from Hoxon as I can. "None of which appear on Wilford." Post pool, trek to the office to ask for some butter. Officer: "There isn't any." Talk to (Wilford) Rod in the dining area and ask him what the score is. "As soon as anything arrives, it gets pinched."

Wilford is a desert island within the desert island that is Hollesley Bay. And I'm in it.

Tuesday, October 11th, 2011.

Noise wise last night, it would have been simpler bedding down during a rock concert. The "officers" did nothing about it. An example of what I'm surrounded by: In the dining room there is a sign saying don't do this or don't do that – whatever it is. It ends with "No acceptions" (Sic). Abeam this signal there was butter but no bread – so went to the office. Roll-check is done here by visiting the white-shirts and singing out your room number. Once "three zero" had been voiced the lack of bread was raised. Like an apologetic estate agent who can't get a door to unlock in an unfamiliar property, the officer went rummaging in some back-stage area and produced a loaf of white.

0800: Geordie encountered on my walk to work. I don't know how I look at the moment but everyone keeps asking "are you OK?" Snippets of the soap-opera that is my new home are previewed and a message for Hoxon's Heston relaying what a sterling job he does is passed. Belmarsh Rod joins the scene – same conversation. He advises me "to put in an app (!) to move back."

Healthcare. Philip is tending to limping Al who asks "why did they move you?" Then: "There are still four empty rooms on Hoxon."

0830: Mopping. I feel more at home on Healthcare than I do at Wilford. Renee the dentist's assistant arrives. "Good morning, Jonathan." Nice to hear my name.

0845: Elk showing three newbies around. "Morning Captain" – I pang for halcyon Hoxon.

0900: Robbie arrives. "Are You OK?"

He concludes poignantly: So close to Tag and the carpet has been whipped from below me. He remarks that I have been "no trouble" and voices that the "youth club atmosphere at Wilford is not correct" for me. Furthermore he announces very regretfully that any progress with him is "now out of the window." He is "astonished" by the threat of "do it, or handcuffs," saying it was "out of order." The "threat of adjudication" if I demanded to see a Governor: "Even more out of order." He says leave it with him and he'll make some calls.

Rounds. At Stow, the Terminator on duty. "Are you OK?" Alert him of my new address. He seems shocked. He offers me a room on Stow "but sharing." I say thanks but no thanks. I want to try to get back to Hoxon.

I tell him off the record that he is needed at Wilford. He gives me a knowing look...

Wilford. Leapt on by WTWFO, the female officer. She needs to see me "further to my talk with Robbie." I realise that Robbie has spoken to someone in a very white shirt who has delegated talking to me to a less white-shirt. She is told that my head is spinning and I'll come back to her.

I now have a coffee supply in my room. Gordon and Andrew have advised me to "larder items when they appear." I feel lowly to do this. I don't want to play these bloody silly games. Why can't it be like Hoxon and civilised?

Healthcare. Converse with Robbie and inform him I have been jumped on by WTWFO who has said she wants words. He replies that "the buck has been passed but run with it."

1130: Leave the haven of Healthcare for Zara (Top). "No news" – please can I come back this afternoon?

Wilford. Lunch with Gordon and Andrew. The dining room now full of loads of loaves of bread. Andrew tells me to take one and some butter to my room. I sit debating whether I should really play this game but survival kicks-in and there is now a loaf of bread in my wardrobe and some butter packs in my fridge – the windowsill.

Number 30. The "Youth club" in full swing. Various CD machines playing different tracks, all at different volume, from a multitude of different rooms. All of which have their doors open. One youngster is sitting outside his abode eating his lunch off an ironing board.

1250: Tannoy: "Mr Robinson to the office please." WTWFO explains that officer someone-or-other has asked her to get to the bottom of my problems further to a call received from Robbie, saying I am distressed. I go through the whole story. She listens to everything and lets slip that the staff refer to me as the "posh pilot." I have been called worse. She "will be in touch."

1330: Healthcare. Philip, bless him, wants an update. The latest revealed, he looks mystified. As we speak we are surrounded by chaos in the building. New management are in evidence plus a new dentist, a female, wearing VERY high heels. Philip and I ask Renee if that's the new dentist. Renee: "Yes." Philip and author (in unison): I have toothache. Renee laughs before saying "idiots."

Rachel tasks me with "finding the Handymen team" to remove all the notice boards on the walls "so they can be painted."

On my walk Rod is spotted. Boy, am I pleased to see you. "How are things?" I summarise: Savages, filth, noise, animals, no discipline, awful and worse than Bedford. Rod: "Stay in your room. Write your book.

Ignore them. Do your best to get moved." As I fill him in on the latest inroads of attempting such a repositioning, a police car slows on the public carriageway and has a look at us. A real *Z Cars* number. Rod chuckles and tells me his first instinct was to grab me and hide in the bushes as he "forgot where we were…"

Handymen HQ. Inside are found three very disinterested tea drinking prisoners (The Three Stooges) – one of whom is Geordie – who only perk up when they realise my request comes from Rachel. As an added bonus the new dentist – and her shoes – are articulated. "We'll be there in ten minutes."

1410: Healthcare. Relay to Robbie the meeting with WTWFO. He asks me to keep him advised and makes an appointment for Friday with me.

1415: Handymen team turn up. All complaining of toothache.

1435: Zara (Top). "Still no news, but no panic – please come back on Monday."

1444: Adjacent to my room is a two man berth with the Christian Bale mirror guy from Hoxon who likes saying "sweet." His roommate is another Hoxon expatriate (Brendan Fraser). He's from Leiston – down the road – but lived in Aldeburgh till he was four.

1530: Snoring Killer is here. On the other side of the Unit – thank God.

1531: Called to the office. Within which two senior officers slumber. I am invited to sit down. One, a top chappie – from the main hub "production office" – sits the other side of the desk and the other – the holder of some nebulous title – sits by the wall looking disinterested and elides me. They vaguely introduce themselves and all the facts are gone through again. The Governor request/adjudication/handcuff saga is sort-of apologised for after I voice my incredulity of events. The officer doing the talking is very careful to point out he wasn't there and thus my story cannot be substantiated. I am told my corridor will be monitored. A start I suppose, but this is the sabotaging kibosh on any move back to Hoxon.

1550: Plot with Robbie who says "sleep on it" and report back to him in the morning. Finally get the Selenium drugs for my hand.

1635: A knock on the door. Tony, the Anthony Hopkins, circa *Magic* gym Orderly, who is the "Elk" of Wilford, comes in to say hello. He has heard some of the details and is sorry that it "has been a ****ing mess so far."

Following dinner an order for the *Sunday Times* for the remainder of my weekends at the Bay is made to keep my sanity.

1855: Snoring Killer has kept the brotherhood of prisoners rolling by giving me three tomatoes.

Wednesday, October 12th, 2011.

"If you're going through hell – keep going," said Churchill. We got married in a room named after Winston. God I hope you-know-who reads this.

0600: I am in case you hadn't gathered, surrounded by noisy louts. The symphony of yelling makes the Window Warriors of Bedford sound like sophomores. The what-sounded-like-a-riot eventually stopped at about 2330, with absolutely no attempt by staff to stop it. A complete 180° from Hoxon. The chamber music of Wilford seems to be bedlam.

0715: Downstairs, asked an officer for more coffee – got it. Half of it is now in my room. I also received my *weekly* loo roll (singular).

People here seem to stay in bed much later than Hoxon. It's 0726 now and all is very quiet.

0745: Healthcare. Today is "redundancy D day." Reading between the lines, Philip and Dave appear safe. WD, Sue and the hurler of rucksacks are on thin ice. Our interior is being blitzed by painters and removal men. In the ensuing carnage, I empty the bins.

Dave comes out with what pretty much sums up the running of what I have seen so far in the management of Her Majesty's prisons by remarking that he's had to "give a health certificate to a prisoner to go off-site to paint – yet contractors are coming inside to paint…"

0845: Reading my book upstairs. I confess to Philip that I feel guilty doing nothing. "Sit there and read!" Our current student nurse asks how things are and tells me that I'm "not like the rest" and I'll "get through it."

I *know* I'm not like the rest and I know that I *should* have known better. *What* a tit I am.

At 0900 most probably the *strangest* things happened to me to date in my time in prison. I defy any prisoner to admit to being asked what I was asked, whilst "working for Her Majesty," open conditions prison or not…

Renee appeared from the kitchen in her nurse's outfit. I don't argue that the scene resembled some very third rate outline for some dodgy film with me being a prisoner sitting there and she *certainly* didn't help the cause of ceasing what was to rapidly unfold as a skit from the *Benny Hill Show* by muttering "Jonathan, help me." I didn't get out of my chair, I didn't have time to. She was already right next to me – and whirled a semi-pirouette. Her back to me, the problem became apparent. And that wasn't all that appeared. Her zip was stuck scintillatingly close to knicker level and I was confronted by my first bra strap for what felt like an awful long time.

I straight away got to grips with the situation.

As the zip went up and I bade farewell to the bra, I asked Renee if there was a hook and eye at the top. "No, but thank you. I didn't know what to do."

Renee, any time.

Anyone else done that in prison? I thought not.

Later on the soft-porn set it was manic. A mass throwing out of stuff for the painters' invasion. The "waste team" turned up to take away some old filing cabinets. I longed for a bit of cake to put in one to quote that fabulous Fletcher line: "First time in prison that a file has been found with cake in it."

Wilford: A reply from one of the agents. "Thanks – but no thanks." A nice letter. Told me to "write to other agents" (!) as "there is nothing stopping me writing to more than one agent at a time." Considering I've probably put half of the county of Suffolk's postmen's backs out with the amount of mail sent out about this blessed book, this tickled me.

I have written to *every* agent. All with the same letter.

Healthcare: In my notes it says: Move. File. Vacuum. Shred. Stairs. Heavy. Bags. In short: mayhem. Julian arrived for a "fit for Home-leave" certificate and asked me if Wilford is as bad as he's heard. He took on board my review (he especially liked the weekly loo roll bit) and formulated a plan. He will meet me outside Wilford this evening, between 1720 and 1740 with a "Red Cross parcel" of goodies liberated from Hoxon.

Rounds. More social respite came in the shape of bumping into L.A. and Stuart. They too have picked up my Mayday and will get a Red Cross parcel sorted. Thanking them, I Told them that the very least I expect is a hamper from Fortnum and Mason.

L.A. said he "is gutted" for me.

1115: Wilford. Strangely, more post and another letter from an agent saying "send it in." I also received a memo to attend a "worldwide volunteering seminar" on October 19th.

Lunched with Gordon and Andrew. Afterwards I put my pudding on the windowsill in my room. To defrost. This just before being jumped on by one half of the senior management of yesterday's interview who "wants a word." Back into the office we went. He asked if I'm OK and if I have "settled in." I was compelled to ask if I could talk frankly. He nodded.

And looked apprehensive.

The meat of my comments were factorised so: There is no discipline on Wilford, the prisoners rampage-rule the Unit, all the doors are open on B corridor well past 2200 playing loud music. There is no food available in the servery, the filth, one can't walk from A to B in the lurid dining area without stepping in something, no cleaning appears to take place, plagues of dirty plates are everywhere, the showers are filthy, the loos not cleaned and on the exigency went... I put it straight to him by asking why don't we have a cleaning rota, like on Hoxon?

His answer: "The Home secretary has taken away his rights to make us do stuff." The cleaning "only happens on Hoxon because people want to stay there." He nondescriptly admitted that "Wilford is the dirtiest Unit on site." His lacklustre solution – voiced with perverse virtuoso:

"Grin and bear it."

Lord I hope that one day someone with some clout reads this book. Please: *Get prisoners working*. I thanked him for listening to me and left – being careful not to step in any spilt food.

1305: Rounds. Medical mail plus the dropping off of an old fluorescent light tube at the waste area. This thing was nearly seven feet long and as I walked, looking like a Luke Skywalker reject with a faulty light sabre, I came across Darth Vader in the shape of EBV. "Where you been?" Described to him the dark-side that is Wilford and advised him to under no circumstances move there or he'll commit murder with or without use of the Force. His riposte – with a Death Star stare: "Fuckin' 'ell."

I don't recall Darth Vader using that terminology.

Healthcare. Yet more letters for Rounds. As I walked past Wilford for the umpteenth time, the dining room floor was being mopped. The senior officer who I had "spoken frankly to" stood and supervised...

Round the next corner was Mathew. He warned me to "be careful and not to talk about the book to anyone on Wilford," then asked me to investigate what the deal was on smokers' patches. I set off for Hoxon – the first time as a non-resident. On arrival the officer said "I don't know why they moved you."

Healthcare. Prodded Dave about Mathew and smokers' patches. He suggested I went to get the patient "to sort this now." As I left Healthcare *again*, Philip was asked if there was any news on the promised emails about their future roles at HMP Hollesley Bay.

"No."

Bricks. Rod busy being Hadrian again and said in *true* Jason Statham style that if I needed him to "have any words" with anyone on Wilford to let him know. Located Mathew in the middle of some mortar and announced that Dave would see him now so off to Healthcare we trod. Left the wannabe ex-smoker in Dave's capable hands and returned to woeful Wilford at 1520.

1700: Dinner with Gordon and Andrew again and an "IPP" guy (Chiwetel Ejiofor). "IPP" means some serious crime was committed and an "open" tariff was passed down. A form of sentencing now discontinued I understand.

1720: Like some Cold War spy film I'm stood under a tree waiting for Julian and supplies in the pouring rain. He arrives at my Checkpoint Charlie bang on time.

1800: There can't be any supplies left on Hoxon. They are now all on my bed.

Thursday, October 13th, 2011.

Overnight this production's Foley Artists' ambient sound effects caustically created continued calamitous continuity.

It has dawned on me that the Peter Sellers NGBTYCATAWYHDTS type should be called NGBTYCADOWYHDTS because he says "dwell," not "think" but I will stick to the original acronym so as not to confuse the reader. The author is already way past it.

0715: Work. Neither Philip nor Dave have heard anything of their future employment and are "technically out of work." Philip explains they are "not insured without a contract." Dave tells me he is fed up with the whole situation. "This place is falling apart," he despondently declares bereft of all hope.

1030: Unit. The officers' door was locked so loitered downstairs as unable to retrieve my key. Read the minutes of a prisoners' forum from 2010: *"Mr (prisoner) has asked Mr (senior officer) about the poor hygiene standards and excessive noise on Wilford."*

1200: To Hoxon to pick up Canteen, where I am now an alien. Get served by Neil as part of his vans job. I return to behind enemy lines with my cigarettes. On repatriation lunch is over but an officer tells me to go to the side door of the servery where my meal is waiting. Find a plate on a shelf with a bit of pizza on it.

Dine al fresco by myself on *the* bench. Pizza revolting.

I have mail. From one of the agents...

She starts off with "sorry to hear about the food. So near and yet so far from the Butley Orford Oysterage." So a good sense of humour. I shall write back and send in my "MS" when I'm out. "MS" is writer-speak for manuscript. I'm learning. Although I confess I did have to look it up in the *Writer's and Artist's Yearbook*. I thought it might be something to do with Michael Schumacher.

Coffee on my bench. Before long I will be talking to it like Pauline Collins spoke to her kitchen wall then her rock whilst on her holiday in *Shirley Valentine*.

My wife used to refer to holidays as "holibops." *Christ* I miss her.

Library. Read the papers, including the *Daily Mail* and show Stuart the hidden wife picture that Mac the cartoonist normally includes in his work. You-know-who and I would always race each other to find it. Thing is, the money I had used to buy the paper in the first place wasn't mine. Live with it Robinson.

1320: Work. A visit from Rod who says he's just passing but I know he's checking up on me. His orders: "Sit in your room and make the book better." He then adds "come and see me at Bricks any time and we'll have a cup of tea." Thanks Hadrian. Dave is asked if any emails have been forthcoming. "No." He has "left a voicemail on the area manager's phone," and given him a piece of his mind. So too I gather, has Rachel.

The area manager is *dead* lucky that WD is not in today…

Not much for me to do – around the hectic goings on of the painters – so retreat outside with Geordie and the rest of the Handymen team – one of whom looks just like Stratford Johns, who I think played Abel Magwitch somewhere along the line. They are aware that I am struggling at Wilford and protectively place me in the centre of our makeshift quincunx firing-off support and terrible jokes. They point out it will soon be over and I "don't really belong here." I correct them and say I *fully* deserve to be here. But they persist. I'm clearly "not a professional criminal" like they are. I admit that no one has yet taught me how to crack a safe.

Dead silence.

One perks up. They "don't want to turn me," but he does enliven me on how to get past a certain type of lock. And no, I'm not going to give the game away – you'll have to use your imagination. Or go to prison.

(Please do the former not the latter).

1415: Rounds. The state of the fish on Cosford a disgrace. Suggest to the officer that he gets in touch with Rick the Fish.

1500: An appointment in a cubby-hole backstage of Zara (Top's) office. This lady (Yootha Joyce) is unaware of my Tag date (worrying). She gives me some paperwork to fill in by Thursday of next week.

NGBTYCATAWYHDTS is spotted on the return leg. All he seems to do is forage about the prison always dressed in a short sleeve shirt. Does anyone know who he is?

1645: Managed to peel off the un-franked first class stamp from the envelope of the oyster-lover literary agent. A good omen? Or a bad one for stealing again?

After dinner there was a mad Wilford tsunami-like rush for Canteen. Deliveries here are much later than Hoxon. Another disadvantage. A deal was then closed with the Unit barber, Scotty (Eminem). My hair is shaggy enough to cut now and the rest of my sentence is also long enough for it to grow back if it's another disaster. (Sorry Dennis).

As I write with the door open – in attempt to get some breeze through here – I hear snippets of "Wilford conversation":

"No, I pay someone to do my washing and ironing."
"How much?"
"A score a week." (Me: How much is a score?)
"A week?!!!"
"Yeah."
"Hang on." [Knock on another door] "Oy_____, you know how you're a bit hard up – well this geezer wants his washing and ironing done every week and he'll pay a score."
[Noise of door opening rapidly].
"A score a week?"
"Yeah."
"Twenty quid?" (Me: That's how much a score is then.)
"Yeah."
"When you need your washing done, put it in a bag and give it to me."

End of business transaction.

Friday, October 14th, 2011.

0745: Tannoy: "Roll-check reminder."

Everyone is still in bed...

0750: Working around the painters the floors are mopped. On the return to Wilford it's not difficult to notice a prisoner standing outside on the upper terrace (the fire escape) eating his breakfast nonchalantly from his royal balcony watching the world go by like some scene from *The Lion King* such is the rampant attitude displayed. The Lording-it effect added to by the fact that he is wearing his dressing gown.

How does one spell Wilford? There are two signs outside: one saying Wilford, the other Wilforde. Various official paperwork also utilise both spellings. Ah, prison.

1200: "Break pads" for lunch. In a bun. There is now a new loaf in my bread bin. The wardrobe.

1530: Wilford, following a 40 minute chat with Robbie about my "futile move." His words, not mine. He informed me that he "had spoken to the handcuffs threat officer pre-move," on the phone. This individual "did not deny saying it," but balked at discussing it further.

The sun-belt in the garden of Wilford withered so positioned myself around the corner – tea in hand – near Reception. A female officer approached me... "Mr Robinson, you look most peculiar standing there." I expatiated that the sun was long past the yard-arm at home which she shrugged off. I asked her how she knew who I was. "I'm the head of security. I know everyone's names."

In the mealtime queue an individual who is always to be seen Blitzkrieg sweeping the main gate area (no name) grinned and told me that he saw my "bollocking for standing outside" with my cup of tea. I confided in my confidant that she knew my name. "You are obviously on radar then," he said with the *most* quintessential professional prisoner voices.

Well, it's nice to be popular.

After Dinner the corridor is enveloped in pure noise. Music, shouting, yells and smells. I decide to hell with it and make myself a cup of coffee and escape outside to the exercise field.

It's cold out here so warm my hands on my cup. Lennox and Brad Pitt are amongst the different clans of talking, walking, sitting, standing, moaning prisoners. They paw at each other like young cubs. The "Hands down front of trousers" mob congregate. NGBTYCATAWYHDTS walks brusquely – solo – in short sleeves. Gordon and Andrew walk together, eating choc-ices. They look like two ladies on Brighton Promenade. Stuart spots me and through sign language invites me to walk with him and his gang. I show him my cup of coffee. I think he knows I'm just here to take it all in.

Saturday, October 15th, 2011.

Is this book flippant? Does it come over that way? It does not mean to do so. I screwed up. I lost everything. I'm sorry. To the people I let down and hurt. To everyone. This book is all I have. What started as quite possibly escapism from the shock to my system is now a serious attempt to flag the shock that *is* the system.

0900: Outside sounds like Brands Hatch. Sure enough, a wide shot reveals a starting grid of prisoners in their cars, waiting to leave on "self-drive" Home-leave. Some are "flash" motors. Some are "clunkers."

Some are commercial vehicles.

One is a Security Services vehicle. The occupant, poacher turned gamekeeper...

Library. Find the usual sleepy L.A. on the bridge backed up by both Stuart and Library Brett running the ship. I read the paper then trudge to Healthcare. On entry am knocked sideways by very strong smells of fresh paint. No one aboard the Marie Celeste. Tap on the Treatment room door. No reply. Well, I tried.

Wilford. Two letters greet me. One with a 2nd class stamp (a Christmas one!) which is unfranked, on a business envelope. That'll be an agent then. The other looks like a prison envelope. It is. It's from Teevee and (unadjusted) reads as follows...

How you doing mate, sorry it's taken time to write back, I'm back at Ranby now, same pad same wing, got there in the end. I'm back on my course which starts tomorrow, industial cleaning so business as usual LOL. My Cat D review in a few weeks so I'l see how I get on, I've also applied for rotal which is simmuler, it means I can stay here and work outside and also intiles me for home-leave and garnaties me tag so fingars and toes crossed, other than that I'm good and times going fast.

I'm glad you'l liking Cat D and staying positive, what ever dos'nt kill us only makes us stronger, innit mate. Before you know it it'll be time to go home and you can leave prison behind you, it's just another story for the book or the lads LOL.

Alrite mate, I'm gonna get off now

Take care, keep in touch
And keep your head up

Your friend TEEVEE

P.S. They can lock the locks, but they cant stop the clocks, tick tock, tick tock, tick tock.

The other letter is an agent's reply. The meat of the matter: "I'd be happy to look at opening chapters… send outline… many prison memoirs published, including Jeffrey's… yours will need to be different and distinctive if it is to stand a chance… harshest publishing climate in 40 years… give it a go. What can you lose?"

The underlining is mine.

1145: Chris Moyles is outside delivering lunch. The telly's on with a new British Airways advert: "To fly to serve." I lie awake in bed most nights wondering if once I've served will I be allowed to fly.

Whilst queuing for lunch I found myself standing next to a gentleman who I nearly knocked over earlier in the week by opening a door as he tried to come the other way. To date the only thing he has said to me is "fucking hell." I enquired how his hand is, that being the limb I got him with. He smiled and asked "how long were you on Hoxon then?" I tell all. This is Clive (Billy Ocean) and he's done 14 years and is affable. And a musician – he "plays the sax." He works in the kitchen and "practices anywhere that he can."

During lunch a Governor did a fair amount of poking-around. As he went about with a senior officer pointing at one pile of mess after another, he looked most unhappy. The S.O. looked plain uncomfortable.

After lunch I locked myself out of my room. The officer who was asked for assistance looked unimpressed when I announced my plight. His declaration: "Fucking hell."

1300: A Jet Ranger (type of helicopter) just flew over. Someone gloating? I've written back to Teevee and also penned a note to Ben who has gone quiet on me.

Such a beautiful day induces me go and sit in our "garden." The inverted commas because... well, you should see it.

I don't mean that, please *don't* come and see it.

Library Brett is sitting on "my" bench. As I near I wonder if he is asleep. Like a dog by the fire, an eye opens to see who is invading his space. "Oh, it's you."

He is an alumnus of HMP Bedford. A week in, then out, then back for two weeks, then out. Why? "Broke bail conditions." His next parole board – "failed two already" – is next summer. He is very bitter and tells me of the vast amounts of vodka he would get through – but he's "fixed it now." Stupid he is not. Just very, very angry. If the lead from *Look Back in Anger* ever went to jail, I am conversing with him now. I steer him back to his Bedford days. He broke bail conditions by texting an ex-girlfriend the first time. The second recall was for putting a birthday card through her letter box. These "breaks of bail" may sound harsh if it wasn't for the original crime.

He had set alight to her house. Whilst she was in it.

As Brett and I chase the sun around the garden, two prisoners come outside. One is the gentleman who breakfasts flouting in his dressing gown – on his "balcony." He's in his dressing gown now. Wilford's version of "AP." This duo carry a chess-board. Library Brett and I witness "Dressing Gown" ("AP2") move a chair to sit opposite his opponent. However something is not right with the chosen furniture and it is flagrantly hurled away. AP2 picks another one more to his taste. The chess game starts. The upturned flotsam chair floats alongside with *nothing* other than gross effrontery.

1600: The chess game is over. Its players departed. Two chairs still sit opposite each other. It's the set of some Pinter play before the actors come on stage. The abeam upturned chair remains capsized consummately spotlighting my gaze.

1604: Upturned chair now the right way up. How do some people make it to Cat D prisons?

1700: Dinner. Don't ask. *Back to the Future* is on telly. I will at last be able to find out what the name of the baddie is to finally close the chapter on who I thought Barclay, of B wing at Bedford – the cage fighter – reminded me of.

1730: Biff!

1745: Buzz has his flight test booked this week. A very odd feeling – one of "mine" in the hands of someone else, somewhere else. But I am somewhere else. And locked up. We've agreed to reconvene – on the phone – on Sunday evening to go over some things he's going to need to brush-up on.

Sunday, October 16th, 2011

Dave revealed first thing "that a very high amount of cases of upset stomachs are reported from Wilford." He "rang the Unit to make sure the banisters were regularly cleaned and spoke with an officer but didn't get anywhere." Many of my fellow guests muster around the microwave at night cooking food from Canteen. I don't ever see much hand washing going on as they gather around their kill like hungry jackals. Living here is like residing on some God forsaken street corner.

0720: Roll-check announced on the Tannoy.

0745: A final call for stragglers.

0750: A "final-final-call" for the remaining two. In desperation the voice asks – pleadingly – that someone knocks on their doors. I don't know why the officer doesn't take them tea and toast.

0841: Another race win for Seb. Red Bull Racing 2011 Constructor's Champions.

1005: Library. A sleepy L.A. says to me "we have your treats." They have been on the "scrounge." Stuart grins – they look like schoolboys who have raided an orchard.

1030: Number 30 and I open my bag. Noodles, crisps, Yogurt, ginger & lemon tea all equals kindness.

A conversation with one of the "twins" (Matt and Luke Goss of Bros) followed. I met one of this duo the day I arrived on the Unit not knowing then that we are blessed with a pair. It was one half who was asked where I could find a mop after initial inspection of room 30. Later that day I saw him and passed thanks for his help but received a blank stare back before (the other one) said "you must have talked to my brother." As days have passed I have seen them both together. It must be very strange being in this situation with a family member. Especially one who is identical in appearance. I ask him what that's like.

"It's okay – but I didn't do it – he did."

Sensing some vast plot for a huge miscarriage of justice – I dig for more information. "Me and me brother and me girlfriend woz walking in this park and this geezer slagged off me missus and attacked her. I does kick-boxing, innit. So I gets the geezer down and he stabs me so me brother gets to it an' puts 'im in a coma, innit." This all said like you or I would discuss a shopping list. What time of day? "Lunchtime." Ever seen this guy before? "Nah." Did you upset him or say something to him? "Nah. We got 5 years. Both out March, innit."

1155: Lunch and Roll-check both in the can. Literally.

1340: The Microwave club hard at it at full throttle. Many of that clan also seem to be in the Hands down front of trousers ("HDFOT") mob. Both parties are equally difficult to understand when they converse and seem most content to do so by yelling without constraint in an almost ship to shore fashion.

1410: Thursday's paperwork for Yootha done.

1430: Scotty and I have agreed on Thursday night for him to sheer my locks. I asked what he wants in payment (expecting him to say the dreaded tins of tuna) but he said "anything." I wonder if a mention in this book will suffice?

Only the author can settle down outside at 1450 as the sun disappears behind Wilford. A knock on the window upstairs tapped distraction from the shade and I could just make out Sweeper Man gesticulating to me. He made a "I'll come down to you" signal. A pleasant chap, always friendly. He's probably a lifer.

He is a lifer and he is Ray (Steven Berkoff). He tells some pretty horrific fables of his past supplied with exceptionally type-cast-to-the-hilt rough diamond dialogue. It transpires he's been "in" since Job was a lad but has now given up and wants to go home and be a grandfather to his children's offspring. He asks how I'm getting on and yet again the subject comes up as to why they moved me. Ray's theory is that I was shunted to be a "calming influence to some of the young idiots." He tells me that if "even if one changes then the system works."

He reveals "gang culture has been brewing on the Unit and they are trying to nip it in the bud." My views on this can be found in a well-known expression about bolting horses and stable doors. Bud? It's a huge – worthy of Kew Gardens – flowering-in-full-bloom rose bush.

Dinner. Sax Clive makes a guest appearance at our table. What prison has done for us is debated. Gordon: not a lot – he thinks what he did wasn't really illegal. "Naughty yes, but not bad." Andrew: It has given him the chance to do his "painter's qualifications." Clive: "The chance of doing a degree." Me: The discovery of me and I can be quite comfortable being... me. Clive – the most "sensible" person at the table turns to me and says "prison has worked for you then."

Now *there's* something to make you think.

1800: Buzz rung. His "skills test," the final grilling that makes the applicant a qualified pilot, "is booked for Friday." OK – although I'm in prison – let's see where my friend (first) and student (second) is on the preparation stakes.

Various technical questions are fired down the phone. Most are met with "no idea." Another broadside of salvo shot at him and the same response. Although I'm in jail, I tell him he's not ready for the test. Who's fault is that? Mine. A few more fairly basic questions are worded. He knows the bare bones but not much else.

This is all no one's fault but mine.

Buzz promises he will submerge himself in the books – and I will ring him on Wednesday. We will then decide whether it's a "go" or not.

What he needs is me. I'm still working for Her Majesty though. Ma'am – will you excuse me?

Monday, October 17th, 2011.

T (Tag) minus 31. Woke at 0720 having been up for an hour at about 0300 with a massive anxiety attack. It has carried over this morning. The reason? I would give anything in the world to talk, just *talk* to my wife.

0730: Dale Farm on the news. *Again.*

0810: On the commute Andrew's story recounted yesterday over dinner rolled around my head. He's in a similar boat to me. A new (second) wife who has also been married before. "Her previous husband wealthy and successful." Andrew says he got concerned when he heard stories about things her previous spouse had been able to afford for her. Feeling inadequate, he helped himself to company money to boost his wife's estimation of him. The inevitable happened. His sentence is much longer than mine. His wife stuck by him though. The irony? His wife said to him "it wouldn't have mattered if you'd just been *you*."

Mine said exactly the same to me.

At work Dave mulled. Same old Dave – always on the verge of holding his hands up and giving up – but never does. The promised emails have arrived. He, Philip and WD are staying. "The rest are being made redundant by the new management." Get an appointment out of Rachel to see Robbie at 1000 on Tuesday. Let's see if we can get this back on track.

Wilford. Do I or don't I write my wife a letter? Or is this one long letter? Someone give me a sign.

0955: Stuart thanked for the rations on my walk to Nacro. Entering the office complex an Orderly, some staff, one officer (who looks about 10) and Zara (Top) are within. I loiter. Zara spots me and waves me over. She's made some calls and wants me back tomorrow. "Will 1500 be OK?" She gives me an A4 envelope for Yootha's paperwork and I make my exit.

Venture to Victoria's empire – two doors down. No one home – not even the Orderly. I'm sure our Empress said she was back this Monday.

1010: Unit. My brain tells me not to write to my wife. Let this book suffice. Love will conquer all. Think positive thoughts.

1200: Lunch. IMB on site. "French stick with cheese" and salad. But no French sticks. Cheese salad then. Chocolate bars are being given out as pudding with a very near sell-by date.

1240: Tony – Wilford's Elk – is standing on the top tier of the dress circle (smoking a cigarette!) evaluating Emperor penguin like the ecology of the dining area. I inquire if he's keeping an eye on the "youth club." With fag in mouth he says "yes, and it *is* a fucking youth club."

Infiltrate the library. L.A. harbouring at his post and is thanked for my supplies. He as usual, looks washed up but is still clinging to the wreckage. I read the paper. HMP Hollesley Bay's Head of Education comes in showing a new member of staff around. He sees me, blanches and departs.

Tramp to Victoria's office. Still, as the theatre industry refers to a closed establishment; "dark." Zara's office is diverted to and asked if anyone has news on our impresario. The word is that she is supposed to be back today but no one knows where she is.

1329: To Healthcare for work.

1330: Leave Healthcare. No work required. Return to worrying Wilford to write.

Backtrack to Healthcare in case there's something to be done. Rick the Fish netted. Did he get the message about Cosford's fish? "Yes" – but can I get Cosford staff to ring Hoxon staff – because initiative is not permitted in prison.

1600: Scotty sources me. Can we change Thursday night's haircut to Wednesday?

1645: *The Four Feathers* (original) on Film 4. I think my late father's favourite film. He must be turning in his grave about me.

Tuesday, October 18th, 2011.

T minus 30. More torture last night. On top of the *unbelievable* noise, every TV channel either had a program "we" used to watch or a film we had seen. I am getting close to completing a thorough search of my room with the certainty I shall find hidden cameras. Why doesn't the system go the whole hog and send me a photo of her having dinner with some guy?

0615: Attempted to Roll-check myself (to a different officer than normal) but I was "too early."

0705: I can see WD's very shiny car. Scenes of Panzer tanks rumbling across battlefields near Arnhem flash through my mind.

0725: The dining area full of rubbish. Chicken carcasses from dinner last night are on the *window sill*. Other remnants of food from the Militia Microwave club masterly make up the scenery. By the toaster a prisoner blows his nose next to me. He has no hankie. He uses his hand.

0730: In my room eating. Trying not to cry. Roll-check announced.

0733: Attend Roll-check. The "officer" clad in jeans.

0745: Tannoy: "Roll-check last call."

0755: Tannoy: Names of the stragglers read out.

0815: A two-hander with Library Brett. I think he detects my mood. "Jon, despite this place being run by idiots for idiots at least we can go outside whenever we want." A very timely reminder and I suppose a good kick up the arse. All jails, he says, "are the same." He concludes with "you don't know how lucky you are."

Work. WD furious that Sue got redundancy and she didn't. She wants out.

Rachel is hinted at that people are making noises about taking over my job when I go – would she like a referral for anybody sensible? "No. They may be sweetness and light with you but we might know something about them that they have not told you." Clean upstairs and go home.

0950: On the path to Robbie. NGBTYCATAWYHDTS appears. Still in short sleeves, he spots me and pretends to talk into a radio. "The suspect is heading towards you," he says to his "control." I grin.

1000: An episode of *Cracker*. He asks how I'm getting on. I describe the disturbed sleep, the bits of chicken this morning, the guy blowing his nose in his hand and Brett's timely reminder. Every time I find myself either laughing or feeling sorry for myself I remind myself why I'm here and think of all the people I've hurt or let down or disappointed or all of the above. I am awash with guilt. My conscience is eating away at me like a canker. Robbie responds he "wants to take my head off" and let my "body walk about for a few days to have a rest." He thinks I'm "black and blue inside."

I relay to him that I do not want to go anywhere near my old feelings of needing to impress people – with stolen money – again and that prison has been good for me in that baked beans and the real Jonathan are better than a "fancy" place and the fake meretricious Jonathan any time. He remarks that "it is clear" I have been "doing some serious thinking." I describe Dennis' very profound observation that my sentence is in my head. He grunts approval and agreement. I add – they could have locked me up in the Ritz and I'd still be wringing myself out internally.

My initial fears of being told I was going to prison are rallied. Being "tall and posh" would make me a marked man. But it never happened. There is no class-conflict here – it's just: Get on with it. I compare trench warfare solidarity with prison life.

Future prospects are covered. I hope the CAA will let me fly again. He digs at what I think the likelihood of that is. My bones say it will be OK. The helicopter industry is very small and I'm sure that the bush-telegraph has been busy. I've got to hold my hands up, admit to being a tit and try to show that I mean business.

He engages matters matrimonial. "Has there been any contact?" I've written letters, emails, spoken to her best friend but got nowhere other than barge-poles. "A classic defence mechanism," cords Cracker. The last time I called, her mum answered, but when she heard my voice she put the phone down. I dilate that Dennis said he would email her explaining where my mind is. Still not a sausage though. I would give anything, I tell him, to have her sit in that empty chair and talk to her. I love her and I'm sorry. I promised her before we married that I'd never leave her. Ever. I'd always fight. "Maybe she finds it tough to have any association with someone who is now associated with HMP." I know. But if the roles were reversed I'd be camping in a tent in that field over there.

He is thoughtful for a bit. He voices that he wants me to relax more and "to stop punishing myself." Homework is set for me. I am to make a mental list of the "best case scenario."

It is tough trying to remember everything after the event. Oh, he did say that within prison "mental healthcare is still looked at by the powers that be as Victorian."

I seriously considered asking Robbie to get in touch with my wife. I didn't though. Wednesdays at 1000 have been diarised for future confabs.

1150: Lunch queue. Overheard from the HDFOT brigade: "You eatin' that food? It's shit blood." (Translation: lunch is not looking terribly nice old chap.) One of his fellow club members, nodding in agreement asks for some food from his friend's private cache because he had already given him something. Response: "You never gave me nuttin."

Lunch: More of yesterday's job-lot of chocolate bars were dispensed.

1315: Library. I have taught Stuart the Mac cartoon game and he is very eager to race me. If this is the highlight of his day then he is in trouble. I find Mrs Mac (in the leaves of the trees) but he can't see the wood for the trees. Another paper is perused until he triumphantly shouts "got it!"

Victoria's office and her Orderly has a line: "I hear Wilford is a youth club." HRH materialises. She has "received everything and all is in order." She accedes to a further audience before I leave the Bay.

1335: Healthcare. No work for me. Robbie about and "is now away next week so can we re-start our program on November 2nd at 1000?" I leave work and return to Wilford as the man overboard.

1440: Off to Zara (Top). And *what* a top today.

All sorts of forms were filled in – although we can't sign it off till we get my National Insurance number – which I don't know. An appointment was made for me to see Yootha this Thursday, "who can look it up." Worryingly, we are "still waiting for something from Probation" (????) Zara rang Judi the Tag lady, who down the phone passed the message *do not panic*.

1600: Tea and toast with Margaret Rutherford. (*Blithe Spirit*)

1615: Healthcare. Julian back among the ranks. I passed enormous thanks for the Red Cross parcel and advised him that I will leave his bag – that is in my room – in the library tomorrow.

All this for some loo paper…

1700: Dinner. "Kebab." No comment. In the post dinner chaos we were mugged. I spied the servery staff surreptitiously taking a *sack* of oranges upstairs. Oh, this was in full view of the officer who was with us this morning – in jeans, and is still in them – and officer Blakey – so named because he reminds me of the same character in *On the Buses*.

Showing my age again.

Wednesday, October 19th, 2011.

T minus 29. On the news: Dale Farm "D day."

Like that witty comeback you think of after the event I woke remembering something else that Robbie touched on yesterday. When I was doing my persistent theft did I not think about the consequences? I told him I'd be a fool not to but I very cleverly managed to bottle it up and store it away so deep in my mind that It didn't bother me.

If I understand correctly, Robbie wants to utilise this skill in my mind management to some sort of positive thing. Oddly enough – in my job, where the wrong decision will be catastrophic – I've never had this problem. Therefore I must adjust my personal thought process and tandem it with my professional "check list." Like Archimedes leaping out of the bath, it has dawned on me this morning that if I can do this – it's failsafe.

0750: Work. WD on good form and being very nice to all the patients and conspicuously nice to me too. So nice that I ask her if she has either won the lottery or if it's her birthday. She even laughs. She's OK. Just blows hot and cold.

Whizzing around my mind is my earlier brainwave: Realigning personal decisions to my professional decision process. Why have I not thought of this before?

I am wearing my bright orange young offenders' sweatshirt – the same colour as the sun which is streaming through the windows. I sweep up with a broom with my mind still turning over. Robbie manifests and is asked for a quick word.

We walk away from the painters, but frankly, I am not bothered if people hear or not. He is questioned that once he's received the requested best case scenario list I presume a worst case itemisation will be called-for. He looks at me like I'm not as stupid as I look.

No one could be that stupid.

I go on. In my flying role, some important decisions face me including the call as to whether or not a student is ready to fly solo. This is no trivial thing. I'm pretty good at this in that the number of people who have gone up matches the quota that came down, *without* gravity in the driver's seat. Thus, why can't I make self-decisions using the work-ethos-process?

Robbie is "totally shocked that neither of us had thought of the usage of this template before." He remarks that when I called him – he had his back to the sun – I looked like a "form of fireball" with the "light blazing" at me in my bright orange shirt. He is "genuinely thrilled" that I have worked this out for myself. I still feel stupid that I know my past behaviour was not to be *bad*. I wanted to be loved. He says "everyone has that." Mine though, is "warp factor 10."

Right. If I can start a process where *every* single decision is made using the "shall I get out of this aircraft and let this guy go?" method, I might have a chance.

0905: Unit. A desperate pleading request on the Tannoy for the "people on the wing who have cleaning duties, to please, if they don't mind, get started on their cleaning."

No reaction whatsoever.

0920: A quick visit to Healthcare to make sure all well before my 1000 meeting. NGBTYCATAWYHDTS wanders – wearing a sweatshirt! It must be cold. He stops and we actually converse. He's from Canada – but has British teeth. Eight years done in his home country and one here. Born in the UK, hence the last lap here. How were Canadian jails?

"Much better. Initiative is widely encouraged. Inmates are given their own budget to buy food (outside but supervised), do their own cooking (inside and supervised) and there is much more onus on prisoners than appears here – even in open conditions." What's the reoffending percentage? "Much, much less."

Muster for the Worldwide Volunteering meeting with a most motley crew. Victoria hovers and introduces us to our hostess, Michelle (Obama) who, when we are all seated, goes through how helpful volunteering can be. Not so much slanted towards the good it will do for the end users but the volunteers themselves – they will "be able to get a reference after three month's work" – which can be "as little as one hour a week." Ten minutes into our presentation – one prisoner gets up and walks out... (Hollesley Bay a *resettlement* prison? Ha!) A few minutes after that, two members of the HDFOT brigade – one is Spitting man, shuffle in. No apology for being late. No interest. No... *anything*. At the end of the briefing our hostess says if any of us want to see her individually she will make an appointment.

Mine is at 1415.

1200: Lunch. The bustling barbaric HDFOT brigade jump the queue. I watch at the servery as they signal fellow members and get extra meals. All with an officer stood there only interested in ticking names.

1255: Library. Give Julian's bag to Stuart. L.A. on set. Tomorrow he has one week to go.

1320: Go to Healthcare to work.

1321: Return Wilford.

1415: The interview with Michelle. What did I "think of this morning?" The carrot of a good reference seemed to be a good hook for my colleagues but that I was staggered that here in a resettlement prison someone got up and walked out in the middle of her speech. She exclaimed that she had forgotten that and "will speak to Victoria." On behalf of my fellow morons, I apologised.

She asked how and why, I thought I could be of help. My full story followed, from beginning to end. If she has any use for a tall posh **** to help people stay out of prison – then I'm interested.

Michelle was amused by the book and surprised by J.A. writing to me. She was very sympathetic about the wife situation and asked if "there is any chance?" I told her I'm doing all I can and this book, as well as a journal of all events in clink is also possibly the world's longest love letter.

We chatted for so long that Victoria came in to make sure that all was well. Satisfied all was hunky-dory (Michelle could *talk*) she brought us both a cup of coffee. Michelle revealed that other prisoners have told her their life-story before and "some have even been in tears." I began to try to wrap things up as I didn't want her to think she'd have to get the Kleenex out. We got up to leave and continued chatting outside the door – so much so that she said "let's go back in again." Back in we went and continued the scene.

What's it like ringing up organisations saying that she works with ex-offenders? "The phone gets put down a lot." How am I "going to deal with that" and will I "tell everybody?" It's going to be difficult plugging a book about prison without admitting where I've been, I said and she laughed. The only way I can deal with this (on release) is to say: I made mistakes. I've been punished. I'm trying to do the right thing now – I can't do anymore. "Good for you," she encouragingly responded.

As I walked out of the building I got a stark reminder of where I am by noticing a sign by the door which read: "Please do not spit, other people use this area for tea breaks."

1700: Dinner. Pizza. HDFOT brigade playing up – one in particular. This charlatan approached Andrew and broached with glee if "he'd like a bet as to who amongst us will be the first to come back to jail." The wager was declined and I secretly wished for Rod's presence.

1730: This week's Canteen sheet appeared under the door.

1800: Made the call I was dreading to Buzz. Caught him walking the dog. Kicked-off with a question about height and speed which he didn't know. Tried a different tack with a "high landing" and "high hover" question (to any helicopter pilots – what's the difference between HIGE and HOGE): "No idea," his honest answer as he shouted at his hound. A final question – which he half knew the answer to. But the standard was not high enough. I gripped the phone, gulped for the voicing of my verdict and told him that he wasn't ready…

He was adamant though and told me he's "thoroughly cheesed off with the whole thing." The costs incurred to date have been enormous. Not helped in the least by his idiot instructor being removed from him. It's his birthday on Saturday and he's "going for it" on Friday. I tried my best to explain what it was I had grilled him on and where he needed to boost his knowledge.

Felt useless after the call. And very guilty again.

1820: Haircut from Scotty on the landing now in the can. The shiny prison corridor floor was soon covered with a carpet of black – and a noticeable amount of grey.

2000: The best thing of today – and my entire stay in prison – is the plan to incorporate any decision making in the future in line with helicopter decisions – end of.

Thursday, October 20th, 2011.

T minus 28. I couldn't believe my eyes last night. One of the larger members of the HDFOT gang was audaciously juicing the oranges from the sack meant for all of us in the dining room in full view of the not-at-all interested officers. The mountains of discarded peel everywhere kept the continuity of the always trashed refectory look like the after effects of an explosion in a marmalade factory.

0615: The Dale Farm eviction continues but doesn't have a patch on Wilford. My "boss" (and hostess) HRH Queen Elizabeth II has gone to Australia. No doubt standards will slip even more here…

Healthcare. Do the loos and bins. A quick two-way with the student nurse upstairs in the kitchen. Originally from Dorset but now local. She's curious about what *I'm* doing here. Transmit the abridged version including I've learnt a lot and don't want to go back to my old ways. "I like your enthusiasm."

0930: Enter the Nacro office to see Yootha. The Orderly, Sid (Victor Banerjee, circa *A Passage to India*) tells me to have a seat. In frame are two "Resettlement" officers. One talks to a prisoner. I gather this is the staff member whom I had correspondence with about the 6 week lie-down not being required for community work. After he has finished with his customer, I ask him if it was he to whom I wrote. It is. He palpitates "that of the 350 or so inmates of HMP Hollesley Bay, lifers and IPP's get preference for the 100 or so available placements." I question why we are not more self-sufficient. "It used to be," he sighs. "Pig farm, milk farm" and the "greenhouse did really good business" but "those days are over" since the "Governor stopped all that."

Shortly I'm sat opposite Yootha. She looks me up on her laptop. I write my NI number down, thank her, wave to Sid and return to wasteful Wilford.

1135: Post. A "no." A standard letter – mostly of discouragement ending with "if you have genuine ability (I do not), persist (I will), the odds are less fearsome than they might first appear." The good news is another reusable stamp. I stuck it on the envelope which will be the carrier pigeon for today's lot of lines.

1200: Lunch. Tuna and French sticks. With last week's missing French sticks finally turning up there was a Biblical amount of bread in the dining room. Some of them are now in my larder…

1245: Library – and Mathew holding Court. I get some of the abuse aimed at me too: "Stealing money whilst flying a helicopter." Welcome back Mathew! After reading the paper and the habitual Mac race, said bye to L.A. who is "starting to crap himself" with all the things he has to deal with on his release and returned to the wing where I now write.

As quietly as I can.

Because everyone is asleep.

1430: Rounds. At Cosford, as per Rick the Fish's request, get their staff to ring Hoxon's office as their fish tank is now totally turbid.

Hoxon. (Not nice going there). The pristine dining room looks like an operating theatre. Walter rallies and tells me of a new resident who sounds like he'll be a prime candidate for the HDFOT club – and wears his trousers halfway down his underpants "like they all do." He apparently asked this gentleman this morning WHY he does it?

"Coz I is from London."

Return to full blast music on Wilford, which I want to re-dub Wembley.

1530: "Gaddafi dead." Pretty harrowing images on TV.

1645: *The heating is on*. I feel guilty. Plenty of people on the outside can't afford it. The Arthur English £700 a day per Unit infests within me…

1700: Roll-check and dinner announced. Completed the former but opted not to eat. Took one look and no thank you. I will eat later. Besides a film is on telly that I feel *has* to be watched whilst I am in prison. I have seen it many times but cannot let it escape me whilst it is on where I am…

The Colditz Story.

Friday, October 21st, 2011.

T minus 27. Got up at 0600. I write, first thing, in my boxers. It's roasting in here with the heating on at full-Fahrenheit-chat.

0645: Downstairs Tony and I discuss the filth. "Apart from the Unit staff being unable to tell us what to do, the other problem," he says "is that the majority of residents have it in their mind that they don't live here and therefore have no interest in doing anything." Thing is, says Tony "we *do* live here." He makes my morning by saying moving from Hoxon to here is "like moving from Park Lane to Brick Lane," although Brick Lane is "quite tidy now."

0710: Work. Dave on duty. All very quiet. Do the loos and vacuum Rachel's office, which has been painted and a huge parachute sized dust sheet covers her desk and computer. Dave and I discuss the inactivity. I tell him it's because everyone is still in bed. He seems close to despair.

0800: Return to the escarpment of Wilford on my railway line like route. The place full of sleepers. Those actually up in their dressing gowns.

0950: Work. Full of prisoners and no staff. The painters – whose ladders are everywhere – are nowhere to be seen. Rachel's door is wide open inviting anyone to help themselves.

1045: Unit. One of the twins knocks on my door. "Do I know anything about publishing?" (!) I *am* being filmed. He's been "writing poems and maybe raise some money for charity?" I suggest to him to write to some poetry organisations with three of his best. He asks me to pick some from his works.

This morning I was a prisoner writing a third rate book. Now I'm a poetry judge.

He returns with some dog eared A4. The best three are *Pigeon*, *Bliss* and *Politics*. But what the hell do I know? Good for him though. Certainly the twins' intelligence between them supplies about 50% of the grey cells at Wilford.

1135: Found a twin and making sure I was talking to the right one, told him I thought they were jolly good. Gave him some addresses of Poetry organisations from the J.A. book and told him that it's nice to see someone here using their brains. I think, as I write at 1720 – he's still beaming.

1145: In my room with post. The corridor being bombarded with music. Five of the HDFOT clan sway hypnotically to a "gangster" tune. Two responses from literary agents. One "send it in." One "don't send it in."

1200: Lunch. The second and last "Black history month" meal. Homemade rather than reheating something. Delicious. Why-oh-why can't the prison use all the local land to provide both stuff for our plates and work for our inhabitants? Sax Clive gave me a heads-up to avoid dinner tonight – he will supply me with seconds direct from the main kitchens.

Waddled to the library. Read the paper. Gaddafi clearly murdered. Looked like a lynch mob. Stuart on good form. L.A. sleepy as usual. We all do the Mac race. I win. Stuart confesses that yesterday they all had a sneak peek to beat me.

Rounds. Delivering new spectacles. Four officers on Stow all sit in the office chatting looking bored. One has a nose at the glasses and mutters with the perennial distaste that so many of the white-shirts display under his breath: "Who pays for these then?" Tax payers do, I tell him. He doesn't look impressed. I can understand his way of thinking. If the system changed and we were all working...

Hoxon. Rick the Fish is asked if he got the message that he can go to Cosford to do his thing? "Yes, and went this morning." The reason that the fish on the *Crossroads* set look so unfit is that "there is no pump in their tank." He "spoke to staff but no interest was shown." I think for a second. I'll speak to Rachel on Monday morning. I know her jurisdiction does not include fish but she is sensible. And can kick ass.

1500: On the Unit bored so return to work. Sue says there's a few letters to go but they can wait till Monday. I plead with her to let me do it now – and off I go again.

1700: Attend Roll-check at dinner peeking at what's on offer to those not lucky enough to be given food by kind Clive.

2030: The glory of eating a proper meal at a proper time. Clive came by – like a good head waiter – and asked if I was enjoying my meal.

You bet I was.

Saturday, October 22nd, 2011.

T minus 26.

0645: Wilford residents *can* get up early. When there's Home-leave...

The news full of Libya, where clearly *someone* needs to do some explaining... St. Paul's Cathedral is to be shut for the first time since the Blitz due to protestors camped outside. Some poor couple are due to get married there today.

Hope the Groom hasn't stolen a bunch of money.

A social from Sweeper Ray until 0745. The poor man all over the place and most fragile. Not helped by "someone smoking a Moroccan woodbine" on his landing last night and he doesn't "want a nicking by staff smelling it is his room." The whole corridor was I gather, as high as a kite.

A call to the office. The main-hub senior luminary returns to these pages and asks "how are you getting on?" After confirmation that I am at liberty to speak openly I convey that the Wilford experience is the worst of the whole shooting-match so far. If I could have a magic wand I'd be ANYWHERE but Wilford. The officer's response: "That's because they're all scumbags here."

1050: Attempting to connect with civilization, Buzz is rung. Voicemail. Happy Birthday is recorded but more vitally I want to know what happened at yesterday's flight test.

1115: Another call to the office (I'm popular today). This time "Unit HDC (Tag) paperwork." The first time I've seen correspondence on my Unit with reference to November 17th.

1200: Lunch. Don't ask.

The afternoon sun blazing down on Wilford's postage stamp garden. Tony is already there and he invites me to sit with him on "the" bench. Before I know it his précis comes my way – with no prodding from me...

This is his second sentence. "8 years." His first: "10 years." The gap between them? "7 months."

I am astounded – and tell him so. How can he do 10 years and only last 7 months before going wrong again? "Oh, I started work straight away. It just took 'em 7 months to catch me." Tony's work? Robbing banks. I'm sitting with Butch or Sundance. Except he looks like Anthony Hopkins. He knows he's "been an idiot" and assures me it's not going to happen again. Besides, who am I to judge? I embark on attempting to get him to tell me he won't be going back to his local Barclays with a shotgun.

"It wasn't a shotgun it was a pistol."

"On leaving prison the first time with the small amount of money they give you," he "decided to go for it." After the first "return to work," Tony decided "this is easy – and carried on." I dig for background information. In and out of Borstals all his young life. "Stealing motors" – which by the sound of things – he wasn't very good at. "First one I nicked – I couldn't drive at the time – so got caught in it." The second time he "made it to the gate," the third a marathon "ten yards." How far did he get on his most successful car heist?

" 'bout 50 yards."

By coincidence he was sent here when it was a Borstal. What was it like? "Miles better," before they "sold off" all the land. "Everyone worked." The food "was all self-produce" and the "Borstal boys even showed the Suffolk Punch horses." Enthusiasm was rife. Learning to deal with horses was a "handy trade and very useful on the outside." Discipline was good. Timed circuit training at the end of any young man's sentence had to be "considerably quicker than the one on arrival." Or you "wouldn't get out." Now though, "the youngsters don't give a toss." They "want everything now and have not learnt respect." They have been "put among the older folk" (Tony is in his 50's) to "try to have a calming influence on them – which hasn't worked."

Tell me about it. The only thing missing from gangland culture on my corridor is drive-by shootings.

I ask him why he's not on Hoxon like all the other sensible folk? He was – "for some months but got thrown out." Why?

"Vodka party."

Some of the "clear stuff was bought in." Tony invited "some close friends to a party." I imagine it's quite a trick to get 5 people into a room in Hoxon. Even tougher when they're drinking vodka. "A litre each." With no ice, drinking out of plastic cups and no mixers, I remark to Tony that there must have been quite a need. Of course, when you've been in that long, receptacle and temperature doesn't become a factor. How did it all go wrong?

Tony realised he had "had enough by about 2100" and went to bed "pissed as a Judge." No problems. "Good as gold."

All was *not* a bed of roses the next morning. Tony got up with a "cracking hangover" and "still pissed, went to get coffee." As he staggered past the room of one of his drinking partners, things didn't bode well as two officers sat sentry like. Matters got worse on surveying the dining room. "Smashed up chairs, tables and even a broken window," created the composition.

"Everyone was breathalysed." Tony's result was "three times over the limit and this was the next morning." All the revellers were summoned to see a Governor.

Tony did not get shipped-out to closed conditions because he confessed to "supplying the lubrication" and mitigated that he had no idea that his pal was going to react the way he did. The Governor told him that he "had used his 9 lives." Four were sent back to closed conditions. Tony – to Wilford.

I still think his punishment the harshest.

1700: Dinner. Gave it a miss. Noticed oranges were being given out and was allowed to take two. Hung around for seconds. An officer "guarded" the bag of fruit... Before "extras" (prison-speak for seconds) were announced I witnessed one of the servery team pick the bag up, take four oranges out of it and put it down on a side counter. With smoke and mirrors the bag then... vanished.

Straight to the orange end of the counter where the lone 4 sat I journeyed. The officer was asked if I could take one. He looked down – then jumped out of his skin. "There was a bag of them there a moment ago," he said in a Manuel type confused waiter voice. I smiled, took one and said thank you.

He'd just been mugged.

Sunday, October 23rd, 2011.

T minus 25. Why does everything I touch go wrong? On picking-up my *Sunday Times* after a nothing-required-for-me-to-do visit to work all the inner sections were the wrong newspaper. Befittingly, I have no *Culture* or *Style*. Sat disappointed downstairs reading in what I've dubbed "café corner" whilst simultaneously being interrogated by Clive. Do I ever read *The Guardian*? My response lead me to believe that there won't be any more food from him...

To the library to ask Library Brett if anyone amongst us takes the *Sunday Telegraph* (!) in the hope that if they do – I've got their paper and they may have mine.

See the blank stare.

On recovering from my question he suggested a visit to the main gate if on the off-chance, they had the rest of my newspaper. Spoke to a female officer – who looked like one of the evictees from Dale Farm – and recounted my problem. Whilst recognising this was probably a first in her prison officer career, she looked at me like I'd landed from Mars. As I write now at 1920 – I'll wager you she is sitting with her pint-sized glass with her non pint-sized partner (most female officers are not the "marrying" kind – if you get my gist) saying "you'll never *believe* what a prisoner asked me today..."

Loads of Tannoy announcements on the Unit. The Arthur Mullard type officer ("AMTO") is on today. Most of his messages broadcast to us end with "innit."

Within our county's prisons a "Listener" prisoner-peer-to-peer Samaritans type scheme is supposed to exist. I attempted to sign up as a volunteer at Bedford but never got the chance... Ray has come to see me and it is apparent that he needs a pair of ears. "Listener's" keep everything confidential and I am not going to break their code of conduct by saying any more.

Outdoors pre-lunch in yet more Indian summer I get talking to a friendly face (Dev Patel) out in a year or so. Towing the line and how prison can be good for one is the topic. Many of his young colleagues tell him he's "no good" as he's "never been sent to the block" (the Cooler). This guy's name?

"Rod."

Another one.

Lunch. The "Number two" Governor – the Rodney Bewes one – is in our presence and observed poking around all the filth that is our dining room. He doesn't look terribly impressed. Our regular table is close to the main entrance and an officer is stood there – no doubt making sure we eat all our vegetables. The proximity of his position makes it easy for me to hear their lines...

The Governor says "the standard of cleanliness simply isn't good enough." The officer's response nearly makes me choke:

"The cleaner is ill today."

1430: *In Which We Serve* on telly. Noël Coward wants "an efficient and happy ship…"

1700: Dinner and Roll-check announced. I check myself "in" but don't fancy the food on offer.

Later, with my door open, Clive walks by and stops. He's obviously forgiven me for my choice of newspaper and giving one of his infectious smiles says in his very broad Brummie accent that I'm "always writing." He is told of this book. His response:

"You've only been in prison ten minutes."

Monday, October 24th, 2011.

T minus 24. Up at 0600. On the news, the Queen, our "boss," is still in Australia. This week's "night officer" is always on the phone – and I mean *always*. Is he reporting in to Australia? The same officer never lets me Roll-check myself for the Appell until the "day shift" starts at 0700.

Dale Farm (now empty) is *still* on telly. The personage in control of its destiny look rougher than the people who were living there.

0720: Outside Rachel's office two living-room television sized cardboard boxes linger – which I'd noted on my visit over the weekend. Pick the first one up to take to the dustbins and realise something is in it. I open up the top – it is not sealed – and find one of those briefcase sized first-aid cases within. I pick it up and shake it. There are things in it. Strange. The rest of the box is examined to see what else I have found. There's another container – about a 1/3rd the size of a shoe box. Its contents clearly marked.

"Hypodermic needles."

Realising the severity of what I have found – and these boxes have been sitting in the open area *all weekend*, where prisoners come and go, I open up and look inside the second box.

It is *full* of drugs. And NOT Paracetamol…

The consequence of this is no different to finding a loaded Kalashnikov – in a prison. Dave doesn't seem to know what to do. The term rabbit in headlights will give you an idea. We look for documentation to see if anything is missing. "That's me for the high jump," he says. He'll "need to call security." Dave cannot understand how or why they got left there although "there was a delivery on Friday."

Do the loos, kitchen, stairs, the Treatment room and the waiting area, now re-dubbed "needle exchange."

0900:   To Zara (Top) to give her my NI number. Is there anything else I need to do? "No." Thank her and head to Healthcare. Nothing doing there – no drugs or needles to be moved… Return to Wilford at 0915.

0945: Revisit work. Rod roaming. "Fucking hell," his reaction to the needles story. Rachel is understandably *almightily* stressed by the saga. So I *really* help matters by contributing on matters fish. "Go to Hoxon, find Rick the Fish and speak to the staff there." En-route I pass Elk ("morning Captain") and then stumble across a BT man looking down a hole in the ground by the chapel.

My line to him: You've found the tunnel.

Hoxon. Two non-regular officers are on set. I identify myself, explain the situation and luckily one of them says that he "normally works on Cosford and is aware that the fish are fucked." Can you please Tannoy Rick so he can liaise direct with you? "What's Rick's surname?"

I have no idea.

Tannoy: "Calling Rick the Fish, calling Rick the Fish. Can Rick the Fish come to the office please."

Now I've seen and heard *everything*. Rick turns up bemused. The officer asks if "Cosford staff showed any interest?" Negative – Rick says that he was told "they don't want 'em." The officer replies that the "Governor is aware of the situation and has ordered a new pump." I thank him, saying I'll be on to the RSPCA on Thursday. He laughs but looks worried.

Wilford bound, Elk is passed again and then go by a now *very* concerned looking BT man scratching his head still studying the hole.

1155: Veggie curry.

1235: Library. In another world with a newspaper from nowhere comes *the* most *almighty* kick to the sole of my right foot. I jump out of my *skin*. When gravity has placed me back from whence I launched, attempt is made to establish who my assailant is…

Mathew stands grinning mischievously like a pantomime villain. *When* my heart re-starts I wish him good afternoon and enquire how the cessation of smoking is going. "Tremendous," he replies before posing "have you got any tobacco?"

1700: Dinner queue with Sweeper Ray. I moan that I'm bored. He tells me to shut up – as I'm "now on countdown."

Any chance of an earlier blast-off?

Downstairs later to borrow the office hole-punch – a daily ritual for this lot – two lead members of the HDFOT brigade were "going to the gym."

Minus their kit.

I witnessed an officer (Jack Hawkins) – one of the snowflake-on-icebergs more sensible ones – who speaks with a Norfolk accent asking them where they were going ("they must think I was ****ing born yesterday," he murmured to me). HDFOT 1 feigned deafness and HDFOT 2 simulated the licking of his nipples.

After this somewhat bizarre piece of playacting I asked the officer how on earth *some* people get moved to open prisons. I suppose his answer should have been of no great surprise…

"Other prisons get so sick of some people that they sex-up their records just to get rid of them…"

Tuesday, October 25th, 2011.

0645: Foot. Foot. Foot. I have not lost the plot – yet – but my right foot is giving me *hell*. My ankle has swollen up like a football. Hobble downstairs and greet another night officer who I've not seen before. Relay that I'm walking wounded and can he Roll-check me now? He reluctantly agrees. Re-climb the stairs noting I have to touch the banisters – which I normally steer well clear of.

My immune system must be working overtime in prison.

0715: Sitting in my room pondering what to do. Too much pain so decide to go to Healthcare. Putting on my sock and shoe – agonising. As I limp to the infirmary daylight is beginning to emerge. Clamber up the steps and find three other patients waiting. One of them is Snoring Killer.

I must stop calling him that. He is always incredibly friendly and apart from the wall rattling week or so he spent next door to me he has never done anything to deserve such a harsh title. From now on the call-sheets will simply dub him Snorer.

Dave is on and concerned by my inability to walk. He helps me take my shoe and sock off and examines the inoperative ankle. Once amputation is discounted he prescribes that age old prison remedy: Paracetamol. He straps me up and I'm "grounded."

Wilford. The officer is told I'm not much use to anyone (story of my life) and will be in my room. "*Jeremy Kyle* for you then," he says. I go back to bed at 0815, full of pills.

Sleep till 1010. Unheard of for me.

1056: The mail is in. I have a letter. From Jonathan Aitken. Despite the fact that I am *certain* I misspelt his surname in my communication to him. The highlights of his epistle are:

Many thanks for your letter... First and foremost I wish you well for your forthcoming release on a tag on November 17th... During my own journey through the criminal justice system I found coming out of prison almost as difficult as going into prison. A period of decompression or adjustment is usually necessary on the road back to normality. So I always recommend taking post release periods slowly and cautiously. Perhaps one way of illustrating what I mean is to send you a copy of an article I wrote for The *Daily Telegraph* about one of the jailed MPs who was recently released. Perhaps you may find some of the thoughts I expressed in the article of use and help.... Concerning your aspirations to become an author, again I wish you well. Good books about prison are comparatively rare.

The "small steps" advice in the newspaper article seems very prudent. Like so many things on the outside, I must consistently remind myself "one step at a time." His key factor of family support scares me. Especially the caveat of "which may require forgiveness from the nearest and dearest of the one who turned their lives upside down."

Andrew absent from lunch. The painting party are daubing the officers' Mess and are resting their easels at that canvas to eat...

12.45 – 1330: Limped to the library. Stuart and I do the Mac race. All other prisoners present think we are absolutely barmy.

1600: One member of the HDFOT battalion, dubbed by Andrew as Mouthy, due to toxic-tones that you can only *imagine* is back from Home-leave. How pleased I am.

1645: *Those Magnificent Men in their Flying Machines* is on telly. Yet another film I watched with you-know-who. And she loved it.

1700: Dinner. Some very greasy chicken. Have a few mouthfuls but can't bear it. Grilled Andrew on what the food was like at lunchtime in the Mess. "Very nice – had chicken stir fry in the grounds." How the other half live...

1740: *TMMITFM* still on. Sad sad sad memories. A knock on my (open) door. Someone who has never spoken to me before – "Have you got any spare burn?"

No.

1741: Another knock on the door – I'm popular tonight – Snorer with a whole home-grown cucumber.

1815: Cucumber sandwiches in my room. Normal service has resumed on the corridor...

1905: Had a good cry at the end of the film.

To you-know-who: I *pray* that one day you read this. You have *no* idea how sorry I am.

1950: Roll-check announced thus: "Spliffs out – mobiles away."

2100: Finished letter of thanks to Jonathan Aitken. Nearly asked him to write to my wife. Very nearly.

Wednesday, October 26th, 2011.

T minus 22. Up at 0600. L.A.'s last full day. Sweeper Ray comes to my room at 0700. My "listening ears" have to be switched on. As usual when he is done, he gives me his "bless you and thank you."

Wish I had someone to confide in myself. Guess that's you, Dear Reader.

At work Dave shows genuine concern to his patient and demands an inspection of the offending ankle. He seems satisfied that I'll live and WD starts calling me Peg Leg. I retort that I'm going to let the tyres down on her car – which I add is very smart. "It was a present from my husband which means I must be a nice wife." This statement causes Dave – behind her – into stifled silent hysterics.

Wilford. A notice is up about the Joanna Trollope lecture and announcing that another writer – whose name doesn't ring any bells – is coming to address us the week after. Both "fresh from the Southwold Arts Fair."

Last time I was in Southwold I bought my wife an ice cream.

0900: Back to Healthcare. Rod arrives. There's nothing for me to do so wait and walk back with him. Decide that it's bloody silly that I can't invite my friend onto the Unit and tell him to hang on whilst the office is asked if I can bring a Hoxonite on board. Very reasonably, secure a "yes." Five minutes later we're in my room. Statham somewhat surprised that there is no sugar on the wing. Wilford's cast has pinched the caster.

In one of those prison brotherhood moments, he thanks me for guiding him on his decision making procedure. He's "changed a lot since we've known each other." I'm touched by this and relay to him that it's not going to stop on the outside. He'll be sick of me calling to check up on him.

I hope someone will do the same for me. He says he'll make a sign for me: "Do not give the pilot any money."

We decide to de-camp to Hoxon where the view is considerably nicer. Walking up a playful debate takes place on which of us is going to ask staff for the author's permission to come on board. The upshot of which is him. After all, I am now a guest here.

The green light given I'm immediately surrounded by familiar smiling faces like dancers around a maypole. Greg, Heston, Big Len, "first in queue" Oliver and L.A. appear. Even an officer comes out (!) and says hello and asks me to "let him know" when I'm returning to my Unit. (November 17th suits me) Rod goes off to make coffee and we go to sit outside.

I remember that view.

And the evocative cleanliness, friendliness, decency and... well... the *atmosphere* of the place. Rod updates me: "The Casino got closed down by the deputy Governor when he raided the dining room one night." All the chips (cardboard circles) "were confiscated and all the players interviewed," who – with massive Bambi eyes – all insisted that no bets were made and it was just a bit of fun. Staff were satisfied that "no gambling was taking place," says Rod adding "that Charles owes him £16 quid."

Big Len is given the hokum of wasteland Wilford. Rod tells him with gusto "he's right – I've seen it." The "old days" are nattered of with nostalgia. I voice that it was probably a good thing that I was moved from the merriment. Hoxon was too easy for me and I was having too much fun. Wilford with the gangster music playing, noisy, filthy, HDFOT lot that is my home is a jolly good reminder of why I'm here.

An outbreak of mirth caused by my use of the word "jolly."

Julian appears. I cause additional amusement by announcing that I wouldn't mind meeting him under the tree again. He deftly requests my shopping list and we make a time for the transaction – this Friday at 1330. Heston is informed that he would have a heart attack if he saw our servery. All seem incredulous as to why prisoners are not made to do stuff. Heston with his pertinacious common-sense orchestrates "squaddies are made to clean their shoes."

Although we are all *prisoners*, from different backgrounds and in for different crimes and assorted sentences – we are *all* in agreement that more discipline is required. Too many people are "just along for the ride" and giving "two fingers to civilisation."

Those are quotes by the way.

Someone far more able with a pen than me once scribed that the degree of civilization in a society can be judged by entering its prisons... If that still rings true good LORD are we in trouble. If, by some miracle someone with some clout reads this – are you listening? This is *prisoners* doing the mud-slinging. Our answer? And we should know – it is paramount to get rid of the perfunctory staff, fill prisons with Mr MacKay's and give them Mr Mackay peremptory power. Then get us working and make prisons endogenous.

Some *leadership* might imbue personage who are (quite rightly) within prison. There is quite a lot of *potential* in some of my cast members. Hitherto, not a lot is being done in the luddite climate to nurture it... HMP Utopia will never happen – but Lordy Lord with some reform, *boy* could there be a turnaround...

Lennox appears. He's being shipped-out to Stow. He's pleased as punch because he's being reunited with Brad Pitt.

1120: "Home" from my Home-leave. Another letter from the nice literary agent: "I'm frantically busy trying to get ready for a short break in Italy." I picture Lady Bracknell sitting next to the Leaning Tower of Pisa with a large bunch of manuscripts in one hand and a larger glass of Pinot Grigio in the other. Her pre Lira last lines: "Don't try to be too funny" and "send 40 pages," ending with "things in publishing are utterly dire."

They can't be that dire if she's jetting off to Italy.

1200: A lot of whispered collaborating going on at another table during lunch. Enough for me to notice. I must not forget where I am. Hope I'm just being neurotic.

1320: Rounds. At Stow, the officers – who tell me they "run the mother ship" – will "pipe me aboard on my next visit." Bump into L.A. who – out tomorrow – is now looking overwhelmed. He has been in six years. "They have flown by," he says. And the last two weeks? "Dragged."

1400: In room. *Brief Encounter* on. You know why I'm watching this.

At work I gather that Dave is going away for a bit – but back before I wrap. He's got various family "do's" on including a daughter getting married ("to a sensible one") and much driving around the UK. I wish him well. He gives me a Mr Barrowclough look. I think he'd rather be here.

1700: Dinner. Won't even begin to tell you.

1725: Canteen sheet. And gangster music.

1745: Got off the phone to Buzz. During said conversation there were TWO helicopter pilots on the line. Buzz passed his skills test! I am *thrilled* for him. He *very* graciously said that I "did the hard bit." I am SO pleased and SO proud of him. He thanked me – lots – for telling him what and where to mug up on further to our last call.

I feel very stupid and ashamed where I am calling him from.

Thursday, October 27th, 2011.

T minus 21. 0750: Tannoy: "Second and last call for Roll-check. We don't want to be late for work do we?

0755: Healthcare. Philip back with a continuity destroying haircut and wants to look at my foot – comparing it with the good one. WD peers at my pads as well. They both seem of the opinion that the tubular grip is doing more damage than good and it is taken off. I immediately feel better.

Patient hat off. Orderly hat on. Get vacuuming. Do room 10. Nothing else for me, so return to Wilford and sit in our dining room with some toast. Sweeper Ray cleaning it (not his job) and muttering about "the animals."

0930: Leiston comes to 30 for a social. "Back from Home-leave and full of cold." He's been in 2 years – out in June and has a job, a home and a family waiting for him. How have the family been? "Very supportive." And her family? "They think I'm working on the rigs." This makes me think for a moment… How he would feel in 20 or 30 years if his daughter was living with someone in jail and was pulling the wool over his eyes? "Not impressed." I proffer to him that when he's out, he should sit his missus down and offer her the opportunity of talking to her parents and telling the truth – and then starting with a clean sheet of paper. I watch him as the project whizzes around his head. I think I've hit my mark.

Return to the crease of Healthcare for an innings at work. Heston at the wicket. Out for a duck as nothing required. He and I tread back to our pavilions and rhetoric of items on the market within HMP Hollesley Bay takes place…

I know nothing about drugs. People today seem to enjoy a variety of things that I have never heard of. In prison a new type has been introduced to me – I hasten to add in name only:

Spice.

I gather that it can be purchased for £10. Cash only. Not Canteen credit or unbelievably even tins of tuna. Only a ten pound note. Real cash in prison is worthless to me because I do not go out. Many prisoners do though…

Body searches or pat-downs – even at Bedford – never include the gentleman's area so it needs not the greatest of imagination to deduce where things are stashed. Remember where Stevie used to hide his goods at B 2 5… My two full body strip searches on arrival and departure at that establishment never included the full Monty.

And there was even an x-ray chair at Bedford. Why don't they make *everyone* have a seat?

1150: Post. A letter from Ben.

Dear Jonathan,

Sorry for the delay in writing back to you I just got your second letter! Despite the poor quality of your jokes I have not excommunicated you just yet. I am still in Wandsworth, it is a black hole that swallows you up never to be seen again. I have managed to get moved to the super enhanced wing and there is a far better quality of prisoner there than in Bedford E wing. E wing is the Induction wing and the super enhanced or Annexe workers all take care of the first night centre, equivalent to

Bedford's C1 but much larger. I don't think D cat prisons exist, in fact I think you are really at home writing to me as part of your release conditions to continue the ruse! I am in Court again early November. This should mean I end up back in Bedford afterwards. My tag date is the end of November so I reckon I will end up going full circle and will get my tag there. Let's hope they get me back on E wing sharpish.

Best wishes Ben

1200. Lunch with Gordon and Andrew, who is now back to reality with a crash and having to dine with us lowly subjects.

L.A.'s replacement in the library is as well-suited to the role as a prison officer at the opera. Raced Stuart at Mac. I won. And again he told me he tried to cheat but couldn't find the cartoon!

1530: Back from a bit of bin emptying. WD told Philip that I threatened to let the tyres of her car down. I think he thinks I'm really brave. Or stupid.

The company over dinner was much better than the food. "Pie" with veg. Made sure I ate all the veg. The pie is currently on the way to pie heaven. (Pie in the sky?)

In the Canteen queue I find myself behind someone I most definitely have not spoken to before. He's reading the flyer promoting the forthcoming writers' lectures. "Who the fuck wants to know about literacy?" he demands. I answer with my eyebrows. "All them do is... write fucking..." Books? said I. "Yeah... fuckin' books."

1720: Paid Scotty for my haircut of the other day – now that I am in receipt of this week's Canteen. The account was settled by the usual prison currency: two tins of tuna. When I am released I am going to avoid the tinned-fish aisles of supermarkets like the plague.

1745-1900: Wilford's evening at the library. I am the only Wilford resident here. Whatever I take out will probably be the last book in prison that I read, so I really should get my hands on something sensible from which I might learn something. *How to win your wife back* is already out. So pick something else. A book with an apt title...

Robinson Crusoe.

Friday, October 28th, 2011.

T minus 20. Upstairs, an officer comes to get a prisoner to show-a-leg at 0705. I wasn't aware we had a morning wake-up service. Stick the news on. St. Paul's Cathedral is the new Dale Farm and has been occupied by people reminiscent of those we saw rioting all those weeks past.

0730: Tannoy: "Breakfast and Roll-check." The response: Crypt silence.

At work Limping Al pootles up. "How's the book?" All good, although I'm not sure people are going to agree with me on discipline – or rather the lack of – in our prisons. "No," he says. My views have "been discussed by-one-and-all" and the general consensus is "that everyone agrees with posh Jon." Ironically a "Unit meeting was held on Hoxon this morning" and "officers have noted a slip of standards of late" and if people don't "pull their fingers out there will be some privileges removed."

Wish we had similar at Wilford.

1045: Ironic that as I sit on my desert island – "the" bench – I'm reading about a chap who is going to end up on a desert island. A quote jumps out at me: "Young people are not ashamed to sin – yet ARE ashamed to repent."

1130: A message from the nice Norfolk officer ("NNO") that my presence is required at Hoxon this afternoon. Rod "needs my writing services." It's a cunning ploy to get me back to civilisation for a bit. NNO gives me a wry smile and says "just make sure you're back by tea time."

1200: Lunch. "Pizza."

1240: Jaunted to the library. The new guy... well let's just say I don't think he's cut out to be a librarian. Bedford's Glenda would have *fit*.

1320: Under my tree to meet Julian – not for booze, funny looking tobacco or pictures of ladies, but bare essentials (rather than women) of razors, loo-paper and washing tablets. He appears very French resistance like at 1325. I feel like I should offer him a smoke from an empty packet or start some Psalm for him to finish to confirm he is the "right" man.

1327: Back in my room to inspect my contraband. Julian's a bloody hero. Splice to the library to give Stuart Julian's bag and go to work at 1330. On the way, pass the Nacro door with the "Please do not spit" sign outside. A prisoner stands there. Spitting.

1332: Rounds.

1335: "Work" complete so head up to the solace that is Hoxon. Arrive at the oasis and herald my arrival to Blakey. After he's clipped my ticket I pass down the bus to Rod's room. Afternoon pleasantries are exchanged and a letter to him is plonked in my hand. It's a response and it's good news. They want a few more details to get the "T's" crossed and the "I's" dotted. We go through the facts and I point out that some of this will need to be rubber-stamped by Victoria. Rod immediately remonstrates in a flash of pique that he feels spurned by her and "she doesn't want to help." All this is recounted *most* Guy Ritchie character like. I apprehensively tell him that I think he is talking rubbish and point out that Victoria has bent over backwards for me and perhaps his customary ad hoc expatiating to her has been a little heavy handed. Bless him – he listens as I make it crystal clear that Victoria is the *last* person anyone wants to piss off here. Rod fatalistically twigs that perhaps I may for once be right. He discloses that relations are not too brilliant between her office and him so we agree that I will attempt to broker a peace deal. I warn him that it sounds like an apology is due. He looks like a niggled nine year old boy next to a broken window on that comment.

Paperwork complete we retire to the "terrace" for coffee. The subject of moving me back to Hoxon is discussed. The only way I can see this happening is if I get stabbed. "Can be arranged," says Rod deadpan. Instead, I opt for a game of snooker with him. Unbelievably, it comes down to the black. This despite the constant barrage of very funny film quotes.

1640: Time has flown by. The scenes completed here full of friendly faces, laughter and cleanliness (not the jokes). Rod makes me laugh by telling me about "people who live in caravans, making them posher by putting a three foot wall around them." I laugh so much that I lose the game. Ever the impeccable host he walks me to the door. He aptly says my departure to Wilford will make me realise how "good it was" at Hoxon. "It's good punishment for you," he concludes as he shakes my hand. Sid zooms over and asks me to take a poster with me for "Volunteering" for the walls of Healthcare.

With poster – I return to Wilford and get in the dinner queue.

1700: Dinner.

1702: Dinner in bin.

Saturday, October 29th, 2011.

T minus 19. Up at 0645. Slept well despite the *stupid* heat. Our "boss" has completed her successful tour of Australia and is coming home. She'll be furious when she sees her oil bill. The clocks change tonight – an extra hour in prison.

0745: Sid's poster up. Philip is told about the "baby steps" Aitken article and tutors me that "troops returning home after action have loads of anxiety about fixing everything now." I reveal my comparison between the brotherhood of prisoners with soldiers – except on Wilford – and he agrees with me. Empty the Treatment room bin – the rest of the place looks not too battle scarred and go home.

0859: The starting grid of self-drive Home-leave prisoners forms outside as I watch the starting grid positions being sorted out on television for tomorrow's Grand Prix. The Security Services van is going out again. I wonder whose site he will be guarding tonight?

Having anxious thoughts. I could make a list right now longer than this book of all the things I need to sort out. But can't right now. Baby steps Robinson, baby steps.

1030: Seb on pole.

1120-1140: A visit from Sweeper Ray. Have to put my "Listener" hat on. I'm not at liberty to reveal what was discussed but I hope Ray finds it helpful talking to me.

1200: "Lunch."

1220: Healthcare. Deserted outside because of "Lockdown" for visits. Chat with Philip about the gang culture which is Wilford. "Wilford Unit has been in trouble for the last three months," he discloses.

1410: Outside in the garden with *Robinson Crusoe* on my *Shirley Valentine* bench.

1500: Too cold so came inside to read. Stayed downstairs.

I don't like listening to other people's phone calls but it's difficult not to when one of the HDFOT clan is on the blower. This call apparently warrants two of them to be on the receiver at this end. Snippets caught: "Blood cous, bruv, uh?" "I can't be bovered." "Sort it. Ah, cous. Yo bruv." "I sorted it blood, innit." "Anything. Easy man." "She ain't coming." "She's just trying to wind me up, innit?" "Serious." (The other person hangs up. Caller re-dials). "You didn't make me finish talking." (Other person hangs up again). "Ah, fuck." "Smiff n' Wesson blood." "Yo cous."

1700: "Dinner." Meals seem now to always be in "inverted commas."

1800: In room with John Wayne (*Brannigan*). Having a terrible anxiety attack. I so badly want to communicate with my wife. So tempting to write to her. Although I am of course. Every day. This book.

Sunday, October 30th, 2011.

T minus 18. Up at 0600 (GMT). Downstairs a bomb site: Bread, half eaten toast, noodles, noodle packets and milk cartons. And that was just the floor. There is a sign on the wall saying "Leave the place tidy – or IEP review."

No one – but no one, gives a toss.

Staff included.

One good piece of news is that the heating has *finally* been turned off.

0700: Showered. No hot water. So that's why the heating is off. Roll-check myself to NNO and ask if he can pass on a message that when they fix the boiler – can they leave the heating off. Expecting to shock him on the daily cost of the Unit's heating, he trumps me: "The establishment's bill is £10,000 per week," and adds "Hoxon is melting."

0750: Tannoy blithely broadcasts: "Just a little reminder, Roll-check, please, for …." Ten names followed.

0915: Pick up newspaper from NNO. "I don't want to see you for the rest of the day," he smiles, passing me half a tree's worth of paper – return room. Right stuff in paper!

0930: Race starts.

0940: Heating back on. (Sorry tax payers).

1103: Seb's race. Only one more GP before Tag if all things fall into place…

Lunch not worth wasting what is now becoming valuable biro ink – and paper. There is none left downstairs and I only have about 1cm worth in my pile.

1225: To "work." There is nothing to be done so Philip and I walk to the door. He surprises me outside by producing tobacco. I didn't know he smoked. He tells me that he "gets an extra £130 a month, bang-up money" as he exhales.

1250: Unit. A social from Library Brett. All is not well with the "new" library guy. I ask him if Stuart is in agreement on this one. "He is." Brett – under Sally – runs a tight ship.

Perhaps Brett should run Wilford.

Robinson J, Robinson C and "bench" spend some time together.

1520: Conference with Sweeper Ray after a visit from his wife. All my talks with him are private but I will reveal that at the end of this chat I point out to him how loyal his other-half has been and he is a very, very lucky man. Above all else – when he does finally get out – he must stay out.

He wants me to write a letter for him after supper.

1700: Dined with Gordon and Andrew and HMP Bedford was the menu of topic. These two had a very different welcome on landing there to me. Their opening night – and in Andrew's case – opening nights – were had on the "Induction wing" with unbelievably, "single cells." You know what? I don't think my first night in prison by myself would have been terribly good for me.

Gordon and Andrew are applying for single rooms on my departure. It will be like splitting up Morecambe and Wise.

1800: Dictation of letter by Sweeper Ray. Then the writing of it on "good" paper. Like a good assistant, I am very loyal and discreet. And that's all you need to know.

1905: Quick game of pool with Eric and Ernie.

1915: Deliver letter to Ray for onward postage.

Monday, October 31st, 2011.

T minus 17. Happy Halloween to you. I heard fireworks last night. I imagine they were in the village but knowing the standard at Hoxon they were probably there.

They'll no doubt have a bonfire on November 5th. And sparklers.

At work Philip accumulated. Young Jimmy shuffled in for his fit-for-work certificate. I asked him how he's getting on in Aldeburgh. "Really well" and I was "dead right" in my description and more importantly, my advice on "do's and don'ts" – he's enjoying himself. He also appears to have matured somewhat.

Mop anything shiny. Healthcare now looks like a new sixpence. Wilford like... well, Wilford... As I enter the sauna which is my room – checking all the windows are still wide open – my top comes off and the door is jammed open in attempt to reduce the Malaysian jungle effect. A long list of stragglers is relayed on the Tannoy at 0745 and I get writing as I simmer.

0755: Tannoy: "Final Roll-check."

0805: Tannoy: "Final, final call for Roll-check," then a vague hint that "the Unit is dirty and could the Unit cleaners please get up."

The Harry Enfield character who is always friendly but very noisy is away on Home-leave from Friday. He's most excited. Not as excited as me. I'll be *that* laugh free for a blissful five nights. I can't wait. I might actually get some sleep.

0845: Work. Report to Philip. Nothing to do.

0850: Zara (Top) to keep abreast (sorry) of any news but she's not in yet.

Victoria's Royal household – to attempt to arbitrate the Rod feud. Knock on door. The Bond heavy Orderly Private Secretary is asked if Her Highness is in. "Do you have an appointment?" No – but can I trouble her for two minutes? Victoria hears my voice and leans back on her chair and says "come in." *Nearly* bowing, I do. And sit down. The door is left open. Victoria, I'm going to say two words which I think are going to make your eyes roll. "Go on," she says.

Rod_____.

The Royal eyes roll.

She testifies prima facie of all that is wrong with Rod. His brusque "I want it now" and "I'm entitled to this" followed by "you must do this for me," chronically scores no points with anyone.

I open my defence for Rod. I know he comes over as a rough diamond – I've been trying to polish the edges away like mad – but I believe there is eclectic potential buried somewhere deep-down in there. He's working like a Trojan on all his BTEC stuff and he's worried about his home situation when he leaves (sounds familiar). I know he's been creating a rod for his own back. Victoria: "All he does is come in waving bits of paper to be signed – and tells us how to do our jobs." By now, the Bond heavy – whose ears are flapping like sails – is stood in the doorway and voices that Rod "won't listen."

I plead – to them *both* – that I know he doesn't help himself – he's doing his bull in a china shop routine. Can I get him in for an appointment – get him to apologise – and *listen*?

Victoria says with empathy "it's good someone is sticking up for him." An appointment is made in the Royal Diary for Friday. I thank them and go to seek Rod at Bricks to cement some sense into him...

The whole episode is recounted to him but *very* gently. I play my ace of reminding him what he said to me the other day about being a "calming influence." I have to battle through quite an obstinate reaction. "I've done nothing wrong – they're here to help me." I tell him to shut up and listen. Not just to me – but to them. They know more about this than he does. I close with another board meeting with him is on the cards *before* his meeting with Victoria – and that everyone is *trying* to help him.

1015: Unit. The chief whip of the HDFOT clan – Mouthy – is having a "conversation" with a member of the same clan but from a different Unit though a closed window. My ears are still ringing. The dialogue ended with "See you later blood, innit." This gentleman leaves prison the same day I do. (If I get Tag).

It's my leaving present to everyone else.

1030: Work. Mathew there – attempting to get a dentist's appointment. Two letters needed to go, both for Hoxon. Mr Kelly departed with me and alerted me that Limping Al "threw a wobbly on Saturday" and "will be shipped-out to another Unit." Elk was walking from the gym to home so I asked him to take my letters up to Hoxon. "No problem, Captain." Elk is now my mule.

Zara (Top). Is there any news on anything? "No. Just sit tight and wait." Frank was outside the building. He relayed the same message and told me to come back and see him "on Friday."

1120: Outside for a smoke. Sweeper Ray brushes by. Was the letter OK? "It's posted." Another prisoner overhears this. "Are you Toe by Toe?" Yes. "Can I have some help?" Of course you can, knock on my door anytime. "Cheers mate." His name? "Roland" (Gift).

In the post a "no thank you" from a literary agent. He "likes my humour" but "not for them…"

1150: I am now a dab hand at peeling off un-franked stamps from rejection letters' envelopes.

1200: Loads and loads and loads of salad.

1235: Overheard: "A touch though, £76 worth of *stuff* for a packet of burn."

Library. A big queue outside – but no staff are about. Stuart arrives expecting "new library guy" to be up and running – or more to the point, sat down and scanning. It appears that "new library guy" is now to be referred to on the call-sheets as "ex-library guy." Stuart does a good impression of Corporal Jones' best "don't panic, don't panic." I leave to locate Library Brett.

On the short hop I catch limping Al who is NOT himself and "wants to be shipped-out." I advise him to hold fire, calm down and go and have a chat with Robbie in Healthcare. He's very "all over the place" and I've never seen him like this before. After more pressure from me he agrees to converse with Cracker.

Brett is on Wilford and the non-even keel library situation is revealed. He rolls his eyes and thanks me for coming to get him. We leave together back for the rudderless library and find a now calmer coxswain in Stuart. I sit down and read the paper. Helmsman Stuart and Commander Brett conclude it's just the two of them now and chat about whatever It is that prison librarians talk about (I'm retired now).

Cox Stuart is coaxed to update me on the Hoxon situation. "People have been shitting in the toilets" (and he doesn't mean IN them). It gets worse: "Someone killed all the fish," by putting "washing up liquid in the tank overnight." There's more: "The youngsters have been getting at Limping Al." I sit shell-shocked. Mostly about the fish. What *sort* of *person* would *do* that?

"Three Governors turned up at lunchtime to address the Unit. There was lots of effing and blinding." They said that "Hoxon is supposed to be the flagship." The Unit was told that "if prisoners want to behave like this, they can, in closed conditions" and "that *the* Governor said that this address is using three Governors' time," which could be spent "filling in forms to help prisoners" and he's "not effing having it." Anyone "who knows anything about it" can "fill in an app" (!) and "see him personally." The Commandant apparently closed his speech with "I've got 400 Cat D prisoners all waiting for a space at Hollesley Bay and I'll quite happily ship the lot of you out."

How is Rick about the fish?

"Taken it OK."

I really am beginning to give up round here. Go to "work." Nothing doing. Speak with Robbie: "Can we do tomorrow at 1000 rather than on Wednesday." Fine. Return to the Unit.

Get told someone has "shat in the shower" here. I go and check the fish.

Fish OK.

1430: Go to my room to write and escape. What IS going on?

As I scribble, a Gregory Peck film is on Film 4 (*The Gunfighter*, 1950). His character has asked his ex if she'll wait and give him a year to "sort himself out."

She said yes.

1510: Going to Healthcare.

1520: Back, my presence not required. On bed with Margaret Rutherford.

1700: Dinner. Most of the talk in the dining room was "who shit in the shower" (Sic). There is talk of a DNA test.

1720: In room. Thoroughly depressed.

1730: Library. Brett materialises at the same time that "ex-library guy" ("ELG") makes his entrance. A row ensues – nothing of any consequence. I study my shoes as insults fly to and fro. ELG exits, stage right. I'm still sitting in my chair admiring my footwear when a voice – the type of which I have *not* as yet heard in prison omits "and who is that gorgeous creature next to you Stuart?" I look up. Brett has turned *purple*. Camp Freddie (I have no idea what his name is) notices me and adds "ooooooh, one even nicer!" gives a "wiggle" and prances off. Who the hell was that? Stuart's line (very matter of fact like):

"Oh, he's the ex-priest. Just arrived."

Tuesday, November 1st, 2011.

T minus 16.

The corridor was beautifully quiet last night. I think every room was basking in the delight of the £76 worth of "items" swapped for a packet of tobacco yesterday.

At work the normal status quo projected itself with Philip. I made up the action by vacuuming. We got talking about long-haul flights – I don't know why – and Philip let slip where he was educated.

The last-hoorah humbling humiliation Hollesley Bay hurls in my direction is when in jail you bump into someone who went to the same school as you.

0815: The heating in my room – and the whole Unit – remains on at full blast. On the news: "People are struggling to pay their heating bills."

0950: Rachel hands me some letters for Rounds. I go upstairs to wait for Robbie armed with them and the Aitken article, which I hope may be of use to him for other prisoners.

1000: Cracker invites me to sit down. A comedy sketch is enacted by stripping-off our tops and opening the windows. The radiators festoon with feverish heat. Does he know the Bay's heating bill? On a shake of the head the figure is released causing him to fatalistically permeate "madness" – with *horrific* similarity to James Donald's last line in Lean's *The Bridge on the River Kwai*. He enquires how things are on Wilford. The nadir is narrated of the on-going filth, the gang culture, the never to be seen senior officer and so on. Revealing that I watched *In Which We Serve* recently, there is not much – if any – respect for our Captain. Indeed he's never to be seen out of his office. Robbie asks if I "know what the staff call him." No idea. "Bungalow Bill," Cracker smirks. "Because he never goes upstairs."

He seems exasperated and incredulous by what I tell him of the Unit. I invite him now to come and see the bedlam and pandemonium. Prisoners prevailing in bed, the odious repulsive food littered around the battleground dining room set-dressed by huge slovenly quantities of unwashed plates making up the scenery. He looks embarrassed. I go on. If three Governors can go to Hoxon to read the riot act – why can't they come to Wilford? Robbie doesn't know what I'm talking about so I fill him in on the dead fish satire ("so, I'm looking for someone who pulled the wings off flies as a boy"), the crap in the loos, taking the piss out of Limping Al and so on.

He bows his head.

I tell him of yesterday's "gift" in Wilford's showers.

He remarks "that Hollesley Bay is falling apart and has been for the last two years."

He concludes that "Wilford is flashing a warning signal within the system." I don't know whether he means solely tantamount within these walls or to the suits that run our country's prisons. I hope both.

I pray that by the time you read this, Hollesley Bay is a thriving, self-sufficient, enthusiastic working prison whose occupants deserve to be there (open prison) and put back in what they've been given. I hope there are enthusiastic staff who give praise, good leadership and to quote *In Which We Serve*, it is an "efficient, happy ship." I'm afraid I won't remember it so.

Cracker exclaims that "it is lunacy" that as I prepare for re-entry I have "resorted to survival mode to stay out of the way of the street-like culture."

We shift subjects. He proclaims that my plan to retrain myself to use the same thought process in my "personal life to a flying check list, a *very* good move."

The best case scenario possibilities that he asked me to prepare are itemised. With regards to flying, the lines in my scene with Michelle are repeated. I know I'm lucky that I have the drive to attempt a "bounce back." I know if anyone can do it, I can. "That sounds good," he nods. The Aitken article is handed over – baby steps will be order of the day. He scans it and makes noises that every prisoner – who can read – should be "made to digest it before being let loose on society."

With a sensitive mien he asks if there is "any progress on the wife front" and "what the best case scenario there?" All I can do is press on with the book and hope that one day she reads it. I stress to him that I'm not trying to sound like I'm in a state of self-pity but prison has taught me a lot. I would just like her to know I've changed. That I'm sorry. And that I love her.

I have to confess that I got a bit tearful at this stage. I apologised. Robbie said that it's "perfectly OK." I should be kinder to myself and I "have to stop" beating myself up.

He brings up my comment from previous pages of the script that if the roles were reversed I would be "camping in the fields next to the prison." I stress to him with no misconception that the only person who is at fault is me.

At this juncture, the floodgates opened-up Hoover dam like.

He "wonders what should be done." I've offered talking with her parents, with a mediator, with anyone. This was of course, before I went to prison – and bucked up my ideas. He takes the rug from under me by suggesting that *he* "gets in touch with her." It's strange you say that because I nearly asked you to do that at our last session.

"I nearly suggested it."

Cracker continues: "It's very apparent" that I need "to talk to her – from one human being to another." He asks for her details. I write them out and give them to him.

A chance, a small glimmer of *chance*.

In my "remaining time here" (assuming I go on Tag) He would like to see me "on Tuesdays *and* Wednesdays." Christ, are you that worried about me? "No." He wants "to build a good safety net" and that I have "more insight that anyone he's ever met in prison." He says that he is sure I have learnt my lesson "and will not be back" (not likely – they can get someone else for the sequel).

Rounds. This will do me good. The fresh air will blow away the millions of "what ifs."

Nothing of great interest to report on the circuit except at Stow, the Terminator asks me how Wilford is. If he "was a serving prisoner," he would "refuse to live there…"

Lunch back at the ghetto. Ham salad. Andrew at the officers' Mess. The author's mind in a mess.

1230: On key-drop a new (to me) female (?) officer is encountered. Clearly Hollesley Bay's Rosa Klebb. Her demeanour was the same as her namesake at Bedford but the match on any close-ups would be catastrophic. I will have to keep her in long-shot and hope the dungarees and Doctor Marten boots keep the continuity going.

At my asylum – sorry, the library – read the paper and then depart for "work" at 1305. Nothing other than a couple more letters.

1320: Wilford with one letter for a resident. The female (?) sarcastic officer ("F?SO") still on site (eating crisps). I reach for the hole-punch (to puncture the letter in order to hang it on that room's hook) without asking. BIG mistake – loads of unrestrained sarcastic comments erupted out of her. I ignored them.

I wonder where they've been keeping her? I suppose, from her appearance and manner they dug her out for Halloween and have neglected to pack her away again.

1445: Work. Rachel would like me to arrange for the notice boards, taken down for painting, to be re-erected. Can I please collate the Handymen. Off I go to the backwaters of the "Industrial" area. The tributary arrived at five minutes later. For the scene, two prisoners are sitting on upturned crates smoking cigarettes and drinking tea. "Ere – it's that writer," says one, burping. "Fuck me," replies the other, lifting one cheek and farting. Any idea where the Handymen are? "One's fuckin' well behind you mate." I spin around and there's Geordie, grinning. Rachel's request is divulged. His team "will be there first thing in the morning."

An officer walks by, carrying an *enormous* soup ladle. This is like a missing scene from *Porridge*. Either Burper or Farter says "afternoon Gov," and sings "yo da laduloeeeeeee."

1700: Dinner. "Curry with rice." Got a piece of chicken. No rice arrived at the Unit. Managed to get my hands on two oranges though.

Wednesday, November 2nd, 2011.

T minus 15. Up at 0620. The grumpy-always-on-the-phone-night-officer on the phone. I don't understand, our "boss" is back from Australia. On the news: "The St. Paul's eviction has been postponed." Showered by 0700. Had a VERY close inspection of the floor before I stepped *anywhere*…

The heating is still on full blast.

0720: Work. More "old school" talk with Philip. Very, very, very strange. He rather excitedly – I can't think why – announces that the new dentist is starting today…

0755: Rounds (Bosnia and Wilford).

0825: Toast in café corner.

Healthcare. Three Handymen stand outside smoking. Their down-tools simply because of "not having any tools." Their "Gov is away" and they "don't know what to do." What, for some screwdrivers? They nod. Does Rachel know? "Yes" and "we'll go and try and find some."

I watch them pass the HDFOT lot standing on the corner. All spitting.

Inside I grin at Renee. The new dentist grins at me. We look like a toothpaste commercial. Rachel asks me to "hang-fire" for the Handymen to return "tooled-up," a rather unfortunate coin of phrase as a lot of my colleagues are here for going places similarly equipped.

Rachel is in a panic as she's on her own with no doctor and the waiting room is packed.

0915: The doctor is here, but at Bosnia "dealing with an emergency." I sit on one of the chairs and think about something else Robbie said to me yesterday: "When this is over," I'll think "*what* was that?" I must constantly remind myself what brought me here.

Waiting prisoners eye me suspiciously as I make notes.

0945: Still waiting. Philip returns from Bosnia and gives me a raised eyebrow "what are you doing here?" I reply with a raised eyebrow "waiting." He goes to see Rachel who raises both her eyebrows when the doctor arrives with furrowed eyebrows.

0950: Rachel now boiling over: "GO AND FIND THE HANDYMEN!" Geordie lives at Bosnia so set-off for there. Another of his team is outside the Unit. "We went for tools – got told no – so bollox to it, went 'ome." Return to Rachel to update her but she is on the phone. I sit and wait.

1010: Rachel off the phone. Relay to her that the Handymen were not allowed to have tools as their "Gov" is away. More eyebrow action. The phone is picked up and someone is shouted at. The phone then *slammed* down, she orders me like a 60's Bond baddie to "get the Handymen. NOW."

Bosnia's office – which has all the ambience of some gaudy bookies'. One officer and one prisoner within. Hello, I'm after the Handymen team. No reaction. Try to explain further but still don't get anywhere. The prisoner is asked if he knows anyone here who works on that team. "I don't know what the fuck you're talking about." The officer says do I have any names? I only know Geordie as Geordie. Does he have a list of where people work? "We're a bit disorganised here."

Suggest to him that he Tannoys the Handymen team. He likes this and does his best Gladys Pugh – alas with no xylophone. The floor creaks as disturbed-by-Tannoy prisoners all turn over in their beds at the same time. However, Geordie appears and I convey that Rachel has sent me for him NOW.

Rachel's office. Geordie relays to her the sequence of events so far. This causes frantic eyebrow action. She picks up the phone again and *firmly* communicates that one of the Handymen is with her NOW and PLEASE can "he have some tools." She gets an affirmative and dispatches Geordie to fetch them. We agree to reconvene after lunch.

Wilford. Roland – who asked for Toe by Toe help – presents himself. What's the score? Get a very confusing yarn about him "being late from a Home-leave, then a nicking and adjudication, all coz the trains were fucked." He shows me a half filled out appeal-form which to his credit, he has done his best to complete. This guy doesn't want assistance with reading but legal aid...

NNO is bench-approached for counsel. "Speak to the S.O. – less of a paperwork trail" (He has as much faith in "apps" as I do). Roland asks in his best elocution if it would be OK for me to speak on his behalf. NNO: "That is acceptable. Grab the S.O. when he's back on Friday."

So, I need to converse with Bungalow Bill...

Lunch and the accumulated acoustics accompanying it were revolting.

1310: Healthcare. The Handymen team, including Geordie, all dramatically drill holes. Geordie's best line: "We got wor tools."

Probe Philip ("off for four days"), Rachel and Nurse Sue if there is anything else. "No." Wish Philip a good few days off and return to Devil's Island.

1530: WTWFO – who seems to have been away for ages – is back among the ranks. She is asked when somebody MIGHT start talking to me about Tag – which is on the 17th. "It's best to talk to the S.O. on Friday." I enquire how can the S.O. make any decisions about me when he's never spoken to me before? She gives me a knowing look and says "he goes on what we say."

1700: Dinner was also revolting.

Later, Roland turns up. The "facts" are: On his last Home-leave – when he was due back at the prison by (at the *absolute* latest) 1530 – his train did not arrive at Ipswich until 1544. "Another prisoner was on the same train which was late." On landing at the gate they were both "nicked." The next day, both were called for adjudication by a Governor. The other prisoner pleaded "not guilty," his mitigation that the trains were late. He was found not guilty. Roland "got in a fluster." He "was asked repeatedly" if he "was pleading guilty or not guilty." In his confusion – he tells me – he pleaded guilty. He got a loss of 10 days Canteen – "which will lead to an IEP review" – which will "hurt further Home-leaves."

I feel like Perry Mason. I ask him who this other prisoner is and get given a name. I'll go and find this guy tomorrow – he is billeted on Hoxon. If he confirms Roland's story he might have a case.

Roland is happy with this plan. He shakes his "brief's" hand. Mine.

Thursday, November 3rd, 2011.

T minus 14. 0620: Night officer-always-on-the-phone on the phone. Who *does* he talk to?

Hoxon. I explain myself to a very sleepy, still in his underwear prisoner. I give him the story the way I've heard it. His version reveals a *completely* different chain of events. Starting with "is this Roland"? On my nod he continues: "I've told him a million times"…

0735: Healthcare. WD serving prisoners. From the mood I can hear that she's in, I wish Philip was on. After "treating" her customers, I ask her to unlock upstairs. Knuckle dusters, grenades and some sort of liquid powder drink are picked up by her and she ascends the staircase ahead of me.

See the stairs creek.

Upstairs is unleashed and I'm asked where Rachel is. I've no idea – so get busy mopping…

Healthcare for prisoners is 0700 – 0800.

0800: WD has locked the front door. *Sweet Jesus* I'm stuck in the Bates' Motel building with Kathy Bates. Mopping the Treatment Room's floor I ask as nonchalantly as possible if she's locked the door. "Yes." She wants to "teach the stragglers that rules is rules."

Soon enough there are prisoners tapping on the window asking for admission. WD doesn't let them in (!) One says he's "got to be seen now" as he's "going to work outside and doesn't come back till late tonight." "Oh yes?" says WD, in a tyrannical disbelieving voice. "And where do you work boyo?"

"The kebab shop, innit."

She's not budging and not letting anybody in either. Including one of the twins who is half hanging off the window in order to establish two-way communications explaining that he's "done his leg in." WD: "Oh well boyo, Healthcare is open 0700 – 0800." (I'm in a siege with a Dragon!) Twin 1 or Twin 2 rationalises "I've only just done it," still dangling in order to be in shot. "I'll ring your Unit," WD says, standing her ground her side of the bastion that is the locked door.

An expletive is made out from whichever Twin this is.

WD shoos them all away. I finish as quickly as I can and vacate the Dragon's lair as fast as my legs will carry me.

0820: Toast, coffee and *Robinson Crusoe* in café corner. As I finish, a Tannoy from NNO asking for volunteers to help in the dining room. The piles of rubbish do not require volunteers – they need mountaineers. Trying to be of help I report to the office and being so good at bins, I put myself down for my awry expertise in the garbage disposal business. He thanks me and asks me what I'm going to do now with Roland's case. I tell him that I've concluded that he was late due to no fault of anyone other than himself. NNO nods. Roland's 10 days loss of Canteen and 14 days loss of "private spends" is not, in my opinion, too harsh. He agrees but points out that because of this, it is likely that Roland will be "demoted from enhanced to standard for a month or so – and he would need to be enhanced on December 1st for his Christmas-leave to be approved."

He philanthropically suggests that Roland asks for "his status to be reviewed between now and November 30th and in the meantime, to keep his head down to re-enhance himself before the cut-off date." I thank NNO for his heads-up about Roland's head down and weigh-anchor to empty the bins.

0950: Healthcare. The Rucksack Hurler in picture – and stressed. "Where's Kathy?" she fires at me. I've no idea. A new doctor (Sir Lancelot Spratt) harrumphs in the waiting room. Prisoners wait. The Hurler goes-a-Dragon-hunting and returns with a positive sighting. "She's upstairs with the other doctor." Sir Lancelot sidles up to me and says in *the* most James Robertson Justice fashion "who are you and where are my patients?" Before I invite him to come and scrub up with me I identify myself as the *Orderly*. We all (!) go upstairs followed by the waiting prisoners who join the wagon trail without any prompting whatsoever. On the first floor is another prisoner, waiting for the doctor who is in with WD. The first floor is now occupied with lots of confused looking people – the author included. Sir Lancelot tries to get into one of the loos – but his Holy Grail is locked. Prisoners ramble and scramble like stampeding cattle causing chaos. WD ejects from the other doctor's office like a champagne cork. "What's going on?" she demands Sybil like. "Where's Rachel?" I respond Basil like that I have no idea as we are surrounded by jostling jail birds and one doctor who clearly needs the loo. Hurler twigs that if she doesn't do something quickly then the Orderly – me – will shortly be mopping up a puddle and admits him to one of the locked lavatories. He's thinking that he wishes he'd worked harder at medical school. WD keeps asking me where Rachel is. I keep repeating that I don't know…

Hurler pats me on the arm around the convict circling circus-ponies and says "probably best if you come back after lunch."

1010: "Home." Roland on the range. We need to talk. He says OK and he'll be along in a minute. Go to my room to compose myself. I suppose like a barrister does before Court – like an actor preparing to go on stage.

A knock on the door. Roland sits down. Without beating about the bush I tell him more Judge like than any advocate mode that I have spoken to his Co D and that Roland's story will not carry any weight in an appeal because *his* train was not late. *He* was late. The only timetable skirmish was the other chap's and that was at the Birmingham end of proceedings. Roland lives in East London (as do so many of my urbanite colleagues – one way of clearing it for the Olympic site I suppose). I warn him that because of this it's likely that his status will be downgraded and when he is considered for Christmas-leave on December 1st, because of his lower rating, he'd better start thinking about letting Santa know he'll be in Suffolk.

I propose to him that he keeps his nose clean and requests a review of his conduct prior to the end of November, in the hope that by turning a new leaf, someone in power here recognises his efforts and rewards him. This is the core structure of society in this prison. I've read it somewhere in the bumf. I remind him that he owes this not just to himself but to his missus and kid – both of whom I am sure are busting a gut to see him over the holidays.

He then rather took my breath away by disclosing something else that had occurred. What followed almost made me cry in despair.

"Well Jon, coz I was pissed off like with all this lot I smoked a couple of joints, innit." *Wonderful*, I think. "And then I had a piss test, innit. Results back next week. I'm fucked." I asked him if it was "Spice" – which I know from my vast experience of things medical at Healthcare go undetected in both MDT's (Mandatory drugs tests) and VDT's (Voluntary). "Nah, it was…" and then the name of something I've never heard of. He is indeed fucked. Or will be when the results come back. I try reasoning with him to play the game. The fact that he is here (in an open prison) means that they want him "out" – they need the space – but he *has* to reciprocate by showing he means business. Whether this sank in or not I have no idea. Roland leaves Court at 1030.

My solution to this? MDT's for *everyone* each day. Even the "posh pilot." Anyone with a hint of anything stronger than a roll-up is out – back to bang-up. Same goes for prisoners who don't pull their weight. This is prison for Pete's sake, where once inmates have reached Cat D open conditions, they persistently take the piss. Flip that over: take the piss out of them and test it. If it's positive: back to a Victorian jail.

1110: Downstairs to see if I have mail. I could do with another amusing "no" from a literary agent. Also I'm short of stamps. That's a lie – I'm out of stamps.

No post. NNO asks me if I'm "dropping the case."

Yes I am. He says "the system WILL help if it's a genuine foul up by the trains." As it is he who has flagged the system – and this officer actually warrants his title (an endangered species) – I jump on the bandwagon and probe. Do officers ever get a chance to voice their ideas? "No," says NNO. "If we do, we are shot down." The only way to develop a notion of possible value "is to let a suit think a good idea originated from a suit."

1200: Lunch queue. A touch of handbags at dawn between Roland and Mouthy. Uncharacteristically, Roland took exception to Mouthy queue-jumping. I don't know what triggered him to protest on this occasion. Mouthy does it all the time. No one normally says a word.

Not even the officers.

Went to the library and read the paper. Stuart asked me to chase up a dental appointment.

1300: Work. WD put Stuart on the list. Nothing else for me to do and was despatched. Still no sign of Rachel. Returned to the library to tell Stuart he's on the relevant bit of paper. Hung about post "official" library hours – Stuart made me laugh by saying "it's a lock-in."

1330: On the news, the Pakistani cricket fixers have all been jailed from between them, 6 months to 4 years.

Some prison cricket team or other should be rather good next year...

1510: Work. The place deserted apart from the Hurler and WD. Both of them displaying huge "we don't care anymore" signs. Do they need anything done? The reply – blank, disinterested stares. Have they heard from Rachel? Shrugged shoulders. Should we be concerned? They drop a bombshell on me by saying "she's leaving anyway. But she doesn't want anyone to know."

In my room writing. *Zulu*, on Film 4.

1700: Attended Roll-check but gave dinner a miss. I have some soup and French bread which I will eat later.

Picked up Canteen, including a grapefruit which I'll have for breakfast in café corner.

Friday, November 4th, 2011.

T minus 13. Sweeper Ray came round late last night but I was in bed with Idi Amin (*The Last King of Scotland* before you get worried).

Last night one "gentleman" was trying to get the attention of another "gentleman" by repeatedly shouting down (or is it up?) the corridor "yo Stag," delay. "Yo Stag," delay. And so on.

"Stag" never answered.

Harry Enfield is on Home-leave as of now. Five days respite from THAT laugh. Esther Rantzen is on telly campaigning for OAP's heating bill assistance.

My windows are wide open to try to reduce the uncomfortably warm temperature in my room.

0710: Roll-check myself to an unfamiliar officer with my familiar Three zero. His peevish riposte: "Is that the same as thirty?" It's going to be one of THOSE days then. On the walk to work, get soaked in heavy rain. On pouring myself into the building WD is serving seven saturated prisoners. I dry-dock and wait for WD to unlock upstairs.

0750: WD still too busy so give up and go "home." EBV stops me and asks me to chase up his dentist's appointment. The fitting of metal teeth probably. On key pick-up the "is that the same as thirty" officer is looking at his rota on the computer – as so many officers seem to do here. All day long.

0810: Second attempt at "work." Sweeper Ray outside. Sorry about last night. Is everything alright? "Wanted to sound-off but better now."

Healthcare. Mouthy musters. So does another member of the HDFOT lot from Wilford. Mouthy is prattling-on about how "someone stole his things, innit." Before I know it Mouthy jumps a queue too far and upsets his fellow club member and we are all witness to a physical skirmish. Punches are not thrown but plenty of a-pushing and a-shoving occurs. WD is on the radio for "back-up" as quick as a flash whilst Mouthy is shouting the odds at his opponent who has objected that "he was first" and firmly orders "do not touch me." The harangue is over in seconds. Mouthy retreats from the premises post sideshow having been chastised by WD.

Limping Al is in the waiting area too and we give each other knowing looks after whip-panning to this dramatic sequence. WD removes herself from behind the Treatment room door and asks the gathered ensemble if we know "that prisoner's name."

Amnesia blankets the room. Both Al and the HDFOT player give me the "prisoner's look" of "say nothing." WD looks at me. I really *don't* know his name. WD: "Security is on its way over anyway." I hiss in her ear that she mustn't ask prisoners questions like that in front of other prisoners – no one wants to be a "grass."

Snap-zoom to the penny dropping.

Officer Shouter walks in like the cavalry. His aloof demeanour as much use as Charles Hawtrey to a rugby scrum. Unbelievably, Mouthy – doing himself no favours at all – follows him in. He and his fellow HDFOT wrangler are called into the Treatment room to explain themselves.

I then hear a grovelling, pleading – and *very* different to the "gang leader" persona normally portrayed – apology to the S.O, WD and the HDFOT queue rival. They are both despatched. WD points at me and says to the S.O. "he saw everything." The S.O. has the sense not to ask me anything on the altercation but says that he understands Mouthy likes queue jumping.

He's gone as quickly as he arrived and a visibly shaken WD says she thought it was "really going to kick- off," which is why she called security. I reassure her she did exactly the right thing and I would have got stuck in if I needed to. Whilst I'm no great fan of hers, I'm even less of one of the unfriendly, arrogant, noisy and unpleasant bully who does not even have the sense to treat his own "club" with some basic manners. WD says it's not my job to protect her but I answer with do you really think I wouldn't?

I bloody well *would* have as well.

Everything settles down as quickly as it boiled over. I do the loos and leave – checking that a still shaking WD is alright. She tells me that when she tells her husband, "he will go mad."

I have visions of that little chap from *The Benny Hill Show* who always got his head slapped.

Reel in Rod on my way to the Unit and instruct him to remember his manners during his royal appointment with Victoria later this morning. He gives me a painful look but I can tell he knows I am right.

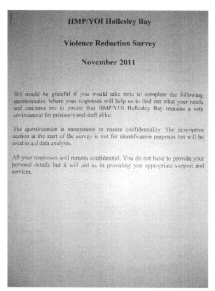

Back on the Unit as I go upstairs Mouthy is telling anyone who will listen in his immutable gangster-LP-cover-front that "the nurse got on the radio very quickly." Ignoring him I go to get my mug. On the trip back downstairs Mouthy is giving his opponent an absolute antagonistic "if looks could kill" vendetta stare. This is not over...

Coffee and grapefruit in my room. Out of the window, across the car park 2 or 3 officers run – with urgency. Something else has happened. I go downstairs and Limping Al is on board the good (?) ship Wilford doing his electrical testing job. Two officers walk from the office with "possession" bags. The large, transparent "prison Gucci suitcases" that are used when we move anywhere.

Like when prisoners are shipped-out...

Al whispers "he's being shipped-out. Did you see those bags?" Are you sure? Because if he is I will run around the prison grounds stark naked. He grins as I depart back for work in heavy rain. Frank found: "No news" and to check with him on Monday. I must keep an eye out for Bungalow Bill.

Nothing doing at Healthcare.

0955: Wilford. On key pick-up I ask an officer if the gentleman who caused the fracas this morning is being shipped-out. The officer confirms that he is.

1015: Work. Some lines of dialogue with the Hurler to sort out EBV's dental appointment. Ventured upstairs to see if WD has a) calmed down and b) if she needs anything done. The doctor that I saw about my hand is with her and she asks how it is. I proffer my mitt. "Oh, lovely, getting worse."

WD tasks me with emptying the yellow bin, the contents of which are due for incineration. I wonder for a second, if I can fit the doctor in it.

1030: Unit. On arrival it stopped raining. Roland roaming and updated on Mouthy now being Ex-Mouthy. He reveals that "someone thumped Mouthy last night." Who? "I'm not saying but someone on this Unit, innit."

1140: Receive a "no" from a literary agent. The stamp franked and the letter boring.

1150: Chow-truck outside. Rod seen talking to Moyles. Shoot downstairs to see how he got on with the Victoria embankment. "Much better." Thank God for that.

1200: Lunch. The dining room *wonderfully* quiet. Still filthy though.

1230: Limping Al back on the Unit for more electrical duties. He sides over to me and says "he's definitely gone then?" Yes, I say. "Come on then...." He says.

I had forgotten that I'd said I'd streak around the prison. We agree that I will just put it in the book.

There you go Al.

To the office to request more prisoners' writing paper. For some reason there's none left downstairs. An officer walks me to their stores cupboard, gives me about 3cm's worth. 2cm of which are now on my shelf. I will have a problem if Tag doesn't happen on the 17th. I suppose worrying about paper is the least of my concerns...

1326: Bungalow Bill in residence. His name is apt. His reticence to ascend stairs is married to his appearance – he resembles a bearded Bill Maynard. The office is asked what the form is to speak to him. "If his door is open, he's receiving guests."

His door is open.

I knock on it and a writing Bungalow Bill shouts – without stopping – "YES?" Bullet points are fired at him on all events to date concerning Tag. He continues to write and "just some rubber stamping then," is said as scribing continues. I thank him and depart.

Was that it? I wonder.

1425: Bungalow Bill sighted climbing the scaffold stairs to OMU, which houses Judi. To see her about me?

1700: Dinner. Would rather go hungry.

1815: A knock on the door from Roland. He's spoken to the S.O. who has agreed that I can speak on his behalf. When? His reply rather shocked me...

"Now."

Audiences with S.O.'s are like busses. You wait 15 ½ weeks and along they all come at once. Like a nervous skew-whiff understudy – who doesn't know his lines – I am pushed on stage. The S.O. invites us to sit down and I – with brain whirring – present the "evidence."

Roland was late. Roland got "nicked." Roland pleaded guilty but shouldn't have as there are "grey" areas. The S.O.'s eyebrows shoot up... The system put the wrong station on his licence.

He digs out the accused's paperwork which mentions a station close to his home. But on his original application – which on approval was *stamped by the system* – it says the station that he DID depart from. The S.O. (whose eyebrows have now disappeared into his hairline): "Do you have that form?"

Yes we do.

We have a case. The S.O. realises this and says "make an app" (!) to a particular Governor and "request an informal chat, in order to set up a formal appeal on Monday." I ask if I can take my "brief" hat off and put my "prisoner" hat on. He consents and sends Roland on his way.

I *gently* ask if he's had any luck with MY paperwork – slightly more important to me, despite feeling rather pleased with myself for finding a loophole for Roland – "yes" – he hopes the paperwork will be on his desk "on Monday." When will I know for sure? I will be "told the result" the day he "gets the paperwork." All good. Let's hope Zara (Top) can find me a home.

I made an "app" to speak to a Governor for Roland...

Saturday, November 5th, 2011.

T minus 12. Happy bonfire night day. I shall be thinking of you-know-who this evening. She loved fireworks night. I wrote that this morning and it's now 1720. *Hellfighters* (1969) is the background noise in my room. John Wayne is wooing his ex-wife. Show me a sign God. I'll know – if he wins her back.

Asked an officer when Governor-so-and-so was expected. "Why?" Updated this relatively sensible white-shirt on the Roland situation and got a most mysterious comeback. "Oh, you're his Mackenzie friend." I beg your pardon? "It's a prison nickname for one who speaks on someone else's behalf." This officer utilised one when he was "interviewed after a death in custody."

0810: Tannoy: "Second and last call for Roll-check."

John Wayne is thumping everyone and not doing very well in wooing his ex...

Schlepped up to work to check up on WD and scrutinise the conditions of the place. WD friendly – I got a smile – and "feeling better" than yesterday after a good talk with her husband. Why do I suspect she had a good talk TO her husband? Did her bins and delivered one letter to Bosnia in light rain.

0955: Library. A "new – new" library guy there – no name yet, sorry, but definitely suitable for a new series of *It Ain't Half Hot Mum*. They can shoot the interiors on Wilford – the temperature's perfect. Read the paper – and then the new edition of one of the freebie newspapers available to prisoners. In it was an interview with the Chief Inspector of prisons. One quote made me reach for my pen...

"My abiding impression was of cell after cell with young men locked in, a makeshift curtain across the window, the light off, daytime telly in the background, sleeping their way through their sentence. It was a truly depressing experience."

1200: Bangers for lunch (the only ones I will see this bonfire night) and toast. The HDFOT players seem incapable of eating whilst sitting still. They dart from table to table, lunch in hand like some bizarre speed-dating gathering.

John Wayne is remarrying his ex-wife. Thank you God.

"Prisoner bullshit" is the expression used at my current address for what you would associate with "Chinese whispers." Over lunch I heard a story from Gordon that – apparently – originated from Alistair about a recent "cell-spin" (room search) where someone with some style had hidden some not permitted possessions. Namely: two bottles of champagne (no ice bucket – bad form) and a certain well-known brand of mobile telephone.

After lunch I went and loitered outside to gather more information on Champagne man from Alistair who works with Moyles on the meals-on-wheels chow-truck. Waited ten minutes and instead of them both rolling up in their Bedford (lorry, not prison), a solitary Moyles appeared. And lo: on foot. "Wot you doin' ere, Jon?" My desire to rack his co-driver's brains was conferred. Why no truck and why no Alistair? "Already done it mate. We're eager."

Another officer was asked when a Governor might get back to me in regard to my "app" concerning matters Roland.

"When he gets back to you."

Early evening a minor kick-off took place between AP2 and an elderly foreign gentleman ("EFG") who quietly lives amongst us. And who wouldn't say boo to a goose. AP2 turning the "A" of his "P" up a notch or two and calling EFG a "cunt." Fortunately a few "sensible" prisoners got involved and the fire was extinguished.

Chow-truck arrives and Alistair grabbed. As per typical prison rumours he didn't know what I was talking about. I made a mental note to only "clock" things when I see them and to disregard any future fables from my peers.

Peered at what had been transported to us for dinner and decided there and then to go hungry.

Had a quiet word with Tony, our "Unit-Captain" about AP2 shouting at EFG. Tony didn't have a clue who I was talking about until I worded the *arrogant* one…

"I know who you mean… I'll sort it Jon."

Later in my room I could hear the fireworks from the village. I opened my curtains, turned the light out and had a private show. I thought about you-know-who and wondered if she was at a display too.

She always loved fireworks.

Sunday, November 6th, 2011.

T minus 11. Individuals still insist on shouting down the corridor from outside my room – to see if someone is in or awake. Always a "yo," followed by a name. This after 2230. At around that hour I heard someone shout *SHUT THE HELL UP*.

I was *very* surprised to find out it was me.

0755: Thirteen (I *counted* them) names and room numbers read out to attend the Roll-check that is supposed to be at 0730.

0805: *Another* call for Roll-check.

0810: Work. WD asked me to have a think about who would be good at stepping into my shoes after my departure. I let her in on Rachel's previous declining of my recruitment consultant services. Having said that, I didn't know then that Rachel is going. And I still don't know that now either. Especially tomorrow, when she is back. Told WD I'd have a think and left for the Unit via the library to pick up my newspaper.

0830: Wilford – and key pick-up. AMTO – pointing at my newspaper – "is that yours?" Yes. "is it today's?" Here we go, I am about to get a "knock down."

Wrong.

"Can I read it after you?"

0850: Café corner. My own little world. Stayed in my oasis till 1000 and returned to the room for a smoke, dropping off the news section to AMTO.

At HMP Bedford all the officers seemed to do was read newspapers. I am now supplying fodder to feed their craving colleagues at the colony.

After lunch some commotion outside my window. A car containing visitors of the HDFOT regiment. They are all talking – sorry, shouting – to someone on my floor who they apparently know as well. It's a small world. My neighbour shouts something even more ironic back to one of the visitors:

"When did you get out?"

1700: Tannoy: "Dinner and Roll-check." Our fare: "Lamb sausage rolls" and ice cream.

Andrew diverts to my room at 1730. His wife has sent him a DVD player which he can't get to work so he is using my telly as a control to see if it's their box refusing to play ball. All they get is a flickering screen. Same result on mine. Eric n' Ernie won't be watching any DVD's just yet.

I go and join them for pool. Midway through it's my turn to make the coffee. In their room to collect Andrew's mug I see pictures of his wife.

Lucky bastard.

Monday, November 7th, 2011.

T minus 10. Philip filled in on the Mouthy incident. On the QT it was whispered that I am aware of the Rachel situation and that WD has tasked me with coming up with some possible suitable replacements. Do we know where Rachel is going? "She has something lined up." Her replacement is going to have his or her work cut out.

Mopped. I have turned into Dennis.

0800: Unit. As usual, no bread could be found in the dining room. AMTO was persuaded to ring the kitchens with the proviso that I'd do a loaf-run. This he did and off I trotted to the gastro-centre of HMP Hollesley Bay. Humming Dvorak's Hovis music on my entrance I thought I'd stumbled on to the set of the final fight scene of *Dr No*.

Enormous stainless-steel humming machines droned Tardis like. Lights blinked. Things not culinary but more akin to a chemical plant whirred. Leiston stood Zombie like, manufacturing sandwiches whilst half asleep. I walked about taking it all in. A gigantic horse trough sized silver metal pan had some sort of pasta meal bubbling in it. It looked like a science experiment. Someone else (Rick Stein but with four days growth of beard and one earring) in chefs' gear panned into shot. I announced that the bread-boy from Wilford had darkened their doorstep and enquired whom I should ask for.

HMP&YOI
HOLLESLEY BAY

CATERING SURVEY

NOVEMBER

2011

PLEASE FILL THIS IN

YOU COULD MAKE A DIFFERENCE

The Catering Department are holding this survey in order to establish, what your views are about the catering at HMP & YOI Hollesley Bay, and how we can make improvements to it.

This survey can be filled in anonymously, so you don't have to enter your name or number on the sheet, but if you can put in as much information as you can when answering the questions, it will help with the compilation of the results.

"Me."

Followed "Me" past more colossal contraptions towards a walk-in larder which was rammed to the rafters with bread. As he started to fill my arms with multiple loaves I asked him if he was one of the civilian chefs. He admitted in a very guilty way that indeed he was. With his depressing gait and speech, he was difficult to differentiate from the rest of the gathered cast who were made up of prisoners. Pillar-box sized tins of tomatoes pillbox surrounded us. As he continued loading me, the close-to-sell-by-date goodies that we've had of late were mentioned: Are they cheaper? "No, just luck of the draw." He explained that the prison has had those supplies in the larder for "some time but because they were getting close to expiry they were used." He went on: "A large supply of stuff is kept aside for riots and bad weather." In either event, how long could we stay self-sufficient?

"About a month."

I probed for his views on the lack of prison reared vegetables, meat and food-stuff. "The tomatoes and cucumbers a great help in the summer but it would be too expensive and difficult with European law for us to rear animals for slaughter here."

I'm no accountant but surely long term it would make more financial sense.

And give prisoners some decent *work*…

Does he find it soul destroying being a professional chef and churning out the stuff he does? "Soul destroying? No. Comical – Yes." I thanked him and lumbered out loaded with loaves.

0830: Rachel's office. A grilling on the Mouthy episode. I filled in the gaps for her, voicing that it's madness that a civilian female is here by herself even in open conditions. They've "been saying that for years." I do not let on that I know she is leaving soon. Nothing for me to do so foray to Frank's office. He's not in. Bump into Rachel again who is going "to fetch another new student nurse." I offer my assistance in this (!) Rachel half rolling her eyes says I "can see her later."

0930: Frank's office. He's heard "zilch," and I should "keep treading water as the system wants me out." I ask if he's in for the week – "yes" – and can I keep pestering him – "yes."

Zara (Top). The S.O. story is run-through and should I start panicking? "In an ideal world this would be sorted" – YOU'RE NOT KIDDING – but she's "going to OMU now and will inquire."

Lunch. Very orderly and well behaved service – and the servery staff cleaned up after the meal as if they were removing evidence from a crime scene. Why?

Because the Terminator was running the show…

1300: Healthcare. Rachel had an "urgent letter for delivery to Stow." Like a military despatch rider I waited as she typed. With the gum on the sealed envelope still damp, routed to my vital destination. The letter delivered, with my heart in my mouth retraced my steps back to Zara (Top). "Still no news" and "come back at 1500," so returned to number 30 for a bit of *Above Us The Waves* on telly.

1410: Surfaced in the library. Stuart and the *It Ain't Half Hot Mum* ("IAHHM") character submerged in the diving-bell of boredom. I got stuck into the newspapers. Stuart asked if he can have my T shirts and IAHHM has earmarked my jacket when I wrap. Told them they can have them both now if the system lets me know what's going on.

1450: Left the library for work.

1451: Left work for Zara (Top).

On the set that is "Resettlement" the scene unravels thus: Zara (Top): "God, is that the time already?" Tries someone on the phone. "No answer." Then: "Have a seat and I'll go and ask." I sit down. Half the office is in darkness. Only when my eyes become accustomed to the dark do I realise that I am not alone. There is a (very young) officer sitting, eyes shut, half asleep in the corner. I enquire if we are saving electricity. "No, I just don't like the light," is sleepily said in a very strong Suffolk accent. Zara (Top) returns. "Zara in Probation has you on her desk (?!!!) but she's not there now." *Another* Zara? "Yes. Come and see me tomorrow afternoon." OK. Which other days is Zara (Top) working this week? "Just tomorrow."

Worry my way back to the Unit. Governor number two – the Newcastle accented one – is in the office dealing with someone else so hover. Ask an officer if I can approach him. "Help yourself." His conversation complete, I sidle over and introduce myself. "I know who are." (Is that good or bad?) Explain the situation. He is sympathetic and I *think* suggests that if "Probation Zara" still hasn't done "her stuff by tomorrow then get an S.O. to deal with it." I take that as the green light to by-pass Zara (Probation) if we need to.

I then bring up the Roland situation and convey the S.O.'s comments on Friday and my "app" to another Governor – to which I have had no response. "That's because that Governor is away."

GOD GIVE ME STRENGTH.

He suggests "not appealing and taking the hit of the loss of Canteen BUT expressing at Roland's IEP review that lateness will never be an issue again." This, according to the Governor "Will then put the onus on the S.O. to pass judgement on whether or not Roland can go home for Christmas." Unbelievably, Roland then appears – from *nowhere* – and listens.

In front of the Governor, I say to him that if he makes it 110% clear he will NEVER be late again – it is highly likely that he will be going home for Christmas. The Governor and I both look at Roland hoping that that the penny has dropped. I thank the Governor, who disappears as quietly as Roland materialised. Message is left with the office that I would like a second with the S.O. who is not in the building but "in the establishment…"

1630: An officer is requested to update me on our glorious leader's movements. "He's not in again today or tomorrow." The plan is now to ask for an alternative S.O. tomorrow. They're making me work for this…

1650: Roland at my door. "The S.O. is here." We shoot downstairs – he's talking to Mouthy 2 –

an enormous Jungle VIP member of HDFOT lot who is the fan of oranges... The S.O. spots me and says that he IS in tomorrow and he'll talk to me then. I acknowledge this as he asks Roland what he wants. He's with me, I say, dragging Roland away. I can take a hint and would rather converse with Bungalow Bill when he's not stressed...

1700: Dinner. The veggie option. Had 2 or 3 mouthfuls then aborted it.

Because I found hairs in it.

Tuesday, November 8th, 2011.

T minus 9. Roll-checked myself at 0720 to AMTO whilst half dressed (him not me). A poster hung at a last- throws-of life-Titanic angle on the wall, so I straightened it out as he fought like an escape-artist doing his act with both his epaulets and the chair as he sat attempting to finish dressing.

0725. Philip presided at work and in a very jolly mood too. And busy. I mopped. I reported that I have said nothing to Rachel – will someone replace her next week? "I hope so." He said it "should be someone who has worked in prisons before." That means it won't be, said I. We both knew that I was probably right.

0750: Unit. The poster I re-hung earlier still up.

0755: Tannoy: "Breakfast Roll-check." (The published time for this is 0730).

0830: Sitting in my room trying to formulate a plan to join together all the pieces I need to leave on the 17th. Namely Bungalow Bill, the lady in charge of internal Probation – Zara, and Zara (Top). I can *list* them. But *they* hold the cards. They *are* the cards. The only ace up my sleeve will be lady luck.

0845: Descend downstairs and ask AMTO if the S.O. is in. "Yes he is." Creep down the corridor and knock on his closed door. Get invited in with a Mussolini "YES" and enter. "Sit down," he barks. A good start. The first line in his script: "I'm *supposed* to be on annual fucking leave." So a *really* good start. I politely try to convey that time is not on my side as Zara (Top) is only here today and we're still waiting for Zara Probation to do something. If I understood correctly, the Deputy Governor said by-pass it. "I'll chase Zara" (Which one?) "And I'll speak to the Deputy Governor," adding that he has a meeting with him later to discuss two prisoners which "doesn't concern" me. I ask him if he's here for the day as time is rather pressing. BB responds with "my day doesn't revolve around you." He closes with "I know it's important to you."

We move on to Roland's situation. He asks how I got on with Governor so and so – the one he told me to make a dreaded "app" to. I explain he wasn't in so I spoke to the Deputy Governor about this as well. He told me that an appeal is futile but it is the S.O.'s discretion as to how long the "lay-down" (The grounding of) would be if Roland holds his hands up and says that he's learnt his lesson. I repeat that the Deputy Governor indicated that if Roland plays ball, he will be home for Christmas.

Whereupon he taps on some memo pinned on his wall saying that the "main Governor has put it in writing that all lay-downs are of a mandatory period." I repeated to him that I very carefully recited to Roland, *in front* of the Deputy Governor that if Roland behaves, on the discretion of S.O. he will be home for Christmas. "I'll speak to the Governor." I thank him and leave still no further forward on anything really.

0845: Key handed in and off to Robbie. Rod was there. Rachel was there. Robbie was not there. Rounds for me. Rod requested help with his CV. Got Stuart a dental appointment for the morning and left for postman duties with our Statham statue who announced he needed me to go to Education with him to use their computer. On arrival there (0900) we found it locked so coffee called. The mail split between us, we agreed to reconvene at Wilford. An uneventful drop-off at Bosnia followed but at Cosford a number of the errant HDFOT team were unsubtly casing the joint – like marauding tomcats waging guerrilla warfare. Something was going down. The next thing I knew, the most enormous prisoner, taller than me and wider than 3 of me, was walked out adorned in handcuffs accompanied by two officers. A ship-out. He went quietly, telling one of the lurking mob: "I'm being shipped-out, innit."

0920: Wilford. When Rod appeared he told me he'd been summoned to work – coffee would have to wait and could I come with him to do what needed to be done. Off we went.

0925: Bricks classroom. Within were three prisoners – four if you include me – and two civilian female teachers, one of whom; Miss Mary – she who knew of my Toe by Toe status on early Hollesley Bay days. "Hello Jonathan," she smiled. I reciprocated the greeting and Rod explained that he'd dragged me along for CV assistance. All the other prisoners talked at once. The individual who I've not met before (Raquel from *Only Fools and Horses*) told me she's "the new head of literacy" and stood by a briefing-board drawing up what looked like a timetable. She asked Miss Mary if "that would work?" and then told me "education is very important." All the other prisoners were still talking both over each other and her. One of them voiced that with her glasses on, the head of literacy "looks like Anne Robinson" (which she didn't).

It turned out in the shambles that the timetable didn't work, as everyone present had started the course at different times and were at assorted stages. Miss Mary looked at me in pleading desperation. I whispered across the table that maybe one-on-one was the best way forward. She and the new head of literacy agreed. Still all the prisoners talked. The subject was now the *X Factor*.

It was *total* chaos. I felt like Nick Hewer watching a team making a muck-up of it in *The Apprentice*.

0945: Nothing was sorted out at all except a crossed-out timetable. Rod, the new head of literacy ("HOL") and I left for "the Pod" – I know that sounds like something out of *Thunderbirds* but it is I learnt where the computers live. We walked through the TV studio like plastering area – where "sets" were being put together. All that were missing were cameras and lights.

All the characters were there.

The Pod. Rod scampered off to make coffee. I sat at a computer and fine-tuned his CV trying to make it less Guy Ritchie like. HOL fiddled with another computer but didn't know the password. In attempt to sound her out I ventured down the Toe by Toe saga at the Bay and the shooting-down-of it by the Captain Mainwaring minded *Head of Education*. I told her that I thought it beyond countenance that he had had barred me from tutoring the program in this prison. HOL responded "perhaps it was a misunderstanding."

Yes. Like Pearl Harbour was.

Rod returned with the coffee. He listened as I revealed this book to HOL and my *overwhelming* intentions to spread the obtuse accountable absurdity of her colleague's actions and my incandescence at his refusal to let me help other prisoners with *learning to read*. She had turned a pale colour by the time I got off my impromptu soap-box.

1115: Unit. Rod and I gossip in my room. He has to produce sugar from his own pockets – leaving a few sachets for next time, as the Wilford supply has gone walkabout, as does seemingly everything not nailed down here.

1200: Lunch. Gordon asks me if I managed to speak Alistair about the champagne man story – Yes I did – and he didn't know what I was talking about. "Oh, it must have been somebody else."

1245: Library. Raced Stuart at Mac. He won.

1300: Work. Rachel: "Come back later." Off to Zara (Top) then. Climb the stairs not worrying at all. Zara (Top) "in a meeting" but her *Blackadder* Darling lookalike Peter comes over and speaks to me. He's "just seen Judi and everyone is still waiting for Zara in Probation." I report that I've spoken to the Deputy Governor last night and the S.O. this morning and politely point out that everyone is waiting and what else do I have to do? "It's a watched pot" (botched lot more like) and "it will all fall into place." If Zara Probation's paperwork is not complete today he "will give Judi the application" for my lodgings "so she can fax it after it has been rubber stamped."

Bearing in mind I am supposed to "move" next Thursday – I am running out of time. Should I stop my countdown?

Can I return later to check on any progress? He reluctantly agrees, sort of nodding and shaking his head simultaneously as he scratches his Peter Gabriel beard. He doesn't help my pessimism with his final words: "I've not seen this before."

1320: Unit. Feeling very low and dejected. Spot the S.O. (boiling a kettle in the staff kitchenette) "I've not seen her," referring to Zara Probation without any feeder line from me. Feel even more dejected.

1500: Zara (Top). "Still no news." She has "just returned from Judi's," leaving my paperwork with her. I ask who in her absence can I speak to? "Only Judi. Things are not looking good for next

Thursday."

Keep calm Robinson. Keep calm.

Frank's office. On hearing the latest update he leaps out of his chair saying he'd "go and investigate" and for me to return in the morning adding that he'd sort it because he's "better looking than me."

1600: Harry Enfield back. Oh Lord – it's THAT laugh again... Wrote till 1700 and dinner. No thanks.

Early evening and downstairs *full* of officers. 3 ship-outs have occurred from Wilford. Went to the library and diarised a time to meet Stuart in the morning to get him on the dental list. Returned to Wilford and spoke to an officer more senior than an S.O. about my predicament and he told me he would follow it up in the morning.

1900: On utilisation of the Unit hole-punch that poster had fallen off the wall.

Wednesday, November 9th, 2011.

T minus 8. Last night I caught the Deputy Governor playing dominos with some prisoners – I believe they won. He probably now owes them a tin of tuna each. I yet again explained my situation to him to which he said "we want you out." He advised me to get hold of "P.O. _____ FIRST thing in the morning" and "the Governor WILL sign it at lunch time."

That's what I went to bed on knife edge tenterhooks worrying about.

0715: Hovering in the car park and The Terminator materialises. He tells me what sort of car P.O. _____ drives to make identification easier adding "obviously I didn't tell you that." No sign of that make and model. Decide a better view will be from my window. For once the ghastly panorama from number 30 is beneficial to me.

0730: Meet Stuart as arranged. My eyes darting for a vehicle of the description I was given. Nothing, so we trudge onwards. On entry, Philip announces "the dentist is ill" and not due back until next week. Plan B for Stuart then – he's put on next week's list.

It's back to hanging around outside for me. Victoria arrives: "Any news on your Tag?" I'm stalking a member of staff now to get the final piece of the jigsaw puzzle put into place. Her line as she reigns off: "If you want anything done around here – do it yourself."

0830: Still no sign so back to Wilford's office and ask an officer to please ring OMU. "Why?" Explain. "Come back in 10." Return in the allocated time and am told I've been given a bum steer: "P.O. _____ is not in till 0930."

0845: Work. All the downstairs doors locked. Eventually find some life and do the bare minimum –

the loos and empty Rachel's bin (which was full of banana skins). Rachel's dialogue was about Sue's leaving present and that she's "put a tenner in." I ask her what the Robbie situation is – I'm supposed to be seeing him at 1000.

Shrugged shoulders.

0900: Unit. Coffee. Window. Ants in my pants. Go downstairs. The more senior than an S.O. officer who I spoke to last night is on site and says "I have not forgotten you." Fill him in on the post dominos conversation with the Deputy Governor and that I'm waiting to pounce on P.O._____. He says he "will still follow it up and by all means pounce on the P.O."

0930: Loiter in the car park.

0935: P.O._____ comes into view. Not by car but on foot wearing a combat jacket. (Has he parachuted in?) The props department has really gone to town and placed a fag in his mouth. I identify myself and tell the whole story, from stem to stern, including what the Deputy Governor said last night. The fag temporally removed and out comes "that doesn't sound right – I'll have a word with our HDC clerk" (Judi the Tag lady) and walks off with his roll-up.

0937: Work. Philip's line: "No Robbie today."

1120: Frank's office. "Nothing mate," his dialogue. Ask him if this is a test. He laughs. "It's the prison system Jonny; it works for some people but not for most."

Another title for this book?

Healthcare. Orange Nicker 2 there. (Being treated for excessive vitamin C?) Ask Rachel, Anything? "No." Ask Philip, Anything? "No." Philip asks me if there is any news on my plight. No.

1155: Unit. In my room trying not to worry. What do I do next to move this along? Who do I have to speak to? What in God's name do I have to do and... Tannoy: "Mr Robinson report to the office." Hmmmm. I wonder...

The officer has paperwork in his hand – odd that I'm being called for post – and hands it to me. One is the "app" I made on Roland's behalf, the other is a letter from Buzz. I'm about to open it when he says "there's your mail – and go next door," adding as if an afterthought "P.O. _____ wants to see you." I walk next door and knock on it. I don't hear the noise my knuckles make on the MDF for my heart thumping in my ears. "Sit down," says the P.O. now minus his combat jacket and cigarette. "I'm going to board you now."

Is he going to waterboard me I wonder?

"You are recommended" – P.O. lingo for "you are going out on Tag." "Your fax will go today for your lodgings." I can only just hear him over my heart beat. "You will have curfew conditions which will be explained to you by Probation. Do you have any questions?" No, I tell him and thank him. I get out as fast as I can before he changes his mind.

So at long last everything has fallen into place. I cannot tell you the sense of relief. Despite being told I will get Tag almost from the end of the first week, it's now been officially confirmed. The last few days of stalking officers in corridors, car parks and at domino tables has nearly finished me. The countdown is back on.

Let's hope someone will house me. Outside the office I read Buzz's letter:

07.11.11

Hi Fletch,

Just a few lines of support for when you're released in ten days' time. Everything out here is much the same as when you left. Everyone running around like nutters getting nowhere fast. But even though nothing out here has changed YOU will have to. I know you will be trying very hard to show people that you are a better person and to win back their trust. I'm not trying to state the bleeding obvious as I know you know all this. What I guess I'm trying to say is you have good friends out here who want to see you "make it"…. Me being on top of that list. You are a good guy Captain so let's get that man back eh??

Let's get you back flying which is what you do best.

Anyway you said you will be calling me this weekend so I will speak to you then.

Captain Lightyear over n' out.

1200: Lunch. Too numbed to eat. Dumbfounded. Relief, relief, relief. Went outside and had a ciggie. An officer out there. He asks me if I'm OK. He knows my news and says "well done." I respond with my trademark fact: Prison has taught me a lot. He takes a drag on his roll-up and says "eye opener?"

An understatement.

1240: Victoria's palace – who had asked for an update. She's in a meeting but the Bond heavy Orderly says "come back in a minute and congratulations." News travels fast. I'll just pop down to see Frank and come back. Frank: "Congratulations" (news travels *really* fast) – and can I come back in 20 minutes. Yes to this and back upstairs to Victoria. I go straight in and sit. The lady-in waiting Barbara present too. "Well, you've got there," says Victoria. Although I do of course still have another week of "shooting" to do. We talk of how it's been. It is without doubt the kick up the arse that I needed and I hope I don't forget what I've learnt when I'm gone. I use the return from a holiday as an example, when one walks in to one's home the day after sitting on a beach at some resort and is obliged to fall back into the real world. I don't want to resort to how I was before. Victoria says "it's good that it seems to have worked" for me.

I tell them about the Aitken article and "baby steps." I reveal this book to them and they are most excited. "Will we be in it?" Yes Victoria and Barbara you are. I thank them for all their help and promise I'll come back to say goodbye before I leave. Their Orderly asks me to take some mail for my Rounds.

Pre Frank went to Healthcare and found Philip, WD and this week's student nurse all lolling in the powerhouse Treatment room. Announced my news and smiles and congratulations flew all around. Philip declared "I'm really pleased for you." WD asked me if I have a partner.

I'm not going to answer that question till – please God – she reads this.

At Frank's fortress he de-briefs me. Grants I can apply for, assistance from all sides and various help-line numbers. I thank him for all his support. His Orderly, sitting in the room overhears me talking about how I'm still beating myself up for being an arse. He points out, like many other people have that I have been punished – and it's now a level playing field.

The stuff Victoria's Orderly gave me is for Stow. Good that I've got to go there as I want to see Rod. I walk up to Bricks. Going in, I'm confronted with loads of prisoners frantically building small walls. Mathew spots me. "It's Austin!" *What*? "Austin Powers – man of mystery. I still think you're a spy." Mr Kelly back to his normal self. "What the fook are you smiling about?" I tell all. "Fookin' great mate." He points out where Rod is. I walk over and tell him. With a huge smile he says "come on, let's go outside."

You name it – for the next 45 minutes – it is discussed. Nostalgia City envelopes us. Tag, baby steps, Limping Al's table manners, Rod's release, the system, Dennis, Young Rupert, Casino Greg, the book and how the sun has now come out. It is a glorious afternoon. As we chat on the wooden veranda type porch – the sort of set-up outside a saloon bar in a western – there are even those wooden railings and banisters where horses would be tethered to – we are bathed in golden sunshine.

I need to convey something to him...

I couldn't have done this without you.

"The place won't be the same without you," he answers.

To the Jason Statham type, when you read this, thank you. For EVERYTHING. You have been my bedrock. Neither a rolled-up Rita or Raquel nor for that matter a rock hammer did you receive request from me. Be of *no* doubt though Rod, you have been my "Red."

The last on that list was never required anyway. I have slavishly used pens to escape. Lots of them – I've *written* my way out of here.

We talk more and lean on the railings basking in the sunshine – he in his "works greens," me in my prison jeans with my ID around my neck still tied to the bit of string that my Hoxon bed-pack arrived with. We could almost be leaning on a bar with a couple of beers, talking about the good old days.

I've learnt my lesson, I say to him.

"I know you have."

Despite the fact that we are at Bricks – tucked well out of the way from the rest of the prison members of the HDFOT club ferociously prowl about in droves doing nothing.

"*Zulu*'s on later," says Rod.

1455: Rounds. At Stow my presence coincided with that of the Terminator and the helpful more senior than an S.O. officer who I spoke to last night. Tell them both my news and thank them. Leave Stow and walk back to Healthcare to see if anything needs to be done. Encounter Heston. Yet *again*, he comes up with one of *his* quotes:

"The sooner you start seeing this with nostalgia the better."

Got to work and completed the mammoth task of throwing out one cardboard box, checking first that it didn't have any needles or drugs in it. Told the gang I'd see them tomorrow and returned to the Unit.

Asked an officer what the form is to get my stuff back. I want to leave here in *my* clothes. He said that didn't sound unreasonable so I asked the best way forward.

"Make an app."

Thursday, November 10th, 2011.

T minus 7. Despite the success of yesterday, Bungalow Bill had to have the last word last night and led me down the corridor to his "headmaster's" office. "Shut the door" (angry Bill Maynard voice). "Why have I been hearing your name all afternoon since P.O. _____ saw you?" I have no idea. I reported to both Frank from Tribal and Victoria from Nacro, both of whom had asked me to come and see them once I was done, otherwise that was all.

"Well I have been hearing of nothing but you all afternoon." Then the penny dropped. Obviously the Deputy Governor, the more senior than an S.O. officer and the Terminator had followed up my attempts to get done what could and should have been done by *my* S.O. a few days ago. Ergo: his problem, not mine.

Slept fitfully due to noise which went on to till 2330. Mostly shouted conversations on the landing. The character with the most dialogue was the *night officer* talking about (loudly) "which was the quietest landing at Wilford."

It's *stewing* in my room. The windows are still wide open. The heating remains on at full blast.

0715: Philip, WD and the current student nurse nattered at work. The former making flu-vaccine flyers for me to distribute around the Units. I mop, empty the bins and leave for Rounds at 0750.

1040: Resettlement. A number of lifers come in — all desperate for outside work — even if it's voluntary. The explanations given for the problems finding them employment are varied. "There is not enough transport for them to commute" is one. "The Governor has a tender in for a further three mini buses," the remedy. "The location of Hollesley Bay" is also a "huge problem." "If we were in Ipswich and prisoners could walk to work we'd be laughing." The idea of using public transport won't do. "£5 a day per prisoner with at least 50 going out — there is no budget for this anymore." The officer explaining all this is proud that he "gets a 100 out a day." He has "more lifers and IPP's on their way in" and he's "already struggling." Alarmingly, he reveals that "Probation — who need to see long-term sentenced prisoners successfully working on their last laps — are having to make do with certificates that prisoner X was unable to get work." The situation has become so desperate that he "has had to turn charities away" — because he cannot get our free work force *to* them.

I sit there taking all this in. I'm not here to see this chap and none of this has anything to do with me. But I still voice my thoughts: Have you thought of bringing Mohamed to the mountain?

"What?"

I understand the problem — but instead of trying to get various different prisoners all around the county, why doesn't the system approach some charities (poppy manufacturing?) and get them to come here where there are plenty of volunteers? As well as the manpower — we have the space. The boondocks area next to Bricks is huge.

"That's a good idea…"

1100: I'm seen for my pre-release "after sales" service. The conveyor belt process that is prison — seems to be closing on producing its product. Me.

Unit. Rumours continue to circulate about the three prisoners shipped-out the other day. I've resisted touching on this to date as it's only prison tittle-tattle that has come my way but I am beginning to think what I am hearing might be true. I need to do some more prodding and poking.

Luckily, Tony is about. He knows about this book — who doesn't — and I make it clear that I'm not looking for anyone to "grass" on anybody — I just want to run the story past him. Like a nervous news reporter to his editor, I rattle off events as I understand them and look at him for confirmation. "You're spot-on Jon." Despite us standing in the furthest corner from the entrance of our dining room, Tony's eyes fluctuate like an oscilloscope screen to see if anyone is listening.

1200: Lunch. The Terminator presided over the dining room. Very well behaved everybody was too. Until he left. *Why* can't the HDFOT section converse and eat at the same table?

1250: Library. An awful lot of prisoners coming in and asking for the local paper. Much more so than normal. Has something happened that may be of interest to the press…?

It is Memorial Sunday this weekend and a display of books has been put out that is topical. I leaf through a monograph on WW1 and stumble across a picture of British soldiers sitting in a trench. Looking at this, wads of regret cover me for any similarity that I have used between people like us – scum – and these brave troops. Especially at this time of year.

The soldiers' eyes look at me accusingly.

Stuart is asked if during his prison career has there ever been a minute's silence on 11.11. "No." What does he think of prisoners having the opportunity to donate a bit of their Canteen spend to buy a poppy? Stuart: "You still have your outside head on – which is a good thing."

A survey is conducted in the library. The first person I quiz replies with a "nah," like he'd been asked if he wanted to wash the Governor's car. The second lectures me on the waste of life and money during the conflict in Afghanistan and the third: "Yes, gladly." Realisation of *some* of the people I am amongst is brought back to me with a bang when someone comes in asking for a national paper wanting to know if there were any riots at yesterday's big student protest in London. A good cue maybe from "him up there" to curtail my poppy survey.

A biography of Richard Beckinsale – Godber – is flicked through. It's no wonder that it's in *this* library but it gives me strange tingles that I've found it here. I remember that episode so vividly of his first night in prison and how Ronnie Barker looked after him. No one could *possibly* attempt to pen a book about (fully deserved) incarceration without a doffing-of-cap to the man who was Lennie in *Porridge*.

1340: Healthcare. There is nothing for me to do. WD, Philip and the student nurse are all on the internet "looking for a good job." Rachel is not in tomorrow – her last day is now Tuesday.

On alighting "Biggles" was yelled. Rod loitered by the "Please do not spit" sign and I invited him to Wilford for a coffee. We passed Frank who was very gently pumped for information about the recent ship-outs and yet more confirmation trickled through. I am aware that I'm letting you Dear Reader, in on this with all the speed of a dripping tap but I don't want this to be another two bottles of champagne palaver.

I *will* reveal that the conversation lead to the standard of prisoners here and Frank came out with what is to date the most sensible thing I've heard any member of staff at the Bay say: "Bring Cat D prisoners here and *then* it can be a Cat D prison."

Room, Rod and roll-ups. His views on my poppy survey are that such things might upset certain factions of prisoners amongst us and like putting up a certain team's football poster on the wall – the prison system "does not want anything to do with anything that could upset the apple cart."

1530: Downstairs. Clive on the scene. Can I go through events as I understand them with him – and when I'm done he can nod if I'm right? "Off you go then, Jon." I do.

He nods.

1700: Dinner. Took one look and no way. I've got Canteen arriving later – I'll survive on grapefruit if I need to.

1730: Canteen pick up.

1815 – 1850: As previously touched on somewhere near the beginning of this collection of commas, films are made in a funny old order. I'm now going to ask you to bear with me and allow me to take you out of sequence. I've just been in the office having a lengthy conversation with AMTO but I'm not going to fill you in on that until you have digested the following. I had originally gone in to attempt to seek intelligence on recent events and gather more facts. This, a bit redundant now, as said activities are in the local (evening) paper.

Sorry for the break in continuity. You've been very patient with me. Your reward is the following story. As I've heard it.

The shipped-out three all worked outside the prison at Ipswich Town Football Club. The Governor is a big fan of the team and supplies three prisoners for general duties – at no cost to anyone as it's classified as volunteer work. The club wins – extra hands for odd jobs. The system wins as more prisoners are doing stuff and the Governor wins at helping out his team. A no-brainer.

They always ate together at the same table. Indeed, they ate dinner as usual, at their normal table the night before they left us. I think I even recently diarised that an awful lot of whispering took place over munching although I had deliberately not gone anywhere *near* describing them within these pages as one of them would be *very* easy to identify.

How can I put this?

Derek and Clive have been referred to in some past chapter of this story – played by the irreplaceable Peter Cook and Dudley Moore. However, the foul mouthed alter egos were not the only characters that Pete and Dud came up with. Another very funny sketch involves a "Mr Spiggott" (Dud) auditioning to a film man (Pete) for none other than the role of Tarzan. All fine and dandy.

Although "Mr Spiggott" has only got *one leg*... Get the picture?

The day they left us they had been taken in one of our (one bus too few) prison mini buses to work as normal. Things however went a little wonky when prison transport returned at the end of the day to pick them up. Not possible, the driver was told. Someone else had already done so. "Who?" asked the driver. "Has the system done it again and sent two transports?" No, he was told. It's not your lot. "Who was it then?" asked the confused chauffeur.

"The police."

It turns out that painting white lines and cleaning kit is not the only thing this gaggle enjoys doing.

They also enjoy a burger. No crime in visiting a certain well known burger joint at all. Nothing dodgy. Unless you're a convicted serving prisoner.

And you rob them.

One security guard "was knocked down but not seriously hurt." The local paper quotes "£18k of takings taken." CCTV was everywhere. After their take-away they returned to work. By now local television news was broadcasting images of three gentlemen that the local Constabulary were keen to have a chat with, one of them our "Spiggott." Back at the club they were rapidly recognised and arrested on the spot. "All gave false addresses" but once they had been properly identified, the local police rang the prison and two and two made four.

The Governor has I hear, gone *berserk*.

There are various *other* rumours doing the rounds concerning this. All I know for sure though is what you've just read. If *what else* I'm hearing turns out to be true, things could get very, very interesting.

Back in time now and the conversation with AMTO. I had gone in to do something – borrow the hole-punch or similar – and dialogue was concluding between our Mullard, sat behind his desk and a prisoner about what everyone is talking about; three lags, five legs and matters burger. As the prisoner departed the scene I picked up on the subject and vocalised that I felt sorry for the Governor. At that, AMTO sat *bolt* upright in his chair and told me to shut the door. He wanted to talk to me.

I closed the door...

"What the fuck do you mean?" I pensively voiced that I thought the Governor trying to help prisoners work off-campus was a good thing and that our ex-residents' not-on-the-menu takeaway had rather let him down.

That pulled the *pin*...

"Let me tell you something, I've been in this job more than thirty fucking years and I've never seen a Governor like it... You've got that all wrong... All he thinks about is himself... Whenever there is a fuck up it's never his fault... He's a selfish bastard who only thinks about himself... I've never seen a prison run like this before... there is *more* going on as well..."

My pen was pretty busy after that.

I will continue to find out if the *more* is true...

2050: Two new freshman faces on Wilford – both besieged Hoxon homesteaders. Poor buggers. One of them IAHHM. Welcomed him and his pal. All smiles back.

"Spiggott," we are hearing, was the getaway driver...

Friday, November 11th, 2011. (Remembrance Day)

T minus 6.

A beeline to Philip for a fillip to confirm the *other* rumours circulating...

Healthcare. To say the atmosphere is "different" would be an understatement. Philip plods about smirking as if he's found Lord Lucan lurking in the dispensary. I stand still and stare at him. We both look at each other almost daring the other to divulge what we know. I go straight to the top diving board and plunge off with what is now public knowledge. He nods approvingly as I recount what still sounds to me like a treatment to the sequel of *Two-Way Stretch*. I do not reveal AMTO's atmospheric sounding off of yesterday – I'll leave that to this book – but I *do* tell him the *what else* I have heard and almost begging him to say "That bit is bollocks Jonathan," he smirks even more...

Philip, is that true?

Smirk.

PHILIP?

A very wistful nod and "yes."

Right – let's emphasise that EVERYTHING in this book is reproduced wholly under oath. It's my witness statement to the whole shooting-match that has been for me prison. Here comes the smoking gun...

The Burger three had as much right to be working outside the prison as I have. They had not yet passed the "Lie-down" ticker tape that is also still beyond my reach as I am not here long enough. The *Governor, wanting to look good at his favourite football club*, allowed the three out *before they were eligible* at his behest, just to score brownie points with his team.

Philip, what will happen? "When this becomes public knowledge, he'll have to go." What, moved sideways to another prison? "No, because of his age they'll get rid of him."

And I thought being in prison during the riots was my peak of political interest. I guess I'm in the wrong place at the right time...

With Philip still shaking his head in disbelief Heston heaves-to, grinning-like-mad at what has happened. He tells me the trio "have been released on bail but are under lock and key at a more secure prison in our locality."

0900: Library. Nothing in the nationals (yet!) – Heston said he doesn't think they'll catch on till it goes to Court – but the local rag is having a field day. "HMP Hollesley Bay would not comment and neither would Ipswich Town Football Club."

Unit. Orange Nicker 2 haunted the hallway looking positively glutinous with his Home-leave stuff packed. 5 days of peace! With a bit of luck – IF I go on Thursday morning (I don't think he has to be back till Thursday afternoon) – I MAY never see him again.

1000: Work. Nothing for me so returned to the library to finish the papers. "Welcome Joanna" posters covered the walls making the place look like a stage for a U.S. Presidential election debate. The "props" department had perhaps gone a little too far to town as copies of her books were EVERYWHERE.

1100: Solo – stand silently in my room for two minutes.

Feel very guilty.

1115: Two letters. One internal, signed by Zara in Probation (she does exist!) Confirmation of my Tag – subject to acceptable accommodation being found for me. The other a letter from a very well-known publisher saying "no." Standard letter – 2nd class post, with no reusable stamp. How long ago did I write to them? They advised me to look in the *Writer's and Artist's Yearbook*…

1200: Lunch. No thanks.

1220: Work. Excused myself this afternoon because of the Joanna Trollope talk. Spoke to Sue who is on over the weekend. Philip briefly made an appearance "who will be back on Wednesday." On the walk back Alistair and one Chris Moyles were doing the food trolley pick-up. Moyles: "Fought you woz gone?" I grinned and announced that Thursday appears to be the big day. "So this is your last Friday," he deduced as some suits walked past us – no doubt here because of you-know-what. We agree that the **** is hitting the fan. "Good for the book though," decides our disk-jockey double with peripheral perception. Moyles then puts the candles on the *top* of the cake, lights them *and* blows them out with: "One of them is my wife's cousin."

1255: Finished *Robinson Crusoe*.

1630: Back in my room having spent the afternoon in the company of Joanna Trollope. As one does whilst in prison.

I was the first to arrive. IAHHM acted as usher. Chairs had been put out in a crescent shape. One table had been struck to make more room for the masses. A table centre stage, altar like, had been covered in what looked like our guest's complete works.

The audience arrived in dribs and drabs. Firstly it was all staff, all of whom were female. An IMB "busy body" lady – who *more* than resembled Edward G. Robinson – sat next to me and started to give me a vocal questionnaire on my views of the library. Sweeper Ray saved the day by coming on scene and I struck up conversation with him to escape further interrogation from the tie-die clad bundle.

I sat centre middle. Sax Clive presented himself close by on the left. Soon she arrived. I can only describe her as someone's great aunt. Pencil thin and our "wardrobe department" wouldn't have to look anywhere other than the blueprints of the dimensions of the late (great) Audrey Hepburn to clad her. I immediately detected a teeny-weeny bit of Margo in her from *The Good Life*. She introduced herself, shaking all our hands and put her bum down on the altar. She opened with apologising for not being a male author and then, because we all looked like a bunch of wall flowers at a 50's dance, asked us to move closer. A bit of chair shuffling later and we all resembled a 70's family peering at the Queen's speech on Christmas day, so close were we to the chancel. "Does anybody here write?" I didn't *dare* stick my hand up. ELG confessed to a bit of poetry ("I does some poetry, Miss") and she was very encouraging. She touched on "writing being good therapy" and seeing as we all have time on our hands, that we "should give it a try."

Research was discussed. One of her characters was a football fan so she visited the terraces of Chelsea – an audible groan went up at this from fellow prisoners who were Arsenal fans. Another piece required military intelligence so she went on manoeuvres with some regiment or other and so on. She was asked what gives her an idea. "It can be an overheard conversation in the supermarket queue" and characters "can be invented from all sorts of people." Her eyes scanned the room – beat – "there are one or two here for instance."

"Observation is the key – and constant note taking" (!!!!) She vocalised encouragement to ask questions so I enquired if there is a particularly productive time for her. Not for the first time, she referred to her age (her daughter is only a bit younger than me) and replied "mornings." She revealed that she has an elderly mother and two ex-husbands – but "loving being single." She moved on to the artistry of writing. "Practicing is good."

She was very out of her depth with what prison is like – our access to the internet was touched on before an internal lamp illuminated within her and she twigged that if we did have use of the worldwide web a great deal of you-know-what would be viewed. As the penny dropped her voice trailed off. Staying on that succulent subject she disclosed that one of her books revolved around two females who had an affair.

Not surprisingly, you could have heard a proverbial pin drop at that point.

Somehow the conversation steered to Ipswich. I – ever the class clown – remarked that I hear there's a good burger bar there and the place fell apart, mostly from the staff I might add. She recognised that she'd missed a joke and I told her that I was sure someone would put her in the picture later or, more likely, she'd read about it in her newspaper – which she told us is the *Guardian*. She appeared incredulous that our "Well stocked library doesn't take the *Times*."

She went on to encourage us that whatever it was that we have done – we can still turn our lives around.

I didn't dare take notes in front of her – which is odd as I'm now perfectly comfortable doing so in front of murderers and prison officers (there's irony in there somewhere) and now I'm frantically scribbling what was said before it gets erased from my tiny brain. Supper was called at 1700 – I whizzed down to be Roll-checked but did not eat.

Back to earlier events and the body in the library; Joanna Trollope. I asked as she writes long hand –

does she get an editor to read what she's done to tweak it? "No," she "knows what works." Hmmm. When she types it…. "I don't type it, my P.A. does…" OK, before she had a PA when SHE typed from her manuscript did she chop and change? "Not really."

I am DOOMED and so is this book.

She changed tack again and touched on relationships. When one has gone off the rails she told us that women feel "ouch that didn't work" and men "feel failure." I must confess I thought it was the other way round. But the list of what I've learnt in the last 17 weeks or so is endless.

As she began to wrap it up Sally came on and thanked her. A polite round of applause cracked around the crevices. I hung around to thank her. Her first question to me: "When are you out?" On revealing Thursday she almost spiritually said "I'll be thinking of you on Friday." I bit the bullet and posed a question of something along the lines of if hypothetically she'd been in prison for 17 weeks would she write a book during that time? Strangely – I thought – she said "yes, but maybe not about jail."

"Is that what you have done?" I shamefully admitted so and revealed that Jeffrey Archer had kindly replied to a letter of mine asking what to do and had pointed me towards the *Writer's and Artist's Yearbook* and there had been a bit of an exodus of late via the prison postal room in the direction of literary agents. "How many?" Ninety something. "Good Lord. Any luck?" I think six or seven send it in responses. "That's FANTASTIC!" Any advice? "Get someone who is *not* afraid of hurting your feelings to read it *before* you send it to any agents."

Any offers anyone?

I think you've probably gathered by now who will be the first person this gets sent to.

Returned to my room, if anything, feeling less confident about this book than I did before the talk. That's odd isn't it? Maybe it's because another prisoner in front of me who also waited to pass his thanks was told by her, and overheard by me: "It's good that you've got loved ones to go back to."

It was that search for love and the asshole way I brought it that brought me here.

1800: Finished writing and dug into some muesli.

The last Friday night in prison? Well, it all depends on Zara (Top). I won't have any news on that till her return to work on Monday.

I read in a newspaper today that stress ages you.

I daren't look in a mirror.

Saturday, November 12th, 2011.

T minus 5.

0755:   There's no more paper or envelopes downstairs. Someone must have been doing a lot of writing…

0800: A request on the Tannoy, as long as the electoral roll, for the stragglers to attend Roll-check.

0850: A plea aimed at WTWFO for more prisoner paper. She gave me a knowing look that she knew exactly why supplies have been diminished so then picked up the phone to ring Bosnia for emergency rations. Still with that knowing look she despatched me to the caravan site.

At Bosnia's office I presented my credential from the Youth Club. The officer gave me enough stationary to last this book a life sentence. I thanked him and set off to "work."

Nothing for me to do other than one letter to be delivered. Luckily, for Wilford. Sue asked me how the Joanna Trollope thing had gone. I gave her a quick synopsis and told her I'd pop back tomorrow.

0900: Library. Not yet open to the general population but I have now become a non-executive member of the board and am let in. Library Brett, IAHHM (whose name I have finally learnt is Frankie) and Stuart are all sorting and piling ordered newspapers into Units for delivery.

Wilford is the smallest pile.

I sit down at "the bar" and read the library papers. The staff departs to deliver the tabloids, much to the irritation of Library Brett who doesn't want me left alone on the bridge. Stuart hushes him and I settle down to a national.

Frankie's back after only a few minutes. I assume he knows about the book – everyone seems to now. Without any prompting from me – out comes his story. And I only came in here to read the paper.

A life sentence. The Court accepted that no "planning" had gone into the crime, and thus did not set a tariff – by which, there was no minimum amount of years that this fellow had to serve. Sometime into his porridge a new Home Secretary decided that there should indeed be a yardstick so a figure was set.

Frankie made his way through the system and ended up in an open prison. He was working "outside and doing rather well" with some sort of financial company. "Staff would visit to make sure everything was above board" and there were no reported problems or hiccups.

With only a relatively small amount of time left to serve – for some reason his "stay was increased." I interrupted and asked if he was caught with a drinks cabinet in his room but he looked me straight in the eye and said no. Regardless, he decided that enough was most certainly enough – and absconded – which is legal-jargon for escaping from an open prison.

If you are an escapee on the run and intend to leave the country you need a false passport. Frankie got one. And went to Spain.

Was that nation selected because of the extradition difficulties that I have read about between the UK and the land of Fernando Alonso? "No, just went there." Was he nervous departing London Gatwick on moody (prison jargon) paperwork? "An understatement," says the gentle giant.

He did rather well for himself under the identity of someone else. He rented an apartment and worked. Apparently his wife "only received one call from the authorities" asking her to "suggest to him he rang them if he got in touch."

Frankie soon suffered Ronnie Biggs syndrome. Simply put: he missed home. And decided, entirely of his own volition, to return to the UK and handed himself in. Did he go out for a spectacular lunch before he did so? "No, I just rang them." Where were you and what were you doing? "I was out shopping." Who did you call? "I dialled 999."

I bet that *throughout* the land that call is used in training sessions for our emergency operators...

He's worked his way through the system again. Would he consider walking? "No."

1010: Wilford. On Key pick up WTWFO is asked if she can have a look at my notes from HMP Bedford. I am curious. She "will have a look" and get back to me.

1025: Gordon is sticking up a photocopied TV guide for the week ahead. On perusal I nearly fall over.

I actually laugh out loud.

Enough for an officer to look up from whatever it is he is doing on the internet in the office. After all the comparisons and all the jokes (?), the biggest irony yet has sprung up. A certain film is being shown on television on my last Sunday – I hope – in prison...

The Great Escape.

1200: A "no" from a publisher proceeded luncheon.

1310: F1 qualifying for the Abu Dhabi Grand Prix. Raced downstairs for a coffee. At the base of the stairs WTWFO signalled me to come into the office. She was in there alone looking at her computer screen. I entered. She told me to shut the door.

She looked uncomfortable.

And turned the screen so I could read it.

These days where the nanny state presides and kids cannot play conkers or throw snowballs anymore, I prepared myself for reams of electronic information about me which would be of use to this book. I wasn't going to be crass enough to actually make notes – all I had was my mug anyway – so I tried to put my brain into gear to take on board the copious information heading my way.

Even if I had a pen and paper on me – I didn't need it. Reams of data I did not get. What I *did* get was:

"Mr Robinson has been working in the library and is moving to Hollesley Bay."

I looked up and witnessed at an even more uncomfortable looking WTWFO. Where's the rest of it? This caused a visible squirm and shifting of position in her seat. She bit the corner of her lower lip. She didn't *say* "that's all there is," she didn't need to – her face did. What the *hell* happens after a suicide when the paperwork trail starts? This made the blood drain from her face. I have not seen someone look so embarrassed since the penny dropped with Rioter Rodney that HMP Bedford was indeed sans swimming pool...

I questioned her again as to what does the system think it's *doing* by being so devoid of interest? I was worried she might burst into tears at this point so I dropped it.

My history at the Bay was only a little more in depth. I am "polite, work hard and try to do my best to help other prisoners." The ex-engineer officer has wished me well – and apparently I kicked up one hell of a stink when I got moved from the Hilton to the ghetto.

1405: Seb on pole. Lewis and Jenson 2nd and 3rd. Both wearing poppies.

1510: Officer Blakey doing the rounds. First time I've seen a Goon sniffing around Wilford. Sniffing being a very useful sense on this Unit – if you get what I mean. I asked him why Rusty the sniffer dog never comes here – like he used to at Hoxon. Blakey shrugged his shoulders.

I think it's because the poor hound would pass out.

Dinner was curry and an out of date (!) Mars Bar. Most prisoners on the Unit are out for Home-leave or Town-visits so the oranges available were plentiful. As I write (2000), there are six on my window sill.

Had a massive anxiety attack earlier about all my possessions. Had to reel my neck in and remind myself where I am. Everything will, when presented to me, fall into place. Good or bad.

First thing I've got to do is get out of here. Not much longer Robinson.

Not much longer.

Sunday, November 13th, 2011. (Remembrance Sunday)

T minus 4. Up at 0630. Overnight it was luxuriously very quiet on the corridor. I assume that someone had brought "something" back from a Town-visit and distributed it to friends/customers as a heavy fog half-blocked the landing when I went for a midnight pee. I made sure I didn't breathe in – in case I'm pulled from the hat for an MDT.

0700: Departing for Healthcare Bungalow Bill had a line: "Where are you off to?" I rationalised that it is an unwritten rule that I call-by Healthcare at weekends to see if anything needs to be done. He didn't reply. They REALLY don't like initiative in prison.

Sue on set. No dramas. Did the bins.

0800: Unit. 2nd Roll-check request.

0805: A long list of names and a plea to "please attend Roll-check."

0835: Got my newspaper and took it with my plastic plate and some bread from my room to café corner. Thirty minutes of escapism later, a tap on the window – from outside. Bungalow Bill beckoning me (what have I done now?) "Can you do me a favour?" (He's not going to ask me for a Rizla is he?) "Someone at Healthcare requires an ambulance." Can I stand in the car park and direct it when it arrives? "It has been called for."

Loiter in car park. Last time it was for a P.O. Now it's for an ambulance.

Directing duties complete and back inside. The Terminator on board – and searching the interior of our industrial sized fridge. On a table near him is a massive flash light that looks like it should live in a watch tower on Alcatraz and a handsome collection of screwdrivers.

I go upstairs. From my window Bungalow Bill is in picture walking up to the gym.

With his sports bag.

As I write the Terminator's dulcet tones are audible on the corridor cornering a prisoner. "Have you got anything on you that you shouldn't have?" "No Gov." A pat-down takes place. The first one I've witnessed at the Bay.

1040: Returned from the library. The Terminator's line on key retrieval: "They don't get my sense of humour on this Unit."

1045: Events at the Cenotaph on TV.

1155: Chow-truck. Keep your head down Robinson. Nearly there. Well, to Tag date. Feel miserable.

Lunch – no comment. In the washing up queue I asked Leiston, fresh from a Town-visit yesterday, if the food is even worse when one has been out. His reply – and he is half my age – shut me firmly up: "We have no right to complain."

F1 Grand Prix of Abu Dhabi.

1441: Lewis' race. Jenson third. Went downstairs to get coffee. Snorer doing the same. He playfully says "last Sunday for you!" I tell him it's going slowly and I am frankly, terrified of all the things I need to sort out in order to get some sort of life back. So many things have been put on the back burner – and now that there is a glimmer of light at the end of the tunnel – I am trying to prepare myself for not attempting to deal with them in a headless chicken fashion.

For any aviator out there for whom my name is not mud, arriving at prison was take-off, E wing at Bedford was cross-wind, Hoxon was downwind, Wilford was and always will be base and I'm waiting for tower, in the shape of Zara (Top), to tell me when I can turn final.

There does appear to still be some pilot in me.

Snorer tells me with great sentiment that he "hates it here" and is struggling but admits it could be because he's spent "so long banged-up." Is he aware of Robbie at Healthcare and why not have a chat with him? He is very suspicious and thinks "talking to anyone will be noted" and earn him "negative points." He says he'll "Think about it."

1700: Dinner and Roll-check announced. Did the latter, missed the former. Or rather, escaped it, as ENGROSSED in the film. I'd never noticed before (and I've seen it a million times) how much they all look *around* when they first get let out of the trucks. The inside of the Cooler reminds me of B 2 5. Funny how the first escape committee meeting is held in the *library*. Is that why it took them so long to give me a job with Glenda?

1940: When the tunnel is found short – Gordon Jackson suggests postponement. Is that what Zara (Top) is going to do tomorrow?

Monday, November 14th, 2011.

T minus 3. Today though, I think will be D day as Zara (Top) will be back behind her desk and will tell me if I have a home to go to.

0715: Healthcare. A two-shot with Geordie, here to pick a-fit-for-Home-leave certificate and "won't be back for five days." With NO disrespect to him I told him that I sincerely hope I will not be here to welcome his return. As he grinned his Tim Healy/Dennis Patterson focus grabbing *Auf Wiedersehen Pet* smile, he said something to me that brought everything – and some – to the most grinding of halts.

"Jonathan, please use your influence, like, to get some changes made round here, like, mon."

Influence???? Now listen here Geordie and listen good. I don't have any influence whatsoever and I...

"Divvn't talk shite mon, the BOOK, mon, make it canny like. Wozza." Like a thunderbolt, Geordie's off the cuff comment made me finally realise in a complete flash that this book has changed from self-therapy into a manifesto for a plea for change in the way our country's prisons are being run. It still however, remains an apology to the individual that I mucked about so inexcusably fiscally.

And I still hope it exhibits my love for my wife. Oh, if only you knew...

I stood there with all of the above tumbling around my mind utterly speechless. Geordie studied me as the words sank in. I apprehensively told him that I would make the book as good as I can and that I hope it makes someone sit up and take some notice. An even bigger smile came my way and we shook hands coinciding with his final line to me: "Why aye mon. Alreet."

WD asked me to come back at 0800 so returned to Wilford which was just beginning to wake up. I remind you that the published time for Roll-check round these parts is 0730...

0749: Tannoy: "Second and final call for breakfast and Roll-check."

0755: Tannoy again... The long list of stragglers masterly mirroring a call-sheet of a Cecil B DeMille production.

0800: On arrival at work the doors were still locked so went for a nose at the gym, the outside of which had loads of loitering lags as its doors remained locked too. On opening, the rush for admittance was filled with nothing other than 100% adrenaline and testosterone. Standing there, taking this in I contemplated what a shame it is that the same energy it is not used for something productive around this place.

What a *waste* of a *free* work force.

Healthcare. Emptied one bin. An *exceptionally* disinterested Rachel was asked if Robbie was in. "Upstairs" was grunted at me. Up, I went.

Cracker was somewhat flustered. He didn't mention last week's absence – but *did* say that he "couldn't commit to anything" with me this week as he "needed to see the Governor." I asked him if all was well – which clearly it was not – but a drawbridge came clattering up. Further to my recent one-on-one with Snorer, it was creatively communicated that I *may* know of a lifer who wouldn't mind a chat. I relayed that this person *might* be reluctant to speak to anyone as he *might* have voiced to me that he was concerned it would score him negative points, which I thought absurd. Surely anyone trying to make positive moves should be encouraged?

"He's right," said Robbie. "Your friend who you *might* know obviously knows the system." A request "will indeed trip alarm bells." He passed sentence further with "anyone voicing a desire to put up building blocks should be seen as good." The best – and only way forward – was to get my man to "put in an app (!!!!!!) to see the psychology department." We both concluded this was madness but "talking and planning" whilst seen as sensibly crucial to people in Cracker's field is "still a negative when noted by the prison system."

0930: Zara (Top) should be in so the bull's horns are firmly grabbed to learn my fate. I climb the stairs on a wing and a prayer and try to ignore the thunderous thumping of my heart. She's in and I loiter by Orderly Sid's desk. I am beckoned over... I am so nervous I don't even inspect today's top... "It's all been sent off." She turns her screen round and lets me read an acknowledgement and confirmation that my request has been accepted and that I am "on the waiting list..."

Initial reaction? I'm going *nowhere*. Is anything else I can do? "No. Just sit tight." Can I come back this afternoon? "Yes of course, but I'm not promising anything."

Buzz's recommendation at the beginning of this journey appears in the sprockets of the projector that is my mind... "Keep your chin up." Right now, I have no alternative strategy to employ. You put yourself here Robinson: keep plugging away. Stiff upper lip. You *can* get through this.

On the walk back to Wilford, realisation sets in. Subject to a miracle, I'm not leaving on Thursday. Right then: start preparing for Christmas in prison. Keep calm. Breathe. Do NOT panic.

Check list, check list, check list.

Snorer sighted. I run the conversation with Robbie past him. He's reluctant to give it a try.

1100: A chat with Library Sally about how JT went. My thoughts? 10/10 for the time and effort. Sally agreed and voiced her frustration that "no male authors had responded" – she has no budget to offer – "not even £5 for petrol." The heating bills that so consummately keep the temperature torrid was disclosed to Sally on that one before telling her I'd see her later in the afternoon for the talk by the other writer and left for Healthcare.

A "no" from Rachel and Sue on any odd jobs. Departing the stage the former was seen talking to an unknown female – her replacement?

1150: Chow-truck heard. Keep calm. Keep calm. Keep calm.

1200: Lunch. One prisoner announced it was his birthday. I asked him if he was going to do anything nice. "Nah mate, spend the day sleepin'..."

1240: Library. Thinking of yet another title for this book: "I was in prison with Joanna Trollope."

Healthcare: Nothing for me. Met our new Rachel. Something familiar rang a bell... Eureka – it's the same medical person who saw me when we arrived at Hollesley Bay – the Sylvia Simms nurse. Once I'd told her we'd met she remembered me. She is only a locum until they find a permanent Rachel Replacement.

1320: Zara (Top): "No news – I suggest you come back here in the morning."

1420: Off to stalk Robbie for an appointment then on to the library for the second writer's talk at the Bay.

En-route Sally was coming in the opposite direction. Had I heard the news? – No. Our visiting author had cancelled. Due to "an upset tummy and many apologies." Sally was mortified.

At work, cornered Cracker and tried to pin him down for dates. Is tomorrow and Wed still on? "No" but he "will get back to me." Not a very positive day so far. Like the *number one* rule in helicopters – if it can go wrong, it will go wrong.

1530: Healthcare. Three letters for Rounds. One for Hoxon, one for Wilford and one for the caravan site.

1640: My countdown calendar says 3 to go.

It's not bloody happening is it?

Tuesday, November 15th, 2011.

T minus 2. Why am I still counting? All I am trying to do every breathing second is fend-off complete panic.

0710: I spy with my little eye WD arriving for work. Of late she has been really kind to me and I feel guilty calling her that. She has explained that "the hard edge of granite" I first saw in her is the "natural shell" she has built up over the years of "dealing with idiot, aggressive and rude prisoners." Regardless, no more WD. From now on: Kathy.

0725: Work. Student nurse and Welsh Dra... Kathy duly there.

Do you believe in karma? Here's a lesson in life. Having elected to say nice things about Kathy I am then rewarded by her inviting me to Rachel's leaving do! I thought at first she was joking but no – she's serious. I tell her I'm very touched and would love to – adding that I hope Rachel doesn't mind. She even tells me they want me to sign a card.

I can't describe how I feel. I might *still* be a human being.

Cleaned, emptied the bins, depleted the Andrex supply, if you follow me.

0845: Wilford. Wrote Rachel a note thanking her for putting up with me and wished her luck. Signed it: Jonathan, Healthcare Orderly (Retired).

0950: Work. Rachel and "New Rachel" there. One letter for Cosford. As I headed for the *Crossroads* set a civilian female was spotted walking that way so asked her to be my mule. (I actually said to her would she mind taking the letter). She said "pleasure," as she took a lit fag out of her mouth.

Library. Stuart and yet another "new library guy" let me in and we all read the papers. Stuart won Mac. Nothing more in the local about the BBB ("Burger bar business"). Sally arrived – laughed at my presence – Stuart and NLG shot to their feet sending newspapers flying and looked busy. Not too far off a previous scene in this epic of prison officers ditching pool cues...

1030: Return from Healthcare. "Shot" a bin emptying scene and signed Rachel's card. Sue was about and I asked her if my attendance at Rachel's party was a good idea. She screwed her face up – not knowing I was on the guest list. I explained that Kathy had invited me. We plotted that Sue will corner Kathy and have a chat as to the most diplomatic thing to do.

1100: Off to Zara (Top). Climbed the stairs successfully despite my knees knocking. Zara (Top) "full of cold." – Can I come back early afternoon?

1105: Kathy "has had a rethink" after her chat with Sue and thinks it's best if I don't come. Easy come easy go. At the library told Stuart I'd meet him under the tree tomorrow at 0730 to walk him up in order to get him on the dentist's list.

Oh – saw Robbie earlier and asked him if he had any news on dates. "No."

1130: No post but my "app" has returned from "wardrobe" about my clothes request: "No, you will be given it on your day of discharge." This despite being told by an officer that it would be no problem.

Keep calm. Keep calm.

1235: Lunch was loads of salad then went to the library. Stuart's line of dialogue: "What a surprise to see you here." Faffed until 1300 so as not to crash Rachel's party and meandered up to Healthcare. The door locked, so rang the bell. Rachel opened it, glass in hand. "We're having a bit of a do." I gave her the letter. She thanked me and asked me to return at 1400.

1355: Left the Unit to do exactly that. Limping Al fiddled downstairs testing electrical stuff. *What* he was testing frightened the hell out of me – reminding me how much longer I *might* be here: Christmas lights.

Healthcare. Sue admitted me through the still locked door. Rachel was upstairs with "New Rachel," the student nurse and Robbie – who was on his knees. I asked him if he was proposing. Various cartons of juice lying about and packets of nibbles gave the place an ambience of a Teddy Bear's picnic. There was nothing for me to do – so across the room said bye to Rachel and thanked her for the gig. It was all a bit stiff and stifled. Very formal and no "good luck" to me or anything. Nor did she make reference to the note I had written to her. Perhaps she was embarrassed. Whatever, an era ends.

Turned to "New Rachel" and told her I'd see her in the morning. Regeneration complete. It's like *Doctor Who*.

I hope I've regenerated.

Heston hid downstairs for his flu jab. Told him the "no" reply to my clothes app. He laughed then Kathy called him in to inject him. He stopped laughing. Off to Zara (Top). Worryingly: "No news." She is not here tomorrow but her colleague with the Peter Gabriel beard will be. That's one bit of good news – I thought that was it for this week but at least someone will be fighting my corner on my last day.

I now doubt very much that I'll wrap on Wednesday.

Zara (Top) suggested coming back at 1545 to see if there is any movement. Decided to go off and see Rod at Bricks for a distraction. Found him sitting stonewalled in front of a computer.

We go outside to set the world to rights. Back on that veranda again which should be in a western – me with my Gary Cooper legs and Rod with his Henry Cooper hair. On updating him in on the Tommy Cooper clothes refusal he says it is my right to have my stuff and instructs me to "go mad with them" to get what is mine. His tirade only falls short of insisting the Governor irons my shirt himself.

His "Gov" appears – I'm probably using too much of Rod's time. He loiters and listens to us chat. I detect him observing me sharpshooter like. After only two or three more of my lines he turns to me and we make eye contact. The silence straight from a western. He shoots his horse-opera line which *spectacularly* flashes me back to early days at Bedford:

"You're a bit of a fish out of water, if you don't mind me saying so."

I am silent for a couple of seconds. My head drops. I raise it again and simply tell him I was a tit and prison is probably the best thing that's ever happened to me.

"Short sharp shock?"

Yes Siree.

1530: Zara (Top). Again "nothing" and come and see Darling in the morning. Right. Went to the library and sat in a corner. First looked at a book on conjuring tricks and then something on the history of space fight.

I now need to either levitate myself out of here or build a rocket.

1630: Jumped on by the Deputy Governor, wanting an update on Roland's situation (what about bloody mine?!) I sought confirmation that Roland's fate is at the hands of the S.O. – "that's right." So then relayed that this was news to Bungalow Bill and would he please set the record straight with the S.O. He nodded at me Bewes like.

Does ANY part of the prison system EVER know what other parts are doing?

Now everyone else's problems were sorted I disclosed that I'd had an unsigned response to my "app" for kit and asked him what the score is on this.

"Not something we would normally do."

1700: Dinner. "Kebab." Say no more. Managed to get 2 oranges. Just as well — Orange Nicker 2, citrus lover numero-uno is back from Home-leave…

Wednesday, November 16th, 2011.

T minus 1. Tomorrow is November 17th. The date I have been watching out for like a slow boiling kettle.

Some lightweight insouciance was required last night and it turned up in the shape of Eric n' Ernie. During their habitual sound thrashing of me at pool the most delicious story was relayed. As previously reported, they are still sharing a room. Picture them both. In bed — please do NOT get the wrong idea — the only action was chit-chat. Somehow the conversation waltzed to Gordon's last "big" birthday where a theme was required. Easy: a salsa evening. Gordon took a few lessons to get to grips with the basics "and enjoyed it very much." Andrew then piped up from his bed that he's "done a few turns" at salsa and he "misses the practice."

Both at this point went quiet.

In their double room there is plenty of space… they could draw the curtains… they could minuet away… A few more seconds passed.

"Never going to happen," said by both.

As he polished off yet another black Gordon then dropped a bombshell by revealing a piece of news which to date, had not reached me.

"EBV failed to come back from work yesterday."

I shot down to the office and addressed an unfamiliar officer. I have heard a friend of mine may be missing off Hoxon. Is this correct? "Two prisoners failed to report" — and that's all he knew. I went back to my room. Two? EBV always hung out with Dennis and… *Robert*.

Last night on the corridor a fog of something not available at your average tobacconists hung like a huge thick eiderdown. The mad giggles made me think for a second that there were some young ladies on the wing.

0623: Night-officer-always-on-the-phone on the phone.

0725: Outside, Stuart was bang on time. Moyles and Alistair arrived in their truck and were grilled on the EBV and Robert situation.

"EBV gone for sure," puffed Moyles. "Not Robert though, as I've seen him today." They couldn't tell me anything else so Stuart and I traipsed up to Healthcare. On arrival, Philip was most bouncy and kept saying "last Day!" to me – I told Tigger I wasn't counting any chickens – then got Stuart on dental list. It was like getting someone an upgrade on an aeroplane.

0800: Mopping complete and Dave is back. How did the wedding go? "All a success."

0807: Back on the Unit both Gordon and Andrew are on the phone.

Booking salsa lessons?

Healthcare again. On set, our "new Rachel," the Sylvia Simms lookalike laboured. Being Healthcare Orderly sure has its perks. Introduced Stuart to Renee, feeling like a matchmaker. She-of-zips told him to sit tight. Heston appeared voicing views on the EBV situation: "He was a player and up to criminal activity."

Bolstered to Bricks to see Rod. If anyone has their ear close to the ground about the EBV saga – it'll be him.

Rod: "He was a lump who never had anything good to say about anything… but I liked him." I responded that our ex-colleague had always been pleasant to me and I knew he was mates with Dennis – and any friend of Mr Waterman is a friend of mine.

Our Statham had a 0930 at the dentist so it was elected to walk up to Wilford for a coffee. On arrival, the officers wouldn't let him in my room, so he sat in the garden whilst I rushed around brewing up. I introduced him to the bench. I don't introduce bench to him though. I think he would have worried about me if he knew I sometimes talk to "bench."

Up to Healthcare we then went, during which he grilled me on the new dentist's skills, only falling short of asking me when and where she had trained. I don't know – she's a dentist for God's sake. "But is she good?" Yes Rod, she's the best dentist in the world. By the time we got there Stuart was outside having been treated and I told Rod to hear it straight from the horse's mouth. Well, Stuart's. The comments were positive and at last Rod relaxed.

Robbie arrived at 0925. I jumped on him for an appointment. "Is 1030 OK?" Perfect. I got given Rounds by Sylvia and headed Hoxon bound with medical mail. During which I encountered Robert…

Chuckling at my assumption that he had departed too, he very patiently thanked me for my concern. He "wanted to be careful" what he said – but "EBV is OK. He is in custody somewhere and Dennis knows about it…" I told him that I was very pleased he was still with us. I'm not sure he wanted to hear that but I think he knew what I meant.

1010: Darling should have his house in order. Here goes. On entrance I am fed one solitary line by the bearded one: "Come back later."

Healthcare. Waiting for Robbie. Rod is recumbent in the dentist's chair. Renee appears. "Isn't Stuart nice?" and then whispers "but he's a lifer," like some character in a Noël Coward play referring to a child born out of wedlock. Her attention switches to me. She knows that I'm due out tomorrow. "What are you going to do?" She's not talking about getting out. She's not talking about next week. Nor Christmas. Nor next summer. She's talking about the rest of my life. I think for a second or two then utter my dialogue:

Try and bounce back.

Upstairs the place is full of strangers in medical uniform talking about suture training. Robbie is making them tea. Once he's sewn that up he is mine. We go into a different room, his being used for human tapestry. He asks for a concise summing up of the "burger three, having been off-radar last week." *Everything* is relayed. We laugh at the absurdity of the situation. Cracker concludes that "if it was put in a book – no one would believe it."

He talks of his "dismay of the lack of morale in this prison, from both staff and prisoners." I recount to him stories from both, and from what I've heard that the Governor is not popular. The vessel in which we serve is not an efficient – or happy – ship.

He agrees. It is "common knowledge" that there are "more phones on Bosmere Unit than at Carphone Warehouse" and of the known "nightly runners taking stuff from Bosmere to Hoxon." The "entire place is in disarray" and is a "huge vicious circle of revolving door prisoners leaving prison – and coming straight back." He goes on: "This is supposed to be Cat D resettlement prison. There are very few Cat D prisoners here and even less resettlement going on," adding that the officer we all know as the Terminator "is needed on all the Units." He goes even *further:* "The only positive thing of the mad house experience" is my "timing and the writing of the book."

His frustration of the out of date system is evident. He makes me laugh by the "make an app to make an app to make an app mentality." "No one is DOING anything" and therefore; "Back to the vicious circle."

Then back to me. He asks if there is any progress on my uxorious urgency. No. I recount how I nearly asked – and he nearly offered – to contact my wife. He suggests that if I've got this far – it's best to wait and to get in touch when JR and HMP are no longer joined at the hip. He tells me that if I have no luck – he will then get in touch with her.

I confess that I've learnt to like me. The basic ingredients are not in fact too bad. I ask him why the HELL that wasn't good enough. Cracker: "Crap insecurity."

Prison, with its multi-cultural, classless society has taught me a very valuable lesson *indeed*.

Robbie says I should be proud of myself. I have survived "not just the sentence but with the living with idiots." He tells me that the Healthcare staff "have talked at length" about me and I have "reminded them that there are some prisoners who are aware and want to make right." They are "few and far between" but I have "given a glimpse to them of why they do their job." I am touched by what he says. I do not intend to let them down.

Or me.

He gives me a contact phone number and email address. I plan to stay in touch with this man.

1200: Lunch. Ate loads of salad. Why can't it be in the rules here that prisoners eat their meals sitting down. At the tables.

1305: Climbing the stairs to Darling. I'm invited to sit down and he makes the call in front of me. I hear of accommodation available in Colchester. It's nowhere near where I want to be but it's a start and a way out. It turns out that the person on the other end is confusing me with someone else. Realising this, Darling looks to me for where I want to go. I tell him and the locale is relayed down the phone. There is somewhere close to where I want to be... Perfect. Things are looking up. Darling asks me to come back at 1430 for the address. Things are REALLY looking up.

To Healthcare feeling very optimistic. Philip asks what the latest is. I relay the news. He gives me his email address. I don't know what, how or when, that the pieces are going to fall into place but clear development is apparent. Sylvia asks me to come back at 1400 for more Rounds. Kathy gives me the thumbs-up.

1330: The waiting is worse than when I worried outside Court on July 25th. At least no one is going on about the state of traffic on the A3. I've returned to the Unit.

1340: Hover at Healthcare.

1400: With ants in my pants, am back in my room.

1405: Back at Healthcare. Sylvia flustered with all the things she needs to do in her new job.

1411: Rounds.

1430: Darling: "Come back in 15." Finish Rounds.

Is this the last time I'll do this? It begins to feel like it just might be...

1450: Darling: "Sit tight." He is dealing with another prisoner. I glance at the clock on the wall. I know that he works until 1600. It's do or die.

1500: Frank lopes in. "You going tomorrow?" Darling is panned to – the Judge and Jury in the Court of my immediate destiny.

"I'd say no."

My balloon deflates.

The other prisoner, thank God, finishes with Darling at 1530. I am summoned to the chair. More calls are made to Judi the Tag lady, the internal Probation department and anyone else either interested or involved. "This would have worked out if it was all in by half two," says he with the beard. It's now nearly 1600.

It's over. I'm going nowhere tomorrow. Accept it Robinson. There's nothing you can do.

When do you think? I ask the owner of the Gabriel goatee. "Friday or Monday – most likely Monday." He's not here tomorrow – so he suggests that I use Victoria to communicate with Judi or failing that, Anna (Ford) in his office – who I am on nodding terms with. He rings Victoria and tells me to report to her tomorrow at 1300. I thank him. And leave. Still a prisoner now and most certainly still a prisoner tomorrow – Tag day. Bastard November the bastard 17th.

Return to Healthcare to announce my retirement is not yet in effect and I will see them tomorrow. Everyone disappointed for me. Robbie: "Is this doing your head in?"

Sort of.

1620: Return room. Exhausted. Mentally destroyed. Made myself eat something. I am all in.

1700: Dinner. Told everyone. All supportive and very disappointed for me.

1800: On the news: "Dale Farm reoccupied."

Thursday, November 17th, 2011.

T minus nothing. Blast off. "Houston, we have a problem."

Up at 0615 and feeling most strange. November 17th has been set-up as the home-straight for so long in my mind – I'm supposed to be "off this picture..." This is another good reminder not to work for this production company again.

Always-on-the-phone-night-officer on the phone.

Wall dots and countdown – odd to see a zero – calendars done.

0635: Night officer off the phone. But consulting a book. The Australian *Yellow Pages*?

0725: Work. Philip and Dave embarrassed about me still being here. I told them it's OK and good training for the "one day at a time" game plan. Then I emptied their bins.

0750: Unit. As I'm still here and my Canteen sheet left blank I asked the office for approval for a

V 1

For Deliveries From 07/11/11
Expiry End 20/02/12

Hollesley Bay

Note: Available Spend Cannot Be Manually Amended

Price	Item	IC	Qty	Price	Item	IC	Qty	Price	Item	IC	Qty
	PHONE & STAMPS			£1.00	Intense Skin Cream 226g	120615		£1.69	Roast Salted Cashew 75g(V)	120524	
£1.00	Phone Credit	PC		£3.25	Palmers CocoButter Formula	093826		£1.49	Fruit & Nut Mix 350g	103563	
£0.46	1st Class Stamp	006207		£3.49	Palmers Coco Butter Lotion	093244		£1.15	Peanuts & Raisins 400g	103564	
£0.36	2nd Class Stamp	098208		£1.99	Nivea Crème 50ml	298071		£1.49	Tropical Fruit & Nut 350g	101672	
£0.01	1p Postage Stamp	125678		£1.83	Johnsons Baby Lotion 200ml	770520		£1.49	Almonds 150g	103562	
	TOBACCO			£1.06	3 Blade Dispose Razors 6s	120616		£0.63	Mini Cheddars Orgl 50g	040341	
£3.56	Amber Leaf 12.5g	108369		£6.01	Gillette Mach3 Blades 4s	065816		£0.60	Caramel Peanuts 80g	086009	
£3.46	Cutters Choice 12.5g	536063		£7.40	Gillette Mach3 Razor	065770		£0.49	Bombay Mix 80g (V)	122522	
£5.21	Turner Tobacco12.5g	092679		£1.52	Shave Cream Tube 100g	096205		£1.09	Soft Pitted Dates 250g	196231	
£3.87	Golden Virginia 12.5g	065158		£4.59	Gillette Shave Balm 100ml	097944		£0.79	Peperami Std Sgl	746214	
£2.26	Red Bull Tobacco 12.5g	093126		£0.85	Cotton Wool Balls 100's	100183			**DRINKS**		
£6.94	Amber Leaf 25g	974940		£0.69	Cotton Buds 100's	100186		£1.00	Red Mountain Coffee 70g	121063	
£7.54	Golden Virginia 25g	481937		£0.60	Sponge	100886		£5.19	Kenco Refill Smooth 150g	116474	
£1.62	HMP Golden Virginia 5g	094783		£0.89	Face Cloth	125867		£0.13	Nescafe Decaf 1 Cup Stick	651180	
£0.92	Hamlet Cigar	420007		£1.01	Toe Nail Clipper	102948		£0.13	Nescafe Orgl 1 Cup Stick	651160	
£3.63	B & H Gold 10's	047222		£2.01	Multi Vita Tablets 60s(V)	095742		£1.29	PG Tips 40's	197746	
£3.37	L & B King Size 10's	362075		£1.90	Cod Liver Oil Tabs 90s(GF)	097872		£1.79	Green Tea Lemon 50's	100662	
£0.89	BBrand L/Slim Filter Tips	116395		£1.17	Johnsons Baby Oil 200ml	446520		£1.29	Red Berries Tea 20's	125117	
£0.20	BBrand Rolling Paper Red	116389		£1.32	Imperial Leather Talc 150g	616680		£1.29	Peppermint Tea 20's	125113	
£0.40	Swan Papers Liquorice	552970		£3.09	Bonjela 15g	261766		£1.69	Earl Grey Tea Bags 50s	113945	
£0.25	Rizla Papers Green	026316		£2.08	E45 Cream 50g	174680		£2.36	Cbury Choc Instant 280g(V)	585595	
£0.56	Lighter Child Restant	081863		£0.30	Paracetamol Tubs 16s	102709		£1.09	Horlicks Or Malt 300g(V)	124696	
£0.15	Economy Safety Match (box)	051905		£1.49	Vaseline Jelly 50ml	107236		£1.39	Coffee-Mate 200g(V,H)	748681	
	BATTERIES			£1.49	Lypsyl Original	121084		£0.35	Horlicks Light Sachet(V)	100616	
£0.80	Panasonic Battery AA(1's)	098195		£1.62	Palmers O/Butter Lip Balm	093412		£2.05	Marvel 198g	007363	
£0.87	Duracell AAA Battery (1's)	045556		£1.00	ES Wet Wipes 80pcs	121975		£0.53	Economy UHT Semi-Skim(V)	989150	
£0.37	Panasonic Battery AAA(1's)	098196			**SWEETS & SNACKS**			£0.55	Economy UHT Milk Whole(V)	989170	
	TOILETRIES & HEALTH			£1.20	Haribo Starmix Bag (GF)	101190		£0.49	Alpro Soya Sweetd 250m(VE)	092831	
£1.13	Branded Toothbrush	068219		£1.20	Haribo Tangfastics Bag(GF)	101326		£1.25	Rob Orange 1ltr(VE)	114130	
£2.03	Aquafresh T.Paste 125ml	095699		£1.00	Bassetts Jelly Babies Bag	101577		£1.25	Rob Apple/Black NAS 1ltr(VE)	114152	
£0.59	Colgate Advance 100ml	114964		£1.00	Bassetts Murray Mints(V)	101625		£0.65	Economy Lemon Squash 1L	072014	
£3.09	Sensodyne F T/Paste 45ml	054826		£1.00	Maynards Wine Gums Bag	101645		£0.65	Economy Orange Squash 1L	081732	
£1.89	Macleans Whitening 50ml	102722		£1.00	Cad Choc Eclair Bag(V,GF)	123188		£0.85	Economy Orange Juice 1ltr	110001	
£1.83	Euthyl T/Powder Freshmint	106544		£1.00	Foxs Glacier Fruit Bag(VE)	116008		£0.65	Economy Tropical Juice 1L	110415	
£1.03	E/Mint Mouthwash 500ml	104705		£1.00	Foxs Glacier Dark Bag(VE)	116032		£1.15	Pineapple Juice 1L (VE,GF)	101250	
£1.32	Wisdom Dental Floss 100m	080835		£0.39	Jelly Beans Small Bag(H)	109435		£1.39	Rubicon Mango Juice 1ltr	666289	
£2.44	Fixodent Denture Crm	116063		£0.39	Fizzy Fish Small Bag(H)	109434		£0.49	Economy Cherryade SF 1ltr	120474	
£1.38	Steradent Tablets Org 30s	980336		£0.50	ES Milk Chocolate 100g	114353		£0.49	Eco Diet Lemonade 1ltr	120476	
£1.29	Dettol Antibac Bar Soap x2	124366		£0.50	ES Chocolate Frt&Nut 100g	115636		£0.49	Economy Lemonade 1ltr	120475	
£0.79	Dove Soap 100g	787415		£1.00	Cad Dairy Milk Bar(V)	113972		£1.67	Coca Cola 1.5ltr (VE)	107920	
£0.66	IL Soap 100g	125249		£0.57	Cad's Bournville 46g (V)	549673		£1.67	Coca Cola Diet 1.5ltr (VE)	107847	
£0.61	IL Roll On Deodorant 50ml	099668		£0.54	Cadbury Crunchie(V,GF)	032557		£1.22	Lucozade Engy Orng 500ml(V)	112711	
£2.93	Dove Stick Invisible 40ml	094741		£0.52	Bounty Milk Std (H,K)	057911		£0.71	Coca Cola Can (VE)	282574	
£2.34	Lynx Stick Africa 50ml	094725		£0.51	Cad Double Decker Std(V)	254911		£0.71	Coke Diet Can (VE)	282673	
£0.70	Economy Shower Gel 250ml	096062		£0.54	Kit Kat 4 Finger	048905		£0.49	D&G Ginger Beer Can	964643	
£1.29	IL Bodywash 250ml	125669		£0.49	Mars Bar Std(V,K,H)	890164		£0.65	Highland Spring Still 1.5L	679084	
£0.59	Radox Shower Gel 250ml	576121		£0.49	Snickers Bar Std(V,K,H)	890168			**CARDS**		
£2.48	Lynx ShowerGel 250ml	516610		£0.49	Twix Twin Bar Std(H,K)	563064		£0.61	I Love You Card 1	103409	
£2.09	H/Shoulder Shampoo Classic	125929		£0.56	Yorkie Milk Orig Std	124302		£0.61	I Love You Card 2	103413	
£3.83	Palmer Coc Oil Shamp 400ml	060592		£0.60	NestleCrunch Wht Choc(V,H)	351775		£0.61	I Miss You Card 1	103415	
£0.50	Palmers Coco Oil Cond 150g	093114		£0.20	Cad Chomp Bar(V,GF)	114957		£0.61	I Miss You Card 2	103416	
£4.24	African Pride Shamp/Cond	094606		£0.15	Chupa Chup Lolly sgl	100260		£0.61	Thinking Of You Card 1	103422	
£3.56	Polytar Shampoo 150ml	098676		£0.15	Skittles Mini	099964		£0.61	Thinking Of You Card 2	103426	
£3.56	O&L 3In1 Shampoo 250ml	067406		£0.47	Polo Original Std(VE,H)	573000		£0.61	Just To Say Card 1	103427	
£2.39	Vegetable Oil Shamp 355ml	094609		£0.73	Fishermans Friend Original	779215		£0.61	Just To Say Card 2	103439	
£0.58	Hair Gel Firm 250ml	071907		£0.45	Walkrs Chse&Onion 34.5g(V)	444300		£0.61	Blank Card	123444	
£3.05	Dax Pomade	094602		£0.45	Walkrs Salt&Vinegar Bag(V)	444290		£0.61	Female Birthday Card	103449	
£4.75	Moisturiser Pink Oil 355ml	094604		£0.45	Walkers Rdy Salted 34.5g(V)	444310		£0.61	Male Birthday Card	103466	
£4.07	Hair,Scalp &Skin Oil 207ml	094596		£0.63	McCoys F/Grilled Steak(V)	964560		£0.61	Mum Birthday Card	103478	
£0.87	Hairbands Thick 6s	124576		£0.20	Space Raiders Beef	100913		£0.61	Daughter Bday Card Child	103464	
£0.35	Hair Comb	102254		£0.20	SRaiders Pickled Onion(V)	186915		£0.61	Daughter Bday Card Adult	103450	
£0.89	Hair Brush Vented	102394		£0.20	Red Mill Tangy Tomato 22g	115723		£0.61	Wife Birthday Card	103496	
£1.00	Afro Comb	093366		£0.48	Doritos Chilli 40g (V)	100641		£0.61	Dad Birthday Card	103507	
£3.96	Clearasil Cleanser 200ml	080203		£0.59	KP Salted P/Nuts 50g(V)	072048		£0.61	Son Birthday Card Child	103506	
£7.32	Clynol Apricot Face Scrub	093403		£5.21	KP Salted P/Nuts 500g(V)	124887		£0.61	Son Birthday Card Adult	103509	

V - Vegetarian   Ve - Vegan   H - Halal   Ft - Fair Trade   GF - Gluten Free   SF - Sugar Free   Ho - Healthy Option   K - Kosher

Price	Item	IC	Qty
£0.61	Open Anniversary	103529	
£0.61	Grandson Bday Card	109194	
£0.61	Granddaughter Bday Card	109192	
£1.32	EID Card 8 Pack	109436	
	FRUIT & VEGETABLES		
£0.25	Banana (HO)	100729	
£0.75	Apples Red 2's (HO)	111544	
£0.26	Orange Medium (HO)	124436	
£0.30	Lemon (HO)	097149	
£0.49	Grapefruit (HO)	111862	
£1.00	Tomatoes Pack(HO)	112933	
£0.80	Cucumber (HO)	113453	
£1.50	Mixed Peppers 2s (HO)	113623	
£0.75	Cooking Onions 500g (HO)	111529	
£0.38	Garlic (HO)	097482	
£1.49	Fresh Ginger 250g	098054	
	BISCUITS & BAKERY		
£0.50	Economy Custard Crms 150g	121002	
£0.50	Economy Bourbon Creams	120918	
£0.50	Economy Digestive 200g	120993	
£0.79	Economy Coconut Rings	121009	
£0.69	Economy Fruit Shortcake	121023	
£0.79	Economy Ginger Nuts 300g	121007	
£0.79	Economy Rich Tea 300g	120994	
£1.00	Economy Milk Choc Dig 200g	120992	
£1.39	Cadbury's Fingers Box	115756	
£0.50	Economy Choc Chip Cookies	104805	
£0.99	Economy Jaffa Cake 300g	089294	
£0.75	Cfords Jam Rings 125g	124853	
£1.85	Milk Choc Hobnobs 300g	124829	
£1.00	McVities Taxi 6pack	115518	
£0.65	GoAhead Yoghurt Break	066813	
£0.50	Nutrigrain Strawberry	114466	
£1.19	Ritz Original 200g(V)	116476	
£0.49	Economy Cream Crackers	116439	
£0.95	Ryvita Crisp/B Dark Rye(V)	113298	
£2.99	Jamaican Honeybun SpiceBun	120715	
£0.79	Plain Pitta Bread 6's	106424	
£0.89	Screen Malt Loaf(V)	107687	
	GROCERIES		
£1.89	Harvest Muesli 1kg	125995	
£2.75	Klg CornFlakes 500g(V,K,H)	066964	
£2.50	Klgs CrnchyNut 375g(V,K,H)	086985	
£2.29	Klgs Branflakes500g(V,K,H)	125439	
£2.35	Klg FruitNFib 375g(VE,K,H)	067281	
£2.25	Klg Coco Pops 235g(V,K,H)	115234	
£1.29	Sugar Puffs 320g	116482	
£2.49	Frosties 500g(VE,K,H)	125366	
£1.49	Weetabix 12s(V,K)	260961	
£0.75	Superfast Oats 500g(VE)	935750	
£1.99	Shredded Wheat 12's(V,H)	065063	
£1.09	Granulated Sugar1kg(V,GF)	295642	
£1.29	Hermesetas 300's	031773	
£1.49	Hartley Sberry Jam330g(VE)	111863	
£1.49	R/bers Orange Marmalade	109075	
£1.99	Econ Sqzy Honey(V)	102755	
£1.85	Smt Peanut Butter 340g(V)	053079	
£3.35	Marmite Squeeze 200g(V)	065678	
£0.14	Nutella 15g Portion	161417	
£1.19	Tuna Chunks in Brine 185g	111694	
£0.75	Economy Tuna Flakes 185g	121144	
£1.18	Econ Tuna Chunks Oil 185g	297770	
£1.55	Mackerel Fillet S/flower	142348	
£1.55	Mackerel Fillet Spicy/Tom	101353	
£1.65	Sardines Oil 120g	833886	
£1.65	Sardines Tomato 120g	833822	
£1.19	Glenryck Pilchards Tomato	835256	
£2.45	Corned Beef 340g(H)	100608	
£1.15	Hot Dogs 400g	834432	
£1.48	Beef Hotdog 400g(H)	098884	

Price	Item	IC	Qty
£1.09	Chicken Hotdog 400g(H)	103866	
£1.25	Pork Luncheon Meat 198g	155200	
£2.49	Stewed Steak 392g	142881	
£0.79	Meatballs&Onion Gravy 410g	116287	
£0.33	Inst N/dle Chick C/Mein	092653	
£0.33	Instant Noodle Mushroom(V)	092659	
£0.33	Instant N/dle Spicy Tom(V)	092666	
£0.33	Instant Noodle Beef 85g	092652	
£0.33	Instant N/dle Curry 85g(V)	092655	
£0.33	Instant N/dle Prawn 85g(V)	062664	
£0.40	Kolee N/dle Chow Mein (V)	092669	
£0.50	Noodle Pot Snack Chic&Mush	102336	
£0.50	Nodle Pot Snack Curry	102337	
£0.99	Economy Basmati Rice 500g	115372	
£2.29	Heinz Tomato Ketchup 460g	092366	
£0.69	Economy Ketchup 470g	118075	
£1.49	HP Sauce Brown 285g(VE,H)	256471	
£1.99	HP BBQ Smoke Sauce(V)	118669	
£0.99	Econom Salad Cream 445g(V)	095492	
£0.99	Sqeezy Brown Sauce 470g(V)	095459	
£0.99	Colmans Mustard Tubes 50g	447193	
£1.05	Hot Sin Stir Fry Sauce	106379	
£1.98	Encona Hot Pepper Sauce	073046	
£1.25	Homepride Curry Sauce(V)	084181	
£1.75	Cup A Soup Golden Veg pk(V)	125083	
£1.75	Cup A Soup Tomato 4s(V)	125654	
£1.09	HZ Tomato Soup 400g(V)	269611	
£0.95	HZ Baked Beans 415g(V,GF,K)	266581	
£0.35	Economy Baked Beans	113633	
£0.75	Branson Spaghetti Tom	013534	
£1.39	HZ Ravioli Tom Sauce 400g	101994	
£0.35	Economy Chopped Tomatoes	113198	
£0.65	Economy Sweetcorn 340g	113295	
£0.99	Peach Slices in Juice 415g	836569	
£0.59	P/apple Slices Juice 227g	110887	
£1.70	Carnation Condensd Milk(V,H)	525972	
£0.62	Carnation Evapo Milk (V,H)	185031	
£0.59	Thick Cream Tin 170g(V.H)	616623	
£1.19	Ambrosia Crmd Rice 400g(V)	122265	
£0.89	Ambrosia Custard 400g(V)	123135	
£0.85	Angel Delight Str/berry(V)	016987	
£0.85	Strawberry Jelly 135g	003004	
£0.78	Ground Black Pepper 25g	578286	
£0.59	RAJAH Chilli Powder 100g	092724	
£0.56	RAJAH Garlic Powder 100g	092727	
£0.69	RAJAH Paprika Powder 100g	092728	
£0.69	Tandoori Masala 100g	750016	
£0.79	All Purpose Seasoning 100g	092752	
£0.65	Cornmeal Fine 500g	092754	
£0.85	Tropical Sun Gari 500g	092755	
£0.79	Jerk Seasoning 100g	092792	
£0.79	Hot Curry Powder 100g	092758	
£0.95	Oxo Cubes Chicken 6's	601580	
£2.29	Xtra Virgin OliveOil 200ml	115704	
£1.59	Economy Vegetable Oil 1ltr	088049	
£1.95	Plain Flour 1.5kg	006893	
£0.69	Suree Coconut Milk 400ml	116183	
£0.99	Smash Original 88g(V)	677180	
£0.99	Mixed Cocktail Olives 70g	110647	
	SUPPLEMENTS		
£1.25	Nurishment Choco 400g(V)	124106	
£1.25	Nurishment Vanilla 400g(V)	124105	
£6.10	Creatine Mondrate 120g(V)	094723	
£7.27	Elite Protin Pwd Banana(V)	094724	
£7.27	Elite Protin Pwd S/berri(V)	094725	
£7.27	Elite Protin Pwdr Vanil(V)	106826	
£6.75	Weight Gain Pwdr Bana (V)	094727	
£6.75	Weight Gain Pwdr Sberry(V)	094728	
	STATIONERY		
£1.20	Drawing Pins Brass 100s	470170	

Price	Item	IC	Qty
£9.04	Clear Multi Punched Pocket	630010	
£0.70	Spreme 10 Wht DL Envelopes	105167	
£1.91	Refill Pad A4 160 leaf	090254	
£1.19	A4 Plain Pad 100 leaf	125392	
£1.83	Ringbinder A4	102464	
£1.20	Coloured Pencils 12k	125373	
£0.19	Eraser	093792	
£1.01	UHU Glue Stick	553640	
£0.61	Writing Pad 30 LF	088772	
£0.30	BIC Cristal Black Med Pen	041126	
	RELIGIOUS ITEMS		
£2.99	Prayer Perfume Frag 27	115977	
£2.99	Prayer Perfume Frag 10	115975	
£0.25	Rosaries Beads	093778	
£1.42	Prayer Beads-Tasbeeh/Subha	094567	
£7.69	Hardback Bible	093779	
£5.61	Hindu Bhagavad Geeta Book	096162	
£16.99	Pagan Book of Prayer	102967	
£7.14	RC Mass prayer book	100519	
£8.89	Quran CD	093644	
£5.57	Arabic Quran with English	094562	
£5.57	Crucifix Metal 2in Chain	096664	
£4.95	2in Cross Chain	099034	
£2.75	Pagan Pentacle Metal	096067	
£5.16	Prayer Mat	094554	
£24.16	White Muslin Gown 52-62	093777	
£1.11	Prayer Hat (Topi)	098793	
£0.56	Plain Tooth stick (Miswak)	098795	
£7.05	Sikh Hair Fix-Weldon&Simko	098785	
	GENERAL ITEMS		
£1.00	Non Bio Soap Powder	107394	
£1.00	Economy Fab Conditioner	115999	
£2.59	Ariel Handwash 960g	789990	
£3.78	Bio-D NonBio Wash Pdr(VE)	095775	
£1.99	Lenor Fab Conditioner	103067	
£1.05	Glade Solid Lily Of Valley	080859	
£1.03	Craft Hobby Brush	094781	
£2.45	Safety Matchstick Cutter	093599	
£2.45	Plain H/less Model Matches	093624	
£0.32	Med Fine Sandpaper Sheet	093623	
£4.53	Acrylic Gloss Varnish	093622	
£2.15	Wood Glue 110g	094506	
£1.15	Alarm Clock	114383	
£1.01	Over Ear Phones	109734	
£2.59	Plastic Can Opener	118668	
£2.54	Addis 3 piece seal tight	065556	
£0.15	MWave Storage Container	051668	
£1.99	Flip Flops Size 8-11	099046	
£13.99	Safety Duvet Cover	103048	
£2.99	Safety Pillow Case	101123	
£7.99	Safety Flat Sheet	100755	
£22.99	Safety Sgl Quilt 9 Tog	123996	
£9.99	Safety Single Pillow	124287	
	SPECIAL OFFERS		
£0.61	Valentine Card 2012	105153	
£0.42	Valentine Card Various	093846	
	Offer 1		
	Offer 2		
	Offer 3		
	Offer 4		
	Offer 5		
	Offer 6		
	Offer 7		
	Offer 8		
	Offer 9		

Total Number of Items Ordered		Total Cost	

All prices include VAT where applicable. All reasonable precautions are taken to ensure that prices, product details, offers and dietary information are correct at the time of printing, but may be subject to change (including statutory tax and duty changes) or material error and no guarantees can be given. Consumers are advised to check products and product labels on receipt to ensure they meet their requirements. When printed with personal details, this document is categorised as PROTECT.

smoker's-pack and yet more prisoner paper as the "production" that is this book has run out. The Unit has run out of "film…"

0815: Tannoy: "Mr Robinson, Mr Robinson." Are there two of us now? Please can I go to Hoxon to "pick up some photocopied writing paper and some more Unit apps." I *nearly* asked them to make an app but didn't dare. On my way up came across Rick the Fish. "Any news?" It's tomorrow or Monday. Got a thumbs-up and "good luck." Greeted Greg next. "Good luck mate – got a missus and a home to go to?" Told him I'll be OK and shook his hand. No aces fell out of his sleeve. Heston was next in shot. Filled him in and got a big smile. Next on the line was Stuart. "You going?" Transmitted the latest. Limping Al brought up the rear. "Is the dentist is in today?" I don't know. Why? "A friend of mine had treatment and is in agony." Who?

"Rod."

Hoxon. Rod sitting at one of the tables stuffing his face with toast. The dental emergency I had been told about didn't seem so dire. "Uncomfortable," was the voiced update on his condition – said with Marmite on his cheek. I've obviously been brainwashed by the prison medical system because I heard myself say to him to take a Paracetamol. He gave me a real Bricktop look for that one and then beckoned me to come closer for "private information."

"I am being moved to Bosnia."

What?! When? How? "Called to the office last night." Why? "Numbers." (Prison-talk for ethnic balancing). Shit Rod, that's bad news. I'm sorry. When? "Lunchtime." At least you've got Chris Moyles there. Another prisoner listening to our conversation interrupts him "When are you moving?" Rod replied Cooler-King like: "It was a secret, till I told Jonathan."

Sorry Rod.

Some appallingly poorly photocopied prisoner paper and "apps" were collected. About a centimetre's thickness of the former and about half that of the latter. In the office the "Handcuffs" officer lurked together with his ex-engineer colleague, who shook my hand. "Handcuffs" was as nice as pie to me – nauseatingly so – and told me that as soon as he'd got the OK I could come back and pick up some smoker's-packs.

To the Resettlement office. Both Zara (Top) and he with the beard were absent – as notified – but Anna, the other person vaguely involved in the skulduggery to get me a home was stationed at her desk. She smiled and said "see you at 1300 for more news (!) and what time are you seeing Victoria to ring Judi?" 1300. "OK." Popped by Victoria's to remind her. "I'm glad you came because I'd forgotten."

REMINDED her and returned to the Unit at 0900.

0935: Tannoy: "Mr Robinson, Mr Robinson." Is the echo that bad?

The office and a smoker's-pack scene: "If you're going Friday, you can have one pack. If you're going Monday, two packs. When are you going?"

I D O N ' T K N O W. I will know more at 1300.

1035: Orienteering to Healthcare, Lennox was traversing the car park with a member of the HDFOT club. Someone had been shipped-out from his Unit today and I was curious as to why. Lennox didn't really know or was reluctant to tell me. His walking partner – who glared at me as Lennox and I conversed – said to me "did you arrange it?" *Full* of supercilious stony eyed froideur he was. I must be on my guard. I begin to think I have got too blasé asking questions then writing things down. I suppose I have become complacent. An officer saw me scribbling on my knees the other day and rolled his eyes at me... I don't think that there is *anyone* here who *doesn't* now know what I have been up to.

Healthcare. Dave asks me to go to the gym to source some plastic bin bags. Off I go and am given a small handful. The bags deposited to Dave, return to Wilford at 1050. On entry to the office to pick up my key, WTWFO says "hold on" and passes me a letter. A hand written envelope with my name, prison number and Unit. She is as white as a sheet. "You are not going tomorrow (Friday) or Monday." I open the letter as she speaks.

"You are leaving on Wednesday."

Shit, shit, shit. That's a week behind schedule. You bloody fool for focusing so much on November 17th.

Think positive. At least it's something in writing. With a date. Everything else has been "maybe." Look forward.

Right. Get a grip. There's nothing you can do. You put yourself here. Onwards and upwards. End of. Get off your arse and do something. I've been told I can pick up smoker's-packs so get yourself up to Hoxon and press on. On arrival, the handcuffs officer (an inordinately irritating waiter working for a tip played by Robert Newton) is even more helpful than this morning and obliges me with two packets of tobacco.

Stuart met on the way back and told him Wednesday. I could see the disappointment for me in his face. At least I now have it in writing.

1135: In room looking at the calendar. Wednesday is the 23rd. Six more nights. You CAN do this.

1145: Tannoy: "Mr Robinson, Mr Robinson." What now, I think. Thursday? Friday? Never? WTWFO: "Can you do me a favour?" Sure – what? The "apps" I brought back earlier are "not enough" (!) so can I go to "Main Stores and pick some more up" – AND some DECENT prisoner writing paper. Get told to ask for "Rod" (!) Is that cast or crew? "Just ask for Rod!" Shoot upstairs to get my jacket. On the way down pass Bungalow Bill on his way upstairs.

Nearly ask him if he needs a guide...

The interior of Main Stores resembles any run-of-the-mill depot. Ask for "Rod," get "Rod" (how many of them *are* there here?) and am given thick wedges of both paper for prisoners and paper for prison officers; dreaded "apps."

Outside Wilford one of the prison Padres (Joyce Grenfell) was positioned. Not the one I spoke to on arrival at HMP Hollesley Bay but someone I have seen around. We grin at each other. "Everything OK?" she asks in that way that people of the cloth do in prison. I tell her I'm fine, that I should have gone today and that I've now learnt I'm going on Wednesday. She makes positive encouraging noises and I confess that on my first full day at Bedford, the resident God squad (I didn't say it like that) chief came to see me to offer support – but I felt it would have been highly hypocritical to ask for it. She is kind and says just me "thinking like that is good."

I tell her of my guilt and the havoc I've caused.

"It's nice to hear a prisoner talking so frankly," she says then adds that I'm "one of the few making the right noises at the end of their time." She wishes me luck for Wednesday. If Wednesday doesn't happen I'm going anyway. "Ooh don't do that. I don't want to see you on *Newsnight*."

1200: Lunch. Wilford is either filthy or once in a blue moon vaguely clean. Today, some bright spark has ordered the dining room floor to be polished. The best made plans though have failed as the polishing detail neglected to check the time and only started at 1145. The floor is unwalkable on. Plan B kicks-in and everyone is told to walk around the edges of the room. The first time anything remotely resembling an orderly queue has ever been seen within these dreary walls.

Due to all the tables being in the hallway we ate like we would pick at nibbles whilst standing up at a cocktail party. As I dined, NNO wandered over. What he had to say nearly made me drop my cocktail sausage. Andrew and Tony, both nearby, listened in.

"I've got someone on the phone wanting to know how you're getting home on Monday."

I have a letter upstairs saying my release is on Wednesday and I don't understand. He repeats that they want to know my method of transport on MONDAY. Like a tennis match, I lob back that my paperwork says Wednesday. Before this turns into Wimbledon, we agree the best thing is to talk to the "producer." We both go to the office. Whoever it was has rung off. WTWFO is in there so I ask her to explain to NNO what the paperwork says. She listens and then with typical female practicability, lifts the phone up and calls Judi the Tag lady. At this time another officer walks in. It's three versus one. I've plonked my plastic plate and cutlery on a small filing cabinet and perch on the side.

She gets through – and asks – what is going on. She reads back what she is being told. It's been moved forward.

It is now Monday.

I put my head in my hands.

I am leaving custody on Monday November 21st. 21.11.11. Even writing this feels good. Lord knows how I'll feel when I type it. I cannot imagine that anything you read in ink will make you have any idea how I feel.

Went upstairs in an utter daze. Got a ticking off from Tony. "Jon – when they say to you Monday – it means you're going on Monday." He's guiding me of course – trying to help. He adds he'll be a couple of weeks behind me having been picked up in a fast car. "Me brother in law's Bentley."

If you got overtaken by a smart motorcar, southbound on the A12, at speed, sometime towards the end of November – it was Tony.

Faffed in the library for a bit. Too drunk on the news to remember what I did. Knew I had 1300 meeting with Victoria and Anna.

1250: Victoria: "I hear you're going on Wednesday." Fill them in on lunchtime's events. They both look at me like I'm lying through my teeth or mad or both. I can hear them thinking "the paperwork says Wednesday." As we talk the royal computer flashes. An email. "Ooh, you're right – it's Monday." Thus I tell them that I don't need any middle-men to communicate with Judi.

Healthcare. Locate Robbie and relay the whole story. "This place beggars belief," he says with true Cracker reverence. There are "three letters to be delivered downstairs" for me. Descend the stairs and knock on the Treatment room door. Dave opens it. Philip is in there tending to someone. Also draping the scene – like a marquee – a most official looking lady (Cruella de Vil) dressed head to toe in black who surveys me with the *utmost* distaste. "Oh, Jonathan," says Dave with all his usual cheer, "just the man." Can I move my mind back to Sunday 23^{rd,} when I "found those boxes." Ah. That's why this lady is here. An investigation into the help yourself to needles and drugs (in *prison*) incident. I correct Dave, telling him I actually looked inside them on Monday 24th. I know, because I wrote it down. Dave then says, still brimming with Brummie bonhomie, "we've got to be careful with this one as he's writing a book." Dave's eyes turn to her. So do mine.

See the thinned lips.

I recount exactly what happened (now see the *very* thinned lips – they've disappeared). She thanks me. I ask her, if she doesn't mind, telling me who she is. "I'm from the new Healthcare service provider."

Rounds. During which I spotted Philip, called his name and jogged over. I hope I haven't dropped anyone in it. "No, not at all, it's got to be looked into." Who is she? "Top brass. Ex-medical and now a legal lawyer."

Bosnia. Come across a newly re-homed Rod – not looking happy. How is it? About six times he tells me "it's fine." By his repeating of the state of the nation it's obviously not so instruct him to hang on in there. We agree to meet for a coffee at Wilford after I have completed the mail-drop. He eagerly accepts. When a coffee on Wilford sounds good – things must be bleak.

At Stow a female officer (Michelle Ehlen) complains that she has to "do a ship-out to Chelmsford prison in a Sweatbox." She is not too thrilled by this concept but perks up when she says "at home there's lots of alcohol to help."

1445 – 1530: In my room with Rod – now in the know about Monday – coffee and numerous roll-ups. We talk about me. I've learnt being myself in prison is quite simple: Just be myself. The old JR would have said when we meet up, "I'll buy you dinner." The new JR will say come and have *baked beans*. I have learnt that naked honesty is not that difficult. He gives me that very encouraging "Rod" look.

Towards the end of our heart to heart – and I know we are going to miss each other – a knock on the door. A young man asking me about my job. Once the "no drugs" tracer issue has been sorted out, I learn he is Noah (a very young Phil Lynott) – and tell him I'll walk him down to Healthcare and introduce him to Philip. Soon I shake Rod's hand and walk up to work with Noah. Philip and he talk business. We agree the best plan is that Noah shadows me tomorrow to see how everyone gets on.

Elk appears. I thank him for all his help and support and shake his hand. He's off on Home-leave tomorrow and I won't see him again. "Have a nice life" his closing farewell. Noah and I leave the building.

The wind-down has begun.

1645: Sweeper Ray comes for a social. *Unbelievably* – to me – he wants to move to my room when I leave.

1650: Alone in number 30. A sudden attack of the disgrace that will meet me on the outside world.

1700: Dinner. Not for me. I'll eat later. Ask NNO what time he finishes tonight. "2100 and not back till Tuesday," so make myself a mental note to find him later to thank him.

2015: Went downstairs to locate NNO. Night "phone officer" in. NNO gone. Damn it. Plan B then. I'll write to him, and others, over the weekend.

2220: Finish this. I'm not supposed to be here now. But I am. Another day done. Keep going Robinson. Keep going. God I'm tired.

Friday, November 18th, 2011.

T plus one. Never thought I'd be writing that. Bloody idiot.

0615: Night-officer-always-on-the-phone on the phone. Did a plus one on the countdown calendar, another dot on the wall and circled the 17th on the Bedford bookmark calendar. Dates between July 25th and November 16th are crosses. From now until re-entry they will be circles.

These life shattering events are important in prison.

I'm trying hard to keep in check within my railway-sidings thoughts all the issues that will need to be sorted/shunted when/if I get out. Whenever I think of one – about ten more roll along. Like railway carriages.

It's a glorious morning. The sort of day in my past life that I would be up early to meet with an enthusiastic excited helicopter student in order to teach them to fly. This morning I am meeting with Noah, an enthusiastic excited prisoner, in order to teach him how to empty bins and mop floors.

Noah appeared bang on time at 0730. A good sign. As we walked up I briefed him, starting off with a warning about Kathy – who I knew was not in today. On arrival introductions were done and Dave came out with a delicious Dave-comment; "Well Noah is much better looking than you Jonathan and have you warned him about Kathy?"

Cue the *Omen* music. Sorry Kathy – but it was very funny. We did the bins, floors and opened all the windows to try and get rid of the heat. Philip voiced that he still needed to talk to Frank in Tribal to rubber stamp the transition of power from me to Noah. I took this as the medical staff's acceptance that he is the right man for the job. I think he'll be fine.

We agreed to meet for the second shift at 0930.

0820: Frank's office. I rattle off my list: a heads-up for him about Noah and Healthcare – he "already knows." (Bloody hell!) Second point: I have nothing in writing about Monday. The housing confirmation says "see map" but there is no map. Frank: "See your Unit staff." (*Thanks* Frank). Third point: I've heard via WTWFO from Judi that I have to go to Probation on Monday afternoon. Where? When? Who? Can I have a map? Frank: "See Unit staff." (Thanks *again* Frank). Fourth point: WTWFO asked me to get in touch with someone or other to arrange travel – can he do that? Guess what: "See Unit staff."

Thank *you* Frank.

Unit. The female Chelmsford Sweatbox officer ("FCSBO") from yesterday is on. The list Frank dodged is sprouted-off to her. FCSBO: "I'll call Judi and get back to you."

0930: Noah and I walk two by two to Healthcare. Philip has spoken to Frank and "all is sorted." Noah is the new Healthcare Orderly. I am unemployed.

0950: Unit. FCSBO tells me "all done." Still no map of where either "home" or Probation are located.

1015: Back in the room following more dialogue with FCSBO on what the form is for Monday. I will be "called at about 0930 to go to Reception." Do I get changed there? "What do you mean?" I don't have any kit. My only clothes are in Reception. I filled in an app asking for their return but got a no…

A roll of her eyes followed that and a phone call was made. I can pick up my stuff this afternoon. I am NOT to wear my suit over the weekend. Furthermore, I must make an appointment with Healthcare to get a fit-for-discharge medical certificate.

1020: Healthcare. Philip will do the paperwork with me "on Sunday and will offer me condoms but they only have extra-large in stock, so probably not much use to me."

Thank you, Philip.

1130: Still nothing in writing about Monday. The only written documentation in my possession is for departure on Wednesday. I have only been *told* that I am leaving Monday.

1145: Rod in the car park and complaining (still) of toothache so up to Healthcare we marched. I left him in Philip's capable hands.

1155: A regular Wilford officer back on the wing and told that my release paperwork is all dated Wednesday but apparently I'm wrapping on Monday. Can I please have something in writing? His response: "It's all taken care of – they're professionals."

1200: Lunch. Pilchards and salad.

1240: Library. Stuart in. Mac race. I won then moaned at him that I still have nothing in writing. He, trying to be helpful said "the library will be getting the discharge list for next week later this afternoon if that's any help."

Healthcare: Whinging to Robbie and Philip about how I still have no idea about what is going on. Knowing smiles from them – they've seen it all before. Philip gives me a letter for Wilford. I playfully tell him I don't work here anymore which results in Robbie shouting "he hit me!" and Philip yelling "high-security prison for you!"

The lighter note continues when a delivery of drugs arrives in more TV sized boxes. Philip and Dave open them. Then start swearing. Something's gone wrong and twice the amount ordered has arrived. It's the hard drugs substitutes that are given to prisoners with serious issues. They show me the invoice. £1500.

Rod told me later the street value is £10,000.

Philip to Dave: "Let's get this in the safe quick."

My line: Why don't we leave it in the corridor like last time?

Unit. FCSBO is asked if there is any news on anything. She looks at me blankly and reaches for the phone. A few words are said and the receiver is put down. The officer types on her keyboard and then turns the screen so I can see it.

Release date 21st. I've seen it in writing. I don't have it in writing but now I have seen it. Progress.

"Go over to the main gate" and I can "pick up details for Probation." She tells me to "give it five." I go upstairs and ponder what Monday – and beyond – will bring me. Most doors on the corridor are open. All watching *Jeremy Kyle*.

Main gate. There is initial mad confusion as to why I'm here. A member of staff thinks I'm Stuart – sorry Stuart – but soon someone appears with paperwork for my meeting with Probation on Monday. When should I get there by?

"As soon as you can."

Unit. Drop off the map and walk up to Healthcare to report the latest. Rod there. And Robbie. Rod's toothache worse and Philip is trying to source a number for assistance. I tell all it's looking good for "go" on Monday. Philip finds the 24 hour emergency number and rings. They are closed.

1700: Dinner. No thank you.

1730: Gangster music playing at full blast.

1650: Tannoy: "Robinson, Robinson." Down I go. "Go to Reception." 10 minutes later I walk my suit, shirt, belt and tie into my room. The shirt is very carefully taken out of the cover.

I want my suit to stay in it as it hangs in a prison wardrobe.

Downstairs, found a washing machine vacant and put my shirt in the wash.

1820: Pool with Eric, Ernie and Sweeper Ray. Lost. Big time.

My shirt now clean and only slightly damp decided that now was the time to iron it. Located Wilford's ironing board and iron and got busy on the landing at the top of the stairs. Gordon was on the telephone about ten paces away. When he rang-off he came over as I un-creased my cuffs. "Jon, do you need any help with that, do you know what you're doing?" I put the iron down and smiled. Gordon I know I look like a moron but I do know how to handle an iron. It's awfully kind of you but I'm OK. "Oh that's OK then. I was worried you didn't know how to use one. You know, I thought you probably had someone do that sort of stuff for you..."

Christ, do I come over that regal?

Saturday, November 19th, 2011.

T plus 2. Up at 0650. Night-officer-always-on-the-phone on the phone.

0750: A deserted ghost-town car park negotiated. A huge rising sun on the nose reflects off Bosnia like it is the surface of a body of water. Dew drapes on the grass that is the exercise field. Mole hills are everywhere – or very poor earth disposal from Bosnia's tunnel men. Enter the brighter than normal red brick building that is Healthcare. Philip parades dealing with a customer. The waiting area still intact, without too much sign of devastation. Mutual mumblings of "how are you?" the lines in everyone's scripts. Communicate to Philip that it's a strange feeling – almost like the last days of a holiday. I ask him if it's normal for me to feel a bit sad about leaving. "It's only human," he explains.

That's what I want to be – a normal human who can be himself.

Rod rolls-up. He Looks brighter but still with the malady of molars. Philip idly chats with him as I do the bins. We all go upstairs so Philip can open up for me. "Very clean and tidy up here," says Rod rather Ritchie like. I ask if I can use him as a reference.

Upstairs sorted, I return to the Treatment room. Philip is now on the phone to the emergency dentist. I leave them to it and walk past the overly bright painted doors of the "music school" on my voyage back to the just still afloat Wilford. As I pace, the typical public institution look of the Bay enrols my attention. The disused clock tower and the monstrosity of an industrial chimney plonked next to what was designed to be an attractive set of buildings fill my vision. Around me, autumn orange is everywhere. On the horizon, Sweeper Ray brushes busily with a broom.

On key pick up at 0820 over the noise of washing machines on the cycle that is spin I ask the officer behind the desk if before I go, I can give the office some internal mail – I would like to leave some letters. "Yes," the reply, accompanied by raised eyebrows.

0945: To the library. Outside, Rod is by the main gate waiting for transport for a trip to the dentist. At the library, Stuart, IAHHM and Library Brett referee events. IAHHM – Frankie – has a line in his script that *completely floors* me: "Jonathan, you are going to be my guest tonight for a farewell dinner." Goodness Frankie, I don't know what to say. Thank you very much. What can I bring? I don't have anything. "Just bring yourself."

Prison has taught me *so* much...

Library Brett is holding the discharge sheet and after teasing me for a bit with whether or not he's going to let me feast my eyes he hands it over. With a wry smile.

I'm on it. For Monday. The first time I've seen it on a bit of paper...

Heston and Gordon turn up. I relay to Heston that if I don't see him again I will be in touch. "You'll see me tomorrow," his reply. The Deputy Governor walks in. All tunnelling activity ceases. He has a bit of a sniff around, makes some comments about how literate we all are and sidles off.

Wilford. Two letters greet my arrival. One about funding post release and the other...

Written confirmation that I am leaving on Monday.

1130: I've vaguely started to pack. Will be returning the duvet to Rod – via Eric n' Ernie. Library Brett wants my towels and Stuart has requested all of my T shirts.

I also need to write letters to Rod, Victoria and Barbara, Frank, NNO, Sweeper Ray, Eric n' Ernie,

Stuart, Philip, WTWFO, Darling, Zara (Top) and Robbie. I'm going to add the officer known to one and all as the Terminator to the list too. Everyone who has been an ally is getting a note of thanks. I plan to do this during the afternoon. I must also write to Buzz. I have written to my wife. Or rather, I am writing to my wife.

It's this book.

1200: Over lunch Andrew grills me about flying — I transfer as much information as possible, surprising myself with the knowledge retained in my brain box after so little utilization of things aviation.

In the washing up queue a slight skirmish occurs with a member of team HDFOT who attempts to get in front of me. Gordon looks on somewhat bemused I think, that I let rip — verbally. A bust-up right at the end BUT manners cost nothing.

Healthcare. Philip is busy re packing the job-lot of drugs delivered in error yesterday and "will get a full refund." (He won't — the system will).

1300: Start writing letters.

1535: Still penning like mad. IAHHM grandly announces that dinner will be served at 1915.

Am I going to miss prison?

1615: Still doing ****ing letters.

I have not written to "bench." But I will go and say goodbye before I leave.

1700: Dinner and Roll-check called on the Tannoy. Only the former is done as I'm dining out. One letter to go: Buzz — the receiver of all things book. I should probably thank his postman.

1800: A knock on the door: Andrew inviting me for pool. We get to the tables but the games room door is locked so downstairs I go to ask an officer to open up. I was going to do a Fletcher and walk in and say "balls" hoping to get a response like "what!?" and then reply "balls, sir, key required for the playing with sir" but I didn't as WTWFO is in there and she's decent.

And isn't always reading newspapers...

I do reveal to her what I was *going* to say. Weirdly, she doesn't understand — she's "never seen *Porridge*." I am *aghast* — and relay so. She "doesn't watch telly." With five years done in the prison service — I am gobsmacked that she has not even heard of Fletcher. Friends of hers "recite lines" but she "laughs to be polite." She is told to tune-in next time an episode is on as I make key signals with my hands.

WTWFO: "Oh, balls."

On the first floor, she opens up for business and like a genie the Deputy Governor walks up. His greeting makes me tingle.

"Anyone for a game?"

You're ON I tell him. Off comes his jacket whilst Andrew asks if he plays for chocolate bars – "no," replies the Governor, "but I used to play for money." How about playing for time? I quip. Concentration envelopes me like swaddling for the next twenty minutes. This is one game of pool that has to be won…

I am pleased to report that whilst in prison, I stuff the Governor. OK, it was his Deputy and it's at the pool table. But I thrash him.

I have now beaten bad ****er ****ers in Bedford and senior staff at Hollesley Bay. Fletcher WOULD be proud of me.

He bids us a phlegmatic goodnight and leaves with his tail between his legs (he did swear a lot whilst he was talking to us – and swore even *more* as I polished him off). As I watch Eric n' Ernie play IAHHM glides Hudson like onto set and announces that dinner is served. I promptly rush to my room to get my plate, bowl and knife and fork – feeling very guilty for bringing nothing to the table – and tell him so. He repeats his earlier statement that all I need to bring is *me*.

If only I had learnt this lesson before – I wouldn't be here.

IAHHM has done a fish curry. With "normal" (non-prison) rice. The fish is *magnificent*. His ingredients – more than you probably have in your kitchen – are dotted around one of the counters. His mate Sam (Kelly) joins us. We wash this wonderful meal down with a very nice little number.

Robinson's Orange Squash.

They both know about the book – and it is remarked that this meal should really be tomorrow – the last supper. I tell them it is a *real treat* and was without doubt the best meal I've had in the last seventeen weeks. They are both lifers. The combined time they have both spent behind the door takes my breath away:

"More than fifty years."

I'm offered second helpings. I take them. *Unbelievably*, IAHHM has also made a Raita – a favourite delicacy of mine in any Indian restaurant. Where did he get the yoghurt from?

"I made it."

Words cannot describe the tastes, the experience of the company and the extreme measures these two have gone to. Their piece de la resistance does not come until the end of the meal though. "Jonathan, would you like some cheese and crackers?"

I'm surprised a bottle of port is not produced.

Towards the end of the feast a young man – who I've been on nodding terms with – gets chatting to Frankie about the recipe for his Raita. Much Chef conversation takes place. He talks to me a little – he knows that I'm "the pilot." He is curious why helicopters cannot fly at aeroplane speeds so I run through dissymmetry of lift and retreating blade stall (one half of the rotor disc in Hoxon heaven, the other in wonky Wilford for non-pilot readers). He picks all this up very quickly (quicker than a lot of students, in fact).

He asks me my name – which I tell him. "Hello Jonathan. I'm Rod." Of course you are. Isn't everyone here?

Sunday, November 20th, 2011.

T plus 3. The last full day. After I'd dropped off last night, I think at about 2230, I was woken up. By machine gun fire.

Things hadn't got quite that bad – someone playing a computer game in his room. By himself with the volume on full-whack and his door wide open. Up I got, sweat trousers on and marched to the source of the noise to order a cease fire. I was not disturbed again.

Until just before 0600 by an owl. Rose for coffee.

Night-officer-always-on-the-phone NOT on the phone!

Sheer panic about all the things I need to attempt to fix on release. Caution myself. One step at a time. Basic panic list is: Will I ever have a life again? Can I get back to work? Will people know I am sorry? How do I tell them? How can I show them?

0725: Work. Give Philip his and Robbie's letters. Philip: "You didn't have to do that." We talk of people's reactions to me back on mother earth. There will, Philip cautions me, be three types of reaction. "Oh my God – I don't want to know," then "oh my God – suck it and see" and lastly "oh my God." For sure – everything will be down to me. We do my medical discharge certificate formalities: "Are you fit?" Yes. "You can go."

Decline the condom offer – I've got bigger fish to fry. A dish called culpability.

No work is required so I announce that I'll pop back later to say farewell. Return to the Unit and coffee. IAHHM is up and about and I thank him for dinner.

It's time to go to Hoxon to say some goodbyes. On stepping-off woozy Wilford Heston and Big Len are going to the gym. A wave. A speeding van breaks to a halt. Neil. A quick handshake. On the walk up – and this is for the last time – I think of all the other times I've done this. I arrived here in the summer. I'd been in Bedford for weeks before that as well. I've been in prison. I'm still in prison. It's all so weird.

Don't forget WHY though Robinson.

The village church bells are audible. Fallen leaves are everywhere. It's cold and damp. The dew on the grass is like moisture on a cold glass in a beer commercial. Two friendly faces walk by in the opposite direction. No names but still: "Hello Jonathan."

Shit. Am I going to miss this place?

I lapse by the green Cathedral. The sun is behind it. Trees separate the distance between me and the sinister structure. The sun shines through the gaps of branches like a film projector in a smoky cinema. I pick a mark in the light and stand there. In the scented air's silence. The bells have stopped. It's a Spielberg scene. A lone pigeon and I are the only signs of life around the building that never gives *any* hint of habitation. Yet it has 30 or so young people in it.

I arrive at Hoxon, clearing myself on board and go to find people I know. Lots of new faces make up the scene. The mail board is checked to see if number 48 is occupied. It is. A foreign name. Lucky bastard.

Neil arrives – "been up since all hours." Neither of us has eaten so we decide to take breakfast. I never thought I'd eat on Hoxon again. Even the toast tastes better. We go to his room for a smoke. He's upstairs now. Pretty much right on top of my old room – a few doors down but with the same spectacular view. We touch on the mountain of things I've got to deal with. He tells me at least I'm "square with the house" – I've no one "to answer to after the punishment." I have "stood in the corner long enough."

My logic is dissecting what he's said. My emotions contradict his theory...

I log out with the officer – "don't come back," he says as he shakes my hand. Outside the front door is always-first-in-the-queue Oliver with some other (unknown) prisoners. He wishes me well. I leave Hoxon. As it goes out of sight – unisons of Hoxon residents all seem to collate. I am aware of pretty much the entire ship's company disembarking to the steps. I glance over my shoulder not daring to turn fully for fear of a lachrymose tidal-wave of water works as a shout is made – by *all* of them.

"DOORS TO MANUAL."

We don't do any of that nonsense in helicopters – but their shouts don't half moisten my vision.

Healthcare: Rod on set and looking much better. The dentist "did the trick." And he's had a shave. Chris Moyles arrives – we loiter outside in the sunshine. It's like the old times. Nostalgia nibbles nicely.

Rod and I decide one last coffee together. He returns to Bosnia to get his ID card – mandatory to carry at all times, he never does though – and I tell him I'll see him at the youth club in 10. At 1015 we are in my room.

He is very quiet today. I don't know what's up (me going?) – but I don't think it's serious. We make a deal to meet in the morning at 0830 for a final farewell. Coffee consumed, we opt to go to the library. I jump into a Sunday paper. Nothing of any great interest. I read a piece about a prisoner who has been released on Tag (it's not me thank God) and the paper wants blood.

Judges know that depending on the sentence – when a prisoner will become eligible for Tag. I feel like I've short-changed my punishment and dodged a bullet.

1200: Lunch. Make myself eat as it has a good bit of meat in it.

1220: On my departure from Wilford for Healthcare WTWFO is given the internal mail I have written. She promises that she will make sure it gets to all the right people. At work, Philip gives me two letters for Rounds. I wonder if I'm going back to Hoxon again but no – Bosnia and Wilford, the Wilford one for Snorer. Philip and I shake hands. His final line: "I hope it all works out well."

I thank him. For everything.

1240: Unit. Give Eric n' Ernie their letter, together with other prisoner letters for them to distribute. It is agreed that I will give them a knock in the morning and deposit my duvet, sheet and pillow case with them to return to Rod.

1300: Tannoy: "Anyone wishing to move to Bosmere or Stow please let the office know."

1445: Tannoy: "If anyone wants to move into room number 30, please let the office know."

Can I move OUT first?

Ask IAHHM which room he is in so I can later give him my jacket. He tells me Stuart will see me in the library first thing in the morning.

1530: Sweeper Ray pops by. He has got my room which is what he wanted. Why – I have no idea. It's nice if you like car parks.

So the end is nigh. And for you too, Dear Reader. Thanks for sticking with me so far. Sorry if it's a load of drivel.

My thoughts?

First of all. I was an arse. I'm sorry. If it makes you any happier, the punishment exerted has been emotional hell and Lord did I get my comeuppance. It has frazzled me psychologically with relentless determination. Prison is deep dark horrid. It's loan, scary and walled by razor wire. The main punishment despite all this though has been in my head: how I hurt and let people down.

Prison can have walls and nets like Bedford, or fields and sea views like here. But it's still prison. And the mind plays havoc. Believe you me, that during bang-up, makings apps, the food, losing my home – and the despair of being unable to do anything about it – seeing all the drugs, all I ever had in the back of my mind was the guilt and sorrow, and all the potency of the baggage that comes with it.

Prison has taught me a good lesson. I think and hope I've been a good student. I've attempted to give my all in the heart-searching department. I've tried to stand my ground facing the *entirely* self-induced adversity – hand on heart. I think I've kept my sense of humour – look at the haircut Dennis gave me. The fact of the matter is that I committed my crime to be loved. I bought it with other peoples' money. I was a fervent tit.

I remember the fear within me on arrival. In complete contrast to what I imagined was coming my way look at the friends I have made.

The slamming of doors. More tonight. The Window Warriors of Bedford have to be heard to be *believed*.

The chilling internal questioning of why are they moving me to a prison so close to Aldeburgh?

The staff. Some good. The idiosyncrasies of most; terrible. That day when I was *desperate* for an officer's attention and I put a note under my door. I will never *ever* forget Rosa Klebb's face as she kicked that bit of paper back into my cell.

Male prison officers all seem to look like Parker from *Thunderbirds*. The times I've *winced* at their unparalleled degage whilst on duty…

I won't even *start* on the Head of Education at my current abode…

The cohabitation comedy of living with Albert Steptoe and his curious conclusion that I was some form of fifth columnist.

This book. That scene in *The Great Escape* when Richard Attenborough tells Gordon Jackson *that* line. "All the organisation – the tunnelling – kept me *alive*." That is what well-nigh this book has done. If it's rubbish – sorry. You try going to prison. You try writing a book. You try writing a book in prison.

PLEASE DO NOT.

I have made good friends. I hope. I have been accepted by who I am and how I am. Not what I am. Perhaps the greatest lesson prison has taught me. There is genuine comradeship here. Some of them may be a trifle uncouth – some apathetic – but there is some decency here.

I hope for three things. That my wife reads this, that I can make amends for my crime and that someone with some clout in the hazardous shambolic running of our prisons – actually reads this.

I know that when I cross the boundary tomorrow – I've done it. It's the end. Or is it the beginning?

1700: Roll-check and dinner. Not surprisingly, I don't eat. WTWFO thanks me for my letter. All my prison gear, apart from what I'm wearing – is in a huge washing bin downstairs. Tomorrow I'll dress in my own clothes.

I'm going to IAHHM's room to give him my jacket.

2000: Back in room. IAHHM said a lovely thing. "Thank you" and "it's been worn by a good man."

Monday, November 21st, 2011.

0500: What did you expect – a lie in? 17 rows of 7 dots complete. I'm in bed – the subject matters on my mind indescribable – listening to the owl outside. I think he's saying "goodbye – and behave yourself." 'Bye owl. And I will.

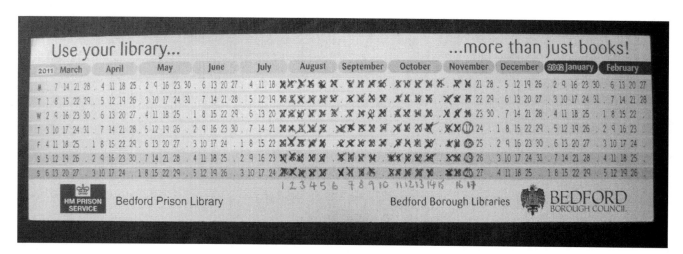

Downstairs for a first coffee. Night-officer-always-on-the-phone, not on the phone! In fact, he stands outside the office and he even has a line of dialogue: "Leaving us today – not happy with our company?" – I presume he's asked the person on the other end to hang on.

0634: Sweeper Ray at my door. Can he move a few of his things in? Before I know it, *eight* huge HMP bags are on my bed – leaving me a doormat sized perch to sit on. I've got squatters.

0655: Dress in *my* shirt and don *my* suit. On go my shoes too. The pair I wore all through Bedford. The shoes I got married in. Find in my trouser pocket the piece of paper I took to Court with Buzz's phone number on it.

More stuff arrives in Ray's hands. Boxes, (more) bags, a radio, a duvet, clothes and enough pornography to erect a tent. The car park starts to hum. I need to return my library books – one of which is the *Writer's and Artist's Yearbook*, which I will owe the publication of this to. And Jeffrey Archer. More Sweeper Ray belongings arrive. I now can't move in my room.

0720: Take books to IAHHM's room. His corridor is semi darkness. In the reduced visibility one prisoner says "morning Gov."

That's why Bedford wouldn't let me wear my suit.

Return room – put duvet, sheet and pillow case into an HMP bag and go to Eric n' Ernie's. Knock on their door which opens in a flash and two big grins fill the screen. I wonder if I've interrupted salsa practice...

I go and stand in the pool room and stare out of the window. The view like that from the bridge of a warship. One of the twins, I think the poet, joins me. His comment from our crow's nest: "I'd give my right arm to be leaving." Moyles mobilises into view. I tap on the window to get his attention. A final wave and thumbs-up his reciprocation.

Mystery twin and I talk about Hollesley Bay. Frank's satirising quote of the place never being a Cat D establishment until Cat D prisoners are housed here is revealed. He strongly agrees and despite being about the youngest person here, despairs at the gross immaturity of our colleagues. His parting words to me: "Don't come back."

I'm downstairs now by Wilford's front door. Eric n' Ernie arrive – on their way to work. I thank them for all the support, apologise for my pool playing standards and tell them to look after each other. They shake my hand.

0820: Standing upstairs again in the pool room. Catch sight of Victoria arriving in the car park and rush down to say goodbye. The first time I've been OUTSIDE in my suit. Victoria does a double take because of my appearance. A big smile and "good luck."

I'm going to need it.

Stuart's on his commute to work. I walk towards him. He's looking me over. I must look very different in human clothes. Enter the library with him. IAHHM in there already. We say our goodbyes and all shake hands.

Everyone is saying how smart I look. Another reminder that emotionally naked JR is just fine.

0830: Office. Can I go to both Healthcare and Bosnia (dressed) as I am? "You're leaving – you can do what you like." Tread to Healthcare. The walk I've done so many times but this time feeling like a normal person. On arrival, Kathy does a *monumental* double take at my appearance and exclaims "good GOD." Dave is on site too and reacts like I've walked in wearing a dinner jacket. Noah makes up the ranks – mop and bucket by his side. I playfully question Kathy if she is being nice to him. A knowing look, her return to my serve... I reveal to her that I've done my best to train him up, appealing to her to carry over her recent jolly manner to the new administration. Kathy and Dave's hands are shaken and they are thanked. On my way out tell Sylvia that I'm sorry if I've blemished her record by the Orderly walking out on her second day. A big grin. Give Noah a wink – and step off HMS Healthcare for the last time.

Bosnia bound for Rod, I am convinced that he has overslept – or forgotten that we said we would meet. On my way to the wobbly caravan site, three prisoners say "morning Gov" to me. No wonder the easiest way to walk out of Colditz was to dress-up as staff…

At Bosnia – double takes from everyone – Rod "is out." I was wrong – sorry Rod. He is probably outside Wilford cursing my timing and wondering where the hell I am. I scuttle off. Spot IAHHM delivering papers wearing my "Escapee" jacket. I catch up with him and as we walk together I see Rod, right at the other end of the car park – outside Wilford.

He walks towards me. His face tells me how strange I must look. A massive grin portrayed once I've been inspected. "You look different," his favourable conclusion. It's still me, I reassure him.

This is heavy going. At Bedford I had cell-mates. Here I've had a soul-mate.

Rod, I have changed in prison – I hope, for the better. "So have I," he counters. I describe to him the help that he has given me and get rewarded with "you've helped me." Still checking me out he observes that I look "like a Governor" and dares me "to challenge a prisoner for their ID." He makes me laugh by saying someone will be watching us from afar and spread the word that Rod "was grassing to a Governor."

I start to feel guilty about leaving all the friends I have made in the lurch. However – I need to get out and try to start fixing the things that put me here in the first place.

Mathew walks up. "What a coincidence," says Rod with his more than observant observation on life. Yes, I agree, I tell him. I thought that too yesterday when he and I talked to Moyles. Mathew's line hits all nails – mine anyway – right firmly *and* squarely on their heads: "Get back flying and stop stealing."

Another apt title for this collection of gibbering gobbledygook.

Mathew is far too "Northern" to remark on my attire. I ask him how he is. "OK, but a meeting with the victim's family is on the cards." How do you feel about that? In typical Mathew style he is non-committal and the barricades are *not* coming down. I shake his hand. Then Rod's – who gives me a big hug. Holding back the water works I tell them to look after each other. Mathew answers as only Mathew can.

"I'm not fookin' looking after him."

Which in Mathew-speak, means he is. I give Rod my "I will be in touch" look. His eyes are *willing* me success. Before I turn on my heel he *unbelievably* generously allows *me* the final quote from his Ritchie repertoire… As I say the line I see in his face the recognition that he knows it's a bow to him…

It's been emotional.

At the doorway of number 30, Sweeper Ray is mopping what is now, his room. I rib him it was a ruse — that I'm not really leaving — it was just a way to get my room mopped.

See the nasty look.

Harry Enfield walks by. Think he's just got up. I shake his hand goodbye. I have warned Ray about the noise. He WANTED to move to my room... The times I have wished for a Lee Enfield...

0910: Sitting downstairs in the dining room. By myself. I am waiting to be called... The final scene needs to be shot.

0920: Tannoy: "Mr Robinson to the office please." Into the office I go. "Reception are ready for you." I ask the officer to Tannoy Sweeper Ray so I can say goodbye. This done and Ray descends the stairs. I shake his hand, telling him I will write.

I leave Wilford...

It's now damp and breezy outside. The 30 yards or so to Reception is paced feeling... interesting.

0925: Reception. I stand at the desk where I was processed on arrival. Officer Blakey handling me. "ID card and fit for discharge cert," his request. Hand over the card — still attached to the bit of string. He reaches for scissors — with a snip, the noose is no more. I find the medical sheet and hand that over.

Another prisoner stands next to me. He's being processed by another officer for Home-leave. I am the only person "checking out" today.

I am given back my property. My wallet and bank card. I'm given £40 plus unspent earnings which in total comes to £90. More than I arrived with. It's strange to handle money. I am asked if I'd like any clothes. As the smart arse in me is about to say three silk ties and a nice overcoat, I spot the look in Blakey's eye. I shake my head and say no thank you.

A file is produced. A4. Not very thick. He opens it and produces five (!) copies of my licence. Printed on the awful prison paper that is one step away from British Rail loo paper circa 1975. As I am signing everywhere he instructs me to, he flicks through the file — my eyes are on what it contains — not what I'm signing. An official looking document appears. Very official — what is at its top stops me from doing anything, let alone signing my name...

"*Order for Imprisonment*" is its header. I feel like a Dickens character. I ask if I can see it. He lets me look. I handle it. Suddenly this all seems very real. My actions made society put me in *prison*.

I have to change my *behaviour*.

Many autographs now completed, Blakey mutters that he doesn't want to release the wrong prisoner and asks me some questions. My previous address. My date of birth, and how long my stay has been. I ask if the wrong prisoner has ever been released. "Not from *here*."

The through fare – if such a thing exists in prison – is getting busy. It appears quite a few of my soon to be ex-colleagues are going out on Home-leave. They are all very excited.

I'm numb.

I hear one of them being briefed "no drugs, alcohol or gambling."

I'm told to have a seat and wait. No problem. I've been waiting 17 weeks...

I keep having to tame the floods of internal items that explode in my mind that have to be sorted when I'm out. I repeat to myself WHEN. I can't do anything now. One step at a time. And remember to hit the nursery-slopes first. Don't go mad. Easy tiger.

Heston appears from nowhere. Like a surprise guest on *This Is Your Life*. He simply walks in, wishes me luck and shakes my hand. Then disappears.

The numbness now leading to nullity. Soon I won't be a number.

The officers finish with everyone. I take the chance to ask them if anyone ever becomes emotional on release. Blank stares back, then a "no."

Someone of the demob happy division asks if we can smoke whilst we're waiting. We're all walked to the other end of the building and the gate is opened. This is where I had my first smoke on arrival at Hollesley Bay. Other prisoners stand at the top of the steps. I excuse myself from the hubbub and walk down the stairs so I can stand where I stood last time. Someone gives me a roll-up. I inhale the view and atmosphere. When I was here before it was the start. Now it's the end.

Transport is declared here. We all traipse out of the main entrance. A white mini bus. Home-leavers all have loads of baggage.

1000: About 10 of us board. My feet leave HMP Hollesley Bay. The driver is a prisoner.

1001: The engine starts. A commercial radio station is on. Adverts playing. I'm scribbling notes whilst at the same time looking out of the window. We set off. Still commercials play on the radio. We navigate through the car park leaving Healthcare behind us to the left. Wilford is on our right. We stop at the gate. The prisoner driver jumps out – I suppose to report the numbers to staff. Still adverts.

Unbelievably a prisoner sitting behind me asks me if he can borrow my pen. Passing my Bic to him is like handing over my oxygen supply. I look out of the window.

1002: Our driver re-appears coming down the steps. The Deputy Governor follows him. Still adverts on the radio. The other prisoner is still using my pen. Is the Deputy Governor coming to check the numbers? Is he coming to tell me they've changed their mind? No. He walks by.

1003: The engine starts. We move off. We pass the library. My pen is handed back to me. Still adverts. The urgency of the other prisoner's pen requirement becomes apparent when he passes a felon in front of me what he has written. Bank details. One owes the other money. No doubt for "interesting smokes." The adverts have stopped and a song is starting.

Dee dee dee dee dee dee dee dee dee dee dee dee dee

I spot the prison boundary. We're picking up steam.

Doo doo doo doo doo doo doo doo doo

Noisy engine but can still hear the radio.

Dee dee dee dee dee dee dee dee dee dee dee dee dee

We cross the boundary as the words start:

"And here's to you Mrs Robinson."

Epilogue.

I think it's only correct that I open this closing with an apology to one and all. Hand on heart I know I have behaved *appallingly*. I got what I had coming to me – boy did I – and I am truly sorry. I acknowledge the justifiable censure against me and somehow hope the words within these covers successfully display that I wish to readdress the balance.

At the end of Niven's book he talked of wrapping it up by bringing it up to date. He seemed rather adept at this writing lark so I shall try to do the same. Originally it was all going to end with the crossing of the border but too many things have happened of interest since I got out.

On the day of my release and after addressing Aldeburgh issues I later attended the body that is Probation. Where trainer clad feet left footprints on the lino floor and around the dog eared posters customers dressed in hoodies huddled over their mobile phones trance like. One waiting gentleman used his phone as a drumstick on the metal park-benches in the hallway. Another one paced impatiently. When I was spoken to, the scene was Clouseau like. "Who are you?" was followed by "why have you come here?"

After I had persuaded them that I was indeed supposed to be on the premises I was assigned a pleasant young man as my Probation officer. Regular appointments have been set up.

He always seems very unsure of himself as he reads from a crib-sheet file on "Citizenship" during our meetings. He often comes out with things like "I haven't done this before" and "I'm not sure what we are supposed to do next." One event took the biscuit. An appointment was made for me on the day of the public sector strike...

That day I as usual turned up with plenty of time in hand. As I neared the building it became obvious that it was under a Dale Farm siege by way of the fact that it was surrounded by people congregating clad in camping gear holding picket signs. One of them was my man – who had made the appointment for me to come and see him. When he saw me he went the colour of a prison officer being addressed by Glenda of HMP Bedford's library. I approached him – grinning – and alerted him to the fact that he had requested my presence this morning. As I said my line the "we will not be moved" chants decayed to a mild murmur as his colleagues' rallies rather tailed off. Clearly his reaction to my address to him was under militant observation. "I can't talk to you now" was whispered in *the* most uncomfortable style. "Go inside to the reception and make another appointment" was then said still in severely hushed tones. A roar of approval went up from his fellows – most of whom looked like customers past from HMP Bedford.

I "crossed" the picket line and made another appointment.

Another rather amusing tale was a conversation with him about me moving from the hostel – of which more later – to another address whilst still "on Tag," of which also more later. I alerted him that I had been told that the necessary paperwork in order to move house whilst still attached to the electronic apparatus would take a month. "Oh no," he said most indignantly. "It won't take a month.

No way." Great, I thought. How long will it take then?

"About four weeks."

Having elected pre-release to be transparent with their service, he was *most* interested in this book. He asked what I was going to say about the Probation service and I relayed that within early pages there was a reference to me seeing them before Court, that prisoners seemed very suspicious of the body and that there would be some brief outline of my experience in the wrapping up of this story – you're reading that bit now. I also recounted one of the officer's observations about Probation having certain parts of their bodies up certain orifices and not spending enough time at the coal face. He asked me what I had said about that. I replied that it seemed rather peculiar that the two parties perhaps rather vital in the sorting out of prisoners' futures didn't seem to be working too well together…

The Hostel… What can I say? I bet you don't know what's coming…

It's *perfect*. A three bedroom house shared with two other guys. One also on Tag and the other on bail. Both sensible, although the latter finishes every sentence (the vocal type) with "blah, blah, blah, blah" – and I mean *every* sentence – and the other gets more electronic messages on his mobile than the triumvirate that is/was the KGB, Cape Canaveral and News International PLC.

The organization that Zara (Top) worked her magic with to get me a home has supplied me a sort of mentor/hand-holder/support Rep. He is Siegfried – and is super. Apart from when he calls me "dude." Great fun and very supportive. When I told him of this collection of words he almost physically man- handled me to a computer so he could read it. *Always* on the other end of a phone and… How can I put this… Let's just say a lot more approachable than the body that is Probation.

Example: Siegfried returns phone calls. My Probation officer does not.

I am still a prisoner because I am on Tag. And under curfew. I must be within the walls of this house between 1900 and 0700. Someone asked me the other day if I am struggling with that. Absolutely NOT. I could still be in B 2 5. Or E 3 8. Ye Gods, I could still be on *Wilford*…

Without inviting myself for a lynching from my fellow "cast" members I think *everyone* who gets out of prison should be under some basic curfew conditions to help and aid them with the slow transition back to the earth's atmosphere. Jonathan Aitken's time-lock "baby steps" again…

I attended Aviation House at Gatwick airport the day after my release to be de-briefed by the CAA. Complete with my Tag. Instead of being told to consider a new career, their response to me, my electronic ball and chain and my experience somewhat threw me. More doors opened from senior management than I have ever seen and out flew comments like "how was it?" and "what was it like?" They treated me like Douglas Bader post Colditz.

One *very* senior boffin said to me "you should write a book…"

I learnt that another aviator had visited the building only the previous week with the same sort of attachment on his ankle. It seems I am not alone. The Authority, as the CAA refers to itself – pilots use a different title – cleared me to return to the skies. I later learnt that they had been in touch with Robbie who had said that I had "used prison as a positive experience." A Cracker.

As I write I have not yet gone aloft. I have been too busy with the book you are reading. This book...

Hmmm.

I will try and explain...

When I was in the dock and the realisation set in that I was indeed off to *jail* the cataclysmic cliché of *crapping myself* came well and truly centre stage. Be of *no* doubt I thought by the end of that night – mercy saints alive – I was *dead*. Wrong. In fact the diametric prison population that I feared so much, as my rubbery knees attested, turned out to be what both got me both *through* the whole slog and taught me *so* much about myself. Double whammies all round. Once the penny dropped that I was in fact surrounded by people who were not a threat but eager to encourage me, I then opened my eyes a little wider and took in the environment and the way things are done. Simply put, it made me reach for a pen. I may have hit an iceberg with my life but I decided to "go down" writing...

If I have managed to convey that what utterly *dominated* me was the uttermost nothingness of the majority of the preposterous prison staff then I have succeeded. In short HMP needs to be changed to HMS. And it's *sinking*.

Even the band ain't playing no more...

When this lot was transferred from paper to computer, I didn't really see the point in making huge changes. I desired that what was felt and written *then* – be carried over *now*. A lot has been taken out. The Wehrmacht publishing world doesn't like waffle. Perhaps they should run the prison service. I hope I've painted an accurate landscape. Previous pages contain events *just* as they happened. The mixture of comedy with tragedy, I hope is nuanced with levels of poignancy. I have no doubt that any humour was a veil of garbage to conceal quiet panic. I have not added to pathos, tempting as it was.

Prison and Hollesley Bay in particular, especially Hoxon – my hideaway – gave me a canvas to walk about and be myself. It became easy to tell people who I was and why I was there. No one judged me. And more often than not, the listeners were invariably of much longer sentence than me. In jail I met, for the first time, pure brutal open honesty. Where can you find that on the outside?

Between these covers I have attempted to reveal a story of accumulated events during my time working for Her Majesty that are littered with what I consider to be an outlying cry that the King has no clothes on. Notwithstanding the unfathomable behaviour of the *Head of Education* at Hollesley Bay, the cultivated vagueness of the majority of prison staff and the overwhelming lack of motivational qualities that I witnessed are I believe the key issue that makes the prison set-up so devoid of success. The existing dithering erratic process of the system sitting on its hands and the *unbelievably* busy revolving door of returnee customers is only just short of scandal.

It became very obvious that prison officers had not been cherry picked – rather collated from personage that one might see collectively around a cherry-picker. You know – the churlish disinterested ones. One tabloid fan was asked during my time on E wing at Bedford if he thought the lavish furnishings – DVD player, remote control et al, were a good idea. "Makes our life easier," he grunted – and then probably checked the odds at Kempton Park for the 2.55. Occasionally I would ask a non-Fleet Street addict how and why he had got the role. Far too often they would honestly confess it was because "there was nothing else" available to them. Whilst I totally acknowledge the difficult times that we live in – surely it is *crucial* that the stepping stone between prisoners and the retribution/rehabilitation game-plan be fulfilled with some *passion*? Officers weren't burdened by ironmongery – one key seemed to fit all locks – just weighed down by disinterest and irreverence. The prison system's relentless blundering down a well-trod wrong turn on the map seems to me, baffling.

What are the top brass of the prison system thinking? Can someone please explain why the on-going enigmatic rearranging of the furniture on the Titanic is allowed to perilously persist with such priority?

I completely acknowledge though, that my life saw me hurtling towards the ground and that as I plummeted, prison pulled my parachute. I so *hope* that this book relays that fact.

I'm writing this on 24th December, 2011. Better known as Christmas Eve. I've been typing a lot since I got out. My goodness, what a lot of words were written in prison. This yuletide will be spent not doing what others do, drinking and eating too much, but typing. I'm by myself in my accommodation. This time last year, almost to the minute, my wife left me. I *can't* describe the pain. Tomorrow – Christmas day – is going to be exceptionally hard work so I am going to keep working away at this.

On visits to the local town I enviously see couples in love kissing. I'm so lonely without my wife. Prison is over – the living hell that is the punishment of her silence goes on. Lord knows where she is as I sit working at this. She was my Camelot and all that came with it. My flawed behaviour whipped the sword out and hurled it away. I deep down within my very soul hope these pages win her back.

Throughout most of the early part of my sentence I felt full of wasted potential. Then I started to take stock and learn. I pray that the climacteric transition that occurred within me is apparent in this book. I hope the ripple effect it may cause within the system is married and indeed matched to it. The only change that has not occurred, apart from my shedding the arse in me, are my thoughts for you-know-who.

Wife, I love you. So much so it's now even for sale in the local bookstore. I'm sorry I was such a ****.

In early December Ben rang me – now also at liberty on Tag. A bit like *he* told me that I was moving from Bedford to Suffolk, he informed me that I was lunching with him the following day. Ben always seems to know what my future holds.

Lunch with him and his wife was lovely. It was terrific to see him and very nice to meet his good lady. During the meal I supplied the last piece of my jigsaw and confessed about the wife situation. Ben's better half admitted to me that she was still hurting due to his stupid actions and then said "he's always been a wanker but I love him."

To my wife: I was a wanker too – in loads of ways. Things that shall remain private and not revealed between these pages but good God woman *I am sorry*. Are we not worth another shot? I promised you I would never give up. Can't you remember the chemistry? Give me another chance. I bet you haven't met anyone yet who makes you laugh like we used to. Mrs Robinson, I love you. And I always will do. And I *know* you *know that*.

I can sometimes do a whole two minutes without thinking about you.

"The most anxious man in a prison is the Governor," wrote George Bernard Shaw. That's quite possibly true at the current time for the Viceroy of HMP Hollesley Bay. The rest of the time it was most *certainly* the author.

What happens next? That's another story.

Thank You

I *have* to communicate heartfelt thanks for their help, guidance and support the following: Jeffrey Archer, Jonathan Aitken and Joanna Trollope for their encouragement both during *and* after my imprisonment, my agent Jane Conway-Gordon for putting her faith in a complete idiot, Philip George for being the cavalry – *always* there, Lisa Cronjé for being brilliant at deciphering my unreadable writing, Alison O'Regan for being the best mentor in the world and *everyone* who encouraged me not to give up.

I have not. Innit.

9329493R00180

Printed in Great Britain
by Amazon.co.uk, Ltd.,
Marston Gate.